SEA OF FAITH

BY THE SAME AUTHOR

Back to the Front
The Perfect Heresy

SEA OF FAITH

ISLAM AND CHRISTIANITY
IN THE MEDIEVAL
MEDITERRANEAN WORLD

STEPHEN O'SHEA

Douglas & McIntyre
Vancouver/Toronto

Douglas & McIntyre Ltd.
2323 Quebec Street, Suite 201
Vancouver, British Columbia
V5T 4S7
www.douglas-mcintyre.com

Published simultaneously in the United States of America
by Walker & Company, New York

For information about permission to reproduce selections from
this book, write to Permissions, Walker & Company,
104 Fifth Avenue, New York, New York 10011.

Library and Archives Canada Cataloguing in Publication
O'Shea, Stephen, 1956–
Sea of faith : Islam and Christianity in the medieval
Mediterranean world / Stephen O'Shea.
Includes bibliographical references and index.

ISBN-13: 978-1-55365-179-6 · ISBN-10: 1-55365-179-0
1. Battles—Mediterranean Region—History.   2. East and West.
3. Mediterranean Region—History, Military.   4. Islamic Empire—
History, Military.   5. Europe—History, Military.   I. Title.
DE84.O84 2006a   909′.09822   C2005-907791-3

Jacket design by Jessica Sullivan & Naomi MacDougall
Jacket illustration courtesy of Kathleen DiGrado/British Library
Printed and bound in Canada by Friesens
Printed on acid-free paper that is forest friendly
(100% post-consumer recycled paper) and has been processed chlorine free.

We gratefully acknowledge the financial support of the Canada Council
for the Arts, the British Columbia Arts Council, and the Government of Canada
through the Book Publishing Industry Development Program
(BPIDP) for our publishing activities.

To
my father
&
the memory of my mother

CONTENTS

NOTES ON USAGE

The goal of reducing obstacles in the reader's path sometimes leads to inconsistency, which, to my mind, is a benign vice when compared to the mischief inflicted on prose by an excess of scruples. As this narrative touches on different peoples, places, and eras, a few decisions had to be made to smooth the journey.

All dates are given in the western manner, with reference to the Common Era and, as tact dictates, not to Anno Domini, the Year of our Lord. Dual dates—one western, one Islamic—for every event would make eyes glaze over. Similarly, the period covered in the book is called the Middle Ages, or the medieval era, for the sake of convenience and familiarity, even if in al-Andalus and Mesopotamia a classical period or golden age existed at some point within the millennium.

Geographical areas are at times referred to by their present-day nation-state names (e.g., France, Iraq) solely as a means of speeding comprehension and avoiding digressions. Similarly, readability—not consistency—has been the guideline in the choice of names of people. The simpler versions of nonwestern names have been retained. Where western versions of names exist (e.g., Almanzor, Avicenna), they have been used. As for the Europeans, not all of their names are anglicized: I simply couldn't call the bad boy of Outremer, as some authors do, Reginald of Châtillon. And if a non-English name is perfectly serviceable—Pedro and not Peter, for example—it has been let stand.

As for the vexed problem of transliteration, I have opted for the simplest form possible. Arabists and Turkophones may despair, but many of the macrons, dots, and apostrophes of scholarly and present-day transliteration have been abandoned. As someone whose surname is no stranger to punctuation, I may be accused of chutzpah in this decision, but, again, the intent is to clear the path of obstacles. I do, however, employ several terms that might at the outset be unfamiliar—*convivencia*, *umma*, and the like. I trust that the reader, as she or he progresses through the narrative, will have been made familiar with these terms. If the writing or the memory fails in this respect, a glossary can be flipped to at the back of the book.

Sea *of* Faith

INTRODUCTION

Mezquita and Ayasofya

Córdoba's white warren of cobbled streets and courtyards stretches out alongside the dull bleached banks of the Guadalquivir River. The old town is a capital of traditional Spanish culture, and its many merchants obligingly peddle the customary flamenco party finery and plastic conquistador gear. Yet in the heart of its historic center, Córdoba defies shopworn narrative through its proud possession of an unusual architectural marvel. The city's magnificent Mezquita—Spanish for "mosque"—bespeaks another heritage, another memory, another story altogether. To those attuned to the historic struggle over Mediterranean identity, this remarkable building offers two encounters—two moments of realization that shape this present work.

The first encounter occurs quickly. Once past the patio of orange trees and through the main portal, the eye and ear are forced to adjust. Intermittent blizzards of flashbulbs lance the dimness, accompanied by the voices of tour leaders shepherding their charges through the sanctuary. But these distractions fade in their turn as the interior takes shape. Row upon row of slender marble columns, twice the height of a man, march across a cool stone floor. For all the regimentation, the effect is not one of parade-ground monotony. Quite the contrary—the exquisite paradox of the Mezquita lies in its creation of dreamlike, shifting expanses along what is essentially a grid.

The capitals of adjacent columns in each row are joined by tall semicircular arches, their building blocks—called *voussoirs*—distinctive for their alternating bands of red brick and white stone. To this shock of color comes an even greater surprise of volume: surmounting each arch is a sister arch, similarly striped, creating a crescent of emptiness between the paired curves of stone that is endlessly reproduced throughout the mosque. The peekaboo succession of spaces enlivens perspective no matter which way the visitor turns, the candy-cane interior seeming to shift repeatedly, all at once, like a Muslim congregation at prayer.

Abd al-Rahman, the Cordoban grandee who commissioned this astonishing mosque in the eighth century c.e., had firsthand knowledge of sudden changes and dramatic new perspectives. As an Umayyad, a descendant of the caliphs who had ruled the early Muslim world from their capital of Damascus, he had been forced to flee his native Syria in 750 when a rival clan, the Abbasids, seized power under the leadership of Abu al-Abbas as-Saffah. The sobriquet *as-Saffah* means "shedder of blood"—the Umayyads were slaughtered to a man. Only Abd al-Rahman escaped the carnage, riding the length of the Mediterranean until reaching distant Spain and making it his kingdom.

Interior of the Mezquita of Córdoba, famed for its striped,
superimposed arches and arresting perspectives.

Abd al-Rahman and his successors in Córdoba built and expanded the Mezquita for the next two centuries, the last and largest of these additions occurring under the rule of Almanzor, a ruthless vizier who wielded the real power behind a puppet Umayyad prince. Aside from doubling the size of the Mezquita, all the while maintaining its striped double-horseshoe colonnades, Almanzor added metal lamps that were fashioned from the bells he had stolen in his sack of Compostela, in the northwestern extremity of Spain. That event, in 997, had entailed desecrating the shrine of a saint who would inspire a devotional frenzy in the Middle Ages. The bells of Santiago Matamoros—St. James the Moor-Slayer—hung harmless in Almanzor's Mezquita, illuminating the pointedly unslain Moors as they thanked God for their vizier's victory.

The story of the waylaid bells hints at the second, spectacular encounter on offer in the Mezquita. By the time a visitor reaches Almanzor's extension, it becomes obvious that the Mezquita is and is not a mosque. Squarely in the center of the airy grove of pillars stands a Christian sanctuary, a towering Baroque cathedral that shoots through the roof of its surroundings. An aesthetic gatecrasher, the church displays a riot of figurative ornamentation that could hardly

Religious palimpsest: the figurative devotional art of the Santa Maria Mayor Cathedral within the Mezquita.

be more impolite to its Islamic host. The Christians wrested Córdoba from the Muslims in 1236, but only in the sixteenth and seventeenth centuries was this dizzying addition undertaken—and then, over the objections of the town fathers. When the monarch who authorized the church viewed it, he remarked ruefully: "You have built here what you, or anyone else, might have built anywhere; to do so you have destroyed what was unique in the world."

Whatever the merits of the Mezquita's Santa Maria Mayor cathedral—one recent detractor called it "a great blister of tiresomeness"—its existence is a tangible testament to a rivalry between faiths that went far beyond the artistic fashions of this city on the Guadalquivir. Just as Abd al-Rahman had, in his flight, crossed the entire length of the Mediterranean, so too did this rivalry, this encounter, encompass that sea and the many lands that surround it.

At the opposite corner of the Mediterranean world stands the Mezquita's only peer in dual identity. Rising high above the Hippodrome in Istanbul, its corpulent domes and fading pomegranate-red walls resembling an unruly fruit bowl, the Hagia Sophia represents the last hurrah of classical Christian hegemony. This Church of Holy Wisdom was Emperor Justinian's bid to awe the world and outdo the ancients. "Solomon, I have surpassed thee," he is supposed to

Justinian's Hagia Sophia, transformed into the Ottoman Ayasofya Mosque and graced by four minarets. The structure is now a museum.

have whispered on December 27, 537, as he first walked under the immense dome of his just-completed church. In his enthusiasm, he might also have added that his dome had dwarfed that of the Pantheon in Rome and, by extension, the gods that it sheltered.

Today the Hagia Sophia, like the Mezquita, is an echo chamber of indistinct murmur. Slightly intimidated groups proceed through its luminous gray-gold interior listening to explanations given in a babel of tongues. On the verge of its millennium-and-a-half mark despite earthquake, sack, and the occasional structural collapse (diverse calamities occurred in 553, 558, 989, 1204, 1346), the sanctuary encloses as impressive a volume of space as any bequeathed to us by the builder's art. The crown of the dome floats some fifteen stories above the marbled pavement, held up by four massive piers and two elephantine half-domes to the north and south. Galleries line three sides of the cavernous nave; two of these are supported by graceful marble columns, their capitals a sculpted thicket of acanthus and palm displaying the monograms of Justinian and his empress, Theodora.

For all its magnificence, the Hagia Sophia houses a relative dearth of artistic treasure—a few fragmentary mosaics in the galleries hint at the glory that is gone. Some of this absence can be traced to the great iconoclast controversy of the ninth and tenth centuries, when holy images were deemed heretical and thus worthy of destruction. The opponents of the iconoclasts—the iconodules—eventually won the day, but much of their subsequent legacy disappeared just as definitively. To understand this latter spoliation, one need only note an inscription in the southern gallery of the church. At knee height, a solitary gravestone in one wall displays the name of Henricus Dandolo, the doge of Venice who, although blind and in his eighties, led an army of crusaders in a devastating pillage of the church and its city in 1204.

Aside from this unholy irony tucked away in a gallery upstairs, the main reason for the absence of Christian iconography concerns the same rivalry so arrestingly on view at the Mezquita. Immediately on entering the sanctuary the visitor sees that the Hagia Sophia is no longer dedicated to Christ. As with the Cordoban monument, the great building accommodates a monotheistic intruder, but here the roles are reversed. Justinian's great cathedral of 537 was transformed into Mehmet the Conqueror's great mosque of 1453, the year in which Constantinople, as Istanbul was then known, fell to the Ottoman Turks. The Hagia Sophia became the Ayasofya.

Graced outside by four soaring minarets constructed by successive sultans, the Ayasofya remained a lodestar of Islam until 1932, when the republican government of Kemal Ataturk converted the building into a museum—an act of secularization that has not been considered in Córdoba. The building's 479 years as a mosque left their imprint but did not deform the space within. A few elegant additions—the loge for the sultan, the *minbar* (the pulpit for Friday prayers), the *mihrab* (the niche indicating the *qibla*, or the orientation toward Mecca)—are hardly noticeable under the eye-catching flourish of bold Kufic

Ayasofya: Byzantine engineering of the sixth century and Ottoman piety of the nineteenth. The round wall hangings are the levhas.

script that covers the dome. It reads: "In the name of God the Merciful and Pitiful; God is the light of Heaven and Earth. His light is Himself, not that which shines through glass or gleams in the morning star or glows in the firebrand." Somewhat less successful, if equally hallowed in their time, are the six *levhas*, giant shieldlike wooden wall hangings painted with six sacred names: God, Muhammad, and the first four caliphs of Islam. The monograms of Justinian and Theodora look decidedly small in comparison.

Still, the architectonic marvel created by Justinian's engineers undermined any attempt at religious palimpsest. The master builders of the Ottoman sultans used their talents on other constructions, Istanbul's greatest Islamic temples— Suleymaniye, Sultanahmet (the "Blue Mosque")—paying imitative flattery to the great dome of the Ayasofya. One present-day Byzantinist has compared these giant mosques of the Ottomans, of which Ayasofya was the first, to "clouds pinned down by the enormous needles of their minarets." Yet to reach this peaceful state, these buildings first had to displace and usurp, just as the Christianity of Constantinople replaced the gods of old Byzantium and, not incidentally, just as the Mezquita of Abd al-Rahman took elements of the Visigothic church that had stood on the spot—and which, in its day, had used as its pillars the columns and capitals of the pagan temple of Roman Córdoba. The Mediterranean world, already rich in the strata of overlaid faiths and cultures, would become immensely richer from the meeting between Christianity and Islam.

Emperor Justinian the Great died on November 14, 565. Five or six years later, according to tradition, the Prophet Muhammad was born. For a millennium thereafter, from the seventh to the sixteenth century, Islam and Christianity would contend for primacy in the Mediterranean world, a competition on dramatic and permanent display at the Mezquita and the Ayasofya. At times acrimonious, at other times harmonious, the encounter between the two creeds in the Middle Ages provides a backdrop to much of what informs, and misinforms, public opinion on present-day conflicts. Although remote in time, the principal events and locales are worth recalling—or at the very least, ordering accurately in one's mind. A shared history should be familiar to all, especially in a day when the idea of an inevitable civilizational clash has once again gained currency. And as in the admirable Mezquita, the two protagonists must be seen in shifting perspectives, in order to do justice to a long history that combined both conflict and coexistence.

War, of course, forms a large part of the story. The two faiths were brandished

as battle standards by the civilizations that rose and fell around the Mediterranean. The two moved men to action, inspired feats of bravery, brought God
into the affairs of siege engineer and swordsman. They gave respectable cover
to the workings of age-old cupidity, by making the mundane violence of a feral
time seem supernatural and sublime and by extending a blessing to even the
most wanton instances of warrior atrocity.

Seven battles, selected from a much larger pageant of violence, exemplify the
military aspect of the encounter between Christianity and Islam, either epochal
turning points in the view of scholarly consensus or events celebrated or deplored in popular historical traditions. The first two, Yarmuk and Poitiers, represent the beginnings of the encounter, a time of mutual ignorance, when the
Muslim armies seemed to have arrived out of nowhere to change forever the
culture of the Mediterranean. The middle three—Manzikert, Hattin, Las Navas
de Tolosa—are the high-water mark of conflict, when many of the combatants
saw themselves as fighting for their faith against the infidel. Religion would
never play a greater role in the conduct of warfare around the inland sea than it
did from the eleventh to the thirteenth century. Constantinople and Malta, the
final two, occurred at the cusp of the early modern period, as the old religious
justifications were slowly being eroded by the dawn of the Atlantic era and the
workings of hard-headed commercial interest. By the close of the sixteenth century, the Mediterranean could no longer be called a sea of faith—a sea of trade
or piracy, perhaps, but certainly not faith.

The martial canvas stretches across the entire Mediterranean world. The modern locations of these battlefields are, in the chronological order in which they
came on the historical stage, Syria, France, Turkey, Israel, Spain, Turkey again,
and Malta. Given this geographical range, different peoples came to the fore in
different epochs. Over time Turks replaced Arabs, and Franks replaced Greeks
as protagonists, while Normans, Berbers, Slavs, Mongols, Italians, and Spaniards
all played a role. If the names of some of their leaders have entered universal
history and folklore (Saladin, El Cid), other figures, just as colorful or influential, are renowned only in a local setting (Serbia's Prince Lazar, Turkey's Alp
Arslan).

At the same time conflict was not perpetual. Eras of coexistence and
commingling—what the Spanish call *convivencia*—make up another facet of Islamic and Christian contact in the Middle Ages. From Córdoba to Istanbul,
from Cairo to Palermo and Toledo, the course of Muslim-Christian complicity
skips around the entire Mediterranean basin, just as scholars, translators,

merchants, and clerics wandered that world and contributed to its halcyon moments of cultural exchange. A continuum of cooperation, audible as a kind of ground tone upon which the more martial music of narrative history must be played, convivencia informed the entire medieval millennium, even those epochs that opened or closed with battle. Four great centers of convivencia— Umayyad Córdoba, Christian Toledo, Norman Palermo, Ottoman Kostanti- niyye (Constantinople)—represent the workings of the medieval Mediterranean as accurately as any jihad or crusade. By combining the epochal battles with the eras of convivencia, a clearer picture of the complex encounter of Chris- tianity and Islam emerges, one that combats the selective, agenda-driven amne- sia that has settled over the subject among some of the religious chauvinists of our own day.

To be fair, the obscuring of the Christian-Muslim encounter of the distant past may not be the result solely of cultural tunnel vision—that is, learning only those histories that redound to the benefit of whichever society happens to be setting the curriculum. (One need only think of how little the brilliance of Muslim Spain colors the western view of the Middle Ages.) Much of our un- familiarity arises from not knowing the Muslim sources for the period under study, those voices that lend balance to what was, after all, a two-way relation- ship. Thanks to the work of professional historians in the last half-century, these sources have been made available in translation, although much of their content has yet to be presented to the nonspecialist reader.

And finally, no matter how resonant in the present, the shared story of Islam and Christianity in the first centuries of their interaction remains impossibly far away in time. Fortunately, the setting for this history is supremely evocative. Fernand Braudel described the magic of the Mediterranean: "Simply looking at the Mediterranean cannot of course explain everything about a complicated past created by human agents, with varying doses of calculation, caprice and misadventure. But this is a sea that patiently recreates for us scenes from the past, breathing new life into them, locating them under a sky and in a landscape that we can see with our own eyes, a landscape and sky like those of long ago. A moment's concentration or daydreaming, and that past comes back to life."

The great historian's assessment is correct. Visiting old battle sites and vener- able cities of the Mediterranean world, with a view to understanding what hap- pened there long ago, adds a sense of place that can only deepen appreciation of a distant time. Whether a story of long ago is full of death or full of life—clad, as a Cordoban shopkeeper might say, in conquistador garb or flamenco

Paris

Tours

Poitiers

Cluny

Angoulême

Milan

Santiago de
Compostella

Bordeaux

AQUITAINE

Venice

Genoa

Ravenna

León

Dax

Auch

Moissac

Avignon

Florence

Burgos

Roncesvalles

Pamplona

Toulouse

Narbonne

Marseille

Pisa

Aₐ

LEÓN

ARAGON

Pyrenees

Toulon

La Garde-Freinet

Ligurian

CASTILE

Zaragoza

Corsica

Rome

Toledo

Medinaceli

Barcelona

Lisbon

Sagrajas

Calatrava

Badajoz

Alarcos

Córdoba

LA MANCHA

Sierra Morena

Seville

AL-ANDALUS

Las Navas
de Tolosa

Jaén

Valencia

BALEARICS

Majorca

Balearic Sea

Sardinia

Tyrrhenian

Strait of Me

Mazaro
del Vallo

Palermo

Sicily

Granada

Gibraltar

Strait of Gibraltar

Algeciras

Tangier

Ceuta

Oran

Algiers

Carthage

Tunis

Pantelleria

Mal

Marrakesh

MAGHRIB

IFRIQIYA

Sidi Oqba

Kairouan

Sufetula

Kerkennah

Jerba

Libyan

Tripoli

N

Vienna

Budapest

BALKANS

Belgrade

Nicopolis

Varna

BLACK SEA

Kosovo
Polje

Novo Brodo

Ragusa

SERBIA

Sofia

THRACE

Bosporus

Erzurum

Manzikert

Adrianople-Edirne

Constantinople

Chalcedon

Ahlat

Thessalonica

Gallipoli

Sea of
Marmara

Nicaea

Ankara

Lake
Van

APULIA

ari

Taranto

Dardanelles

Dorylaeum

Caesarea

CALABRIA

Preveza

Lesbos

Aegean Sea

ANATOLIA

Edessa

Lepanto

Athens

Konya

Aleppo

Ionian
Sea

MOREA

Mystra

Dodecanese

Antioch

SYRIA

Rhodes

Hama

Homs

Cyprus

Crete

Tripoli

MEDITERRANEAN SEA

Damascus

Hattin

Yarmuk

Acre

Bosra

Sea of Galilee

Jerusalem

Ascalon

Dead
Sea

Damietta

Gaza

Alexandria

Beersheba

SINAI

Bilbays

Cairo

EGYPT

finery—meaning can be gleaned from what is on the ground today and from how the past is represented. Something can even be learned from the way the wind blows through a cypress tree. The mullah and the bishop might balk, but seeing is believing.

⤙ ⤙   ⤚ ⤚

From Mezquita to Ayasofya then, from Andalusia back toward the distant shore, through the Balearic, Tyrrhenian, Ionian, Adriatic, Libyan, and Aegean seas, past the islands of Majorca, Corsica, Sardinia, Sicily, Malta, Crete, Rhodes, and Cyprus—the Mediterranean is an irregularly shaped historical stage, punctuated by peninsulas and bounded by three continents, a succession of intimate cove, treacherous current, and terrifying emptiness, wine-red or *grand bleu* or the White Sea (Akdeniz, in Turkish). When in 260 B.C.E. the sailors of the Roman republic defeated the Carthaginian navy in the battle of Mylae (Milazzo, Sicily), the victorious crews are said to have cried out, *"Mare nostrum! Mare nostrum!"* And it was "our sea," or rather theirs, for hundreds of years thereafter.

But the mare nostrum of the Romans meant more than just the sea itself. As its Latinate name announces—*medius terra*, "middle land"—the Mediterranean includes the territories hemming it in. By the second century C.E., the dominion of the Roman Empire encompassed the entirety of this Mediterranean world, and all of its constituent societies were influenced to some degree by the Graeco-Roman model of thought and societal organization. It was a formidable accomplishment and, were it ever to come undone, a precious legacy to inherit.

Inevitably, disintegration did occur, and the Mediterranean slipped the traces of Roman control. From the fourth through the sixth centuries, the principal beneficiary was the Eastern Roman Empire. Centered in Constantinople, the new Rome constructed on the site of ancient Byzantium by Emperor Constantine in 330, this survivor of antiquity ruled much of the mare nostrum well after its former landlord had fallen. (The year of old Rome's collapse is commonly taken to be 476.)

Over time the eastern inheritor of the mare nostrum changed the nature of the imperium. The language of its rulers was Greek, not Latin, and the prism through which the world was viewed had radically altered. A monotheistic religion became the guarantor of legitimacy. For most of its imperial centuries old Rome had deified its emperors, but its Mediterranean had nonetheless accommodated many faiths. In the Mediterranean of the Byzantine Empire—as the Eastern Roman Empire came to be called by historians—a potent belief system became the handmaiden of power, and attempts were undertaken to make the peoples of the Mediterranean into a community of like-minded believers.

The faith was Christianity, a movement of Jewish sectaries that had, over the centuries, established a claim to universality. Its avatar, Jesus of Nazareth, was seen as a divine being by most of his followers, whose proselytizing would transform the spiritual landscape of antiquity. A stepchild of Judaism, Christianity as disseminated through the Greek-speaking world claimed that Jesus had been the Messiah awaited by the Jews and that the sacred books of Judaism— known to Christians as the Old Testament—were precursor texts to his teachings. And whereas the older faith suffered a grievous blow in 70 C.E., when a Jewish revolt in Palestine was ruthlessly crushed by Roman authorities and the main temple of Jerusalem destroyed, Christianity weathered fitful persecution in its earliest days to thrive the length and breadth of the mare nostrum and eventually overtake Judaism in the number of its adherents.* On its adoption as the established religion of the Roman Empire, both east and west, in the fourth century (following the favored status granted it by the same Emperor Constantine who built Constantinople), Christianity had arrived, both as the arbiter of the ontologically correct and, more important, the medium through which authority flowed. A spirit of transcendent legitimacy floated over the affairs of the Mediterranean, which had become, as is often said, "a Christian lake."

The waters, however, were not placid. The Christians of this new Mediterranean differed noisily on the precise nature of their savior. Christological debates echoed throughout the mare nostrum, causing pogroms to be prosecuted and councils to be convened. At Chalcedon (Kadikoy, Turkey) in 451, orthodox Christian doctrine was spelled out yet again: Jesus, it was decided, had had two natures, human and divine, complementary yet intertwined; moreover, Jesus was part of a trinity of divine personae. Although the emperor placed his stamp of approval on this decision, dissident Christian doctrines—Monophysitism, Arianism, Nestorianism—held sway in Syria, Egypt, Armenia, western Mesopotamia, north Africa, Spain, and much of Italy. The cacophony was such that one visitor to

---

*Judaism is thought to have had millions of adherents outside Palestine in the first century C.E.

Constantinople remarked: "Everywhere, in humble homes, in the streets, in the marketplace, at street corners, one finds people talking about the most unexpected subjects. If I ask for my bill, the reply is a comment about the virgin birth; if I ask the price of bread, I am told that the Father is greater than the Son; when I ask whether my bath is ready, I am told that the Son was created from nothing." Adding to these violent disagreements were the oft-times contentious relations and pecking-order disputes among the early Church's five seats of patriarchy—Alexandria, Antioch, Constantinople, Jerusalem, and Rome. As the pagan historian Ammianus Marcellinus noted, "[n]o wild beasts were so hostile to humans as most Christians were in their savagery toward one another."

For all that, by the middle of the sixth century a certain Christian commonwealth had been realized. The barbarian peoples who toppled old Rome—Vandals, Visigoths, Ostrogoths—had been either put in their place or convinced to help create a fledgling Christian civilization in the west. A Byzantine general of talent, Belisarius, had reconquered Italy and north Africa for his master, Justinian, thereby lengthening Constantinople's reach across the Mediterranean. If a threat to this new world order were to come, it was expected from Mesopotamia and beyond, out of which the armies of the four-century-old Sassanid Empire of Persia had long been venturing to skirmish with the Byzantines and their allies. Little did the peoples of the Mediterranean realize that a far greater rival was about to emerge and that their Christological talk-shop would soon come crashing down about their ears.

A new and equally cogent religious worldview arrived on the shores of the mare nostrum in the first half of the seventh century. It had originated in the Hijaz, the west-central portion of the Arabian peninsula. Its exponent, Muhammad, a merchant of the well-established Quraysh clan of Mecca, claimed to have had serial revelations from the angel Gabriel and from God, revelations destined first for the Arabs and then for humanity as a whole. These visits to Muhammad were seen to be the final in a series of supernatural interventions that had begun with Abraham and continued through the prophets of the Hebrew Bible and Jesus. The resulting religion, Islam (meaning "submission"), with its divinely dictated book (Quran, "recital"), took the revelation granted to the Jews—and later appended by the Christians—and incorporated it into what Muslim believers held to be the perfection of monotheism. In this new view, the two older faiths had corrupted, in some ways, the original revelation.

Abraham (Ibrahim), in being the first monotheist, was the first Muslim, and the stories of his exploits and those of his descendants found in the Hebrew Bible were reinterpreted in the light of the Quranic dispensation. Thus, in a fundamental distinction from Christianity, the sacred texts of Judaism were not embraced by Islam. The message given to Muhammad, the last in a long line of prophecy, improved and supplanted all that had come before.

The Mediterranean would thenceforth witness a formidable encounter between two claimants to universal spiritual legitimacy. Mutual incomprehension marked much of their meeting, at least in its early stages. Byzantine Christians first viewed Islam as yet another heretical variation on a theme, a new voice in the shouting match over the nature of the divine. It is doubtful that the revolutionary import of Muhammad's message was at all evident even to the most sophisticated of Christian thinkers of the time. Muslims had a more nuanced view of the Other: they were specifically enjoined by the Quran to respect Jews and Christians as people to whom valid, if woefully incomplete and partly corrupted, revelations had been given. Despite this injunction, the idea of Christians as pagan idolaters was difficult to suppress. Muhammad had been tireless in stamping out polytheism in Arabia—"There is no god but God" is the preeminent Islamic affirmation of faith. The tenet similarly central to the Christian credo—"I believe in God, the Father Almighty, the Creator of heaven and earth, and in Jesus Christ, His only Son, our Lord: Who was conceived of the Holy Spirit"—suggested to the Muslim, and any other non-Christian for that matter, that these quarrelsome Trinitarians might be worshiping more than one god.

When incomprehension gave way to hostility, the force of arms often prevailed, despite the message of brotherhood preached by both Jesus and Muhammad. Christianity, at first an outsider, pacifist creed, came to don the martial mantle of empire; as the Middle Ages progressed, it would put on the armor of kingship, hold the pennon of crusader knight, make warriors of its monks and saints of its pirates. Islam, on the other hand, was political from the outset: Muhammad had been very much of this world, fighting battles to unify the Arabian peninsula under his rule. Each of Muhammad's successors (or *khalifa*, "caliph") was considered a spiritual and temporal leader whose actions in the world of the here-and-now were divinely sanctioned, however transparently political those actions might be. This supposition of supernatural guidance might have translated automatically into rigid despotism if Islam, owing to its electrifying notion of an egalitarian brotherhood of believers, did not implicitly

invite questions of legitimacy concerning the person of the caliph. If a bad
Muslim, or a bad general, was he a true caliph? Whereas Christological concerns were the Achilles' heel of early Christianity, quarrels over the succession
of Muhammad would dog the younger faith, raising and dashing dynasties and
creating schisms.

Despite their internal divisions, both faiths thrived and profoundly influenced
the thoughts and actions of kings and emperors and sultans. One historian,
writing confidently in the heyday of twentieth-century skepticism, stated that
"when modern man ceased to accord first place to religion in his own concerns,
he also ceased to believe that other men, in other times, could ever truly have
done so, and so he began to re-examine the great religious movements of the
past in search of interest and motives acceptable to modern minds." Such a
breezy claim about the triumph of the secular is not as easy to make in the present day, but the idea of inquiring into the materiality of faith-based historical
moments remains valid. Certainly, in the event, the encounter between Christian and Islamic societies was not exclusively of a religious nature. Sparks flew
for many reasons, the greatest of which was the belief in war as the ultimate arbiter of politics and policy. Greed, geopolitical rivalry, imperial or familial ambition, individual megalomania and sociopathy—all played their customary
roles as well. Internecine warfare among Christians, and among Muslims, did
not cease until the questions raised by the Islamic-Christian encounter were
decided. Muslim dynasties had at each other with at least as much gusto as they
would reserve for wars against the infidels. In Christendom the same was true—
in 1204, to return to the Ayasofya, the crusading Latin Christians, not the Muslims, sacked Greek Constantinople.

That warfare was such a central fact of life everywhere at the time should not
obscure the fundamental importance of belief in the meeting between Christian
and Islamic societies. From what can be gathered across the chasm of so many
centuries about the character and outlook of individual historical actors, varying levels of spiritual conviction were at play. Saladin, for example, the Kurdish
hero of Hattin and vanquisher of Jerusalem's crusaders, appears to have been a
genuinely religious man, deeply offended at the Frankish interlopers in what he
thought should be a Muslim-controlled Palestine. Charles Martel, on the other
hand, long celebrated for saving Europe for Christianity through his victory at
Poitiers, seems to have had about as much religious feeling as the average war-
horse. These inferences, even those that extend to societies at large, do not diminish the very real spiritual consequences of the actions of the powerful,

however earthbound their motives. We take for granted the confessional geography of the Mediterranean, that is, which countries are, in their majority, Muslim or Christian. Yet there was nothing inevitable about Turkey being overwhelmingly Muslim, or Spain being overwhelmingly Christian. This geography of belief was decided in the millennium of the Middle Ages, through the contingencies of battle and the actions of men.

The ramifications of this confessional geography are difficult to overstate. Law, language, art, the role of women, the tolerance of minorities, education, the very organizing principles of a society—all were influenced by the dominant religion, whether Christianity or Islam. In that light, Judaism cannot enter this story of the Middle Ages but peripherally, since it did not rise to the imperial prominence of the other two monotheistic faiths. Jews, although important actors in the various societies informed and controlled by Islam and Christianity, played a vital but nonetheless secondary role in the unfolding of the drama and appear more in descriptions of convivencia than in accounts of conflict. Their relegation to the periphery is in a sense paradoxical, since Judaism is central to the genesis of the other creeds. If any faith may lay claim to paternal authority, it is Judaism—consequently, the competition between Islam and Christianity can well be viewed as a sibling rivalry writ very large. Although this may not sit well with acolytes of the two junior revelations, one metaphor for the great encounter is inescapable: that of two sons struggling over an inheritance. That this inheritance—the mare nostrum—far exceeded the actual grasp of the father matters little, for the monotheism first expressed in Judaism is as much a legacy of Mediterranean antiquity as the writings of Plato and Aristotle. From the seventh century on, as the two brothers quarreled and composed and quarreled again, a world, an inheritance—and a god—were at stake.

CHAPTER ONE

YARMUK 636

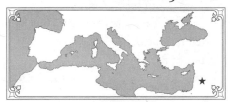

*The rise of Islam; the fall of Christian
Syria and Palestine*

In contrast to the refinements of rivalry on display at the Mezquita and the Ayasofya, the place that ushered in the era of confessional competition for the medieval Mediterranean seems decidedly raw. The upland bordering the Yarmuk River, a scarified terrain of black basalt boulders, looks in many spots less world-historical than lunar-historical. The battlefield, from the year 636, is no killing field turned picnic ground, as at Agincourt or Waterloo, for contemporary politics have combined with natural infelicities to make the area particularly inhospitable. To the north of the canyon carved by the Yarmuk stands the Golan, a sun-bleached highland bristling with the instruments of war.

Very little is even faintly bucolic or artful about this place, the junction of Syria, Jordan, and Israel. The smaller rivers of the region are wadis, bone-dry creeks given to the occasional flash flood. If the caprices of the wadis have long bedeviled cultivation—the local ones, Ruqqad, Allan, and Harir, have now been thoughtfully dammed—the gorges in their lower reaches have disheartened even the goatherd. The plateau is one of hardscrabble farms and cinder-block villages and kibbutzes, the occasional spinney of eucalyptus combining with great black boulder barriers to lend some order to the prospect. In unexpected spots, solitary hills rise to well over a hundred meters in elevation, giant, isolated thimbles of vegetation in this patchwork of stony field and sudden gulley.

The canyon of the Yarmuk, Syria's border with Jordan, closes off the southernmost sector of the old battlefield with finality. To flee the unruly yet cultivated plateau of the Golan is to rush headlong to the brink of a steep slope. The drop to the canyon floor is two hundred meters. The Yarmuk seems then a fittingly dramatic stage for a momentous event, something beyond the ordinary warring that a watercourse inspires in the peoples of a parched land. And the river, which winds dozens of inhospitable, cliff-lined kilometers westward before meeting the Jordan just south of the Sea of Galilee, did indeed witness an epochal occurrence, an instant of bloody encounter that would profoundly alter the civilization of the Mediterranean.

For all its importance past and present, no monument or statue commemorates the fateful battle at its site. Near Nawa, a Syrian town within artillery range of

The death trap for the Byzantines: the Yarmuk River valley, looking west.

the Golan Heights, two hills are recognizable landmarks from the Battle of Yarmuk. The northernmost, Tal al Jabila, almost certainly overlooked the staging ground of the Byzantine army. South of Nawa, another lone prominence is known locally as the Hill of the Gathering, an allusion, it is thought, to the massing of the Muslim forces in the spring of 636. Yet however telltale these features, present-day visitors come here for reasons that predate that victorious year for the Companions of the Prophet.

One afternoon in November 2003, east of the two hills, a lipstick-red tour bus with Lebanese plates raced through the dusty village of Sheikh Saad on its way to a shrine just out of town. The vehicle came to a halt, then disgorged several dozen young women who walked up a small rise in the plain to enter a low, whitewashed building of indeterminate age. Inside was a small sanctuary, built around a bier draped in silken green flags. The women, their flamboyant makeup at odds with their demure headscarves, fingered the flags reverently, then caressed their faces. Smiles were exchanged, pictures taken, cell phone calls made. This was Dar Ayyub, the burial place of Job, the biblical figure famed for being lucklessly piled on by destiny. His reputation for patience seemed to be the drawing card for these marriageable girls, the exploits of their ancestors at Yarmuk forgotten amid nervous giggling about future mates. Their imam, a handsome young fellow attempting to look sterner than his charges, eventually glanced at his watch and signaled that the visit was over.

Their bus pulled away, perhaps to go to nearby Nawa, where Noah's son Shem rests similarly in peace. As the sound of its engine grew ever fainter and the silence of the scrubby plain took over, the interplay of past and present on this landscape was inescapable. The road they were traveling traced the route of the old Roman thoroughfare that linked Damascus and Jerusalem, and although certainties are elusive in dealing with distant events, the world-changing cavalry charge of Yarmuk likely took place here, in front of the biblical gravesite patronized by these thoroughly modern Muslims. If so, Dar Ayyub is also the tomb of the Christian East. A historian from the early twentieth century, expressing the "Orientalist" sentiments decried in its latter half, gave a valediction to antiquity in considering the process made possible by what happened in these fields: "after ten centuries, at one stroke of the Arab scimitar, everything collapsed overnight: Greek language and thought, western patterns of living, everything went up in smoke. On this territory, a thousand years of history were as if they had never been. They had not been sufficient for the west to put down the slightest roots in this oriental soil. The Greek language and social customs had been no more than a layer, a poorly fitting mask. All the Greek cities which had been founded and grown up, from the banks of the Nile to the Hindu Kush, any real or apparent implantation of Greek art and philosophy, all of it had gone with the wind." That passage smacks of hyperbole—a nice Greek word—but the importance of Yarmuk cannot be gainsaid.

 ≺≺ ≺≺   ≻≻ ≻≻

The road leading to the clash at Yarmuk had passed through a turbulent time of chaos, plague, tyranny, famine, and war. In the years surrounding the death of Emperor Justinian in 565, apocalyptic horsemen had been cantering at will around the Mediterranean. Much of Italy had slipped from the grasp of the Byzantines, victim to the vigorous Germanic barbarians known as the Longobardi (Longbeards), or Lombards, who had begun their migration southward from the forested fastnesses of eastern and central Europe. Spain was claimed by the Visigoths, Provence by the Burgundians. A ferocious Turkic tribe known as the Avars had crossed the Danube to wreak havoc in the Byzantine Balkans. When not losing provinces, the Greeks lost people: the buboes of pestilence carried off as much as half the population of Constantinople.

Grief came from all quarters, even from the center. In the early seventh century an illiterate Thracian sergeant usurped the purple and, as Emperor Phocas, proved that outrageous cruelty and paranoia were not confined to such reviled old Romans as Caligula and Nero. Blinding an adversary, or even someone suspected of being an acquaintance of an opponent, became commonplace under Phocas, as did the use of the rack to wring confessions from innocent and guilty alike. To worsen matters, his reign saw the long-dreaded threat from the east materialize. The Persians, under King Chosroes II, a onetime friend of the emperor who had been decapitated to make way for Phocas, shattered the fragile peace between the two empires. Ruler of a proud and belligerent federation centered on what is now Iraq and Iran, the Sassanid dynasty of Persia saw its chance in the commotions on its western borders. As Phocas blinded and beheaded enemies real and imagined in Constantinople and sowed discord between Christians and Jews in the Middle East through indiscriminate persecution, the armies of Chosroes attacked the outlying provinces of the Christian imperium. Upper Mesopotamia, then Armenia, then Syria, Palestine, and Egypt—the raids of conquest and plunder met little opposition from the garrisons demoralized by the cruel ineptitudes of Phocas and his cronies. Clearly, the crisis cried out for new leadership.

It came from Heraclius, the son of the Byzantine governor of Carthage. The North African city, the once-mighty capital subdued in the days when the phrase "mare nostrum" was first uttered, had become a provincial outpost of the imperial metropole. In the first decade of the seventh century, Carthage endured the depredations of Phocas and dutifully continued to serve as a granary of the empire. Under Heraclius, the grain ships of Carthage changed into a fleet of revolt. In the year 609 the handsome thirty-five-year-old aristocrat set sail on the Mediterranean, passing through the Aegean to the city of Thessalonica. He wintered and summered there, gathering troops and allies and communicating with plotters in the capital, before finally heading off in the autumn of 610 for the Hellespont. In October his ships crossed the Sea of Marmara and dropped anchor in the Golden Horn, the inlet that meets the Bosporus and the Marmara at the thumb-shaped promontory occupied by the great city of Constantinople. The outcome of the uprising was never in doubt. Emperor Phocas, bereft of allies and beset by enemies, was stripped of his splendid robes and bundled down to the harbor, where his visitor from Carthage, enjoying the threadbare spectacle, is said to have sneered, "Is it thus, O wretch, that you have governed the state?" To which Phocas replied, "No doubt you will govern it better." The repartee was not appreciated: Phocas was instantly executed, his body skinned and cut up into several manageable pieces to be roasted in an oven before a crowd of raucous ill-wishers. Later in this eventful day of October 5, 610, Heraclius was crowned emperor and then promptly wed a Byzantine princess, Eudoxia. With the passing of time, Heraclius and all of his successors would insist on being called *basileus*, the Greek title of kingship that replaced the old Latin honorific *imperator*.

Heraclius had taken control of an empire in tatters. So large was the task of overhauling it that more than a decade would pass before he took to the field in force against the enemy. As a good soldier, he divided the old mare nostrum into a multitude of protofeudal military districts that doubled as units of civic administration. This reorganization, each district being known as a *theme*, would serve the Byzantines well for the coming centuries of conflict, for the soldiery settled in these lands received an inalienable land grant in exchange for compulsory service in the army should the occasion arise. As basileus, however, afflicted with the Byzantine knack for Christological hairsplitting, Heraclius meddled in matters religious, persecuting those he deemed heretics and, at one moment, enacting an edict that outlawed Judaism. Moreover, his private life was public scandal: on the death of Eudoxia from what is believed to have been epilepsy, Heraclius official-ized an outrageous liaison by wedding his beautiful niece, Martina. The royal couple's succession of sickly and sometimes misshapen offspring in the years to follow was viewed, quite understandably, as divine retribution.

For all his outsize flaws, Heraclius nonetheless managed to set his empire aright and gird it for battle. In particular, he was successful in compelling the wealthy Orthodox churchmen of Constantinople to bankroll the army estab-lishment he was rebuilding. It was past time for the Byzantine basileus to take on the *shahanshah*, the Persian king of kings, who ruled in despotic splendor from Ctesiphon in Mesopotamia.

The epic stories of Darius and Xerxes, whose armies Athenian hoplites and sailors had defeated at the dawn of the classical era in the landmark battles of Marathon and Salamis, have overshadowed this later Greek-Persian rivalry in the twilight of antiquity. The Sassanids, already a dynasty four centuries old in Heraclius' time, had fought the old Romans in their day and were now intent on taking on the Greek Christian soldiers commanded from Constantinople. The buffer zones of the Syrian desert and the mountains of Anatolia had been breached constantly by both sides, in an age-old struggle between east and west for control of the Fertile Crescent. Endowed with a civilization as glorious as that of the Byzantines, the Sassanids saw themselves, not as epigones of the great Persians of a thousand years previous, but as the superiors to all other peo-ples of their own day. One Sassanid wrote of this self-evident truth:

[Iran] is the navel [of the world], because our land lies in the midst of other lands and our people are the most noble and illustrious of beings. The horse-manship of the Turk, the intellect of India, and the craftsmanship and art of Greece; God has endowed our people with all these, more richly than they are found in other nations separately. He has withheld from them the cere-monies of religion and the serving of kings which He gave to us. And He made our appearance and our colouring and our hair according to a just mean, without blackness prevailing or yellowness or ruddiness; and the hair of our beards and heads neither too curly like the Negro's, nor quite straight like the Turk's.

The tone of self-regard mounted in official correspondence. In letters from the Persian king to the Greek basileus, the salutation alone gives an idea of what might be called, charitably, their relationship: "Noblest of the Gods, King and Master of the whole Earth, Son of the great Hormisdas, CHOSROES, to Heraclius his vile and insensate slave." The goading might have been tolerable to the basileus, had not Chosroes, through his great general Shahrbaraz, sacked the great cities of the Byzantine east—Antioch, Aleppo, Damascus, Alexandria. At Jerusalem, Shahrbaraz torched the Church of the Holy Sepulchre and made off with some of Christianity's holiest relics, including the True Cross, which landed in the royal treasury at Ctesiphon. The Persian insult had gone beyond the personal, the political, and the economic—the god of Constantinople had been defamed.

Accordingly, in 622 Heraclius gathered together a great force and crossed the Bosporus to take the battle to the very heart of the Persian empire. He was the first emperor of the Byzantines or Romans to lead an army in person in more than two centuries. The occasion was hailed as momentous, especially after Heraclius handily won a battle in Anatolia and then, to avenge Jerusalem, destroyed a complex in Ganzak, an Iranian fire-temple sacred to the faith of Zoroaster, whose teachings formed the basis of the Persian religion. Success followed success for Heraclius in a long and bloody campaign. For Byzantines of the time, the year 622 might thus have marked an auspicious new beginning: victory in the field and for their faith provided by a great basileus.

If they entertained such thoughts, they could not have been more mistaken. Few instances of historical irony are as pitiless as that attendant on the timing of Heraclius' offensive to rescue and reinvigorate the Byzantine Empire. The same year, 622, witnessed the birth of a far graver threat to the Greeks, one that would relegate their great conflict with the Persians to the status of a mere warm-up. The force born at that moment would blindside the Sassanids, wiping them from the slate of history in less than two decades, and provide the Byzantines with an ideological adversary for more than eight centuries. In September of that year, in the Arabian peninsula, a few dozen acolytes of an obscure visionary named Muhammad Ibn Abdallah slipped out of the hills surrounding Mecca and made their way northward to Yathrib, the oasis town now known to us as Madina. It was the time of the *hijra*, or emigration, the Year One of the Muslim calendar.

-+- -+-   -+- -+-

Nothing presaged the succession of events that would eventually give rise to a religion that today numbers more than a billion adherents worldwide. At the dawn of the seventh century, according to most of the traditions (*hadith*) re-lating Muhammad's life and deeds, the man who would be the Prophet was outwardly ordinary, his material situation unenviable. His early life seemed unlikely to foster a destiny of any distinction, much less one that would change the world. Even when his vocation manifested itself in middle age, the better part of a decade passed before he would influence anyone outside his immediate circle of family and friends. His journey from the outermost margin to the up-permost summit of history has few parallels. Muhammad's closest peer in seis-mic piety is Jesus of Nazareth, but the latter's life, or at least the mortal portion of it that everyone can concede as having occurred, ended in the ignominy of crucifixion as a criminal. Not so Muhammad. His message was widely accepted by the end of his life; the Quran, the first book to be written in Arabic, was compiled within a generation or two of his death in 632. Jesus died alone, exe-cuted by a provincial governor. Muhammad, in his final days, knew himself to be a success, the patriarch of a large and loving clan, the master of much of Arabia.

Even a cursory biography of the man astounds. An orphaned poor cousin of the Quraysh tribe of Mecca, born in 570 or thereabouts, he had been raised in boyhood by a benevolent uncle. As a youth, Muhammad first eked out a living in the employ of his more successful relatives. At the time Mecca was an impor-tant trading center and pilgrimage site. Its precious well, Zamzam, stood near the middle of the *haram*, a sacred precinct in which bloodshed was forbidden. The oasis settlement was controlled by several families belonging to the Quraysh. Muhammad's branch of that clan, the Beni Hashim (whence Hashemite), had among its members several guardians of the haram—a source of some revenue—but only a few prominent men such as his uncle engaged in the caravan trade. Meccan merchants organized the spice, crafts, and slave caravans that received Indian and African goods and captives in the port of Yemen and hauled them up the torrid Red Sea coast—the sea itself was infested with pirates—and on to the rich Byzantine entrepots in Palestine and Syria.

Muhammad's luck changed when he was charged with accompanying a cara-van partly financed by Khadija, a wealthy widow of Mecca. Although any as-sertion about his life fairly begs to be hedged for want of a consensual narrative, by the time he took charge of Khadija's business Muhammad is believed to have traveled throughout the Byzantine Near East and visited such important centers as Damascus and Jerusalem. The Prophet's first biographer, Muhammad Ibn Ishaq, claimed his subject had an important encounter in the provincial city of

Bosra, in southern Syria near the Yarmuk River. There, according to Ibn Ishaq, Muhammad the merchant was recognized as a putative prophet by a Christian mystic.

Eventually Muhammad wed Khadija, who, although more than a decade his senior, would bear him four daughters. It was a marriage fertile in other ways as well, for the newly comfortable Muhammad had the time and leisure to find his calling. Years of meditation followed and, it has been hazarded, conversation with the monotheists of the region—in pre-Islamic times Jewish and Christian tribes were present among the pagan majority of the Hijaz, as well as many seekers of monotheistic truth outside the two older traditions.

The heretofore unremarkable spiritual itinerary of the merchant took a dramatic turn in the year 610, when the angel Gabriel paid him a visit and said, as recorded in a *sura*, or rhymed chapter, of the Quran: "Recite: in the name of thy Lord who created, created man of a blood-clot. Recite: and thy Lord is the most bountiful, who taught by the pen, taught man what he knew not." Henceforth Muhammad would be visited by an angelic emissary for the rest of his life, causing him to utter the words of God (Allah) during episodic trances that were as spiritually ecstatic as they were physically painful. Not to belabor the workings of coincidence, but the year of that first, momentous revelation was the same one in which Heraclius went sailing to Byzantium.

From 610 onward Muhammad elaborated an ethical, monotheist view of the world that would do away with the metaphysical indiscipline of the desert animist and the political anarchy of a people riven by blood feuds and narrow tribal beliefs. In descriptions of the creed, attention is usually lavished on the five pillars of Islam (profession of faith, ritual prayer, alms-giving, fasting, and pilgrimage), but other features characterized the new dispensation as well. Among the most important: a permanent exhortation to lead a life of personal piety and probity, a clear description of what awaited in heaven and hell, a project for constructing a society and system of law, and, critically for its subsequent universal appeal, a call for brotherhood and decency in dealings with others, a decency that cut across tribal and eventually ethnic and even religious lines. Islam was seen as perfecting what had come before; Muhammad, then, was the conduit of a god giving his final and complete revelation.

The Prophet's first convert was his wife, Khadija. She was followed in her faith by a few members of the Beni Hashim family as well as some of the dispossessed of Mecca. Timorously at first, then with increasing confidence, Muhammad brought his message to the Quraysh at large, urging them to destroy the

idols cluttering Mecca. He deplored that the haram's cube-shaped Kaaba—a
building said to have been erected by Adam and restored by Ibrahim (Abraham) and Ismail (Ishmael)—had become a site for the worship of al-Lat, al-
Uzza, and Manat, the goddesses revered as the daughters of God. While some
of his listeners from within the Quraysh converted, most remained unmoved.
They were comfortable with what is called henotheism, that is, belief in a
supreme god that does not exclude the existence of other divinities.

At one point, no doubt hoping to win over the stubborn, Muhammad came
close to admitting the validity of God's associate gods—but he soon back-
tracked, claiming that these "satanic verses" had been dictated by an evil presence imitating the divine voice that visited him. Instead, Muhammad grew
more uncompromising in his monotheism and resumed hectoring his kinsman
into abandoning the gods and goddesses of their fathers. At this moment, his
standing in Mecca must have resembled that of Socrates in Athens—a loqua-
cious local irritant who eventually inspired mortal enmity.

Old photograph of the central courtyard of the main mosque at Mecca. The black building
surrounded by pilgrims is the Kaaba.

Although constrained by tribal custom to respect their own, some of the Quraysh finally had their fill of this monotheist innovator, whose preaching threatened to disrupt the flow of pilgrims and their purses to Mecca. The unconverted Meccans—the majority—first tried shunning all of the Beni Hashim, whether Muslim or not, and excluding them from the life of the city. When this internal economic exile didn't work—it may even have strengthened Muhammad's hand with the rebellious younger members of the Quraysh—darker stratagems were devised. Muhammad may have caught wind of a plot against his life or simply seen ominous clouds gathering: following a secret negotiation with the men of Madina, he fled Mecca with his few dozen followers. But more than a flight from something, the hijra was a movement toward a goal: autonomy for the community of Muslim believers, the *umma*, under the leadership of Muhammad. Out from under the baleful glare of the conservative Quraysh, Islam could thrive.

Once in Madina, the Prophet proved to be an extraordinarily nimble leader, entering into nearly a dozen politically useful marriages after Khadija's death and exhorting his followers to repeated feats of valor, all the while giving utterance to the social and spiritual precepts to be enshrined in the Quran. When not relying on the innate persuasiveness of their faith, the near-destitute Muslim pioneers of Madina subdued Arabia through warfare, the shrewd division of spoils and collection of tribute, and tactical assassination. First subsumed were their hosts, the two pagan tribes of Madina who had invited Muhammad, as a holy man, to arbitrate a dispute—a custom common in pre-Islamic Arabia among those too tired or wary of its alternative, the blood feud. The Prophet resolved the argument by converting the Madinans wholesale: they are known to historians of Islam as the Helpers, as opposed to his Quraysh converts who are called Companions. The Helpers' long-standing ties to the bedouin nomads of the vicinity swelled the ranks of the Muslim armies. Muhammad had less success with the three Jewish Arabian clans of Madina, who welcomed the newcomers but refused to give up their faith and join the Muslim umma. Eventually they were dealt with brutally—either through expropriation and banishment or, in the case of the unfortunate Banu Qurayza clan, mass execution of the adult males and enslavement of their women and children. They were accused of abetting the Muslims' bitterest enemies, the Meccans.

Defeating those wealthy and obdurate kinsmen became the highest priority for the Muslim émigrés of Madina. Not only did the Meccans' refusal to convert still rankle, but their power and alliances remained a mortal threat. Battle was first joined in 624—the Muslims launched a raid on the caravan of Abu Sufyan, a prominent Meccan Qurayshi, as it passed near Madina on its return from Palestine laden with treasure. The raid was a failure; even more alarming, a large Meccan force, hastily assembled and rushed northward to defend Abu Sufyan, came across the Muslim contingents, almost by accident, at the oasis of Badr. Far outnumbered, the Muslims nonetheless won a resounding victory. Many had been emboldened by the Prophet's guarantee of instant admission to paradise for anyone slain in the service of Islam—an incentive destined to have a long and violent posterity. Badr, the initial blooding between Arabian brothers, sparked a series of skirmishes in the ensuing years, a seesawing campaign of desert dustups marked by the customary horror of fratricidal war. Abu Sufyan's wife, Hind, to cite just one perpetrator, has gone down in Islamic history for eating, after a battle of 625, the liver of Muhammad's slain uncle, Hamza. (Then again, Hind's father had been killed by Hamza at Badr the year before.)

In the latter half of the decade, however, the Muslims prevailed, both on the battlefields and in the hearts of the people. Then as now, it was hard to argue with success. Muhammad's record of unrelenting triumph elsewhere in the Arabian peninsula was an outstanding inducement to convert, as was the Prophet's well-earned reputation for magnanimity toward any who accepted his message, however tardily. In 630 Mecca welcomed back her wayward son and acquiesced in his leadership—although Hind, the liver-eater, is supposed to have heckled him. Wisely, Muhammad held no grudges. In the two years remaining in his life, the prominent people who had so long mocked him were appointed to positions of prominence in the Islamic polity, and the spoils of further wars were freely distributed to former enemies. A new society—a state, in effect—began taking shape, marked by the galvanizing presence of a young faith; a heretofore unattainable unity of purpose among oasis dwellers, quasi-sedentary merchants, and warrior nomads; and most significantly, a willingness to disperse beyond the sandy confines of Arabia. Out in the larger world, where the armies of Heraclius and Chosroes were fighting themselves into exhaustion, where the two great empires reeled from years of battle, opportunity awaited. Muhammad's successors would seize it.

◄- ◄- →- →-

The Byzantines were weary. Their Persian wars were going well, but they bled the treasury dry. Safe behind its massive land walls constructed by Emperor

Theodosius II in the fifth century, Constantinople managed to withstand Persian and Avar sieges while Heraclius, confident in his capital's capacity to repulse assault, was ceaselessly ranging through Anatolia, Syria, and Mesopotamia, co-ordinating three separate armies against Chosroes. Faced with reverses in the field, the vainglorious shahanshah drifted into the neverland of the deranged— at one point he ordered the body of a defeated and defunct general to be packed in salt and shipped back to Mesopotamia so that he could personally supervise the flaying of the corpse. The Persians watched impotently as the cities of the eastern Mediterranean were reoccupied by the Byzantines. By the dawn of the 630s, the Greeks had won.

In victory Heraclius, unlike Muhammad, did not forgive and forget: fierce punishment was meted out to all who had sided with the Persians. This led to a further souring of relations between the Greeks and the subject Semitic peoples of the Near East—Jews and monophysite Christians. At the same time the empire's long-standing Arab warrior allies, the Ghassanids, who had for generations served as Byzantine proxies in defending Syria from Persian incursions and bedouin raids, had a falling-out with Constantinople. Although this breach was patched up by the time the Companions of the Prophet came calling with their spears, it frayed the loyalty felt by the Ghassanids to their Greek paymasters.

A Muslim tradition, or hadith, holds that Muhammad actually wrote letters to Heraclius and Chosroes in an attempt to avert the coming storm. True to form, the embattled shahanshah threw the bearer of Muhammad's missive out on his ear. Heraclius, however, had the letter read aloud: it exhorted him to embrace Islam. His curiosity piqued, the basileus is said to have summoned a non-Muslim Qurayshi merchant passing through Jerusalem and questioned him about the Prophet. The merchant was none other than Abu Sufyan, the intended victim of the attack at the Badr oasis and then still an opponent of the Muslims. (He and his wife Hind would convert at the last minute, on the eve of Muhammad's return to Mecca.) Abu Sufyan, according to the hadith, conceded that Muhammad was a man of unimpeachable integrity with a growing number of disciples, an admission that greatly impressed the basileus.

In a further twist, the tradition holds that Heraclius received an astrological message that told him that the Byzantine Empire would be undone by a circumcised people. After considering, in keeping with his idea of Christian kingship, the murder of all male Jews, Heraclius is supposed to have paused, seized by an intuition—and then asked that the ambassador from the Ghassanids be relieved of his clothes. The envoy, duly examined, explained that his circumcised state was in keeping with age-old Arab custom. The hadith reported that Heraclius, newly enlightened, raced up to Homs, in the Orontes Valley of Syria, and convened an episcopal conclave in which he pleaded for the conversion of all Greeks to Islam, in order to thwart the astrological sentence of doom. The bishops, as might be imagined, thought he was out of his mind.

However much they strain credulity, these stories of foreboding and flightiness suggest that their authors had some sympathy for the Byzantine predicament in these years. As the sands inexorably ran down toward Yarmuk, the Greeks had no idea of what was in store. They were victors over a rival empire, in the manner of Romans of the past, ready to resume the normal peacetime pursuits of trade, the hunt, the games at the hippodromes and, as always, interconfessional bickering. The Persians, their only threat in the east, were neutralized—in 630 Heraclius took the recovered relic of the True Cross back to Jerusalem, rebuilt the Church of the Holy Sepulchre, and as was his wont, ordered a massacre of the Jews in Galilee. He could have had no inkling that at the same time Muhammad was returning to Mecca amid similar scenes of triumph. Notwithstanding the hadith, he might not even have heard of Muhammad. Heraclius, during this last visit of a basileus to Jerusalem, may have been told of a minor action in the south of Jordan—a Byzantine and Ghassanid detachment had beaten back an Arabian raiding party the year previously—but he could not possibly have known, unless he were a prophet himself, that the small Jordanian skirmish had lit a short fuse or that the attackers had been animated by a faith that would soon rival his own.

For the Muslims of Arabia, by contrast, this preliminary period spawned few complacent illusions of the type afflicting the Byzantines. On the death of the Prophet in Madina in 632, Abu Bekr was chosen as head of the Muslim umma. He had been one of Islam's earliest acolytes and had fathered Aisha, Muhammad's cherished child-bride. A man of great devotion to the memory of his revered friend, Abu Bekr hewed closely to Muhammad's example of simple piety and discerning leadership. In staffing his army, he sought to juggle Muslim bona fides—the seniority of a commander's conversion to Islam—with demonstrable talent, even if the candidate in question was a conspicuous latecomer to the cause of the Prophet. Among the latter was Khalid Ibn al Walid, an ally of Abu Sufyan's, whose conversion came a few years after he had distinguished himself at the head of Qurayshi armies inimical to Muhammad and the Muslims. Late as it was, Khalid's conversion was a boon to the young movement—during Abu Bekr's caliphate, he subdued tribe after tribe of Arabians who, on hearing of the Prophet's demise, opportunistically recanted their faith and began touting homegrown imitators of Muhammad. These wars of reconquest, called the *ridda*, established Khalid as a military commander of great ability. Thenceforth known as the Sword of God (Sayf Allah), he was selected to lead the offensive east into Mesopotamia to topple the already-tottering Sassanid Persians—or rather, to take advantage of the uprisings against the Sassanids in the wake of their defeat at the hands of Heraclius. By decade's end, the Muslims would bring Mesopotamia definitively into their orbit.

The caliph Abu Bekr also made the fateful decision to take on the Byzantines, although he claimed to be only fulfilling Muhammad's wishes: had not the Prophet ordered the raid into southern Jordan? No excuse was needed—the Persian and Greek empires both dangled like overripe fruit on the borders of Arabia. The popular western idea of the early Arab conquest as the work of wild-eyed warrior missionaries, converting the quivering masses at swordpoint, should be retired. Islam, the new dispensation, fostered a novel cohesion in a disorganized desert people, who thus far had practiced only the sporadic *razzia* (raid) on the tantalizingly rich civilizations at their doorstep. Under the stewardship of Muhammad and his successors, the umma became a protostate capable of coordinated movement and campaigning. Certainly the new generation was fired by faith, but the motive behind the wars of aggression lies less in the nature of Islam than in the nature of mankind. Weakness and division had been detected; strength and enthusiasm, marshaled—and wealth lay there for the taking. In 634 the Muslims at last moved on Palestine.

The leader of this first expeditionary force, Amr Ibn al As, like Khalid a late convert destined to be lionized by the faithful, chose to make his attack near Gaza. The engagement at the oasis of Dathin was hardly more than a skirmish, but the Muslim victory shocked the Byzantine Near East. The Persians had just been evicted after decades of warfare; suddenly the Arabians, a manageable (and commercial) people, were recast as conquerors. Peasants fled in panic from the great estates of Palestine, the cities swelled with refugees, and the patriarch of Jerusalem, Sophronius, thundered from the pulpit about the "diabolic savagery" of the invaders. Amr and his Muslims pressed their advantage— marauding bedouins plundered the countryside, avoiding the fortified towns and keeping clear of the coast, which the Byzantine fleet patrolled. East of the Dead Sea, on the Jordanian plateau, armies looted at will. Heraclius, from his palace in Homs, called on his brother Theodore, a veteran of the Persian wars, to go south in force and counter this wholly unexpected bolt from the blue. Abu Bekr, from his deathbed in Madina, called on Khalid Ibn al Walid. He was to cease operations in Iraq and head to Palestine. This turned out to be the order that tipped the balance.

In the late spring of 634 Khalid and his men raced directly from Iraq across the hell of the Syrian desert. The ride has entered legend—in one of its variants, Khalid at first denied his thirsty pack-camels any water, then let them greedily overdrink their fill from the Euphrates so that in the desert they could be culled successively, their stomachs cut open, and the precious water within shared out among his warriors. However it was accomplished, Khalid's dash through the scorching badlands concluded with an irruption not in Palestine or Jordan but in southwestern Syria, just a day's ride from Damascus. In a twinkling he besieged and captured Bosra (where Muhammad had been recognized as a prophet by a Christian mystic). The Arabians, whom conventional Byzantine wisdom held to be mere raiders, the martial equivalent of purse-snatchers, had taken an imperial city—and one not on the borderlands of southern Palestine or Jordan but in Syria. Heraclius, sensing his august person to be in harm's way, moved north to the safer precincts of Antioch, close to Anatolia and the sea. Khalid went south: he met up with Amr to take command of the forces mustering to face the army of Theodore, the brother of the basileus.

The first major clash occurred on July 30, 634, at a place called Ajnadayn, which is believed to have been located approximately twenty kilometers to the west of Bethlehem. Although details of the engagement are sketchy, the Muslims won a crushing victory. One account has Khalid's greatest champion challenging the Byzantines to duels prior to the battle, taunting them thus: "I am the death of the Pale Faces, I am the killer of Romans; I am the scourge sent upon you, I am Zarrar Ibn al Azwar." Zarrar lived up to his boasts—he is credited with slaying several Byzantine grandees and shoring up morale at a key juncture in the battle. The defeated Theodore was sent home to Constantinople in disgrace and to the not-so-tender mercies of Martina, his all-powerful niece and sister-in-law.

The Muslim armies probed farther northward, their numbers no doubt growing as tales of booty spread. Throughout the following year the invaders won a series of engagements near the Dead Sea, until finally they broke through in strength into Syria and began to capture its great cities. These age-old desert "ports," outposts of the Mediterranean world that received the caravans from the east, were the key to power. From south to north—Damascus, Homs, Hama, Aleppo—the string of sophisticated trading centers seemed perilously close to slipping from the control of Constantinople. Huddled behind their city walls, the subject peoples of Syria began to look askance at the Byzantine status quo. Did not these invading Muslims promise them freedom of worship? Were they not fellow Semites? With the imperial Greeks, one paid exorbitant taxes but was never sure to be left alone. Under the Muslims, the exactions and tyranny would continue, but synagogue and monophysite church would be inviolate.

Heraclius was reaping what he had sown with his years of cruelty and revenge. Damascus fell, then Homs. The basileus, sensing the faintheartedness abroad in the province, chose to move resolutely. Armies were levied in Anatolia, warriors summoned from Armenia. The majority-Greek cities of the coast provided supplies and more men. The Ghassanid Arabs, longtime allies of Constantinople, gathered their forces. For all its battle fatigue, the Byzantine Empire in its reach and world-beating ambition remained a worthy successor to the Roman; its full weight was brought into play against the intruder.

Outnumbered and perhaps a little overawed, the Muslims beat a tactical retreat. They withdrew from the cities so recently captured and regrouped near the southern Syrian centers of Bosra and Dara. In the latter, interestingly, one of the Arab Jewish clans of Madina had settled after being chased from their homes by the Prophet some ten years earlier. In the sources, there is no mention of hard feelings between these Jews, the Banu Nadhir, and their former persecutors—this clan of armorers and blacksmiths may even have helped equip the Muslim army, so disgusted were they by the intolerant bloodlust of Heraclius. Just as likely, however, the Banu Nadhir Jews of Dara had no choice in the matter—fifteen thousand Muslim warriors, at the very least, were squatting their new homeland by the Yarmuk. They were soon to be joined, in the summer of 636, by a huge Byzantine force.

⤛ ⤛ ⤜ ⤜

Maddeningly, the horizon of history as it bears on this world-altering event is clouded with uncertainty. Sources for the battle range from blame-dodging Christian chronicles to triumphalist Muslim traditions, and the resulting thicket of self-serving tale-telling has left Yarmuk in a narrative limbo. Until recently western scholarship routinely discounted many of the Muslim accounts; credence was given instead to claims that a sudden sandstorm blinded the Byzantines—in the stony terrain of the Golan, no less—and to the customary Greek accusation of Armenian perfidy. One of the commanders at Yarmuk, a hitherto loyal Armenian warrior called Vahan, was supposed to have been proclaimed basileus by his mutinous followers on the eve of battle, thereby sowing confusion in the Byzantine ranks. While not unprecedented for the time (both Phocas and Heraclius had started as usurpers, after all), the tale of revolt seems too tidy a manner of explaining away the Byzantine defeat. What can be asserted with certainty is that Byzantine Syria and Palestine in the fourth decade of the seventh century were divided, weakened, captious provinces—and that the advancing Arabians had overcome tribal animosities to form a disciplined fighting force.

The Byzantines had assembled in southern Syria by July 636. Their main fortified camp was established by a wadi in the western Golan, near Yaqusah—what is now the no less armed-to-the-teeth Kibbutz Meizar. Though hardly the quarter-million-man force described in one Arab chronicle, the Christian soldiery may have outnumbered the Muslim two, perhaps three, to one. Heraclius, from his headquarters in far-off Antioch, instructed his generals to set about Byzantine business as usual: they were to attempt to buy off, suborn, or corrupt their counterparts on the opposing side. As a stratagem it was a shabby but humane way of achieving victory without bloodshed. Indeed, one of the Byzantine leaders at Yarmuk, Niketas, was the epitome of an enemy-turned-collaborator: his father had been Shahrbaraz, the formidable Persian general who had laid waste to Jerusalem two decades earlier.

The Muslims did not bite. Bribes were rejected, blandishments ignored. If anything, some Ghassanid and other Christian Arab auxiliaries of the Byzantines may have found the reasoning behind the refusals compelling. Although Khalid had been deprived of overall command—on the order of Umar, the successor as caliph to the recently deceased Abu Bekr—his prestige remained undiminished. His aura of invincibility, coupled with rumors of a new brotherhood of faith animating the invaders, could not have failed to intrigue. Whatever the dynamic of desertion and side-switching, as the summer of 636 progressed the incorruptible Arabians clearly did not melt away into the desert as expected; instead they gained in strength. And the Byzantines, even if this corner of Syria had long been theirs, began feeling like an army in hostile territory.

Their supply line to Damascus became unreliable; the Christian Arab governor of that city complained long and loud about pouring provisions down the maw of a vast imperial host. He is even thought to have organized a night raid on a Byzantine camp outside Damascus, an incident said to have shaken morale. As July turned to August, the Byzantine generals realized that time, perhaps even God, was not on their side.

In mid-August 636 Vahan is said to have made one last overture to Khalid: if the Muslims decamped and quit the province, a king's ransom would be theirs. The Sword of God demurred. Just after daybreak the next morning—in all likelihood August 15—the signals were given. Various champions from the two sides approached each other over the boulder fields and fought duels to the death as their comrades slipped on surcoats of mail and hardened leather. As custom demanded, the light Muslim archers took a running leap and mounted their steeds. The Byzantine infantryman strapped on his simple conical helmet, with a long strip of metal to protect the nose. Round shields were raised; javelins and spears bristled. At last the battle standards were hoisted, the cross of Byzantium on one, the colors of Arabia on the other. The armies that had skirmished with each other all summer readied themselves for the carnage to come. By noon battle was joined. The epochal engagement at Yarmuk would last six days.

As far as can be determined, the battle front stretched about fifteen kilometers from Nawa south to the Yarmuk River. The Byzantines held the west; the Muslims, cognizant of the local terrain, chose to make their stand in the east, leaving the enemy to take the fight to them. The Byzantine camp at Yaqusah was more than twenty kilometers in the rear, established there because of its superb natural defenses and its position athwart the route that led to northern Palestine. It was the back door to the Promised Land. This eminently sensible strategic setup had one flaw: between the camp and the field of battle—a site of Khalid's choosing—lay the Wadi Ruqqad, which in its southern reaches carves a topographical gash in the plateau rivaling that of the Yarmuk's canyon. To reach the safety of their camp then, in the unlikely event of a retreat, the Byzantines would either have to take a circuitous detour to the north, where the Ruqqad was easily forded, or cross a Roman bridge spanning the wadi at a place called Ayn Dhakar. The bridge at Ayn Dhakar stood a few kilometers north of the Ruqqad's dramatic confluence with the Yarmuk and provided the most direct route back to the camp at Yaqusah. It was a sturdy and reliable old structure but a potential bottleneck if things went awry.

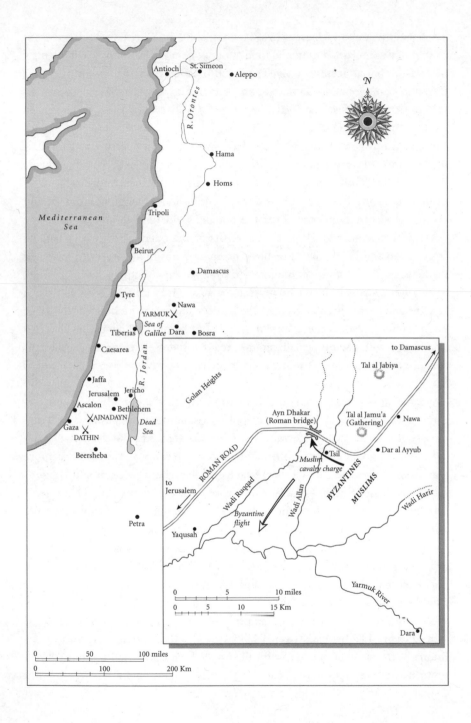

Not that the Byzantines anticipated a military reversal. They had a considerable numerical superiority and, even with ominous dissensions between rival commanders, a long and glorious history of victory in the field. These Greeks were Romans (*Rumi* or *Rum* to their enemies), the rightful proprietors of the mare nostrum. The Arabians, so they still thought, were a rabble.

The Armenian Vahan seems to have coordinated the initial massive attack from his position at the midpoint of the front, near the present-day village of Tsil. Hardwood shields locked and aloft, spears bristling, a cloud of arrows preceding it, the Byzantine infantry would have marched forward in the same hedgehog formation that its Roman forebear had used to subdue a world. The Arabs, nimble in the saddle and lightly armed, fell back before the onslaught, their Yemeni bowmen loosing volleys of armor-piercing bolts as the Muslim lines re-formed. Throughout this first day of battle, scores of engagements raged across the plateau, with many of the dozen or so commanders on both sides joining in the vicious hand-to-hand fighting. By nightfall a sanguinary stalemate obtained, with no ground gained or lost.

The Byzantines attacked the next morning while the Muslims were at prayer—that much they knew about this unfamiliar enemy. The encampments of Khalid and the other generals, especially in the northern section of the battlefield, near Nawa, seem at one point to have been overrun. In some Arab chronicles, the women in the camps made their important appearance at this moment, a peculiarity of the battle that would amplify in the ensuing days. As the Byzantines, in a calculated encircling strategy, drove back first the Muslim left, then the right, time and again the wives and daughters of the retreating warriors came out to menace their fleeing menfolk with sharpened tentpoles, cursing them for giving ground. The redoubtable and by now inevitable Hind is celebrated in these traditions for stemming a rout in the southern section of the battlefield, near the cliffs of the Yarmuk, by leading her sisters in a suggestive song containing the oldest threat of all:

We are the daughters of the night;
We move among the cushions
With a gentle feline grace
And our bracelets on our elbows.
If you advance we shall embrace you;
And if you retreat we shall forsake you
With a loveless separation.

Her husband, the seventy-three-year-old Abu Sufyan, promptly turned around and counterattacked, only to lose an eye to a Byzantine arrow. Another story has a retreating Muslim leader in the northern sector making the same impulsive return to the fray, exhorting his men, "It is easier to face the Rumi than our wives!"

Whatever the truth of these tales, every able-bodied person on the Muslim side must have pitched in to withstand the assaults of the Byzantine foot and horse. They had to hold their ground, having nowhere to retreat but the desert. In all probability Khalid's strategy, risky in the extreme, called for a Muslim attack only when the Byzantines showed signs of exhaustion or disorganization, neither of which the outnumbered Arabians had the luxury of allowing themselves. Despite the inexactness of the source material, consensus holds that Khalid at last saw his chance on the fourth or fifth day of the bloody stalemate.

In the *Strategikon*, a contemporaneous Byzantine military manual, mention is made of a combined cavalry and infantry maneuver to be used to create surprise and deliver a sudden hammer blow to the enemy. Calling for a complex ballet of foot soldiers thinning ranks to allow columns of galloping horsemen passage to and from a point of impact, the maneuver required the sophistication of a long martial tradition even to be considered as a tactic in the heat of battle. The foremost historian of Yarmuk thinks that—in place of the unlikely sandstorm theory—the Byzantines tried this maneuver and botched it. Somehow the cavalry became separated from the infantry, leaving the latter bereft of protection. Khalid had been holding his horsemen in reserve, behind the Muslim lines, waiting for just such a moment. Cymbals crashing and war cries sounding, he raced into the gap. The surprised Byzantine horse, most of them Ghassanids, fled northward, to Tal al Jabila and the lava fields beyond. The Armenian infantrymen, their left flank completely exposed, bore the full brunt of the charge, falling back as wave after wave of sword- and spear-bearing cavalry barreled into them. In these days before gunpowder, it was the mismatch dreamed of by every rider of camel or horse. The left and part of the center of the Byzantine lines were comprehensively massacred.

But that would not necessarily have spelled doom for the Byzantine Middle East had the day not held a second surprise. According to one account, somewhere in the sector, hiding behind a hillock or in a hollow, a small mounted detachment awaited its orders. Its commander may have been Zarrar Ibn al Azwar, the killer of pale faces at Ajnadayn. When word finally came, the horsemen left their place of concealment and rode westward like the wind.

They galloped through the shouts and confusion and broke out into the clear beyond enemy lines. Their destination was the bridge at Ayn Dhakar.

⤛ ⤛   ⤜ ⤜

It is, of course, impossible to locate with any precision where the cavalry commando unit, if indeed there was a contingent of handpicked men, had been hiding: perhaps behind a long-vanished stand of trees; or behind Dar Ayyub, the Hill of Job; or near the more imposing Tal al Jumu'a, the Hill of the Gathering (where a Syrian army observation post now keeps the western horizon forever in its sights). The road, after making a right-angle turn in front of Job's shrine, heads straight westward through empty fields, where the mounted warriors would have certainly begun their ride, toward the distant village of Tsil. Today olive groves eventually flash past on this road, peopled by veiled women beating the tree branches so that the fruit drops into sacks spread open on the rock-hard ground. The men, most of them sporting a red or black kaffiyeh, tie the bags and hoist them up onto the backs of uncomplaining donkeys. Aside from the occasional army jeep trundling into view, the scene would be familiar to the combatants at Yarmuk.

Tsil itself breaks the spell. Half-finished concrete structures hem in a series of starburst road junctions; schoolgirls scramble out of the way of mechanized contraptions that look and sound like great malevolent insects. A helpful shopkeeper first points the way to Wadi Allan before realizing that the Wadi Ruqqad and Ayn Dhakar are being sought. A sly smile greets this information, and a you-can't-get-there-from-here shake of the head follows. And he seems to be right. On each attempt to reach the Muslim cavalry's goal of fifteen hundred years ago, a roadblock materializes, usually manned by a baby-faced Syrian conscript, waving away the anachronistically curious no matter how many official papers are produced. The critical bridge of Ayn Dhakar lies only a few more kilometers to the west, yet the complications of the present conspire to thwart a glimpse of the past. At last an impossibly ancient farmer, his great- or great-great-grandson smiling beside him from atop his perch on an ass, indicates a dirt track leading down a grassy ridge.

The barely passable route descends an unexpectedly steep slope until it meets a paved road to which access had been denied earlier in the afternoon. This T-junction is invisible from the crest of the ridge, where the army checkpoint stands guard. Farther down the slope a plantation of tall trees offers precious shade and further concealment from the conscripts. Less than a half-kilometer on, the road levels off to cross a broad culvert—and there it is, the Roman bridge, unused but unmistakable, standing off to the left. Its friable red-brick rational arches, sturdy stone piers, and humped-back cobbled roadbed—all betray the enduring work of the engineers of the mare nostrum. It, despite the absence of any signpost, will serve as the monument to the Battle of Yarmuk.

The bridge of Ayn Dhakar still spans Wadi Ruqqad, which is now a scree of jagged granite blocks and scrubby bushes. South of this point the river bottom descends deeper and deeper into the plateau until reaching the Yarmuk; north, the wadi's waters now lap up against an earthen berm; east, the old Roman road leads from Tsil and the battlefield; west are the heights of the Golan; and suddenly three white jeeps emblazoned with the UN logo approach at great speed. They are obviously not interested in archaeology—far too much water, apparently, has passed under this bridge.

The Muslim raiders were led directly to the spot by a traitor to Byzantium. Surprise and demoralization did the rest. In no time they had commandeered the vital structure and put themselves in control of the best escape route for the

The Roman bridge spanning the Wadi Ruqqad at Ayn Dhakar, a site of crucial importance in the Battle of Yarmuk.

beleaguered Christian troops wishing to regain their camp. The bridge was no longer a bottleneck; it was securely stoppered.

To worsen the Byzantine prospects, Khalid had moved infantry behind his outflanking cavalry, so that the northern part of the battle front, beyond Ayn Dhakar, became inaccessible to the imperial forces. The circuitous line of retreat to where the wadi could be forded was now blocked by thousands of Muslim warriors—and presumably their wives. The great mass of the Byzantine army was thus stranded on the southwestern reaches of the plateau, between Wadi Allan and Wadi Ruqqad. Getting back to camp at Yaqusah would entail scrambling down and up the gorges, perhaps even trying one's luck in scaling the steep slopes of the Yarmuk.

Disaster turned to debacle. Even the safe haven of camp was gone: the raiders of Ayn Dhakar had ridden under cover of night to Yaqusah and destroyed the Byzantine position in the rear. That they could have done this so thoroughly must be put down to a collapsing will to fight on one side and their own insane bravery on the other. The news filtered back to the front lines. By the final day of the battle, the armies of the Byzantines were nothing more than mobs of terrified men, tripping through the dawn light, hoping to find a way out. Some just sat down where they were and awaited their fate. Some fell to their deaths in the mad jostle to escape. Others made desperate last stands. The Muslims pressed them from the north and the east, ever closer to the chasm of the Yarmuk. Prisoners were not taken; he who was found was slain. Thousands, perhaps tens of thousands, perished.

Yet the Byzantine nightmare was not over. The men who had escaped the bloody denouement, either by deserting early or by fighting their way out as a group, were making their way north toward home, certain that the victorious Muslims would tarry on the killing fields to divide up the spoils of war. This too was a fatal miscalculation, another failure to appreciate just how disciplined a force they faced. The Muslims wheeled away from the battlefield to give chase, making much of Syria and what is now Lebanon into the scene of a wide-open manhunt. Vahan and his remaining troops were overtaken and slain well south of Damascus; retreating soldiers were killed in the Bekaa Valley; Khalid stormed up to Homs, several hundred kilometers north of Yarmuk, where Niketas pleaded with him to accept his sudden conversion to the cause of Islam. The Muslims pressed the hunt even farther north, going into the Orontes Valley, the cradle of Syrian civilization, and then on to the approaches of Anatolia beyond Aleppo. The surrenders of towns and cities came as fast and furious as the victorious horsemen rode. No second battle over Byzantine Syria would be fought. Yarmuk had decided that.

⼁⼁   ⼁⼁   ⼁⼁   ⼁⼁

In the countryside northwest of Aleppo, glimpses can still be had of the world that was to vanish. A series of limestone ridges rises on the horizon once the ancient city has been left behind, the folds in the earth creating hidden valleys and defiles, as if the forces of geology are playing hide-and-seek with the visitor. The human landscape is even more deceptive, the few villages punctuating the windswept hills seeming like sentinels stationed in a wilderness. Yet here and there, and soon everywhere, odd combinations of hewn, honey-colored blocks can be detected against the backdrop of gray rock and purple soil. The weather-beaten stones eventually coalesce as tympanum, lintel, colonnade, atrium—the remains of church, villa, warehouse, and market. More than seven hundred deserted Byzantine villages and towns are here, a grand gallery of ruins, testament to the time when these barren downs were blanketed by olive groves and pomegranate orchards, crisscrossed by Roman roads alive with merchant and scribe, matron and actress, monk and pilgrim.

The most impressive of these ruins sits on the prow of a green escarpment exposed to the west wind blowing off the mountains. It overlooks the last stage of the Silk Route that stretched from China to Antioch. Along the spine of the ridge, olive trees and Aleppo pines cast shade on a path that once was a proud avenue known as the Via Sacra. Nowadays it ends in a great tan jumble of acanthus-carved capitals and half-collapsed archways. These are the remnants of four vast basilicas, arranged in cruciform fashion around a hall open to the sky. In the center of this roofless enclosure stands the base of a large stone column, the nub of a pillar that used to rise twenty meters in height. Atop this column was once a wooden platform, where for thirty-six uninterrupted years a fifth-century mystic named Simeon Stylites lived out a strange life of ostentatious self-mortification, attracting throngs of pious onlookers from throughout Byzantine Syria.

The magnificent rubble of the St. Simeon complex gives an idea of the wealth of Christian Syria and the eccentricities of its otherworldly concerns. In the shadow of Simeon's pillar, the Christological quarrels that mined the Byzantine East from within no longer seem so outlandish. The pilgrimage site, once a rival to Jerusalem in the numbers of the faithful it drew, survived the shock of

Yarmuk but would not get around the long-term consequences of the battle. St. Simeon entered into a slow decline; earthquake and neglect would eventually reduce it to ruin. Even a temporary Byzantine reoccupation of the province in the tenth century would not halt the process of dechristianization. By the year 900, according to most estimates, Islam was the religion of the majority in Syria; by the year 1000 St. Simeon had taken on the appearance it has today: a valedictory in stone overlooking an empty borderland. The saint himself, a hermit besieged by admirers, might find the deserted setting more to his liking now.

If Yarmuk signaled the beginning of the end of Christian hegemony in the Mediterranean, it also marked the start of something new. On Palm Sunday 638 Caliph Umar bin al-Khattab entered Jerusalem, going through the same streets that had witnessed Heraclius' procession a mere eight years earlier. Whether Umar rode an ass or a snow-white camel into the city—this is disputed— Jerusalem's patriarch, Sophronius, showed the caliph the deference due an overlord. Umar had decreed that Jews and Christians would henceforth pay the punitive *jizya*, or poll tax, in exchange for the right to worship freely, if discreetly. The two Peoples of the Book were now *dhimmi*—protected second-class

The basilica complex of St. Simeon Stylites. The nub of his pillar can be seen in the center of the ruins.

citizens whose life and livelihood depended on the sufferance of Muslim authority. The Quran enjoined the faithful to broad-mindedness:

> Dispute not with the People of the Book save in the fairer manner, except for those of them that do wrong; and say, "We believe in what has been sent down to us, and what has been sent down to you; our God and your God is One, and to Him we have surrendered."

Patriarch Sophronius offered to usher Caliph Umar into the Church of the Holy Sepulchre. Although Isa (Jesus) was important to his faith, Umar declined. Should a call to prayer occur while he was touring the site, he told Sophronius, as a good Muslim he would be obliged to prostrate himself within the church—and his followers would then insist on turning the sanctuary into a mosque. Surely the patriarch wouldn't want that, would he?

Mount Moriah was a different matter. Umar would have known that this rocky height of Jerusalem—whose many names include Mount Sion, the Temple Mount, and the Navel of the Universe—was the place where Ibrahim (Abraham), the first monotheist and ergo the first Muslim, had tried to sacrifice his son; where Suleyman (Solomon) had built his temple; and where Muhammad had risen to heaven and returned to earth on his night ride to meet the prophets of the past. It was thus a hallowed spot, surpassed only by Mecca and Madina. Indeed, in the two years immediately following the hijra, the Prophet and his Companions had prayed in the direction of Jerusalem, not toward henotheistic Mecca. As the second of Muhammad's successors, Caliph Umar stood upon this holy place and surveyed the surrounding countryside. These lands were now part of the *dar al Islam*, the abode of Islam and, thus, peace. The Rumi still held sway in the *dar al harb*, the abode of war.

What remained of the Byzantine armies retreated over the Taurus Mountains, to the safety of rugged Anatolia, the Asia Minor of the ancients. Heraclius quit Antioch a broken man, the empire he had saved from the Persians torn apart by a thunderclap from the desert. In the churches of his venerable cities and in the basilicas of St. Simeon, a question was being asked: was the victory of this new heresy a punishment visited upon the Byzantines by the Almighty? The homecoming of the basileus suggested the affirmative. On reaching the Asian shore of the Bosporus, Heraclius refused to board the imperial tender to take him to Constantinople on the European side. He had somehow developed a morbid fear of water. This hydrophobia held up his entry into the city for weeks, until a pontoon bridge was thrown across the Bosporus, replete with view-blocking horsemen and potted palms that allowed the stricken basileus to ride across the strait without once glimpsing it.

Heraclius died in 641, leaving Martina to intrigue with sons and lovers over the succession. Umar died, assassinated, in 644, the first of three successive caliphs to meet the same fate. The nascent abode of peace would plunge into civil war. As for Khalid, he died in obscure circumstances, having been cashiered by Umar shortly after Yarmuk—the caliph may not have wanted his commander's fame putting him in the shade. In Homs, the city of many of Khalid's exploits, an enormous mosque is dedicated to him, rebuilt in grand style by the Ottomans in the early twentieth century. Khalid's bier stands in a corner beside the entrance, bathed in fluorescent green light. A sign in the prayer court reads, in Arabic and in English, "Don't beg, it's not dignified."

CHAPTER TWO

POITIERS 732

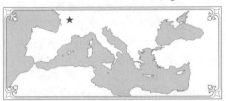

A century of Arab conquest; collision in Constantinople,
North Africa, Spain, and Gaul

S ome passages of writing overshadow the events they describe. In tracing
the extraordinary century following the great clash at Yarmuk, no one has
composed a more memorable flight of prose than that penned by Edward Gibbon about the Battle of Poitiers, at which Charles Martel and his Franks dealt a
blow to the Muslims. Gibbon, an Enlightenment Herodotus, speculated on what
might have transpired if the battle had gone the other way. His was the what-if
scenario that haunted the western mind for generations:

A victorious line of march had been prolonged above a thousand miles from
the rock of Gibraltar to the banks of the Loire; the repetition of an equal
space would have carrried the Saracens to the confines of Poland and the
highlands of Scotland; the Rhine is not more impassable than the Nile or Euphrates, and the Arabian fleet might have sailed without a naval combat into
the mouth of the Thames. Perhaps the interpretation of the Koran would
now be taught in the schools of Oxford, and her pulpits might demonstrate
to a circumcised people the sanctity and truth of the revelation of
Mohammed.

Mischievous and masterful all at once, Gibbon's conjecture about what might
have been if the Muslims had emerged victorious at Poitiers contributed to the
idea that Christendom was somehow saved in 732. The Englishman was not the
only one to promote that idea among Enlightenment luminaries. The French,

on whose soil the battle took place, have a long literature about the importance
of Poitiers. The snide genius of Voltaire, while mocking his countrymen's
exaggerations about the battle, felt compelled to concede in his *Essai sur les
moeurs*: "Without Charles Martel . . . France was a Mohammedan province."
Later artists agreed, in a more flamboyant manner: nineteenth-century tableaux
of swarthy Moors being felled in the presence of underdressed Amazons still
adorn many town halls in France. In our main source for the battle, the *Chronicle of 754*, a new word—*europenses*—appeared in describing Martel's men, a
lexical invention seized upon by those who see Poitiers as Europe's baptismal
font. Even if the revisionism of modern histories has chipped away at the importance of the clash—some see it as just a razzia gone wrong—for many westerners Poitiers remains a touchstone, as pivotal a moment as Caesar crossing
the Rubicon or Copernicus surveying the heavens. The Muslim defeat at
Poitiers neatly closed a period of one hundred years starting at the death of
Muhammad, a century of conquest and expansion that refashioned the Mediterranean world forever. In this view, Poitiers becomes less a high-water mark
than a buoy bobbing in an eddy of change.

At the Church of St. Hilaire le Grand in Poitiers, recalling that the giddy century of Arab conquest touched this place—the Muslims sacked the church in
the autumn of 732—requires a strenuous effort of the imagination, so thoroughly are the sanctuary and its surroundings imbued with timeless Christianity. St. Hilaire is no ghostly St. Simeon, alone in a landscape of swaying cypress
and sun-bleached rubble. The pale Romanesque structure—the current building dates from 1049—stands serenely in a quiet corner of the old city, its weathered stone shaded by a stately yew. Recently on a gray summer Sunday a
handful of parishioners listened to their *curé* celebrate mass in a dank nave that
suggested nothing more than a rainy, uninterrupted Latin past.

Moving out from the old church to the town and its surroundings does not dispel the incongruity of connecting this place to the doings of the Companions of
the Prophet. Poitiers, although south of the Loire, is a mere three hundred kilometers from Paris—and a world away from the Mediterranean. Perched on a
hill overlooking the river Clain, it is a lovely town of spires and convents, their
cool slate roofs having little in common with the warm terra cotta of the south.
Its hinterland—the Poitou—is slide show France, all brooks and copses and
gentle green slopes suggestive of peasant pleasures behind swollen hayricks and
before snug village hearths. That this was rich territory worth a fight is obvious,
and the two other great battles of Poitiers attest to its desirability. In 507 Clovis,

the first Christian king of the Franks, defeated the Visigoths at Vouillé, just to
the east of the city. (He was guided, apparently, by a miraculous light that appeared above the tomb of St. Hilaire.) In 1356 the English and French faced off
during the Hundred Years War; undaunted by defeat at Crécy a decade earlier,
the flower of French chivalry galloped to even greater catastrophe, this time just
south of town. These protagonists fit the Poitou picture: red-faced ax-men
hacking away at each other in the foliage; estranged Channel cousins colliding
in the shadow of castles both claimed as their own.

But the Arabs, the acolytes of a desert visionary, in this setting of waving
grains and wayside chapels? It surprises to this day that they got this far, so fast.
In all descriptions of the distant past, an ever-deepening abyss of time must be
crossed; only at Poitiers, however, do we also confront a chasm of space. Gibbon, in his speculative tour de force, underscored the length of the Muslim victory march from Gibraltar, yet the wild century-long race to this leafy corner
of France began not at that great rock, the Mediterranean's westernmost
guardian, but clear across the sea, on an impossibly faraway shore. From
Yarmuk to Poitiers, the progress of Islam beggared belief.

                              ◄◄ ◄◄   ►► ►►

The century of conquest after Yarmuk began in the richest province of the ancient world. Egypt was an eye-popping prize, a font of food and lucre that
would dazzle any invader, let alone a warrior from the barren Hijaz of the Arabian peninsula. The Muslims may not have known that in the year 610—the
year of Muhammad's first revelation—the treasury of the Orthodox patriarch
of Alexandria had contained an astounding eight thousand pounds of gold, but
the peripatetic merchants among them would have seen for themselves the cornucopia of the Gift of the Nile (Egypt gave Constantinople seven million
bushels of grain as its *annual* tax levy) and been aware of the province's
millennia-old trade with the emerald and gold mines upstream. Even without
the prompting of God, the Quraysh knew what they were after.

The man chosen to lead the attack on Egypt was Amr Ibn al As, author of Islam's first victory against the Byzantines, at the oasis of Dathin near Gaza in
634. Since the heady days of Ajnadayn and Yarmuk, the middle-aged Amr had
settled down, carving out a large estate for himself in Beersheba, once the home
of Abraham and his quarrelsome kin. Abraham's children were once again to
come to blows, as Amr led an expeditionary force of four thousand horsemen

from his Judean property out into the wilderness of the Negev. It was a puny army, given the immensity of its target, but rarely had the greatest territory of the Byzantine Christian imperium been so primed for defeat.

On crossing the Sinai in December 639, Amr and his Muslims found the inhabitants of Egypt in a feckless mood, fed up with the extortions of Constantinople and torn by the usual intramural religious feuding. The vast majority of local Christians—whose name, *Copt*, is a variant of the word *Egypt*—had rejected the decision made in 451 at the Council of Chalcedon. There, in the fateful pronouncement that would cleave eastern Christianity into several factions, orthodoxy had declared that Jesus possessed two natures, one human and one divine. The Copts, unimpressed by Greek and Roman pretensions to speak for Christianity, remained militantly monophysite in outlook (i.e., Jesus was solely divine) and reviled the Orthodox or "Chalcedonian" Christianity of their rulers as heartily as they did their tax-gatherers.

In a six-year-long occupation of Egypt in the 620s, the Persians had shrewdly courted the Coptic leadership at the expense of the Greek elite, but the victory of Heraclius over Chosroes led to the reinstatement of the old, hated pecking order and, predictably, a return of persecution. As a sop to Copt sensibility, Greek churchmen concocted a compromise position in the ongoing Christological quarrels, called monothelitism (signifying that Jesus had but one *will*), but that bit of doctrinal legerdemain met with skepticism in Egypt and elsewhere. Patriarch Sophronius of Jerusalem played a role in discrediting the flimsy olive branch of monothelitism; no doubt his satisfaction at dashing Christian unity was soured when he later found himself playing tour guide around the holy city to a conquering Muslim caliph.

Amr waded smartly through the morass of Christian bad feeling in Egypt. By July 640 he had fought his way inland to the gates of Babylon, the garrison town just downstream from the old Pharaonic capital of Memphis. This major stronghold—not to be confused with the ancient Babylon of Mesopotamia—managed to withstand the Arab siege throughout the fall and winter, even though its commanders and Coptic populace were subject to the divisive leadership of a certain Cyrus, the Orthodox patriarch and thus Constantinople's man in Egypt. It is unclear whether Cyrus tried to negotiate the surrender of Babylon for his own gain, or if he merely destroyed the city's will to fight. Heraclius, enfeebled but enraged, recalled Cyrus to the capital and dismissed him. The basileus, however, died almost immediately afterward, and by mid-641 Cyrus was headed back to Egypt, at the behest of the widowed Martina, who wanted peace above all else so that she could conduct the necessary court intrigues to retain power. This was not to be: by year's end, Martina and her son, Heraclonas, had been exiled to Rhodes, the former with her tongue cut out, the latter with his nose slit open. The wealthiest province of the empire was being attacked while the capital was in an uproar.

Babylon fell to Amr Ibn al As on April 9, 641. He then turned his attention to the metropolis founded by Alexander the Great, the brightest beacon of Hellenism on the Mediterranean. Alexandria, however grand its past, would not last long in its present state. As succession struggles paralyzed the imperial court in Constantinople and, consequently, the fleet it commanded, unpleasant memories were rekindled in Alexandria with the return of Cyrus, who, among other achievements, had once had the brother of the city's monophysite bishop tied up in a sack and thrown into the sea. He was patently not the person to inspire its citizens to die heroically on the ramparts. Amr, as smooth a diplomat as he was accomplished a horseman, entered into lengthy negotiations with the despised Cyrus. The surrender of the capital of Egypt, a city of some 600,000 people, became foreordained.

In September 642 the Greeks sailed away, and Amr and his army rode unopposed through the gates and took possession of the city. Later anti-Muslim writings have Amr's men then sacking the famed Library of Alexandria, in a sort of bedouin know-nothing frenzy, but that tale has been debunked by impartial scholarship: the holdings of the library had been dispersed or destroyed during internal Christian disputes long before the arrival of the Arabs. More to the point is the commentary of a Copt writing only a generation or so after the events: "Everyone knows that the defeat of the Greeks and the conquest of Egypt by the Muslims was in punishment for the tyranny of Emperor Heraclius and the wrong he inflicted on [Egyptians] through the patriarch Cyrus." Sterner still is another monophysite history, written after several centuries under Muslim rule: "The God of vengeance, . . . having observed the malice of the Greeks, who cruelly pillaged our churches and monasteries wherever they had dominion and condemned us mercilessly, brought the sons of Ishmael from the south to deliver us."

Amr undertook to leave the Christians to their own resentments, as long as they paid their taxes. According to one tradition, he wrote to Caliph Umar of the great wealth that would no longer take ship in Alexandria for Constantinople: "I will send to Madina a camel train so long that the first camel will reach you before the last one has left me." That caravan's point of departure was to be a new city, Fustat, built between Graeco-Roman Babylon and Pharaonic Memphis, at the spot where the Nile branches out into a delta. As with the newly founded cities of Basra and Kufa in Iraq, the plan was to have an enclosed Arab-Muslim settlement, called an *amsar*, at the meeting of arable land and the desert. The Muslim warriors and immigrants, their dwelling-places in the amsar organized by tribe, would live off the labors of the locals, who were neither persecuted for their beliefs nor encouraged to convert to Islam. (If they did convert, they were exempted from taxation, thereby inconveniently reducing the kitty to be shared out among the umma.) The organized thievery of the Byzantines was thus replaced by another, more benign system.

Only four years after founding Fustat, Amr was forced back to his Judean retreat in Beersheba. Caliph Umar had been murdered by a Persian slave, and the man chosen as his successor by a council of notables in Madina, Uthman ibn Affan, immediately showed he had no time for a putative rival in Egypt. Amr was dismissed, and a kinsman of the new caliph was named governor of the province. Indeed, kinsmen of Caliph Uthman soon began occupying almost all positions of authority in the young Arab empire. The windfall of conquest brought riches, and riches brought strife—the once lean and hungry Muslim umma had triumphed not only in Egypt, Syria, and Palestine but also in Iraq and the marches of Persia, and the tribute of the wealthy peoples of the Fertile Crescent stoked personal ambitions. However devout the Companions ruling the umma were, they were also not immune to jealousy and greed. Under the new caliph, one clan from among the Quraysh seemed intent on taking over the entire enterprise, a clan, moreover, that had been dilatory in its acceptance of the Prophet in the infancy of Islam. But many of the Companions from the other clans were still alive and possessed of clear memories. Old resentments resurfaced, a power struggle loomed. The road to Poitiers was still very long—now it would be anything but straight.

⤛ ⤛ ⤜ ⤜

Straight Street is the main thoroughfare in the historic heart of Damascus, the oldest continuously inhabited city on earth. Mentioned by name by none other than God himself in the New Testament, the street has witnessed the changing fortunes of many peoples, and after the Greeks came the turn of the Muslim Arabs. Against all expectations, ancient Damascus, not Madina or Mecca, would be the cynosure of Islam's triumphant journey around the Mediterranean.

One can easily see why Damascus has seduced so many conquerors. The city stands in a well-watered valley at the edge of the sown and the sandy, a Fertile Crescent crossroads protected from the winds by a stupendous rock outcropping to its north, the Qasyun Hill. This awe-inspiring height, twelve hundred meters in altitude and now haunted by heavily hennaed bedouin women willing to read palms for a price, is a transcendent presence on the Damascene horizon. The view from atop Qasyun remained the same for forty centuries: far below stood a compact, walled city in the center of a vast, verdant oasis. Only in the last century has the prospect changed color to ashtray gray, the sprawl of tower blocks and satellite dishes having stifled most of the greenery. According to local tradition, the Prophet came to the lookout on Qasyun and decided not to visit Damascus after seeing the beautiful city stretched out below him. Muhammad explained to his perplexed friends that he would rather wait until after this life to enter Paradise.

Others had no such otherwordly compunctions. Foremost among them was Muawiya, the Prophet's former secretary and, after the conquest of Syria, the Muslim governor of Damascus. He looked and—fatefully for Mediterranean history—liked what he saw. Muawiya ibn Abu Sufyan was of the Beni Umayya clan, the same grasping group of kinsmen to which the new caliph belonged. His full name betrays that he was the son of Abu Sufyan and Hind. Incredibly, the Qurayshi couple loudest in their ridicule of the Prophet, the two sterling exemplars of foot-dragging in the face of Islamic truth, begat the founder of the first great Muslim dynasty, the Umayyads. Muhammad's unfortunate uncle Hamza, whose lifeless body had been outraged by Hind, might well have spun in his grave when her son became supreme leader of the umma. Other martyrs for Islam from its early days might have done likewise, especially after Muawiya permanently sidelined Madina as a political center by establishing the caliphate in Damascus.

Muawiya needed several eventful years to achieve his object, for other fronts would open up in the west. After the murder of Umar, Caliph Uthman authorized raids into the Cyrenaica, today's Libya. As the razzia became the norm, the open-throated war cry of the conquerors was heard as far along the coast as Byzantine "Africa"—or Arabic Ifriqiya (Tunisia). Amr Ibn al As was to play a role in these raids, for he had been hurriedly summoned out of his Beersheba retirement to deal with an emergency—a Byzantine fleet had appeared on the horizon and taken back Alexandria by surprise in 645. Under Amr's capable leadership, the situation was quickly restored, and the Greeks sailed away once again, this time permanently.

Straight Street, Damascus, in the nineteenth century.

Amr took this Byzantine reversal, and his renewed prestige, as an inducement
to join in the raids to the west. The most lucrative involved south-central
Ifriqiya, where Gregory, an ambitious Greek patrician opposed to the monothelite party in Constantinople, had seceded from the Byzantine Empire by declaring himself basileus. At Sufetula (Sbeitla, Tunisia) the Arab cavalry made short
work of his delusions of grandeur, slaying Gregory, routing his army, comman-
deering his treasury, and carrying off his followers into slavery. Not all reached
the auction block: legend has Gregory's beautiful daughter, Yamina, deliberately hurling herself headfirst from a camel, preferring death to life as a captive
concubine.

As his coreligionists probed the north African coast in these years, Muawiya
left Damascus and crossed the Taurus Mountains to attack Anatolia, dutifully
following in the footsteps of the Persians and so many other enemies of the
Rumi before them. The news from Alexandria, however, gave him pause. Of all
the invaders past and present to have made life miserable for the empire of the
mare nostrum—Parthians, Vandals, Visigoths, Ostrogoths, Avars, Burgundians, Huns, Persians, Bulgars—few had bothered disputing its control of the sea
itself. Muawiya rightly saw an object lesson in the retaking of Alexandria—
until Islam possessed warships, he reasoned, it would always be vulnerable to
Rumi mariners. This insight guaranteed his greatness.

After winning the assent of his kinsman, Caliph Uthman, Muawiya set about
manning the fleet that for the next millennium would contest control of the
shipping lanes. The men of the desert would take to the sea. Amr Ibn al As, a
landlubber to the last, argued against the idea by warning, "If a ship lies still, it
rends the heart; if it moves it terrifies the imagination. Upon it a man's power
ever diminishes and calamity increases. Those within it are like worms in a log,
and if it rolls over they are drowned." The intrepid Muawiya, supported by the
caliph, brushed aside all such reservations. The desert "ports" of Syria (Damascus, Homs, Hama, Aleppo), and the amsar "ports" of Egypt (Fustat), Iraq
(Kufa, Basra), and Tunisia (Kairouan, founded 670), would henceforth be
joined by the maritime ports of an Islamic Mediterranean empire. It was an inspired decision.

The fleet was made ready with astonishing speed, no doubt thanks to the ex-
pertise of recently conquered seagoing peoples, whether Muslim or not—
Yemenis, Syrian Greeks, and Copts. The Muslims probably engaged the
services of their old commercial partners, the mariners of the Indian Ocean, in
acquiring the navigational skills needed to match the Byzantines. These sailors

from the subcontinent were not only versed in the intricacies of celestial naviga-
tion but would later discover the magnetic compass, an invention of incomparable utility in dashing across open water. By 649 Muawiya and his allies had
weighed anchor, ready to begin the deadly game of island hopping that would
characterize much of the encounter between Christian and Muslim on the inland sea. Crete was raided, and Cyprus fell. In 654 came the turn of Rhodes, an
outpost of Graeco-Roman maritime supremacy since the earliest days of classical antiquity. Its famous colossal statue of the sun god Helios, toppled by an
earthquake in 226 B.C.E. and thereafter left in rusted but respected disarray
alongside the harbor, was sold by the unimpressed Muslim raiders as scrap
metal to a Jewish merchant of Edessa (Urfa, Turkey). Nine hundred pack-
camels were needed to haul it away.

The ships of Muawiya continued their progression up the coast of Anatolia.
After Rhodes came Kos, in the Dodecanese Islands of the Aegean, the stepping-
stones to the Hellespont and beyond to Constantinople itself. The basileus,
Constans II (a grandson of Heraclius and his first wife, Eudoxia), grew alarmed
enough to sail out in 655 to crush the upstart maritime power. Unexpectedly, the
upstarts crushed the Byzantines. Constans barely escaped the naval battle with
his life, having to resort to switching clothes with a brave volunteer in order to
slip away undetected. The Arabs had proved invincible on land; they seemed
unbeatable on the water as well. The entire Mediterranean appeared poised to
go the way of the Fertile Crescent.

Murder intervened. The following summer Caliph Uthman was dead, igno-
miniously cut down by fellow Muslims in Madina. The dar al Islam was thrown
into chaos, the umma profoundly shocked. This was only the most visible sign
of a larger unrest roiling the fledgling empire. The perpetrators had ridden
to Madina from Fustat, where the grievances against the caliph's nepotistic
rule had accumulated into open revolt. In Iraq too dissatisfaction had been
growing—the non-Arabian converts to Islam, or *mawali* (clients), began demanding a share of the treasure and influence reserved for the Quraysh and
their allied tribes in the amsars. The dissident grandees of Islam, who had
voiced their disapproval of Uthman in the latter years of his caliphate, dis-
tanced themselves from the crime. Amr, as might be expected of so slippery a
survivor, had been in Beersheba in that summer of 656, far from both Fustat and
Madina. Aisha, the child-bride of the Prophet who had matured into a formidable widow, had been returning to Madina from a pilgrimage; when she learned
the news, she quickly turned around and dashed back to Mecca. The most

prominent dissident, however, had been present in Madina on the day of the murder—Ali ibn Abu Talib.

Like the millstone of the Council of Chalcedon in the sinking of the Christian East, the rise and fall of Ali would be of utmost importance for Islam's future, and its repercussions in subsequent centuries would play a role in the fortunes of the faith around the world. In the wake of Uthman's murder, Ali assumed the caliphate. It was, to some in the umma, a distinction too long deferred. He was the closest male relative of the Prophet—Ali's father had been Abu Talib, the uncle who had raised Muhammad. When Muhammad's situation improved, he adopted Ali—his first cousin—as a son, then wed him to Fatima, the youngest daughter of the Prophet's union with Khadija. Ali was thus cousin, adopted son, and son-in-law of the founder of Islam, a Companion from the earliest days and a member of the Prophet's own Beni Hashim clan of the Quraysh. It is still argued whether he was the second or third convert to Islam. (The first was Khadija; then came either Abu Bekr or Ali.) A more qualified candidate to succeed Muhammad was scarcely imaginable.

Had Ali been the first of the caliphs, his rise to prominence might not have been disputed. But the council of tribal elders who selected the caliph had passed over him on three occasions—in favor of Abu Bekr, Umar, and Uthman. And in the quarter-century since the Prophet's death, the fortunes of the umma had changed beyond recognition. Although the revived rivalries among the Quraysh were familiar, the brotherhood of believers faced the threatening novelty of thousands of mawali—non-Arabian converts—knocking at the door of spiritual and material legitimacy within Islam. More ominously for overall unity, prominent believers controlled centers of wealth and sophistication far superior to the settlements of the Hijaz. From the opulent oasis beneath Qasyun Hill, Muawiya demanded justice for the murdered caliph, his tribal kinsman. He proclaimed Ali illegitimate and himself caliph, thereby sparking a civil war.

Ali acted with dispatch. He moved the seat of power from Madina, where his enemies were thick on the ground, to Kufa (modern Najaf), an amsar in Iraq. In 658 he vanquished an army of malcontents near Basra at the Battle of the Camel, so called because Aisha, the dissident widow of the Prophet, watched her side lose from atop her mount. A year later Ali's climactic confrontation with Muawiya at Siffin, near the Euphrates in Iraq, ended in a startlingly original fashion. Traditions hold that the commander of Muawiya's Syrian cavalry,

the ubiquitous Amr Ibn al As, after being bested in several days of bloody combat, ordered his beleaguered riders to affix pages of the Quran to their spears.
When Ali's soldiers, devout Muslims all, saw their opponents thus caparisoned,
they dropped the tools of war. Out of the ensuing confusion, an agreement was
reached: a committee of two would decide who should be caliph, Ali or
Muawiya.

Following months of negotiation, Muawiya's representative—Amr, once
again—managed to get a decision that, although far from clear-cut, could be
skewed in favor of the master of Damascus. Naturally Ali rejected the arbitration, but by then some of his own followers had rejected him. Known as the
Kharijites (or "seceders"), these uncompromising purists were disgusted that
Ali had agreed to arbitration in the first place. In 661 two of their number murdered Ali in Kufa. Muawiya had won by default. The son of Abu Sufyan and
Hind became the caliph, thereby further embittering the "party of Ali" (*shi'a
Ali*, hence shia), who looked on his sons Hasan and Huseyn as the natural successors to the supreme magistrature. The groundwork had been laid for an enduring disagreement that would transcend the merely dynastic, as the eventual
elaboration of several schools of sacred Islamic law and the example of
Muhammad's habitual behavior—*sunnah*—came to guide the conduct and beliefs of the vast majority of Muslims, the sunni.

The Byzantines, as might be expected, were delighted by these Muslim woes. For
the first time in decades the pressure had relented. Constans II, freed of the menace from Asia and clad once again in his imperial finery, decided to reverse the
itinerary of his celebrated grandfather, Heraclius. Instead of sailing east, Constans went west across the Mediterranean, moving his capital from Constantinople to Sicily. His reasons were multiple: to escape the toxic air of monothelite
intrigue on the Bosporus, to shore up his possessions in Italy, and to counter any
attacks on Carthage and north Africa. A contemporary source also had him fleeing Constantinople to escape the ghost of his brother, whom he had blinded and
killed two years earlier. Whatever his rationale, Constans set himself up in Syracuse, an important center of Magna Graecia (Greek-speaking Sicily and southern
Italy) since the time of Pericles. There he held court, content to let the Muslims
tear themselves apart and watchful for any threats to the legacy of Augustus, Justinian, and Heraclius. The east might be lost, but the west would hold.

Murder intervened once again. On September 15, 668, as Constans was taking
a bath, a slave brained him with a marble soap dish. We don't know why,

though one historian playfully suggests the murderer may have been nostalgic for Constantinople. However base or noble the motive behind the killing, Constans' experiment with a new western Roman empire died with him. Carthage and its hinterland were pushed once again to the periphery of Byzantine concerns, with irreversible consequences for the future of north Africa. The court returned to the comforts of Constantinople, which, as events dictated, was a surpassingly good idea. In the years following Ali's assassination, Muawiya had consolidated his immense power as caliph and was ready to take up where he had left off. As a Muslim fleet picked off one after another of the Dodecanese islands and a Muslim army advanced through Anatolia, his goal became blindingly obvious: the splendors of Straight Street were not enough; Muawiya wanted a palace overlooking the Golden Horn. The new basileus, an adolescent son of Constans who took the throne as Constantine IV, was called on to defend the city bearing his name.

In the spring of 674 an enormous fleet of war galleys crossed the Marmara and stationed itself in front of the sea walls of Constantinople. Catapults let fly. The greatest Arab expeditionary force seen thus far waited expectantly for a breach to be made in the famed fortifications of the capital of the Rumi. What it could not have expected was to become itself the target of a terrible new weapon—Greek fire. Some time before Muawiya's navy arrived, a Syrian Greek architect named Callinichus had shown Constantine's advisers his diabolical invention: an inflammable substance that could be propelled through metal tubes to splash, ablaze and inextinguishable, on solid and liquid alike. The merits of this rudimentary napalm were self-evident, and although the exact nature of its constituent ingredients will never be known for certain—the secret disappeared with the Byzantines—Muawiya's men were but the first of many unfortunates to be subjected to it. Greek fire was merciless; not only could it set a ship alight, but the surrounding sea could also be made a slick of flames, thereby preventing sailors from saving themselves by jumping overboard.

In a testament to the determination of the attackers, they remained four years besieging Constantinople, even though they had no protection against its incendiary terrors. No less disciplined were the defenders, who had at last managed to make a stand against the invincible Muslims. Muawiya conceded defeat in the fall of 678 and signed a truce with the Byzantines the following year—the first setback for the warriors of Islam since they had ridden out of the Hijaz. In describing this moment, one recent historian of the Byzantines sees Gibbon, then raises him one: "He [Constantine IV] had inspired his subjects with the morale to withstand five years of siege by a power hitherto considered irresistible, and in doing so had saved Western civilization. Had the Saracens captured Constantinople in the seventh century rather than the fifteenth, all Europe—and America—might be Muslim today."

◄ ◄ ► ►

"The last of the Merovingians fell asleep in their ox-carts." A French historian's weary witticism about the lethargy of western Europe during this time of cataclysmic upheaval in the Mediterranean comes as a welcome contrast after the Gibbon-like flight of panic about the siege of Constantinople. The Merovingians, the royal house of the Franks during this first half-century of Muslim conquest, would have been almost entirely unaware of the great changes taking place elsewhere. The chroniclers of their activities, Fredegarius and his continuator, had heard of Yarmuk: in one cryptic passage the Byzantine defeat is attributed to a sudden die-off—52,000 Christian soldiers—in the middle of the night. Yet like Heraclius in Jerusalem in 630, who was perhaps apprised of a minor skirmish in the Jordanian desert against the Arabians, the Merovingians would have had no inkling that hazily distant events had any possible bearing on Gaul. It seems unlikely even today.

A medieval rendering of the delivery and effect of the incendiary device known as Greek fire.

Even without their slumbering insularity, the Merovingians have not been remembered respectfully. French textbook convention holds many of them to be
rois fainéants, or do-nothing monarchs, and one of their number, Dagobert,
owes much of his fame to a nursery rhyme that has him putting his breeches on
backward. Posterity becomes more charitable in considering the power behind
the Merovingian throne—the so-called "mayors of the palace" who led Frankish warrior bands in nearly annual campaigns of murder and rapine. Indeed, referring to northern Europe at this time as Christendom betrays misplaced piety:
many of the Franks' Germanic cousins clung to their traditional beliefs, and
even among those evangelized, the teachings of the Church often got lost in a
thicket of folk culture.

In 678, the year in which Muawiya's charred ships limped away from Constantinople, a mayor of the palace named Pepin of Herstal came to power in
Gaul, following an obscure assassination of a Merovingian monarch in a wood-
land outside of Paris. The advent of Pepin was a godsend to the fractious
Franks, for his lineage, the Pippinids, was to upset the Merovingian oxcart and
assume royal power. (Much later, under their most illustrious descendant,
Charlemagne, they would grant themselves imperial status as the Carolingians.) Pepin began the hard slog of unification that would, in time, enable the
Franks to repel the Muslim invader.

Not that this future virtue could have been divined through the fog of war that
settled upon Gaul following Pepin's death. The series of events is unclear, but
the sons and grandsons of Pepin, through untimely death or birth, showed
themselves incapable of continuing his work. Only a bastard, born of Pepin's
liaison with a certain Alpaïde, seemed to have the necessary belligerence. Long
kept under lock and key in Cologne by his stepmother Plectrude (Pepin's
widow), in 715 he was sprung from his dungeon by plotters unconcerned with
the imperfections in his pedigree.

The freed warrior was past thirty, already a ripening age for an ax-man with
countries to cleave. Henceforth Karl Martiaux—Charles Martel—would forge
a kingdom that covered much of present-day France, western Germany, and the
Low Countries. Martel—the name comes from Martin, not *marteau* (hammer)—embarked on an unrelenting itinerary of violence, forcibly bringing the
eastern and western Franks to heel. Although he was later portrayed as a paladin of Christianity, some of his achievements include deposing the bishop of
Rheims, imprisoning the bishop of Auxerre, and exiling the bishop of Orléans.
An unholy man of war, he would nonetheless turn out to be the man of the

hour. As his reign began, the second half of the Arab century of conquest was well under way, its outriders drawing ever closer, however improbably, to the Pyrenees.

◂◂ ◂◂ ▸▸ ▸▸

If the road to Poitiers was not straight, the struggle for the African littoral—the "west," *al-maghrib*—would show that it would not be smooth, either. In the lands now known as Algeria and Morocco, the Arabian tide of the early eighth century seemed less an unstoppable force of nature, subject to reversal only by self-defeating civil war or technological surprises on the order of Greek fire, than an invading army far from home, dogged by the problems of insurgency, long supply lines, and the vagaries of luck. The customary adjectives used to describe the great Arab conquest—*whirlwind*, *lightning*, and so on—should be shelved for this moment of its history.

As always, events in the eastern affected those in the west. Following the failed siege of Constantinople in 678, the Muslim impetus slowed. One reason was a generational shift: the fire-breathing Companions grew old and died—an octogenarian Amr Ibn al As had closed his eyes in 663, and Muawiya would do the same in 680. The changing of the guard led to a second civil war, this one over the succession, as opposed to the accession, of Muawiya. The forces of his son defeated those of Ali's son, Huseyn, at Karbala, Iraq—an event mourned by the shia to this day. These turbulent years also witnessed the sacrilegious spectacle of Muslims killing each other in Madina and damaging the Kaaba of Mecca.

Only when Abd al-Malik, a forceful scion of a collateral branch of the Umayyads, rose to power in Damascus in 685 was the repressive apparatus needed to stem successive revolts put in place. Even if dangerous resentments simmered in Iraq, Persia, and Arabia—among the shia, the Khariji "seceders," the rival Qurayshi, and the mawali "clients"—Abd al-Malik managed to give the young empire a sense of permanence. He ordered the construction of the Dome of the Rock in Jerusalem; built on Jewish holy ground by Christian artisans for the glory of Islam, it made manifest that the newcomer to monotheism was distinct from the other two beliefs, yet as venerable and authentic in its embrace of all human history. In Damascus the Great Mosque, built by the Umayyads in these years, delivered the same message—and its astounding mosaic facade of figurative art, a masterpiece of Byzantine craftsmanship, showed that a cultural exchange of the highest order was taking place.

Armed with a renewed sense of self-confidence under Abd al-Malik, Islam once again looked to the horizon. Toward the close of the seventh century, according to quasi-legendary accounts, an adventurer named Ukba ibn Nafi made a razzia of epic proportions, racing clear across the Maghrib until he reached the Atlantic near Agadir, Morocco. Ukba, his appetites unslaked after two thousand kilometers of killing and looting, is said to have spurred his horse into the surf and shouted over the crash of the waves: "My God I call you to witness that if my advance were not stopped by the sea I would go still further!" Boasting in this register begs for a comeuppance: on his return journey home to Kairouan in Ifriqiya, he and his men were waylaid and butchered in the foothills of the Aurès Mountains in eastern Algeria. His tomb, Sidi Oqba, is now a hallowed shrine, "a pilgrimage site," one historian dryly notes, "for the descendants of those who took part in his murder."

The agents behind his demise were Berbers, the indigenous peoples of the region, whence the latter-day name "Barbary Coast" for the shores of the Maghrib. The Berbers refer to themselves as *Imazighen*, "free men." Unlike the Christian Arabs of Syria or the Copts of Egypt, they would staunch the Muslim advance for a generation. Long experience with conquerors, from the Phoenician settlers of Carthage through the Romans, Vandals, and Byzantines, had made them a protean bunch, capable of alternating moments of deceptive amenability to foreign customs and faiths with instances of sudden, deadly revolt, their hardened mountain men screaming down from the rugged heights of the Aurès and the Atlas to wreak havoc on the plain among the colonizers of the moment. They had stepped aside in 698 when the Muslims finally reduced Byzantine Carthage to a ruin and founded Tunis in its place, but their reliability as allies—and as suspiciously eager converts to the new faith—was open to question. The greatest historian of the Middle Ages, Abd al-Rahman Ibn Khaldun, a fourteenth-century native of Morocco who studied the Berbers in detail, counted no fewer than a dozen instances of wholesale Berber apostasy from Islam in less than seventy years.

To the worthies in Damascus, the Berbers were toying with the dignity of Islam. Worse yet, the occasional flaring of Berber belligerence had caused the wealth of north Africa—and its links to sub-Saharan sources of slaves—to drift infuriatingly in and out of reach. The most celebrated revolt against the Arabs occurred at the turn of the century, led by a woman known to us only as Kahina, which means "prophetess."

According to tradition, Kahina was the queen of a nomadic tribe called the Jerawa, a group of nomadic Berber Jews living in the eastern reaches of the Aurès. The legends surrounding Kahina make her the most remarkable personage of the century leading to Poitiers. Fearless in battle, she is said to have repeatedly swooped down from the Aurès to assassinate the unwary and strike fear into the new masters of Ifriqiya. Possessed of a temper that made her red hair stand on end, Kahina is credited with uniting the Berbers—perhaps scaring them into submitting to her—and temporarily throwing the invaders back as far as Libya. The Arab chronicles also have her engaging in a scorched-earth campaign that devastated the northern coasts of Tunisia and eastern Algeria—and in so doing, she gradually turned the more sedentary folk among the Berbers against her. Despite her reputation as a virago, Kahina is also remembered in legend, perhaps inevitably, as a loving mother. In 704 or 705, as her army braced for a final showdown near what is now the border of Algeria and Tunisia, Kahina foresaw, as only befits a prophetess, which way the day would go. On the eve of battle she persuaded her two grown sons to slip away from her camp under cover of night and join the other side, thereby saving the lives of her boys. In the morning she died fighting beside a spring; her head was sent to Damascus for the caliph's edification.

Once Kahina was slain, Berber resistance gradually petered out into ineffectual local actions. In the early years of the eighth century, the pace of Muslim progress westward picked up speed, dooming the churches and Christian shrines of the Maghrib to the fate of St. Simeon within a century or two. Christianity would never again be the dominant religion on the south shore of the Mediterranean—the confessional geography of a giant swath of the littoral had changed for good. It is interesting to speculate what the greatest north African Christian, Augustine of Hippo, would have made of this new state of affairs—in his lifetime in the fifth century, the sack of Rome had led him, in *The City of God*, to lament the passing of antiquity. What would he have said of the passing of Christianity?

The new Muslim governor in Kairouan, Musa ibn Nusayr, no doubt had neither the time nor the inclination to linger over such questions, for his problem was, as ever, the unpredictability of the Berbers. He eventually hit upon the solution that guaranteed the pacification of his province. He distracted the Berber warriors from thoughts of revenge by holding out to them the promise of future rewards—not in the next life but in this one, and in an unexpected setting: Spain. When precisely Musa first started sending raiding parties there is unclear, but he undoubtedly gave the fateful order to turn north toward Europe.

Whether his decision was motivated solely by Machiavellian considerations about the restive Berbers can never be known—Musa may also have had empire-building ambitions for himself. Equally uncertain is the question of whether the Muslims received help from complaisant traitors. According to an

oft-repeated and colorful tradition, a certain Julian, the governor of the newly
forlorn Byzantine outpost of Septem (today's Ceuta, a Spanish enclave on the
Moroccan Mediterranean coast), sent out feelers to Musa telling him that he was
prepared to provide ships for the invasion of Spain. Julian intensely disliked
King Rodrigo, the Visigothic ruler of Iberia. One version of the story has Julian's antipathy stemming from Rodrigo's rape of his daughter—an outrage he
surmised after the unfortunate girl, a guest in the capital of Toledo, sent her father a symbolic message in the form of a rotten egg. His anger blinding him to
the consequences of ferrying a Muslim army to Christian Spain, the Greek governor unwittingly opened the door to monumental, lasting change.

   Whatever the historical truth—the conquerors had hardly needed an invitation
anywhere else around the Mediterranean—in the year 711 one of Musa's Berber
commanders, Tariq ibn Ziyad, the Muslim governor of Tangier, made the voyage.
When Tariq and several thousand Arabs and Berbers rowed across the Mediterranean at its narrowest point, a new era dawned. The two great rock eminences on
either shore, long known as the Pillars of Hercules, were about to quit the vague
precincts of Greek legend for the sharper outlines of the century of Muslim conquest. To the south now rises the mountain of Musa, Jebel al-Musa; to the north,
that of Tariq, Jebel al-Tariq, or as we and Gibbon pronounce it: Gibraltar.

❮❮ ❮❮   ❯❯ ❯❯

It took twenty-one years for the line of conquest to go from Gibraltar to Poitiers.
No one disputes Gibraltar as the landfall of Islam in Europe; there is less agreement about the other end of the march. The most likely candidate is a hamlet
twenty kilometers to the northwest of Poitiers called Moussais-la-Bataille, although, owing to the paucity of geographical information in the historical sources,
where precisely the battle named for Poitiers (and sometimes Tours) took place
will never be established to everyone's satisfaction. The claims of Moussais, defended convincingly in a 1966 study by two French historians, are multifold: its
name (*la Bataille* is an old if undated suffix); its proximity to the Roman road leading from Poitiers to Tours (the ruins of Gallo-Roman Vieux-Poitiers stand just to
its north); its eminently suitable terrain for a large-scale battle; and its position just
a few kilometers south of the important confluence of the rivers Clain and Vienne,
which any northbound invader would have had to ford en route to the riches of the
Loire valley—and to which any defender would have barred the way.

   The environs of Moussais, itself an exurban collection of modest homes, still attest to their continued role as a route of passage. Near the village, just beyond the Clain, a high-speed train can be heard hissing past on its journey from Bordeaux to Paris, as can the rushed whisper of traffic on France's main western expressway. The occasional honk of a car horn drifts over the screen of mature trees along the riverbank, proof that a secondary road remains popular with time travelers going in the other direction, toward a successful technological theme park called, bravely, Futuroscope.

In a pasture on the high ground west of Moussais sits a giant chessboard. It overlooks an anonymous field of shorn barley that may or may not be the setting for the battle. Laid out in 2000 by an association convinced of the site's importance, the board's sixty-four squares alternate between a comic-book narrative of the Battle of Poitiers and a series of apposite quotations from thinkers

The Rock of Gibraltar, site of Islam's landfall in Europe in 711.

and artists of the past. The choice of chess is ingenious, for the game, introduced to Europe by the Muslims, involves countless permutations in an encounter where the pieces stand cheek by jowl—much like the variety and
closeness of contact that characterized the meeting of Christianity and Islam in
the Middle Ages. To go along with the memorial makers—to stand on a chessboard under the pale summer sun of northern France and ponder its impishly
presented uncertainties—is to realize that memory is a game of continual reconstruction, and that each generation gets to play.

  That realization is particularly useful in considering the momentous event preceding the battle—the sudden and utter collapse of Visigothic Spain. Here the

A Muslim and a Christian playing chess, from the "Book of Games" compiled for King
Alfonso X (reigned 1252–84) of Castile and León.

modifiers *whirlwind* and *lightning* might be profitably used—the Muslims took only five years to accomplish what had occupied the legionaries of Rome for two centuries. The quarry of Tariq and Musa, the Visigoths, would arrive at the terminus of their journey through history as melodramatically as they had begun it.

A barbarian people of eastern Europe, the Visigoths had first poured over the Danube to escape the advancing Huns and somehow managed, in 378, to shatter Roman power at the battle of Adrianople (Edirne, Turkey) and kill Emperor Valens in the bargain. In 410 the Visigothic king Alaric took Rome itself—the event that moved Augustine to despair. His restless successors moved on, to be turned away from Gaul by Clovis at Poitiers, in 507, after which they consolidated their hold on Spain, where they finally settled down. Although created by the architects of Rome's downfall, their Iberian civilization possessed more than a passing resemblance to the old regime—particularly in its great slave-holding estates—and, in a peculiarity of the peninsula's history, a characteristic of Christian Spanish regimes of a distant future: an intolerance of Jews. The sheer vituperativeness of seventh-century Visigothic anti-Jewish legislation easily rivaled the measures of the sixteenth-century Inquisition.

Once King Rodrigo heard of Tariq's landing at Gibraltar, he raced from the north of his kingdom, where he had been fighting the reliably rebellious Vascons (or Basques), down the entire length of the peninsula to the tip of what is now Andalusia. In a battle near the mouth of the Guadalete River, the Berbers and Arabs won an annihilating victory, perhaps aided by treasonous Visigoths—they were also given to endemic dynastic quarreling. Rodrigo may have been slain at this engagement of 711, for he disappears from history at this point. Whatever the circumstances of his death, he was to be the last Visigothic king of Spain. Tariq then headed northward, effortlessly capturing one city after another on his march to Toledo. Many have conjectured that the Muslims were welcomed as liberators by the Jews of Iberia, but no documentary evidence backs up this assertion—although sustained persecution by the Visigoths and news of fellow Jews living peaceably as dhimmi (protected if penalized non-Muslim communities) in Syria, Palestine, and Egypt would hardly have disposed them to be stout defenders of the old order.

By 716 all of Iberia, save for a few slivers in the north, had been subdued. A few captured Visigothic royals may have been shipped off to Damascus as curiosities; certainly Tariq and Musa ended up there—as with Amr Ibn al As and Khalid Ibn al Walid, the magnitude of their achievement had made them

suspect in the eyes of the caliph. In these years Damascus could ill afford to
countenance rival centers of power.

As Spain was being overrun, yet another attempt had been made to capture
Constantinople. An enormous fleet of eighteen hundred vessels (and 120,000
besiegers) had failed to dent the defenses organized by the redoubtable basileus
Leo III, whose advent marked the beginning of a lasting Byzantine recovery in
Anatolia—and not inconsequentially, the sparking of the ferocious century-
long quarrel over the place of icons in Orthodox religious life. In 718 the fleet
of the caliph, as battered as Muawiya's had been a generation earler, sailed out
of the Hellespont to an even sorrier fate than defeat—almost total destruction
by a wild storm off Rhodes. This was clearly not the moment for Musa and
Tariq, the Muslim conquerors of Spain, to become too powerful.

Success, in the end, was not dependent on their leadership. After taking
Barcelona, then Girona, the Berbers and their Arab masters poured over the
Pyrenees. The Visigothic kingdom of Septimania—Languedoc—fell to them
promptly. In its capital, Narbonne, one later chronicler, mindful of the looming
rendezvous in Poitiers, had the conquering horsemen coming across a ruined
classical temple that, improbably, possessed an inscription in Arabic: "Here you
are, o sons of Ishmael, arrived at the end of your journey! Turn back." This ex
post facto oracle might equally have been inspired by events in Toulouse, where
the Muslim advance on land met its gravest reverse since the days of the
prophetess-queen Kahina. In 721 Duke Eudo of Aquitaine dealt the invaders a
severe defeat before his capital, the Muslim forces escaping extermination
through a fighting retreat organized by a cool-headed young commander named
Abd al-Rahman al-Ghafiqi. Although one papal source claimed, absurdly, that
375,000 Muslim warriors died at Toulouse, we can nonetheless assume that it was
a very bloody affair. For the next few years the raiders gave Aquitaine a wide
berth, preferring to launch lightning strikes up the Rhône Valley.

With Eudo's victory, the already poor relations between Berber and Arab in the
Muslim camp became further strained over a sizable bone of contention: the
greater share of booty, women, and slaves—and the better parcels of land—
had gone to the Arab minority, rather than to the Berber majority, in the
conquering armies. A Berber chieftain named Munuza, dissatisfied with the
division of spoils, set himself up in an independent principality in the vicinity
of what is now Andorra. This unique north African realm in the Pyrenees
was made even more extraordinary when the Christian duke Eudo gave to the

Muslim Munuza his daughter in marriage. Although the temptation to see the union as a love match is almost irresistible—Othello meets Desdemona—the clear-sighted Eudo undoubtedly wanted to secure his southern border through this alliance, for to his north his troubles were multiple, and they all stemmed from one root: Charles Martel.

Since his accession to power in the second decade of the eighth century, Martel had been single-minded in his attempt to win a kingdom for himself and his sons. In the north he had succeeded; in the south stood an independent and prosperous Aquitaine, a goad to his ambition. Duke Eudo's Aquitaine, which had long before slipped from Visigothic control, remained a stubbornly Romanized place, in its customs and laws and language—and undoubtedly in its condescension toward the shaggy northerners ruled by mayors of the Merovingian palace. In the 720s Frankish warriors repeatedly harassed Aquitaine, motivated, according to Martel's greatest apologist (the continuator of the chronicler Fredegarius), by Christian outrage at Eudo's alliance with the Muslim Munuza. This explanation is implausible in the extreme, for Martel's

A fanciful rendering of Charles Martel, the hero of Poitiers.

early career had scarcely a trace of militant piety. As with the Arabian move out of the Hijaz a century earlier, opportunity and cohesion were compelling enough reasons for war in this era of near-permanent conflict: under Martel, the Franks were united, and weaker neighbors, such as Aquitaine, became the prey.

The pieces on the chessboard of westernmost Europe were thus arrayed on the eve of the Battle of Poitiers. The first to be swept away was Munuza. The Arab leaders of Spain could not long tolerate a Berber princeling reserving a large chunk of conquered land for himself. Laying siege to a stronghold in his unique Pyrenean dominion, the Arabs and their allies hunted down Munuza and killed him. Lampégie, Munuza's Christian widow, was packed off to the women's quarters on Straight Street. In Toulouse, Duke Eudo no doubt bewailed his daughter's departure for Damascus, but the disappearance of his Berber son-in-law may have caused him even greater distress. There was no longer a buffer between Aquitaine and the Arabs, which meant the Eudo was beset by enemies in both the north and the south.

In 731 the caliph raised Abd al-Rahman al-Ghafiqi to the office of governor (*emir*) of al-Andalus, as Muslim Iberia was by then known. Abd al-Rahman had saved the day before Toulouse some ten years previously and was reputed to temper his proven martial ability with sincere piety and even-handed governance. Dealing with restive local chieftains in these early years of al-Andalus occupied the energies of the caliph's appointed representatives, unless some larger object diverted attentions and appetites. As Musa ibn Nusayr had done in north Africa—allaying rebelliousness by offering new vistas of loot—the emir chose to broaden everyone's horizons: he called for all able-bodied adventurers of al-Andalus to assemble in Pamplona for an expedition into Aquitaine. The perpetrators of the occasional razzia into France had brought back not only riches but also tempting tales of wealthy monasteries and pilgrimage churches farther afield, stories that would have quickened the stride of Berbers, Arabs, and freelance Visigoths heading to Pamplona.

A large host set out under the emir's banner in the spring of 732. Abd al-Rahman elected to cross the Pyrenees in the west, over the pass of Roncesvalles.* The Andalusi army crossed the Pyrenees without incident and soon

---

*Some sixty-five years later Charles Martel's grandson, Charlemagne, would take the same route out of Spain—and the slaughter of his rear guard at Roncesvalles by the Basques would later be commemorated in *The Song of Roland*, a chanson de geste composed in the era of the Crusades that propagandistically transforms merciless Basques into murderous Muslims.

closed with the enemy. Abd al-Rahman's second encounter with Duke Eudo had a decidedly different outcome. The attackers overwhelmed Aquitaine; several towns of the duchy—Oloron, Auch, Dax—were sacked. A large battle took place near the meeting of the rivers Dordogne and Garonne, its result the flight of Eudo's men and the burning of Bordeaux. Another engagement raged later that summer near the rich settlement of Agen, and once again Abd al-Rahman prevailed. This time Eudo fled north, with the invaders in pursuit, although they tarried a few days to loot and burn the episcopal see of Angoulême. The invading armies had by then heard of the jewel-bedecked shrines in Poitiers and Tours, the latter the richest prize in all of Gaul. For his part, the duke of Aquitaine, having lost his daughter and his lands, was forced to let go of his pride as well—he had no recourse but to appeal to his enemy, Charles Martel, to help him resist the juggernaut from the south.

Ensuring his place in history, Martel moved fast. As the men of al-Andalus rode north from Angoulême, the Franks forded the Loire at Orléans and hurried south. At Cenon they crossed the confluence of the Clain and Vienne, no doubt aware that the Church of St. Hilaire, then outside the walls of Poitiers, had been emptied and put to the torch. Incredibly, the century of conquest had reached the rolling greens of the Poitou. The scouts of the two armies skirmished to the immediate north of the city, then retired to their respective commanders. Abd al-Rahman, electing to leave the Poitevins shivering in fright behind their fortifications, wanted to make haste along the Roman road to Tours; Martel and Eudo, like Khalid Ibn al-Walid at Yarmuk, chose the spot where he would have to come and move them out of the way. The Muslim army swung around the walls of Poitiers, then headed north along what Arab chroniclers later would call *balat ech shuada*, "the road of the martyrs of the faith." The Franks waited. In all likelihood they spread out over a narrow front of a few hundred meters, between a hillock and a river, on either side of the road, below the chessboard at Moussais.

≺⊢ ≺⊢ ⊣≻ ⊣≻

The main battle occurred on a Saturday in October—in the first day of the month of Ramadan—in 732 or, according to some, 733. A prelude of up to a week preceded the decisive encounter as the two sides sized each other up, maneuvering and feinting in the surrounding forests. Little else is known with certainty, although a consensual narrative of the event has emerged, relying principally on the *Chronicle of 754*, so named for its date of composition. The author, whose identity is unknown, appears to have been a Mozarab, a Christian living under Muslim rule in al-Andalus. Believed to be a Cordoban, he was a near-contemporary of the participants and thus may have been aware of how the survivors remembered the clash. Several Frankish annals, many of them less one-sided than the continuator of Fredegarius, recorded the event fairly shortly after its occurrence, while the Muslim sources date from at least two or three centuries later. From these narratives, what happened on that terrible Saturday and strange Sunday can be reconstructed.

The Muslims attacked first. Prayers said, the sun rising in the sky, by the thousands they leaped onto mounts that had been rested and watered in anticipation of this moment and wheeled them around to trot northward along the Roman road leading from Poitiers. Picking up speed in the open fields, they let out bloodcurdling cries—confessions of faith, shouts of encouragement—to discountenance the Franks, who had never faced such an enemy. This was the paradigmatic moment of the early centuries around the sea of faith—two great masses of soldiery, most of whom had no familiarity whatsoever with their opponents. The thought of their being siblings in faith would have been utterly alien—only later, through generations of contact, collision, and commingling, could the notion even be entertained.

Even before the Berbers and the Arabs came into sight, to be espied for the first time by Martel's Franks, they would have been heard, their drums pounding, horns blowing, and cymbals crashing. As the snapping pennants and shining spears of al-Andalus finally appeared in the clearing, in a rolling cacophony of dust, horse, and rider, the Franks must have muttered their own prayers. Martel had ordered them to stand fast in a solid mass, shoulder to shoulder, their shields planted in the ground before them like a palisade, their two-bladed battle-axes ready to be hurled into the onslaught.

The impact of the charge would have been tremendous, confused, murderous. Arab tactics called for dislodging the enemy from his fixed positions, luring groups of foolhardy defenders into counterattack by feigning retreat, then whirling about to surround and submerge them once isolated. In the ensuing melees, an archipelago of fighting far from the point of initial contact, the advantages of lightly armed horsemen came to the fore. Wielding swords or spears, or loosing arrows from their bows, they could swarm and scatter with great speed, weakening and wounding the adversary until even the most compact unit disintegrated into a brace of individuals running for their lives,

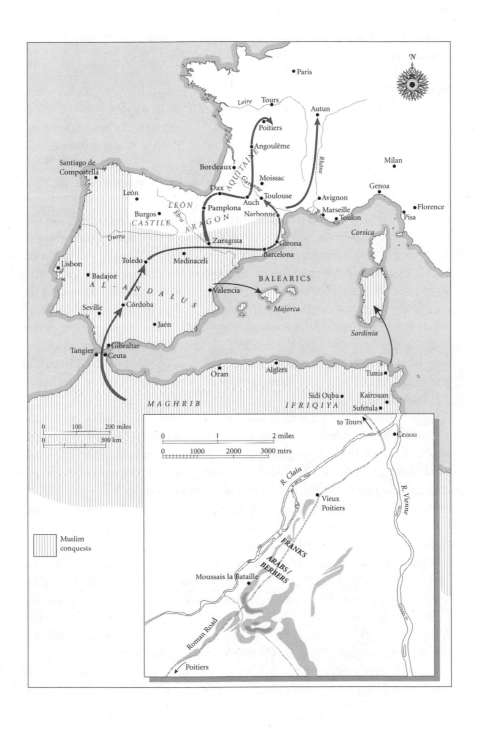

Paris

Loire

Tours

Autun

Poitiers

Angoulême

Milan

Santiago de
Compostella

Bordeaux

Moissac

Rhône

Genoa

León

Dax

Toulouse

Avignon

Florence

LEÓN

Pamplona

Auch

Marseille

Pisa

Burgos

Narbonne

Toulon

Corsica

CASTILE

ARAGON

Ebro

Duero

Zaragoza

Girona

Barcelona

Lisbon

Toledo

Medinaceli

BALEARICS

Badajoz

AL-ANDALUS

Valencia

Seville

Córdoba

Majorca

Sardinia

Jaén

Tangier

Gibraltar

Ceuta

Oran

Alglers

Tunis

MAGHRIB

IFRIQIYA

Sidi Oqba

Kairouan

Sufetula

0   100   200 miles

0   300 km

to Tours

Cenon

0   1   2 miles

0   1000   2000   3000 mtrs

R. Clain

R. Vienne

Vieux
Poitiers

FRANKS

ARABS/
BERBERS

Muslim
conquests

Moussais la Bataille

Roman Road

Poitiers

vulnerable and alone. As a tactic, it mirrored the larger one of breaking up a massed army into unorganized groups of pursuers.

But the Franks, famously, did not budge. They may have staggered back from the brunt of the assault, but they resisted the mirage of pursuit when the horsemen withdrew. The Berbers and the Arabs charged again and again—they couldn't break the Frankish lines. These "Europenses," according to the Mozarab chronicler, stood immobile, like "a wall of ice." In front of them, along the *balat ech shuada*, the wounded and the dying of al-Andalus grew in number, as yet more attacks were ordered and bloodily repulsed. The road of the martyrs to the faith had earned its name.

The gruesome business lasted one long autumn day. At some point a detachment of cavalry, perhaps led by Duke Eudo, dashed out of the yellowing woods to storm the Arab encampment. As this was stocked with the riches looted in the past few months of campaigning, its loss would have been a catastrophic blow to Muslim morale. According to tradition, Abd al-Rahman himself headed the charge that beat back the interlopers. Seeking to rally his men—many of whom might have been content to turn back home with their takings rather than risk battle in the first place—the governor of al-Andalus led the last few desperate attacks as daylight failed. Somewhere amid the flailing of sword on shield, as the heavy Frankish cavalry lumbered forward to help the infantry, Abd al-Rahman was killed.

Night fell. The armies disengaged, carrying off their dead and injured in the gloom. When dawn broke on Sunday morning, the battlefield would have been quieter than it is today. Martel had his men get into formation behind their wall of shields and bucklers. All waited to hear the enemy approaching in full cry. The minutes passed. Scouts were sent out, their horses disappearing from view, then returning at a gallop. The enemy camp, its hundreds of colorful tents still standing, appeared deserted. More Frankish riders tentatively moved forward, ordered to scour the surrounding woods for ambushes and hidden traps. The morning was spent cautiously looking for the concealed adversary, trying to divine the ruse behind his empty encampment. But no—the men of al-Andalus had vanished silently, like wraiths, in the middle of the night. The irrecoverable blow had been the loss of their chief, depriving them of the will to fight any longer in this strange land. They had slipped away in a hushed panic, leaving much of their treasure behind, to be divided among the victors.

However anticlimactic, it was a telling moment. Martel and Eudo had succeeded where Cyrus of Alexandria, Gregory of Africa, Kahina of the Aurès, and Rodrigo of Spain had failed. The momentum of Muslim victory may have been slowing anyway, but the Frankish wall of ice had brought it to a full stop. Only two Byzantine leaders—the young Constantine IV and the iconoclast Leo III—had dealt the Umayyads significant defeats; now a chieftain at the head of a ragged confederacy joined their ranks. Eudo regained Aquitaine; Martel and his son, Pepin the Short, would wrest Provence and Septimania from Muslim suzerainty within a generation. Shortly thereafter Charlemagne would do the same for Catalonia, chasing the conquerors from Barcelona and creating what was known for centuries as the Spanish March, the borderland of Christendom in the westernmost Mediterranean. The lines had been drawn, indistinct and impermanent, but far sturdier than those of the preceding century of conquest. If the Battle of Poitiers was not the cause of this new alignment, it was certainly an agent in helping it come about.

Appropriately, a sense that history changes course at certain moments, in certain places, can be felt at Moussais-la-Bataille today. But its clever memorial also contains laudable reminders that an event is no more important than the way it is remembered and taught, and by whom. On a July day in 2002 a group of Chinese exchange students, on an outing from a summer-school language course at the University of Poitiers, carefully paced the chessboard squares overlooking the empty fields, reading the inscriptions and absorbing the ambiguous history attached to the site. Nearby a bend in the river Clain is named for drowned Moors; no doubt old-timers in the area will remember a local World War II French Resistance unit called the Bataillon Charles Martel. Many of the grown sons and daughters of the Muslim immigrants in the housing projects of Poitiers will probably have heard of a far-right racist cybergroup that styles itself Martel. And even the hardened hacks of French politics can cite a Mitterrand-era stroke of trade protectionism that sent all Japanese VCRs bound for the French market to a customs pen in Poitiers. The administrative order was numbered 732. Poitiers lives on, the chess game of memory continues.

CHAPTER THREE

CÓRDOBA

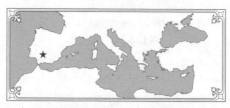

A golden age of coexistence; the mare nostrum
as a Muslim lake, 750–1030

*C*onvivencia is the term given to "living together," a Spanish word with suggestions of conviviality and complicity. Usually used to characterize Christian hegemony over the Muslims of Spain in the later Middle Ages, for our purposes it describes any society where the appetite for war gave way to the taste for intelligent coexistence between different communities of faith. In several parts of the Mediterranean, the bruising century and a half following the Prophet's death was followed by a time of consolidation, when the clash of armies momentarily ceded ground to more humane pursuits. Christian and Muslim and Jew looked at one another over a changed landscape. War and carnage would continue in many quarters, as would the usual brutal power struggles in the capitals of ambition, but the contours of a new Mediterranean world had begun taking shape. Most important, the mare nostrum was gone.

  That reality took a while to sink in. In the lands bordering the northern shore of the inland sea, much of Europe remained in a restless slumber, its Carolingian stirring under Martel's grandson Charlemagne all too brief. The jolts of Viking raids in the north and pirate incursions in the south spread terror throughout the continent, adding to a sense among the literate few that the passing of an old world had meant the passing of the world itself. The final days as outlined in the Book of Revelation, an eschatological phantasmagoria still favored by those unhappy with their times, were thought to be imminent. A commonplace of monastic chronicles and letters spoke of *mundus senescit*, the

world grown old. That glum sentiment would have been deemed peculiar outside of western Christendom. The idea that a dying civilization was "saved," by
the Irish or whomever, is parochial and would have been thought as such by the
denizens of the Mediterranean. By the yardstick of trade, intellectual inquisitiveness, and cultural interchange, civilization was doing quite well in the
eighth, ninth, and tenth centuries, with or without the monks.

In the east during this time, a revived Constantinople turned its attention to its
Balkan and Danubian possessions, its status as Europe's greatest city dented but
not destroyed by the loss of its influence in the world of Arab, Syriac, and Copt.
In Anatolia, still the Greek homeland of Christianity, the armies of the basileus
fanned what had become a low-level conflagration with the Muslims into a blaz-
ing fire only every other generation or so. The age-old animosity between rival
empires of East and West, which predated the rise of Islam, was still keenly
felt—in an opening reminiscent of Chosroes' poisonous letters to Heraclius, a
Muslim caliph addressed the Christian basileus as follows: "In the name of the
most merciful God, Harun al-Rashid, Commander of the Faithful, to Nicephorus, the Roman dog. I have read thy letter, O thou son of an unbelieving
mother." Notwithstanding these bilious pleasantries, successive leaders of the
Byzantines sought to compose with rather than confront their enemy to the east.
The fate of their Italian possessions, menaced by the Lombards and Franks,
were of more moment to the counselors of the basileus than any *revanchard*
dreams of retaking Jerusalem.

Elsewhere a period of adjustment necessarily took place. From the Taurus
Mountains of southwestern Turkey clockwise through Syria and Palestine and
all the way around the great sunny smile of the southern Mediterranean to
the Pyrenees in the west, Islam was in control. The vast majority of its peoples
were dhimmi, that is, Christians and Jews protected by Muslim authority in
exchange for reduced rights and a higher rate of taxation. To spare the sensibilities of the Muslim minority, the ringers of church bells were everywhere enjoined
to discretion; further, churches and synagogues might be repaired but not replaced with new ones; and no one from these communities of People of the Book
might dare insult the Prophet or possess any slave who had embraced Islam.
Aside from having to put up with these and other marks of social inferiority,
the infidel could pursue his livelihood and worship his god with the blessing
of the *qadi*, the chief religious magistrate of the Islamic city. Convivencia,
imperfect and impermanent, was about to flourish. Paradoxically, the conditions for its first full flowering in the Mediterranean—in Córdoba, the capital

of al-Andalus—were fostered by acts that had nothing remotely to do with living together. Once again, Muslim turned on Muslim.

◄◄ ◄◄   ►► ►►

In 750 in Damascus a mob broke into the tomb of Muawiya, the first of the Umayyad caliphs, and scattered his remains to the winds. He had been dead only seventy years. Muawiya's successors met similar posthumous indignities—the bodies of the men who had directed a century of conquest from Syria were unceremoniously disinterred and thrown out into the street. The rulers of an empire that stretched from the Indus to the Atlantic had become carrion. Their descendants barely had time to deplore the insult: following an initial massacre of the caliphal clan, a conciliatory truce was declared, for the sake of unity in the umma, and the remaining Umayyad princelings were invited to a banquet at Abu Futrus, in Palestine. Seventy dignitaries showed up; not one left the table alive.

The perpetrators of this bloodbath were members of a Qurayshi clan descended from Abbas, one of Muhammad's uncles. What distinguished the Abbasids, as the dynastic family is known, from other Quraysh disgruntled by the Umayyad monopoly on power was their ability to harness the resentments of converts to Islam. In Persia and Iraq the black flag of revolt had been raised repeatedly—among the shia and, most important, the sophisticated mawali of the old Sassanid empire, who could no longer stomach the precedence given the Arabian originators of Islam in the exercise of legitimacy and the division of wealth. There may also have been in their attitude more than a little age-old Mesopotamian disdain toward their desert neighbors. Although the Persians, in particular, did not immediately get what they were after—the Abbasids proved as jealous of Qurayshi prerogative as the Umayyads—their backing of the rival Arabian clan brought about one great change: imperial Islam moved east, to the Sawad, where the Tigris and Euphrates come close together.

The Abbasid city of Baghdad or *madinat al-salam* (City of Peace), near the old Sassanid capital of Ctesiphon, was created in 762, the radiating spokes of its avenues nicely symbolizing its newfound location at the center of the universe. In a trice the cultural chameleon that was early Islam left the precincts of the Graeco-Roman world of Syria for the splendors of Persia. Damascus was a memory, though the shift in intellectual and artistic influence was not absolute. Far from it: in the next centuries Baghdadi scholars—Christian, Jew, and Muslim—would translate (as in both "move" and "render into Arabic") an enormous classical corpus of Greek and Roman thought. Al-Kindi, a ninth-century Baghdadi thinker, encapsulated the city's broad-mindedness when he wrote: "We should not be ashamed to acknowledge truth from whatever source it comes to us, even if it is brought to us by former generations and foreign peoples. For him who seeks the truth there is nothing of higher value than truth itself." At the same time as the wisdom of the west came flowing in, others brought to the city goods, techniques, and ideas direct from the wellsprings of India and China. Baghdad became both clearinghouse and producer of civilization.

The city's influence spread into all fields of intellectual endeavor. As their Arabic names indicate, algebra, algorithm, even "Arabic" numerals (in fact an Indian import) would be among Baghdad's many contributions to mathematics. Its researchers scoured ancient texts for medical insights; its theologians wrestled with Aristotle and the siren song of reason centuries before scholastics in the West would do the same for Christian revelation; its engineers and agronomists perfected the waterwheel, improved irrigation, tried new crops; its geographers mapped the world, its astronomers the sky; its artists and artisans rivaled their contemporaries in glittering Constantinople. And its Abbasid caliphs, their world still alive to us through *The Thousand and One Nights*, grew wealthy to a degree that would have shocked the first successors to Muhammad's leadership in Madina. When, in 802, the caliph Harun al-Rashid heard of a remote monarch whose fledgling society might one day prove useful as an ally, he elected to send a gift as a token of his magnificence; the Baghdadi embassy bearing precious silks and leading an elephant named Abul Abbas to the court of Charlemagne in Aachen was no doubt greeted with the awe we today would reserve for a visit from extraterrestrials.

For Mediterranean history, the genesis of Baghdad was an event on the same order of magnitude as the founding of Constantinople. The East, indeed the Far East, had drawn closer to the shores of the inland sea, now unimpeded in its access through the smooth continuum of Islam. If the ideas and innovations of Asia were the first to be felt, its peoples——particularly the nomads of the steppes——would soon venture into the Fertile Crescent and beyond, with untold consequences for the region. Yet even as Baghdad's emergence as the metropole of Islam helped contract cultural distance, the stubborn realities of geography conspired to reduce the caliphate's political influence. Simply put, Baghdad was too far to the east to hold on to the west. Centered at Damascus, the Arab empire had begun showing signs of strain—ruled from Baghdad, it came apart, never again to be reunited. The radiating avenues of the great city turned out to be centrifugal.

⤛ ⤛　⤜ ⤜

The most spectacular instance of flight from the center involved Abd al-Rahman ibn Muawiya al-Dakhil. A Syrian prince, grandson of an Umayyad caliph, Abd al-Rahman had remained in hiding during the Abbasid coup and shown enough sense to turn down the invitation to dine at Abu Futrus. He and his brother, preferring the safety of the upper reaches of Mesopotamia, were nonetheless discovered by agents of the Abbasid usurpers. Abd al-Rahman escaped capture by swimming across the Euphrates; his brother turned back in midstream, believing his pursuers' shouted promises of mercy. Safe on the western bank of the river, the fugitive Umayyad prince watched as his credulous sibling had his throat slit.

It is not known how, exactly, Abd al-Rahman managed to elude Abbasid bounty hounters as he crossed Palestine, Egypt, Cyrenaica, Ifriqiya, and the Maghrib on his five-year journey to al-Andalus. He remained in the dar al Islam, the House of Islam, all the while putting as much distance as possible between himself and Baghdad. One tradition has him holing up with distaff kinsmen in Morocco—his mother had been a Berber slave brought to Syria—until conditions were ripe for him to cross the Strait of Gibraltar and rally his Andalusi supporters. At the time north Africa and Iberia were experiencing revolts that mirrored the upheavals in the east—dissatisfied Berber converts and conquerors resented the privileges of the Arab minority and, like Munuza of the Pyrenees, set up principalities independent of the control of the emirs. Adding to the strife, the division between the two umbrella clan structures obtaining in the Arab world—the Yemen, or "south Arabs," and the Qays, or "north Arabs," to which the Quraysh belonged—was creating havoc in al-Andalus at this time. A factor in all the civil wars to afflict the umma in the seventh and eighth centuries, this distinction was neither innocuous nor folkloric: one unfortunate Qaysite emir of early al-Andalus fell into the hands of his Yemen enemies and ended his reign crucified between a pig and a dog.

On August 14, 755, Abd al-Rahman bravely disembarked on the troubled shores of al-Andalus, earning his *laqab*—official sobriquet—as al-Dakhil (the immigrant). Alerted long before to his imminent arrival and impatient to put an end to the strife, a large force of Umayyad loyalists awaited him. He captured

Córdoba, made it his capital, and proclaimed himself emir, thus setting himself up for a life's work—he ruled for thirty-two years—unifying al-Andalus by mercilessly crushing restive Berbers and rival Arabs and safeguarding his hard-won possession from Abbasid and Frankish intrigue. Before finally submitting to the emir, the leaders of the important northern city of Zaragoza took care of the Franks for him, repulsing Charlemagne and hastening the disastrous retreat through Roncesvalles. (Charlemagne's hostility to the Umayyads explains why an Abbasid elephant arrived at his door as a gift.) As for his former persecutors, Abd al-Rahman proved searingly pitiless: early on in his reign, he had several truculent Abbasid sympathizers decapitated; an itinerant merchant, at the emir's behest, then set off with the severed heads salted away in his baggage and, in the middle of one night, placed them in the main market square of Kairouan, capital of Abbasid Ifriqiya. The cries of horror as the shops opened the following morning eventually reached the ears of the caliph in Baghdad, who was moved to say of the fearsome Umayyad survivor: "Praise be to God who has placed a sea between me and such a demon!"

For all the grisly business attendant on its founding, the unitary state of Umayyad al-Andalus would eventually become a beacon of learning and the arts, its civilization bred of convivencia attaining refinements then available only in Baghdad and Constantinople. The immigrant, known to history as Abd al-Rahman I, laid the groundwork by stabilizing al-Andalus from within and fixing its borders without: after much skirmishing, Umayyad Spain came to occupy a good two-thirds of the peninsula, the no-man's-land (*tierras despobladas*) between the petty Christian kingdoms in the north and the grand emirate to the south stretching, roughly, along the valleys of the rivers Ebro and Duero. By contrast, along the Guadalquivir, Córdoba's river, emerged an everyman's land.

The dhimmi—a majority of the populace of al-Andalus until about 950—played a major role in the life of the capital, participating in its institutions and culture. Mozarab Christians, although second-class citizens and often subject to punitive measures, took part in the government, as scribes, advisers, administrators, diplomats, and soldiers. Christian feasts, themselves adapted from pagan rites, enlivened the life of the capital: the midsummer night's festival of John the Baptist became a citywide celebration.* Other Christian proclivities were

---

*John's story has an Islamic element: his head, as delivered to Salome, is supposed to be underneath the foundations of the Mosque of Abraham in the citadel of Aleppo or in a shrine of the Umayyad Mosque of Damascus.

welcomed as well—the monastic vineyards in the suburbs became destinations of choice for thirsty but discreet Muslim grandees, and encounters between hedonists of different faiths were commonplace in the city's shaded groves of leisure. Out of this cultural promiscuity, however fleeting, greatness emerged.

Few people could have been happier at this turn of events than the Jews of Iberia. After the Visigothic nightmare, they would know three uninterrupted centuries of peace under the Muslims. Al-Andalus was for them Sefarad, hence the term *sephardic*. Given time to develop, a vibrant literature emerged among the Jewish Andalusi commmunity, and its poets competed with their Christian and Muslim counterparts in technical virtuosity and still-haunting flights of feeling. By the tenth century the sacred and once-somnolent language of Hebrew had been dusted off, its use for the study of the Talmud complemented by its employment in profane artistry, prefiguring the synthesis of Kabbalism, a poetic approach to the divine that would characterize later medieval Jewish thought in the western Mediterranean. In more mundane matters, sephardic merchants exploited their ties of kinship with communities scattered throughout the dar al Islam, and Jewish scholars, traders, and doctors served as multilingual ambassadors for al-Andalus. In the tenth century one such physician, Hasday ibn Shaprut, became the de facto foreign minister for the Umayyad ruler, negotiating peace treaties with the non-Muslim kingdoms in northern Spain and, in an unparalleled moment of medical diplomacy, successfully treating a Christian Castilian royal, Sancho the Fat, for obesity within the walls of Islamic Córdoba. Shaprut, ever the weaver of networks, once tried contacting the distant Jewish kingdom of the Khazars, north of the Black Sea. Even after the Córdoba of the Umayyads fell (1031) and al-Andalus broke up into a passel of independent city-states, the age of tolerance continued: in the eleventh century, for example, Shmuel HaNagid, poet, scholar, soldier, and leader of the Jewish community, served as grand vizier, or first minister, to the emir of Granada.

The development of such sophistication took generations. When Abd al-Rahman I first authorized the expropriation of the Visigothic church of Córdoba and began its transformation into the splendid Mezquita, no one could have predicted the near-miraculous burgeoning of civilization that would occur in the following centuries. Indeed, the emir's own writings (or those attributed to him) suggest a backward-looking ruler seized by nostalgia for Syria and sorrow for his slain kin. For Rusafa, his Cordoban country estate named after the Umayyad compound in Syria, the emir imported plants and cuttings from the

Middle East, no doubt hoping to create there a garden of earthly regrets. It in-spired him to write a lament for the displaced that transcends his own plight:

In the midst of Rusafa a palm
has appeared in a Western land,
far from the home of palms.
So I said: This is me—
for I, too, am in exile,
far from my family and friends.
In exile you have grown tall,
and alike we're far from home.

However exquisite the melancholy derived from going back in search of lost time, its expression in al-Andalus was not accompanied by the hand-wringing about senescence and apocalypse common in Christian Europe. For one thing, the Muslims had won, and the Christians lost, a world—an inescapable fact that would have colored thinking about the changed circumstances. Also, the Mus-lim immigrants to the Iberian frontier—more than a million in the ninth and tenth centuries—brought with them the know-how of the old country. Damas-cus was a memory in al-Andalus too, but it hardly ceased to count as a font of traditions and techniques. Add to that the contributions of Baghdad, dynastic enemy but cultural cousin and trading partner (especially for Andalusi Jews), and it becomes easier to understand how al-Andalus made its predecessor, Visigothic Spain, seem like a benighted backwater. To cite just some of the crops the Arab immigrants brought to Spain is to realize how great was the transfer of knowledge from east to west: cotton, rice, hard wheat, sorghum, sugarcane, saf-fron, lemon, lime, orange, apricot, fig, pomegranate, banana, watermelon, spinach, artichoke, eggplant. One wonders what the Visigoths ate.

Under the Umayyads, large portions of the peninsula's wilderness came under cultivation—the *huerta* of Valencia, still one of the most astonishing deltas of agriculture in all of Europe, was fully developed by the Arabs and Berbers. A tenth-century Iraqi visitor, Ibn Hawkal, gave an assessment of Andalusi pros-perity:

There *are* uncultivated lands, but the greater part of the country is cultivated and densely settled . . . Plenty and content govern every aspect of life. Pos-session of goods and the means of acquiring wealth are common to all

classes of the population. These benefits even extend to artisans and workmen, thanks to the light taxes, the good state of the country and the wealth of
its ruler—for he has no need to impose heavy levies and taxes.

Another traveler in al-Andalus noted the abundance there of *norias*, the type
of waterwheel used in irrigation for which the Syrian city of Hama is famous.
By his reckoning, in the valley of the Guadalquivir alone, five thousand were
in use.

  Stomachs full and peace prolonged, the peoples of al-Andalus lived a moment
of grace, one that can be called an embarrassment of sophistication in light of
its begrudging mention in most histories of Europe. In the ninth century, under
Abd al-Rahman II (the immigrant's grandson), Córdoba owed much of its cultural effervescence to the emir's patronage of one Ziryab, a singer, who, the
story goes, was thrown out of the caliph's court in Baghdad by a teacher jealous
of the younger man's voice. Welcomed in Córdoba, handsomely paid, and
housed by the Umayyads for thirty-five years near the immigrant's old estate at
Rusafa, Ziryab (Blackbird) became the cultural commissar of the city, dictating
fashion and dispensing savoir faire as befits any self-respecting metropolitan

The famed norias, or waterwheels, on the Orontes River in Hama, Syria.

dandy stuck out in an aspiring boomtown. Few aspects of social convention escaped his notice. Among his many injunctions, Ziryab instructed the Cordobans how to serve dinner (the composition and order of courses), how to recognize and cook wild asparagus, how to put away their dark clothes for summer whites (although white had been traditionally reserved for mourning), how to coif themselves presentably, how to make the most of their natural assets (he is believed to have founded a beauty institute), how to apply perfume, use toothpaste and deodorant, and generally live an urbane ninth-century life. More important was the effect of his principal talent—said to have committed a repertoire of ten thousand songs to memory, Ziryab influenced the development of Andalusi music, echoes of which can still be discerned in flamenco laments. The mix of love, loss, and longing, so prevalent in the songs performed for the upper classes of al-Andalus society, is suspected to have eventually crossed the Pyrenees and helped foster the troubadour ethic of courtly love. If so, it is a neat little oddity that the first great troubadour, William of Poitou, should have come from, of all places, Poitiers—and that his father attended the consecration of St. Hilaire le Grand, the church sacked by the pioneers of al-Andalus. An even nicer coincidence, given the memorial examined at Moussais-la-Bataille, is what is said to be another of Ziryab's gifts to western Europe: the game of chess.

Alongside a healthy respect for the senses came a commitment to the life of the mind. At its apogee of political and military power in the tenth century, Umayyad Córdoba was also a city of scholars and books. The library of its ruler—by no means the only library in the city—was said to have contained 400,000 volumes, at a time when the greatest libraries in Christian Europe would have counted perhaps four hundred. One of its Umayyad princes, al-Hakam II, seems to have been a veritable bookworm, sending out agents throughout the dar al Islam to bid on the latest manuscripts and to recruit the best copyists. A papermaking workshop, the only one in Europe, was set up in the Andalusi town of Játiva, near Valencia. The omnivorous passions of Córdoba were common knowledge in the Mediterranean: when, in 949, the basileus Constantine VII Porphyrogenitus sent a friendly embassy to the febrile city on the Guadalquivir, it arrived not only with mosaic tesserae to be used in the glittering mihrab of the Mezquita but also with a copy of the works of Dioscorides, the greatest medicinal botanist of antiquity, to the delight of the physician-vizier Hasday ibn Shaprut. Since no one at court could comfortably handle Dioscorides' Greek terminology, further help was solicited from Constantinople, and some two years later a monk named Nicholas arrived in Córdoba. Along with a bilingual Sicilian Muslim, Nicholas worked with a committee of local notables (including Hasday) to make the the original Greek treasure trove, heretofore available in Córdoba only through an incomplete Baghdadi translation, accessible to Arabic speakers in al-Andalus.

Indeed, the encouragement and study in Córdoba of such practical arts as medicine, agronomy, and public administration ended up fostering the habit of inquisitiveness necessary to work an intellectual and artistic revolution. Blessed with plenty and learning, al-Andalus reinvented the individual, a person who had for all intents and purposes disappeared in the latter antipagan and communitarian centuries of the mare nostrum. As the bibliophiles of Córdoba savored the refinements of Baghdad, Andalusi Arabic poets were ringing changes on the classical form they had inherited from Mesopotamia and producing a body of work that, while often less sophisticated and profound than its eastern model, was at times more intimate, robust, and direct. Andalusi poets gravitated especially to the natural world, and sensual descriptions of the cultivated landscape and its objects of desire abounded. New forms were also invented—to some extent inspired by the Romance songs these Iberian Arabs were hearing all around them in the convivencia of al-Andalus. Their achievement represented, in the words of one historian, "the last flowering of an original and personal lyrical poetry before modern times." This was no mean accomplishment, and it would continue to bear fruit in Muslim Spain long after the passing of the Umayyads. Among the non-Muslim communities of the peninsula the taste for innovation was shared. "For the first time since the age of Scripture," noted one translator of the period's poetry, which entered what is almost always referred to as a Golden Age, "Hebrew poets were writing with tremendous power about a wide range of subjects, including wine, war, erotic desire, wisdom, fate, grief, and both metaphysical and religious mystery." Muslim, Christian, and Jew had managed, in the centuries known elsewhere as the Dark Ages, to light a flare that burned true.

Without doubt, then, by the middle of the tenth century Córdoba was the greatest city in western Europe. But Camelot it was not. However broadminded it seems in comparison to its contemporaries, Córdoba witnessed many scenes of civic violence, both endemic and episodic. Of the latter, revolt was usually the cause—and usually the work of Mozarab converts to Islam who, like the Berbers before them, resented their relegation to inferiority within the umma. In 818 the walls of the city were festooned with dozens of crucified leaders of one such revolt, and the suburb in which their supporters lived—on the left bank of the Guadalquivir, across an old Roman bridge that still stands today—was razed to nothingness. Revolts in the provinces also scarred the face of a unitary al-Andalus, the most successful being a quasi-independent principality that lasted almost fifty years in the mountains north of Málaga, the handiwork of a Muslim chieftain, Umar ibn Hafsun, who opportunistically converted to Christianity.

The religious undercurrent to Ibn Hafsun's tenth-century revolt, and that of the Cordoban converts three generations earlier, hints at the flip side of con-vivencia: resentment. A constant in the encounter between Muslim and Christian in the Mediterranean, those who were the most opposed to intelligent coexistence were those who took their religion the most seriously. Refuting the other's faith—a fifteen-hundred-year-old literary cottage industry still thriving—first matured in Iberia, amplified by repeated jeremiads about the dangers of getting along. Many Islamic religious leaders habitually bemoaned as a betrayal of Islamic law the prominent posts awarded to non-Muslims; their Christian counterparts took a similarly dim view, but on the grounds that active cooperation would inevitably end in the Arabization and Islamization of their community. Further, each group thought that the other was a sink of corruption. For the Muslim holy man particularly, the Christian population, its wine flowing and its women bafflingly immodest, represented so many threats to the life of the good outlined in the Quran and enshrined in the *sharia*, the laws derived from the words and deeds of the Prophet. Indeed, the Umayyads had such a preference for blond slavewomen imported from northern climes that many members of the ruling family were noted by contemporaries for their fair hair and blue eyes. The great tenth-century leader, Abd al-Rahman III, is said to have dyed his hair dark so as to appear more of an Arab and thus a member of the Semitic master race.

For the devout Christian, assimilation was the bogeyman. In the mid–ninth century, Paul Alvarus, an Andalusi Jew who converted to Christianity, thundered against Christian youth aping the fashions introduced into Córdoba by Ziryab, the Baghdadi arbiter of taste. Alvarus complained that good old Visigothic Christian culture was being forgotten:

My fellow Christians love to read the poems and romances of the Arabs; they study the Arab theologians and philosophers, not to refute them, but to form a correct and elegant Arabic. Where is the layman who now reads the

Latin commentaries on the Holy Scriptures, or who studies the Gospels, prophets, or Apostles? Alas! All talented young Christians read and study with enthusiasm the Arab books; they gather immense libraries at great expense; they despise the Christian literature as unworthy of attention. They have forgotten their language. For every one who can write a letter in Latin to a friend, there are a thousand who can express themselves in Arabic with elegance, and write better poems in this language than the Arabs themselves.

Although this may sound like the usual reactionary cant about traditional values, events proved that Alvarus was not alone in his concerns about Christians going soft in the embrace of Muslim rhetoricians. In the 850s the city's interconfessional cease-fire was shattered by a succession of fervent Christians who publicly insulted the teachings of Islam and the sincerity of the Prophet—in the hope, quickly realized, of a martyr's death. Although the Christian bishop of Córdoba, at pains not to rock the boat, tried to discourage this sort of self-seeking martyrdom, the pious provocation continued throughout the decade, culminating in the case of Eulogius, a scholar and poet much admired by his Muslim counterparts. After showing him clemency on several occasions for his repeated sallies against Islam, the qadi finally summoned Eulogius before him. One of his councilors pleaded with the obstinate fellow, "What madness drove you to commit yourself to this fatal ruin, forgetting the natural love of life? Please listen to me, and do not rush into this headlong destruction, I beg you. Say only a word in this hour of your need, and afterward practise your faith where you will. We promise not to search for you anywhere." The old Christian disobligingly repeated his insults and was reluctantly beheaded. The bones of these "martyrs of Córdoba" were allowed by the Andalusi authorities to be moved to the Christian kingdoms of northern Iberia, where they quickly became objects of devotion at monasteries then grimly busy, given the prevailing mood, illuminating commentaries on the Apocalypse. Convivencia had its limits.

⊰⊱   ⊰⊱   ⊱⊰   ⊱⊰

In those days a thousand years ago the Mediterranean stretched out blameless under the sun, as inviting and deadly as it had been in Homer's day. Great schools of tuna came swimming in by the thousands through the Strait of Gibraltar every spring, to be corralled and slaughtered with pagan glee by the inhabitants of the islands dotting the inland sea. The many seasonal winds of the irregular expanse—tramontane, mistral, bora, gregale, meltemi, sirocco—governed the livelihoods of the millions of souls who ventured out onto its waters and whose story will always remain untold. Their fortified mountain villages and watchtowers, however, bespeak a time when those who wanted to live well did not live down by the water's edge. If the peoples in the Mediterranean hinterland had, for the moment, settled on who would be their masters, the peoples closer to its shores would know, in the ninth and tenth centuries, an era of upheaval.

The lateen sail appeared on the horizon. Although its name is a corruption of the word *Latin*, the triangular sail—ideal for tacking in near-tideless seas with capricious winds—is thought to have originated among the sailors of the Indian Ocean. Sighting it on the Mediterranean meant that Muslim mariners were nearing, if not to trade, then to pillage. Times had changed since Muawiya first coaxed the men of the desert onto the planks. What had been called *al-bahr al-ʒulumat* (the Sea of Darkness) and *al-bahr al-rum* (the Sea of the Rumi) had lost its terrors for the Arabs. Together with the Berbers, they now ranged through the sea, looking for slaves, riches, and colonies. The men of al-Andalus were in the vanguard: the century of conquest had been checked on land, but it would continue on water.

The islands fell like so many dominoes in a cold warrior's fantasy. In the western basin, the Muslims of al-Andalus conquered the Balearic Islands and Sardinia, opening the way to operations in the Tyrrhenian and Ligurian seas. The Island of Beauty, Corsica, suffered raids but seems to have resisted lengthy occupation—or so the folklore of that singularly pugnacious place insists. In the eastern basin, defended by the Byzantine fleet, the island peoples put up a strong fight, but the determination of the invaders was not long stymied. Indeed, that determination had some desperation to it—the adventurers who took Crete in 825 were the same mawali converts to Islam whose suburb on the Guadalquivir had been destroyed and whose ringleaders had been so theatrically crucified on the walls of Córdoba. These troublesome Iberian exiles, after being made unwelcome in Muslim Alexandria, needed a new home—to Byzantine chagrin, their eyes fell on the rich prize of Crete. The story goes that their leader, on disembarking, gave his men twelve full days to fan out and plunder at will. When they returned to the beach, their appetites sated and their swag bags bulging, they saw that their boats had been torched. Only then did their Cordoban admiral tell them they were not raiders but settlers.

In the central Mediterranean, at the choke point between Tunisia and Italy, the lateen sails scudded northward. The first en route had been Homer's Island of the Lotus Eaters, Jerba, an oasis of greenery just off the harsh shores of western Libya. The fishermen's archipelago of Kerkennah did not resist long either, nor did Pantelleria and Malta. The latter is only a day's passage before a strong sirocco to the most desirable isle of them all, Sicily.

Crisscrossed by Roman roads, embellished by Greek temples put to use as churches, blanketed in olive groves and vineyards and possessed of sprawling estates, fortified ports, mother lodes of minerals, and game-filled forests—even in its dilapidated ninth-century condition, Sicily was scarcely the type of prize to be just given to an enemy. Yet it was. One of the most coveted territories of the medieval Mediterranean world, rivaled only by the Orontes Valley of Syria, the Nile Delta, and the new huerta of Valencia, Sicily was betrayed by a Byzantine usurper. The agent of treachery was a naval commander who, fearing punishment for having had his dastardly way with a nun, killed the governor of the island and declared himself basileus of the entire empire. Backing up this preposterous claim required muscular allies, so, like Julian of Ceuta—who supposedly helped Tariq cross the strait that would bear his name—this desperate adventurer traveled to Kairouan to invite the Muslims on an excursion across the water. Delighted, the Ifriqiyans made landfall at Mazara del Vallo in mid-June 827. Although many years passed before the entire island was subdued—Palermo surrendered in 831; Syracuse, amid exuberant slaughter, in 878—the loss of Sicily spelled an end to the grandest territory of Magna Graecia. Although it would after several centuries revert to Christianity, Sicily would never again be Byzantine.

The islands safely in Muslim hands, the continent came next. To retell all the raids conducted by the Andalusis and the Ifriqiyans in these years would be numbing in the extreme, even if their frequency and ferociousness kept generations of coast dwellers on constant alert. The Muslims made progress in Calabria and Apulia (respectively, the toe and the heel of the Italian peninsula), going so far as to set up an independent emirate for a couple of generations in the Adriatic port of Bari. As much of southern Italy was the scene of endemic feuding among local Lombard lords, the Muslim intrusion added just another element of fear to the tenor of the life there. At least the newcomers' warrior prowess was appreciated—in one clash between ninth-century Lombards, each side hastened to hire Muslim mercenaries, one baron choosing Ifriqiyan Sicilians, the other Andalusi Cretans.

The one event that provoked the most consternation among the Christians was a raid on Rome, in 846. Although the Eternal City by then looked fairly mortal, its fortunes at their nadir, its once-glorious buildings overgrown, its aqueducts shattered, its old stones cannibalized for higgledy-piggledy constructions, the city's status as the see of Latin Christianity was universally recognized. Recognition, though, did not necessarily entail respect, as any given successor to St. Peter might be deemed incompetent or corrupt, or both. The pope at the time of the Muslim attack was the aging Roman aristocrat Sergius II, a sufferer of gout and practitioner, along with his brother, of simony—the buying and selling of ecclesiastical offices. The brothers seemed to have done precisely nothing to prepare the city for an assault that everyone assumed was coming after the fall of Palermo. In August raiders landed near Ostia and proceeded unopposed to the city. The citizenry retreated smartly behind the stout Aurelian Wall—so called for its construction by Emperor Aurelian six centuries earlier. However practical for defense then, these fortifications had the signal disadvantage of not englobing what had become the locus of Rome's newfound role as a capital of Christendom: the Vatican. The Ifriqiyans patiently stripped the shrine of St. Peter (as well as other extramural buildings) of all its trappings, emptied its treasury, and then hauled their glittering take back to the ships. The next pope, Leo IV, closed the barn door behind them by building a string of fortifications on the right bank of the Tiber that gave some measure of protection to the Vatican and the Janiculum Hill. Cold comfort lay in knowing that the raiders had lost all their loot in a storm at sea.

In short, a remarkable chasm existed between the power of Córdoba during these years and the threadbare dignity of its Christian neighbors. The maritime republics of the Italian peninsula—Genoa, Pisa, Amalfi, Venice—were still nascent entities in the ninth and tenth centuries, short work for the organized raiding parties of al-Andalus and Ifriqiya. In 933 every woman and child of Genoa was ensnared in an Andalusi slaving dragnet that descended on the Ligurian port while its able-bodied men were away at war. (The story then has the menfolk rescuing their loved ones in a counterraid on an island off Sardinia.) Even the great were not immune from outrage. The prominent churchman Mayeul, head of the vigorous Burgundian monastic movement centered at Cluny, was waylaid in 972 by Muslim brigands when crossing the Alps en route to Rome. The kidnapped abbot was freed only after the payment of a ruinous ransom. This exploit in criminality was just another in a long series of depredations, many of them carried out by an Andalusi gang that had made its base on the coast of Provence, near what is now La Garde–Freinet. Also called Fraxinetum, it survived for many years as a bridgehead of chaos thanks to its inhabitants' shrewd use of spiky Mediterranean vegetation as a wall to repel any would-be liberators from landward. Only a solitary track, as wide as a man's shoulders and always guarded, led from this haven of banditry into the interior. La Garde–Freinet was, literally, a thorn in the side of Mediterranean Christendom.

In an attempt to ward off further humiliation, the lords and merchants of Europe took to sending embassies to the heathen pleasure dome on the Guadalquivir. The northerners traded with al-Andalus—primarily lumber, minerals, wool, and slaves, a few of the last being made into eunuchs in Verdun and Valencia—and therefore wanted relief from the dangers of piracy. Tact was essential in these diplomatic missions. One delegation from Otto the Great, the Germanic monarch who established the Holy Roman Empire in 962, bore letters that were found to contain disrespectful references to the Prophet. The German monk-ambassadors were placed under house arrest for three full years—until the letters had been returned to sender (Otto's brother Bruno, archbishop of Cologne), revised to eliminate their backwoods Christian earnestness, then resubmitted to the captive embassy in Córdoba for presentation to Abd al-Rahman III. Given the mores of the day, they were lucky to get out of al-Andalus alive.

Most ambassadors were sensible enough not to come carrying in their satchels such potential death sentences. For Abd al-Rahman III, whose lifework consisted of building Madinat az-Zahra, a palatine city to the northwest of Córdoba, a Byzantine delegation thoughtfully brought over scores of classical columns from the empire's limitless supply of spolia from antiquity, to supplement the hundreds more the Umayyads were stripping from monuments throughout Iberia.* At Madinat az-Zahra the art and artifice of al-Andalus went over the top: Abd al-Rahman's audience chamber, the place in which he received many of the cowering delegations from the north, was constructed of translucent marble, its inlaid tiled floor spreading out in geometric arabesques from a large reflecting pool filled with quicksilver. At a discreet signal from the sovereign, a slave would steal in to roil the surface of the mercury, and the room would suddenly become alive as dozens of darting flashes of light refracted onto the already-dazzling walls—an illusion worthy of the Wizard of Oz, perhaps, but one that could not fail to over-awe European emissaries for whom the acme of luxury would have been a spitted boar roasting in a rough-hewn fireplace.

For the ruler of al-Andalus, on the other hand, such splendor was a necessary

---

*The palace complex eventually incorporated 4,313 columns.

trapping of his office. On January 16, 929, at Friday prayers at the Mezquita, Abd al-Rahman III had himself acclaimed Commander of the Faithful—and as such, caliph. This was problematic, as only one successor to the Prophet should have existed at any given time, and everyone was aware that Islam had a caliph, an Abbasid in Baghdad. But by the tenth century Andalusi pretensions were such that the spiritual and temporal inferiority implied by the status of emir could no longer be tolerated. A further prod to this unilateral self-promotion lay in the unsettling developments in Ifriqiya, where an upstart had proclaimed himself caliph nineteen years previously. A messianistic shia faction from Syria—the Ismailis—had wrested power from the ruling families of north Africa and boldly claimed its descent from the Prophet's daughter, Fatima— hence the name of Fatimid for its dynastic footprint. The shia Fatimids believed theirs was the true caliphate because they embodied the occulted line of religious leadership forced, or divinely guided, into hiding after the disastrous events that had given the sunnis primacy. The Fatimid caliphate, a sudden bloom in the desert, threatened the patiently tended Umayyad restoration in Córdoba and its flourishing trade in gold and cereals in the western Maghrib.

War was averted between the neighboring caliphates when the Fatimids turned their backs on the west and set out east toward the strife-riven Abbasid province by the Nile. Fustat, the amsar of Amr ibn al As, was to be superseded by a twin city, founded in 973 as al-Qâhira (The Triumphant) by the Fatimid caliph. The town, its name rendered by westerners as Cairo, would surpass Córdoba in size and, long after al-Andalus had vanished, become the principal metropolis of the Arab world, a primacy it retains to this day. For the all-powerful Abd al-Rahman III and his successor, the bookish al-Hakam, such a development would have seemed the stuff of sheer fantasy.

Yet the Umayyads of al-Andalus did vanish, almost overnight. Within sixty years of its completion as the most luxurious folly in all of Europe, the Madinat az-Zahra was a jumble of rubble to be gawked at by the curious. Walking there today along the cypress-lined gravel pathways laid out by archaeologists who have been painstakingly trying to reconstruct a small fraction of the place, it is nigh on impossible to imagine the palatine city a thousand years ago, its golden fountainheads and whispering date palms, its silk hangings and soft night breezes, its craftsmen's workshops, vaulted kitchens, and spotless stables, its caliphal palace, cushioned women's quarters, and jewel of a mosque—or its twelve thousand loaves of bread baked daily to feed the fish in its ponds. As for Hakam's library, it too would disappear, torn apart by fundamentalist Berber conquerors and, later, consigned to the flames by Christian Inquisitors fearing the contamination of Arabic script. Of the 400,000 volumes, it is said, only one has survived—it was discovered in a library of Fez, Morocco, in 1938.

⤙ ⤙   ⤚ ⤚

If Umayyad al-Andalus can be deemed to have perished in any one place, it is Medinaceli. Although the map shows it as halfway between Toledo and Zaragoza, the village actually seems sited on top of the world. High on the tallest bluff in the desolate uplands separating the basins of the Duero and Ebro, Medinaceli dominates an unforgiving prospect of dun-colored plateaux stretching out all around it. If one squints carefully, a few flocks of sheep can be made out in the distance, bleating faintly as they pick their way along ancient *cañadas*, the cliff-hugging paths of transhumance that are unseen by the motorists flashing past on the expressway in the gorge far below. More likely to be noticed is Medinaceli's Roman arch of triumph, standing against the sky at the brink of the abyss, its lonely grandeur a classical reproach to the highway engineers who have made this historic threshold nothing more than a drive-by curiosity.

A view of a ruin at Madinat a\dh-Zahra, the opulent tenth-century palatine city built for Abd al-Rahman III on the outskirts of Córdoba.

Less conspicuous than the arch is Medinaceli's fortress castle, padlocked and unvisited. It too stands on the cliff's edge, its two squat towers—one square, the other cylindrical—unrelieved by any decoration. Today they guard the village cemetery, a sad little affair in the grasses of the castle's forecourt. Medinaceli—its name from the Arabic *madinat salim* (City of Salim)—was a frontier outpost of al-Andalus, from which campaigns were launched with regular springtime cupidity against the Christian kingdoms to the north. Here, after one such campaign against Rioja in 1002, Abu Amir Muhammad ibn Abi Amir al-Ma'afari, the absolute ruler of al-Andalus, died. He is more commonly known in the west as Almanzor (from al-Mansur, his *laqab*, or official sobriquet, denoting "the Victorious"). The great man's grave cannot be located within the castle, and no sign or plaque in the baked brown height attests to his passing, yet he, in life and especially in death, brought about the undoing of al-Andalus.

Almanzor was the usurper who doubled the size of the Mezquita and changed the bells of Santiago de Compostela into so many ironic lampholders. He was an

The Roman Arch of Triumph at Medinaceli, overlooking an important route of passage between northern and central Iberia.

arriviste of the first order, the Napoleon of al-Andalus. At the outset of his career a humble scribe who nonetheless claimed descent from an old Arab family of Algeciras, he won favor and promotion in the caliph's court in Córdoba through his natural brilliance, iron self-discipline, and Machiavellian cultivation of friendships. Many of those who aided him on the way up would come to sudden and brutal ends, with the exception of Subh, the beautiful Christian concubine of the caliph al-Hakam II, who at his death in 976 became the queen mother of the eleven-year-old heir, al-Hisham II. Almanzor, who was almost certainly Subh's lover, made sure that the boy was sequestered—permanently—while his late father's councilors attended to affairs of state. Thus began al-Hisham's descent into a long, sad life as a sodden wreck, a caliph in name only, lost in a sensual fog behind the high walls of the Madinat az-Zahra.

Within a few years of the old caliph's death, Almanzor had eliminated all his rivals for the regency, masking his naked power grab behind the fig leaf of dynastic continuity represented by the captive boy caliph. He ruled through a terrifying apparatus of spies, informers, and torturers. In just one instance of his Olympian cruelty, Almanzor condemned an unwisely irreverent poet of Córdoba to a life sentence of being shunned—no one in the city was allowed to speak a word to him, ever, on pain of death. For twenty years, until his demise as an insane, lonely old coot, the unfortunate poet lived as a ghost in the capital in which he had once been admired and feted. To have had him executed at the outset would have been more humane—which is no doubt why Almanzor let the poor wretch live. He was known in town as "the dead man."

Almanzor's exercise of absolute power was not confined to such finely tuned malevolence. Under his rule Córdoba saw a flurry of new construction. Not to be outdone by the works of the great Abd al-Rahman III, he decided to erect his own extravagant palace complex in the Cordoban hinterland. Named, confusingly, Madinat al-Zahira (the Glittering City), it rivaled the slightly older Madinat az-Zahra in stupefying excess. We will never know for certain, however; so thoroughly was Almanzor's creation sacked in the civic turbulence following his death that not a stone remains to be picked over by the curious.

Almanzor imitated Abd al-Rahman III in other ways. The scholarly al-Hakam had shown no taste for the raids against the Christians of the north at which his father had excelled; Almanzor revived the tradition with a vengeance, changing what had been a seasonal rite of skirmishing and slave rustling into a near-permanent campaign of rapine and massacre. Athough not trained in the command of armies, he proved himself a natural. The protokingdoms that were taking shape in the north—León, Navarre, Castile, Aragon-Catalonia—would know no peace during his time, and because of his actions against them his name has come down to us, via vituperative Christian chronicles, in a Romance-language form. Almanzor undertook, at one count, fifty-two campaigns of devastation against his northern neighbors, never once suffering a serious setback and utterly destroying, at one time or another, Coimbra, León, Barcelona, and Vallodolid, as well as scores of other lesser towns, castles, and monasteries. His laqab, al-Mansur the Victorious, is well deserved. During his assault on Santiago de Compostela, the holiest Christian pilgrimage destination west of Rome, Almanzor thoroughly leveled the place and stripped it of its treasures, leaving untouched only the gravesite of the apostle James (Santiago), the raison d'être of the sanctuary. Showing such ecumenical scruples might seem odd, until one realizes that the armies of Almanzor numbered many Christians—and that Jesus and his apostles are, in any event, revered by Muslims.

The composition of his victorious armies eventually alienated the Cordobans from their already-unloved despot. The Umayyads had long had Christian contingents as a praetorian guard—not native Mozarabs but mercenaries from the north. Immune to inter-Arab rivalries and ignorant of civic factions, these axmen were thought to be dependably loyal to their caliphal paymaster—as non-Arabic speakers and therefore as effectively shunned as the lonely old poet, they were commonly known by Cordobans as the "silent ones."* Under Almanzor, the door to his campaigns swung wide open to all manner of European freelance adventurer, scandalizing the religious authorities for whom these wars were necessarily an exercise in jihad—a divinely sanctioned aggression against infidels. Even if Almanzor occasionally played to the bigotry of the devout—he organized several public book-burnings of volumes from al-Hakam's great library—the regiments of infidels taking part in what was billed as a Muslim holy war could scarcely escape notice. It is thought that his Christian troops were so numerous that Almanzor made Sunday the day of rest for his armies.

Yet worse than the Christians, in the minds of the Umayyad sophisticates, were the Berbers. Al-Andalus had been born amid bad feelings between Arab and Berber—and it would die in the same bath of ethnic hatred. Almanzor, whose refined and pleasure-loving subjects no longer had the stuff of wild-eyed

---

*The phenomenon was not confined to al-Andalus: the basileus of Constantinople was protected by feral longhairs from Britain and Scandinavia called the Varangian Guard.

belligerence needed for his wars, took to importing entire tribes of Berbers from north Africa—the more barbarian, the better. These were not the Berbers of the conquest, who had long since adapted to the softer mores of convivencia, but illiterate, barely Islamized irregulars, who remained in their tribal units rather than integrating a regular army. The Arab aristocracy, the Mozarabs, the citizenry of Córdoba—all were appalled at what they viewed as a growing horde of unwashed at the city gates. The Berber newcomers no doubt repaid the disdain in kind—some surely thought that these perfumed and pampered Arabs were somehow more despicable than the tough Christian barons against whom they fought in the north. It was clear to all that the loyalty of the Berbers was neither to Córdoba nor to the Umayyads but to Almanzor alone.

All of this was an admirable arrangement for the usurper so long as he, or someone with a similar surfeit of ruthlessness, was around to control them. The Berbers had proved useful in quelling rebellions—one revolt ended in the beheading of his eldest son; another, quite mildly, in the banishment of Subh to a nunnery. (She had tried to rouse her son, al-Hisham, from his torpor.) And the Berbers were indeed as ferocious as their legendary forebear, Kahina, unblinking in atrocity and uncomplaining when ordered to load their saddlebags with the heads of Almanzor's many victims. But in 1002, at the age of sixty-three, gout-ridden and cantankerous to the last, he came to his rendezvous at Medinaceli—"he died in Medinaceli," says one lapidary Christian chronicle, "and was buried in hell"—and thereafter left al-Andalus in a parlous state. Overrun by rudderless mercenaries, rife with long-suppressed rivalries, and coarsened by constant war, the Córdoba of convivencia could not survive his passing. The first minister's quarter-century-long trajectory from Algeciras to Medinaceli brought about the ruin of al-Andalus, principally by devaluing the Umayyad coin of legitimacy. The notables of the great cities of al-Andalus took note— long cowed by an Umayyad caliph and a brilliant vizier, their ambitions could finally be unleashed.

The sad pageant of bloodshed in the years after Almanzor is an unedifying spectacle. Claimants to the throne sprang up like mushrooms, mercenary armies clashed throughout the Iberian peninsula, and what can only be called a revolution by the people of Córdoba occurred in 1009. The following year was named the Year of the Catalans, after the presence of a large contingent of Christians from Catalonia selling their services to rival pretenders. Another year, 1013, saw the restive Berbers go utterly berserk, spending two months in Córdoba looting, raping, and killing comprehensively. By 1031 the Umayyad caliphate was gone, forever. The Madina az-Zahra and Madina al-Zahira lay in ruins. By midcentury three dozen or so independent statelets existed in al-Andalus, of which once-proud Córdoba was but a frail and diminished sibling. A death at forlorn Medinaceli had brought the whole magnificent edifice crashing down with finality.

As can be imagined, a great deal of eulogizing ensued, for a moment of grace had passed. Any place where the good life was so ardently and sensually pursued, alongside its plashing fountains and beneath its spreading palm fronds, could not fail to inspire delicious melancholy among the sensitive. No longer was distant Damascus mourned, as in the days of Abd al-Rahman the immigrant, but rather what he had created on the banks of the Guadalquivir. One Cordoban, Ibn Hazm, author of more than four hundred works of prose, wrote a memoir on heartbreak that can still touch the reader across a millennium. In *The Ring of the Dove* he recalls falling in love with a beautiful slave girl in his household during the days of Córdoba's glory. Forced into exile, he eventually returned to the city and glimpsed his beloved after their long separation. Is it the girl or Córdoba he describes?

Gone was her radiant beauty, vanished her wondrous loveliness, faded now was that lustrous complexion which once gleamed like a polished sword or an Indian mirror; withered was the bloom on which the eye once gazed transfixed seeking avidly to feast upon its dazzling splendour only to turn away bewildered. Only a fragment of the whole remained, to tell the tale and testify to what the complete picture had been.

CHAPTER FOUR

MANZIKERT 1071

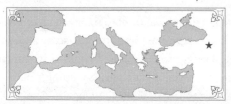

*The fall of Christian Anatolia; the rise of the Normans
and the Turks; the Great Schism*

Some time in the early morning of an August day in 1071, a Greek nobleman by the name of Romanus sensed the tickle of a leather slipper on the back of his neck. He was lying facedown on the ground, a posture he had often seen in others but had never dreamed of assuming himself. Romanus IV Diogenes was no ordinary aristocrat. As the Equal of the Apostles, Co-Gerent of the Earth, the half-man half-god who had inherited the mantle once worn by Augustus and Justinian, he ruled the most venerable empire in the Mediterranean world—yet here he was, as abject as the meanest of petitioners ever to have groveled before him. The moment was a belittlement of incalculable magnitude.

The felt walls of the nomad's tent in which the basileus prostrated himself kept out the rays of the sun, but the Greek's shame—and that of a thousand years of imperial dignity—was bright and blinding all the same. The theatrics of his abasement made plain what had happened: amid the golden summer grasses of the high Armenian plateau, Anatolia had been lost. The Asia Minor of the Graeco-Roman world since the days the Athenians faced down the Persians, the sacred province of the ancients won over, in the earliest years of the Common Era, to a strange new faith that would mature as Christianity, and latterly the rich and rugged heartland of the Byzantine Empire, Anatolia had slipped, permanently, from the grasp of the Greeks. Romanus lay stretched out on the ground, humiliated, his world in pieces.

A question was addressed to him: what would you do if our positions were reversed, if I were on the ground instead of you? "I would have you flogged to death," Romanus answered. The honesty pleased. The foot was removed from his neck and he was told to rise.

We will never know the expression on the face of Romanus' tormentor as the basileus got to his feet, but he would have held a switch in his right hand as a symbol of his authority, its hardened leather handle enclosing a luxuriant wand of horsetail hair. This foe of the Byzantine was the leader of a people on horseback, who had ridden in from the steppes of Asia and conquered all who had stood in the way. Prior to Romanus, the Abbasids of Baghdad had acquiesced in their authority, to be followed by a succession of provincial governors who surrendered power to these bowmen from the east. Converts to Islam, but more at home in the saddle than in the mosque, these newcomers would henceforth occupy center stage in the encounter with Christianity. Much of the continuum of Islam, from the Oxus River to the eastern marches of the Mediterranean basin, was now controlled by the Turks. Their chief, Alp Arslan, allowed the chastened Romanus to stand up. Without too much exaggeration, one can say that Turkey was born on this day. More straightforward is the proposition that a new era had begun around the sea of faith. Strangers no more, Christian and Muslim would, over the next two centuries, engage in an intense series of clashes for primacy in the Mediterranean.

The opening contest of this heightened period of conflict took place, appropriately, at a crossroads. The garrison town of Manzikert (present-day Malazgirt) in eastern Turkey guards the easiest route in from the mountains of the Caucasus and northern Iran to Asia Minor. It stands on a meander of the Murat Su, the river that is the southern branch of the upper Euphrates. The mile-high steppe surrounding Manzikert has been a theater of changing fortunes since the dawn of civilization. Ancient kingdoms—Assyrian, Hittite, Urartan—did battle on this volcanic upland, the snow-tipped height of Mount Ararat looming beyond its eastern horizon and the blue expanse of Lake Van closing it off to the south. In 400 B.C.E. Xenophon and his ten thousand Spartan mercenaries, fleeing homeward from a bungled adventure in Mesopotamia, had crossed this treacherous threshold in midwinter, the account of that ordeal, the *Anabasis*, immortalizing the inhabitants as a rough and unforgiving lot. As a stage for human hardship, the plain around Manzikert has few rivals, its position as a buffer between Europe and Asia consigning it to continual conflict and its seismic caprices making it a scene of recurring misery.

Peopled for most of the Common Era by the Christian nation that came to be known as the Armenians, the region has seen cruelty and upheaval well into the present day. In 1915, near the towns of Malazgirt, Van, Mus, and Bitlis, tens of thousands of Armenians were herded together to begin their death march northeast toward the Caucasus. Nowadays the windswept plateau is home to dirt-poor Kurdish beet farmers and their families, their status in the modern Republic of Turkey a thorny question. Here and there, hundreds of bleached white boulders have been laboriously lined up on the slopes of bald hills to form gigantic exhortations to Turkish patriotism—mind-numbing makework projects for the army of conscripts stationed in eastern Anatolia to keep an eye on the Kurds. Of the Byzantines, there is scarcely a trace left in the region; of the Armenians, little more, save an exquisite medieval monastery standing deserted on Akdamar Island, surrounded by the eerie quietness of Lake Van.

Here only the memory of Alp Arslan is promoted, his distant victory over Romanus Diogenes the sole event to merit present-day recognition. In a traffic circle at the western entrance to the town of Malazgirt, Alp sits astride a rearing stallion, the animal's impossible-to-miss male attributes the sculptor's statement on the manliness of the Turks. Never mind that the Turks, like all nomads from the Asian steppes, rode only geldings and mares into battle, the virile message is admirably conveyed. An inscription on the pedestal plaque, once it has cited the mandatory nugget of wisdom from Ataturk, makes a more subtle, if unverifiable, claim about Alp Arslan's prowess: he, it states, had only 15,000 men; the enemy, 210,000.

East of town, near where the engagement of Manzikert is thought to have taken place, two white monoliths poke up forty-two meters into the sky, like the tines of some colossal tuning fork. This "Gateway to Anatolia" stands in a cleared park—a rarity in this poor region—replete with stone bleachers for performances every August. A guide from the local cultural office explains that the annual festivities consist of a reenactment of the battle put on by a dozen or so costumed Boy Scouts. As is only historically correct, the Rumi are bested by the Turks, to the applause of their parents and the politicians. In 2003 Prime Minister Recep Tayyip Erdogan came all the way from Ankara to watch the show. "The same boy gets to play Alp Arslan every year," the guide says. "He looks exactly like him."

≺≺- ≺≺-　 -≻≻ -≻≻

Shortly after the year 1000 the Turks entered history and stayed there. Long after their Christian coevals in sudden conquest—the Normans—had faded into obscurity, the descendants of Alp Arslan would continue to have their day in the sun. When they first tentatively ventured out of their homeland between the Caspian and Aral seas, no one would have imagined that they would soon be the spearhead, then the bulwark of Mediterranean Islam—the first in wresting Anatolia from the Greeks, the second in defending the Near East against invading Latin crusaders. However unlikely, such was their destiny, for they made their move west just as great change was occurring throughout the lands bordering the old mare nostrum.

The caliphate of Córdoba, torn to shreds following the demise of Almanzor at Medinaceli in 1002, was succeeded by the weakened statelets of a fractious Muslim Spain, prey to fratricidal wars and the malevolent attentions of their newly aggressive Christian neighbors beyond the Duero. Indeed, western Christendom

The Gateway to Anatolia during a recent celebration of the anniversary of the Battle of Manzikert.

as a whole was finally awakening—continental historiography has often used the year 1000 as a benchmark, a starting block for the coming race of events. Some contemporaneous consciousness of the change seems to exist: the eleventh-century chronicler Radulf Glaber wrote movingly of a "white mantle of churches" descending upon Europe around the year 1000. The conversion to Christianity at this time of the Scandinavians, under Harald Bluetooth, and the Hungarians, under King Stephen—two heretofore obstreperous pagan peoples—could not but have given heart to the small bands of educated men toiling in the monasteries and in the entourage of a newly revitalized papacy.

As the century turned, a once-cowering Church undertook to tame the feral energies of its flock: it began negotiating Truces of God, sworn agreements forbidding warfare at certain times and, especially, enjoining the belligerent to spare ecclesiastical property and persons. By century's end, however, the Church had changed tack; it was to channel these energies—both religious and warlike—in an attempt to take back what had been lost so long ago: Jerusalem and the Near East. There the Latins would come up against the Turks.

As few written sources chronicle the rise of the Turkic peoples, much of their history preceding their incursion into the dar al Islam remains hazy. Of the three great groupings of central Asian nomads—Mongol, Iranian, Turkic— the last came to be the most widespread, its many constituent nations (Huns, Cumans, Uigurs, Kazakhs, Uzbeks) each carving its own niche in Eurasian history. Interestingly, given the subsequent Muslim confessional identity of most of these nations, it is thought that the Jewish Khazars were of Turkic stock, but their kingdom—which the sephardic grandee Hasday ibn Shaprut tried contacting from distant Córdoba—had all but vanished by the year 1000, victim to the expansion of the recently christianized Slavs of Kievan Rus (the forerunner of Ukraine and Russia). The disappearance of the sedentary Khazars coincided with the apparition of a nomadic Turkic people in Iran and Afghanistan, led by a warrior named Seljuk. These Seljuk Turks, as they are known, would change the Middle East and Islam.

Their first conquests were the kingdoms bordering their traditional pastoral grounds. Seljuk and his followers had seceded from the larger Oghuz tribe near the Aral Sea and had advanced into Transoxiana and eastern Persia sometime around the turn of the millennium. For several centuries already, the once-unitary umma—at its apogee the Umayyad caliph al-Walid I (705–15) ruled an empire stretching from India to Portugal—had been divided and subdivided into various statelets and dynasties. The center could not hold its far-flung possessions, and local governors broke away from the capital to set up their own royal lines. (The Fatimids of Egypt and the Umayyads of Spain went so far as to claim caliphal status.) Even in the heart of Islam, the Abbasids of Baghdad were a much-diminished force, having fought ruinous civil wars and, by the tenth century, having been reduced to the rank of a shaky first among equals in a hierarchy of competing entities. When the toughened nomads rode into the region on their hardy ponies, they were first hired as mercenaries by the rival powers, only to turn on their paymasters and take control. The Seljuks, having been converted over time to the sunni Islam of their neighbors, promptly subdued western Afghanistan, Iran and, by 1055, were before the gates of Baghdad itself.

Their opponents there were not the Abbasids but the Buyids, a group of Iranian opportunists from near the southern shores of the Caspian Sea who had become the power behind the caliphal throne after capturing Baghdad in 945. The Buyids were shia, militantly so, which caused sparks to fly when dealing with their sunni Abbasid puppets. The entire edifice of caliphal legitimacy was questioned by the party of Ali, especially after the killing in Karbala of Huseyn, Ali's son, during the second of the Muslim civil wars of the seventh century. The Buyids promoted Huseyn's memory and may have established the tradition of *ashura*, the great annual festival of lamentation in his honor. The shia traditions of cursing the memory of the first three caliphs and organizing mass pilgrimages to the tombs of Ali and his family in Karbala and Kufa (Najaf) are also thought to originate from the Buyid stewardship of Mesopotamia. Yet however earnest and ultimately divisive their brand of devotion, the Buyids were also clear-sighted: unlike their shia contemporaries, the Fatimids of Egypt, they did not attempt to usurp the caliphal title, preferring, like Almanzor of al-Andalus, to exercise their power and influence from behind a screen of traditional legitimacy. Thus the Abbasids continued to guide their sunni followers, their actual power waxing or waning depending on the forcefulness of the occupant of the caliphal throne and the intensity of infighting among Buyid grandees.

When the Turks finally arrived before the great city on the Tigris, with their ranks of mounted bowmen willing to let fly in yet another swarming victory, the slave armies of the Buyids were in no mood to be led to the slaughter. They melted away in fear. The capital itself was hardly any more motivated, the confessional tensions of the last century having transformed the city into a series of walled-off warrens of sunni, shia, Christian, and Jewish communities. Seljuk's grandson, Tughril Bey, accepted the acclaim of the inhabitants and threw out the Buyids. He then went north to quell a revolt in the al-Jazeera (Island), the fertile lands between the Tigris and Euphrates in northern Iraq. On his return to Baghdad in 1058, the grateful sunni caliph made him the "King of the East and West." The once-despised nomads—many Turks served as mercenaries and slaves for Persian and Arab rulers—had gained effective control of the huge central swath of the dar al Islam. The caliph, an Abbasid, retained spiritual primacy, but the sultan ("holder of power") ruled the roost.

On Tughril Bey's death in 1063, his thirty-three-year-old nephew, Alp Arslan, succeeded to the sultanate. He was said to have a mustache so long that he had to tie it behind his back before riding to battle (which makes the idea of his present-day Boy Scout look-alike even more intriguing). During his decade-long reign, Alp would have many such occasions for securing his whiskers, for his aptitude and appetite for warring equaled that of his uncle. From Alp's perspective, there were two reasons for driving farther west beyond the al-Jazeera: the heretical Fatimids and his uncontrollable kinsmen. The first stemmed from the young sultan's sunni creed—although the Seljuks had but recently been unlettered infidels, their embrace of Islam was fervent, and their convert's zeal led them to view deviation from the emerging sunni consensus as a stain to be cleansed. Furthermore, the greatest blot on the umma, the shia Fatimids of Egypt, happened to possess a large and rich kingdom, ruling through subject allies Palestine and Syria as well; hence the reward of conquest would not be solely spiritual. As so often occurred around the medieval Mediterranean, the precepts of faith dovetailed nicely with the dictates of greed.

Yet faith was not what led Alp Arslan into his world-changing conflict with the Christians of Constantinople. Rather, the clash came about from the second of his motives for heading west: the pell-mell nature of the Turkish advance. The Seljuks, now partly sedentarized and domesticated, had been fairly orderly in their quest for greener pastures, but their fellow Turks far less so. The eleventh-century migration of the steppe nomads into Persia, Mesopotamia, and Anatolia was a gradual, uncoordinated mass movement of peoples taking advantage of the lack of a cohesive force able to keep them out. Alp Arslan's distant kinsmen, sometimes called the Turkomans or Turkmen, were not interested in the niceties of Islamic doctrine or the lure of Baghdadi scholarship. They simply sought pasturage for their ponies and sheep, and the less severe climes of Azerbaijan, Armenia, and Anatolia seemed splendidly suited for setting up their tents. If Alp wanted to control these unruly nomads, he needed to corral them for organized, coherent campaigns of conquest. Otherwise, chaos on his northwestern border would ensue, perhaps diverting him from his main goal of wresting Syria and Egypt from the grasp of the heretical Fatimids. He planned to help these Turkomans secure their mountain meadows to the south of the Caucasus, then turn his attentions elsewhere. Not surprisingly, the people already living there—the Armenians—did not agree to the theft of their lands, and neither did their sometime friends in Constantinople. This was Christian turf that would be defended. Fortunately for the invading sultan, at precious few times in its history was the Byzantine Empire so ineptly led.

<<- <<-   ->> ->>

Constantinople a mere generation or two before the advent of Alp Arslan had been at a summit of power and glory. A formidable basileus, Basil II, had mercilessly and methodically quashed threats to the empire, earning the sobriquet Bulgaroctonus—the Bulgar-Slayer—by blinding fourteen thousand vanquished enemies on a Balkan battlefield and sending them to stumble home as a warning to all who would dare defy him. Muslim privateering in the eastern Mediteranean had been curbed; Crete and parts of Italy recaptured; an offensive to retake Sicily envisaged. The coffers of the well-managed empire were overflowing. Basil had cracked down on the sharp practices of the wealthy landowners in Anatolia and encouraged the prosperity of small farmers and artisans. Farther east the Armenians had been forced to bend their knee to Byzantine authority for the first time in two hundred years, and even the Muslim worthies of Damascus and Aleppo, alarmed at the loss of Antioch to Basil, agreed to pay tribute to the Rumi. The empire had not covered such a large area since the days before the rise of Muhammad.

Basil's main failing was that he was childless—and mortal. His death in 1025, after a reign of forty-nine years (the longest in Byzantine history), instantly ushered in a carnival of incompetence and intrigue at the highest levels of the state. The empire would never recover from the ensuing half-century of foolishness. Although a sophisticated bureaucracy held the creaking apparatus together, within four decades of Basil's demise the Byzantine Empire was well on the way to bankruptcy, its military establishment reduced to a mere shadow of its Bulgar-slaying eminence, and its woes only worsened by a debilitating tug-of-war among different factions of aristocrats, functionaries, generals, and churchmen.

Basil's brother, a pleasure-loving sexagenarian, had been the first in succession, to be followed by the husbands and adopted adult sons of his two daughters, Zoe and Theodora. Through their short-sighted alliances, the throne passed to the incompetent family of a scheming palace eunuch and thence to aristocratic clans—the Monomachus and the Ducas—determined to drain the treasury in order to shower favor on courtiers. Basil's vast surplus disappeared, and the landowners of Anatolia, freed from his wise practice of preventing estate consolidation at the expense of the peasantry, became staggeringly wealthy, with few, if any, incentives to serve the state. The armies of the themes—the political and military provinces established by Heraclius—became a thing of the past, even though they had been the cornerstone of Byzantine military might for four centuries. Based on citizen-soldiers drawn from the ranks of a landholding peasantry, the thematic levies dried up as an impoverished populace could not meet its military obligations and became little more than serfs on the immense estates of the powerful.

All of which might have stood as a mere case study in bad public policy had not the Byzantine military machine come sputtering to a halt at the very time it would be called upon to meet its greatest threat since the fleet of Caliph Muawiya had sailed into the Sea of Marmara. The basileus Constantine IX Monomachus (ruled 1042–55), a philosopher-king whose erudition and taste fostered a magnificent flowering of art and learning in the capital, proved disastrous in the more down-to-earth matter of protecting his empire. At midcentury the basileus disbanded the thematic army of Armenia—the principal target of Turkoman raids—in order to raise revenue for his courtly amusements. These citizen-soldiers, who should have been the frontline defense of the Byzantine Empire, were dispensed from ever mustering again once they had raised enough cash to send to Constantinople.

Our best historical source for this astonishing period of mismanagement is Michael Psellus, the author of *Chronographia*, a valuable but self-serving memoir. The brilliant Psellus, a bureaucratic infighter of the highest order, was the éminence grise behind the sorry succession of intriguers to don the purple regalia and misrule with zeal. Thanks to their efforts, the undoing of Basil II's achievement came about with stunning swiftness. A once-cohesive and powerful empire was reduced to relying on a cutthroat collection of mercenaries to defend itself, most of whom turned instantly mutinous once, as often happened, the imperial treasury could not cough up enough money to pay them.

At Psellus's urging, an even more incompetent Constantine took the throne in 1059. The reign of Constantine X Ducas made that of his predecessor look like a heyday of good governance: under Ducas, the themes were further disbanded, the treasury raided, the civil list padded, and the military beggared. No longer could a popular and capable general lead a revolt, for the simple reason that no one could field an army. As one historian noted with bemusement: "History provides few such vivid examples of the baby being thrown out with the bath water. At the end of the process the civilian party no longer had anything to fear from the military. But then neither had the Seljuks."

Into the midst of this spectacle of self-inflicted decline came yet another misfortune: a religious dispute fraught with future consequence. On July 16, 1054, Christianity was definitively sundered into Orthodox and Latin. Three papal legates marched into the Hagia Sophia and excommunicated the patriarch of Constantinople before a clerical congregation agog at their cheek. The schism, which endures to this day even though the excommunication was rescinded in 1965, may have been inevitable. The churches of Rome and Constantinople had drifted apart through the centuries of turmoil, and the West was now in a combative, assertive mode. One of the legates thundering out his condemnation of the patriarch—he had called one of the Greek prelates a "pestiferous pimp"—on that fateful day of 1054 was Humbert of Moyenmoutier. This ferocious cardinal from Lorraine was the spiritual godfather of the papacy of Gregory VII, who would lay out a vision of Europe that called for the subordination of all kings and princes to the will of the man wearing the tiara in Rome. To the Byzantines, such a proposition was preposterous, as their basileus already provided the direct link between the temporal world and the almighty.

To be sure, other reasons for the schism existed, some of them resulting from liturgical puzzles (the use of leavened or unleavened bread in the Eucharist, for example), others arising from the complex constructions at the core of the Christian faith. The confusion over the nature of the man-god Jesus of Nazareth had had a corrosive effect on Orthodoxy's relations with the monophysites; yet another trap lay in the nature of Christianity's Holy Trinity. The best-known example of how the Trinity could be a minefield was Arianism, the early faith of the Visigoths and other Germanic tribes—later deemed a heresy for holding Jesus to be a creation, not an eternal equal, of God the Father. By contrast, the contention between Latin and Orthodox concerned the third person of the Trinity, that is, the Holy Ghost, or the Paraclete.

In a controversy known as the Dual Procession of the Holy Ghost, Latins and Greeks differed on a small but critical matter in the profession of faith. In their credo, the Greeks held that the Holy Ghost proceeded from—emanated from—God the Father alone; the Latins, that the Holy Ghost proceeded from God the Father *and* the Son—an important distinction effected by the simple addition of a suffix to the Latin: "filio*que*." This filioque controversy had long envenomed relations between the churches, particularly in the ninth century, when the competition over who would evangelize eastern Europe was at its height. Although the Greeks prevailed and ended up converting the Slavs to Orthodoxy, the filioque matter was never settled. It could be trotted out at any time to inspire exchanges of scalding vitriol between theologians. Such was the case in 1054, only this time the breach proved permanent.

If change had been in the air in the epoch following the arbitrary benchmark year of 1000, by midcentury a strange coincidence of *intra*confessional change was enlivening matters further. The Seljuk capture of Baghdad in 1055, prompting as it would the elaboration of sunni orthodoxy under successive Turkish sultans, is often seen as the event that cemented the formerly inchoate rift between shia and sunni in Islam. Doctrinal disagreements would thereafter trump disputes over caliphal genealogy; and thenceforth each tradition would go its own way, later to subdivide further.

That a similar cleavage occurred in Christendom at almost precisely the same time is a remarkable coincidence; the Great Schism of 1054 ensured that Christian unity would be forever out of reach. By the thirteenth century an Orthodox prelate of Athens, giving vent to the animosity bred of the rift, could write that Latin Christians were less likely to understand "the harmony and grace of the Greek language than asses to enjoy the lyre, or dung-beetles to savor perfume." Clearly, as the result of these divisions from the 1050s onward, the Mediterranean would witness encounters between ever more fractious Christianities and Islams.

⋖ ⋖   ⋗ ⋗

The Christian schism did nothing to bolster the already precarious Byzantine position in the face of the gathering Seljuk offensive. No grand alliance of Christians would fight the Turks. Moreover, another coincidence conspired to distract the dithering elites of Constantinople from the coming storm. At precisely the same moment as the Turks were bursting into the east, the Normans were doing likewise in the west. A nation of terrifying Norsemen who had supposedly been domesticated by the land grant of a duchy in what is now northwestern France, the Normans refused, famously, to stay put. In 1066 they crossed the Channel from Normandy to take England. In Constantinople, news of that event would have been shrugged off as distant barbarian trivia had not those same Normans suddenly appeared, out of nowhere, in the Mediterranean. In the strife-riven territories of southern Italy disputed among Lombard lords, Byzantine governors, Sicilian Muslim emirs, and agents of the papacy and the Germanic emperors, the Normans came first as mercenaries, then as conquerors, in a curious echo of what the Seljuks were achieving at the same moment on the Iranian plateau.

Yet the Norman movement into Italy differed in one important respect from the Seljuk conquests. It was the work not of a nomadic people migrating en masse but of a handful of freelance knights looking for adventure—and one obscure but supremely belligerent family would outdo all others in audacity. That clan was the Hautevilles, from Normandy's Cotentin peninsula. Its patriarch around the year 1000, Tancred, had had the good fortune in his two marriages to have sired twelve strapping sons (and at least one daughter), but the bad fortune not to have been rich enough to provide for them and keep them out of mischief. The older sons, restless with their pittance of a patrimony and aware of opportunity around the Mediterranean, left the fog of Atlantic Europe to fight for and eventually win principalities for themselves in the sun of southern Italy. The first of many Hautevilles to arrive—William Bras-de-Fer (Iron Arm), Drogo, and Humphrey—would have held pride of place in the family annals of ambition had not the eldest of their half brothers, from Tancred's second marriage, surpassed his siblings to become one of the greatest arrivistes of the Middle Ages. In 1046 thirty-one-year-old Robert Guiscard came to Italy with nothing; by the time he died in 1085, he had humiliated popes and emperors, laid the groundwork for the Kingdom of the Two Sicilies (the island and the southern half of the Italian peninsula), and made himself a legend of presumption throughout the Mediterranean.

What Guiscard (the name, a distant cousin of *wiseacre*, means "weasel" or "cunning") achieved through warfare, treachery, and intimidation—even Pope Gregory VII, the ideologue of papal supremacy, was bullied into granting the Norman legitimacy—amounted to nothing less than the extinction of Greek power on the Italian peninsula. As Guiscard, with the the help of his sword-wielding amazon of a wife, Sichelgaita, relentlessly hacked away at their empire, the Byzantines, bereft of the leadership of a Basil II able to counter such a fighter, were mesmerized by his progress. Anna Comnena, the Byzantine princess whose *Alexiad* is an outstanding memoir of her years at the pinnacle of society in Constantinople, grudgingly admired this ruffian from the wilds. High-born Anna, after pointing out that Guiscard was "of obscure origin, with

an overbearing character and a villainous mind," nonetheless could not suppress her fascination for a man "of immense stature, surpassing even the biggest
men; he had a ruddy complexion, fair hair, broad shoulders, eyes that all but
shot out sparks of fire . . . Homer remarked of Achilles that when he shouted
his hearers had the impression of a multitude in uproar, but Robert's bellow, so
they say, put tens of thousands to flight."

Robert Guiscard's roar—he would eventually attack the Byzantines on the
other side of the Adriatic as well—may well have deafened an already-tottering
leadership to the tumult at the gates to Anatolia. The Hautevilles even had
a hand in the Great Schism—the disastrous exchange of embassies in 1054
between the pope and Constantine Monomachus originally arose from concern
over what to do with the Normans. And yet they were far from being the only
troublemakers in the area: the Danubian frontiers of the Byzantine Empire had
grown more dangerous in the half-century since Basil's death, as new tribes
poured into the Balkans to take up where the blinded Bulgars had left off.

In short, the west was an unedifying spectacle of disintegration, while the east
was a disaster unfolding. The Turkomans, with or without Seljuk participation,
galloped far into Anatolia, their nomadic warriors spreading fear and mayhem
well into Cappadocia and beyond. Turkoman bands looted whatever they
found, besieged provincial cities, and lured mercenaries from the tasks assigned
them by promises of ever greater booty. Alp Arslan knew that he had to control
these wild men if ever he were to fulfill his god-given mission to topple the
Fatimid caliphate. A new basileus, Romanus Diogenes, decided on his accession
in 1068 that he too would have to bring the situation under control, if ever he
were to staunch the bleeding of his great, wounded empire.

≺≺ ≺≺   ≻≻ ≻≻

If the choice of Romanus Diogenes can be said to represent the empire's coming
to its senses at the eleventh hour, his ascension to the throne lacked any semblance
of seemly, statesmanlike deliberation from the leadership in Constantinople. A
military man of a rich family from Cappadocia in central Anatolia, Romanus had
served well as the Byzantine governor of Sofia before being disgraced on suspi-
cion of plotting a coup against the basileus, Constantine X Ducas.

The failed coup made Constantine, the old basileus, determined that no
usurper should wrest power from his family. A Ducas, and thus from one of the
most illustrious clans of the empire, Constantine named his brother John as

caesar—deputy emperor—and looked to one of his sons to succeed him, thus ensuring the establishment of a dynasty. When Constantine fell fatally ill in 1067, he put the final touches on his plan to exercise influence from beyond the grave. Before an assembled group of senators and notables, he had his wife, Eudoxia Macrembolitissa, swear never to remarry. Whomever a widowed empress took to bed often ended up supplanting the male heir of her late husband as the new ruler: thus it was of paramount importance to the expiring Constantine that his wife, whom he had genially ignored for his mistress, not spoil the Ducas chance at perennial power by sleeping with any one of their many enemies.

Eudoxia saw things differently. She was young, of a powerful family herself (her uncle had been the patriarch at the time of the Great Schism)—and she was an empress. That last attribute may have been the most important, for Eudoxia saw that her empire was in mortal danger. The Turkish incursions were becoming impossible to ignore any longer: in the latest in a long string of calamities, the great Cappadocian city of Caesarea (Kayseri, Turkey) had been sacked by a Turkoman brigand called Afsin, whose repeated raids left the unmistakable impression that no one was defending the Byzantine heartland. Even some in the civil party—those responsible for the emasculation of the military—yearned for a warrior to wear the purple. Eudoxia must have agreed.

While the Ducas males, as reliably ineffectual as the late Constantine, prepared to take the helm, Eudoxia unexpectedly let it be known that she was in the mood to marry again. This she could most emphatically not do, unless the patriarch of Constantinople released her from her vow and convinced the senators to do likewise. Such an outcome was unlikely since the patriarch, John Xiphilinus, had long been an ally of the Ducas faction, and, in any event, the Orthodox Church frowned on serial matrimony. But Xiphilinus, powerful and thus predictable, was no stranger to selfishness. When a eunuch in the great lady's entourage intimated that Eudoxia's amorous gaze had fallen on the patriarch's very own brother, Xiphilinus had a sudden change of heart. What greater destiny for any family than to occupy both the patriarchate and the throne? Without giving away his game, Xiphilinus took the senators aside in private interviews and persuaded or bribed each in his turn to declare the widow's vow null and void.

Eudoxia then pulled the rabbit out of her hat. She had never really stated who the object of her affections was—the patriarch had been hoodwinked. Romanus Diogenes was summoned from the provinces and brought before her. As a friend described him, the young aristocrat "not only surpassed others in his good qualities but . . . was also pleasant to look at in all respects. His broad chest and back gave him a fine appearance, and his very breath seemed noble, if not divine. He seemed more handsome than others, and this was enhanced by his bright eyes." Whether Eudoxia fell then and there—the same source implied that she abhorred sexual intercourse—is a secret that went to the grave with her. It is said, however, that on seeing the man, "unrestrained mercy took hold on the Augusta [Eudoxia], and streams of tears fell from her eyes." Romanus certainly presented a physical contrast to the late and unlamented Constantine, and his warrior abilities were what the bloated court of Constantinople needed most. On New Year's Day 1068, Eudoxia and Romanus wed. The Greeks had a new basileus.

However capable a leader, Romanus found himself in a scarcely enviable position. Much of the court hated him, particularly the ever-powerful Ducas party, into whose midst he had married. The patriarch, of course, still smarted from having been so thoroughly outwitted. Romanus did not have a strong enough following to undertake the much-needed purging of all his malevolent in-laws— even the Varangian Guard, the brutal coterie of barbarians assigned to protect and look out for the basileus, sided with the caesar, John Ducas. Psellus, in his memoir, fairly spat out his contempt for the new man on the throne. Romanus, according to Psellus, "completely despised the officers of state, refused advice, and—incurable malady of emperors—relied on no counsel, no guidance but his own, under all circumstances without exception. As for myself, I swear by God, the God whom philosophy reveres, that I tried to turn him from his ambitions."

The campaigning seasons of 1068 and 1069 witnessed an energetic Romanus, at the head of a ragtag but still lethal force of irregularly paid mercenaries, ranging through Anatolia in search of a Turkish quarry to engage. Alp Arslan, after having reined in the Turkoman Afsin, had given the official Seljuk imprimatur to the incursions from the east by capturing several border strongholds. Alp and his men savagely sacked Ani, the capital of Armenia, burned the city's scores of churches to the ground, and massacred all of its inhabitants or carted them off into slavery. Skirmishing over other frontier towns, notably Edessa (Urfa, Turkey), marked these years as well, along with a few minor battles in which Romanus got the best of the Seljuk raiders. The basileus, despite chronic defections from his army, could claim to be making progress.

Opinion in Constantinople was not so indulgent. Guiscard the Norman was rolling up Byzantine Italy, critics pointed out, yet Romanus was looking the other way. His long marches through Anatolia were deemed little more than cat-and-mouse chases, never once closing with the main armies of the enemy.

In their telling, he was arrogant, incompetent, and, worse yet, determined to impoverish them all. As Romanus needed great sums of money to pay his hired soldiery, the Church and the aristocracy had been strong-armed into parting with some of the treasure they had amassed under the corrupt practices condoned by successive emperors in the last half-century.

For all of the year 1070 Romanus stayed in Constantinople, preparing a grand offensive and, no doubt, trying to keep his ill-wishers from coalescing into a force that could unseat him. When he was finally ready, in 1071, to make his decisive move against the Turks, he made sure to take a Ducas with him, half-hostage and half-insurance against skulduggery during his absence from the capital. Andronicus Ducas was given command of the rear guard of the army—a position that would put him, fatefully, at the basileus's broad back.

Curiously, this final campaign may have been unnecessary. Tentative peace feelers had been extended between Alp and Romanus, and had they agreed to an acceptable partition of Armenia, both might have felt secure in their borders. Whether the sultan could have kept the Turkomans within them, after they had seen just how weak the Byzantine military was, is another matter. And whether Romanus, surrounded by enemies in his court, could have survived surrendering a part of Armenia—so decisively captured by Basil II and so sedulously despoiled by his successors—is also far from certain. Whatever the case for peace, neither man embraced it.

In March 1071, the basileus ferried a large force of fighters, estimated at between 60,000 and 100,000, across the Bosporus for the trek eastward. They were a motley lot. In addition to the regiments of native soldiers cobbled together from the remnants of the Byzantine regular army, hordes of mercenaries filled the ranks—Franks, Germans, Normans, Armenians, Pechenegs (a Turkic people from the Balkan frontier), and a variety of non-Seljuk Turks with only a notional grasp of loyalty. Added to the untrustworthiness of the troops were the questionable allegiances of Romanus's commanders, some of whom sympathized with the sidelined Ducas family.

Alp Arslan, by contrast, did not have such acute worries. He was planning what promised to be a plunder-rich offensive against the Fatimids of Egypt. After mustering in northern Persia, the Seljuks passed through western Armenia, taking Manzikert and Khilat, an outpost on the northern shore of Lake Van, then pressed farther southwest into upper Mesopotamia. Alp captured or extorted payment from the border towns (Edessa, Aleppo, Antioch) that the Byzantines had garrisoned in earlier campaigns. In short, he was engaged in a preliminary housekeeping operation—shoring up his defenses on a quiet frontier—before heading south with his army to do battle with the shia heretics of Egypt. He appears to have been unaware of the large host lumbering eastward from the Bosporus in the spring of 1071.

Romanus's progress was fitful. His attempts to dragoon further troops as he passed through mountainous central Anatolia met with limited success, and his army began showing ominous signs of truculence, several minor mutinies having broken out during the slow march eastward. More worrying still was the commander's mood. His friend and comrade-in-arms, Michael Attaliates, the memoirist who described Romanus as the acme of male beauty, complained that the basileus had become an unpredictable man, his native self-assurance resembling arrogance and aloofness as he began to "make a stranger of himself to his own army, setting up his own camp, and arranging for more ostentatious accommodations."

At Erzurum, in June or July 1071, a council of war was held. Word arrived of the Turks in difficulty before the distant citadel of Antioch, so the country to the south and east of Erzurum presumably lay open for the taking. Against the advice of at least two of his generals, Nicephorus Bryennius and Joseph Tarchaniotes, Romanus elected to split his army in two. He would march on Manzikert with half of the expeditionary force; Tarchaniotes and Roussel of Bailleul, a Norman adventurer, would take the other half and recapture Khilat, on Lake Van. Subsequently they would meet up for further operations, perhaps deeper into Seljuk territory.

When Alp Arslan first got wind of the vast Rumi army is not known. He did, however, retrace his steps in a hurry, abandoning his siege of Antioch and his plans of conquest to the south in favor of dealing with the immediate menace looming in the north. He sent his wife, in the company of his capable Persian vizier, Nizam al-Mulk, to race ahead of his army and return all the way to Azerbaijan in order to recruit more horsemen for the coming clash. By early August the Seljuks had mustered somewhere in the vicinity of the town of Van. Alp and his forces, in all likelihood, skirted the lake's southern shore—thereby passing within sight of the Armenian monks at their monastery on Akdamar Island—and rounded its westernmost point in their ride to Manzikert. This itinerary, conjectural at best, is favored by historians searching for a reason why the half of the Byzantine army under Tarchaniotes and Roussel simply disappeared.

No consensus of opinion, or definitive answer, can explain the desertion. Tarchaniotes was a capable general; Roussel, a fearsome leader. Cowardice cannot have been the cause. Either they were bested by Alp Arslan—a theory favored by the Muslim chroniclers writing several centuries after the event—or they left of their own accord, through treachery, insubordination, or just plain disgust with tactics of their commander. Our most reliable sources—the eyewitness Attaliates and the Byzantine and Armenian memoirists writing within a generation or two of the event—do not mention any battle; they disagree only on the motives behind the sudden flight. They all concur, however, that no one told Romanus what had happened. No messenger galloped north to inform him that a great part of his army was now scampering back through Anatolia. The huge force he had spent an entire year husbanding the empire's resources to assemble was, in the twinkling of an eye, halved. As the basileus retook a poorly defended Manzikert and celebrated his bloodless victory there, he did not know that Khilat, a day's ride away, was still in Turkish hands—for the very good reason that no one had bothered to attack it. And he did not know that tens of thousands of horsemen under the command of Alp Arslan had taken their places in the hills and were looking out over the plain of Manzikert, waiting.

Great battles do not create or undo nations at a single stroke; their aftermath, however, sets up the conditions necessary for immense change. Such is the case of Manzikert. What happened in this remote corner of Armenia on that day in August 1071 would set off a movement of people and ideas that changed the northeastern Mediterranean decisively. Christianity in the region, slowly but surely, would retreat before Islam, and the indigenous inhabitants of Anatolia would, over centuries, change identities. None of this, of course, could be foreseen by the protagonists—for them, the innocence of immediacy prevailed, and that was troubling enough.

Romanus began hearing strange reports of Turkish skirmishers on horseback harassing his foraging parties out in the plain to the south of Manzikert. Normally the Turks preferred sudden and unexpected attacks, pinpricks followed by a hasty retreat, but these newcomers seemed buoyed by an unusual fearlessness. Perplexed by this information and by the lack of news of Tarchaniotes, Roussel, and their armies, Romanus summoned Nicephorus Bryennius and instructed him to take a small force out to investigate and, he hoped, link up with the half of the army believed to be fifty kilometers to the south in Khilat.

The Armenian church on Akdamar Island in Lake Van, looking north toward Mount Suphan.

Long before he could reach the hills, Bryennius saw that the situation was serious. The enemy was out in force. After some heavy skirmishing, he called for reinforcements, at which point Romanus, displaying the high-handedness deplored by friendly and hostile chronicler alike, publicly berated his general for cowardice. Into the picture then stepped Basilacius, an Armenian commander, who seconded Romanus' misjudgment and vowed to prove that these harassers in the hills were nothing more than a sorry band of marauding Turkomans. Brave Basilacius tore out of camp with a small group of like-minded warriors; the mysterious riders in the hills retreated before them, letting them get farther and farther away from the larger force commanded by Bryennius. When they were well and truly alone, thousands of Seljuks emerged from their hiding places and surrounded Basilacius and his rash companions. Almost all were killed.

Once rumors of this debacle reached Manzikert, Romanus ordered Bryennius to take the whole left wing of the army and find out what was going on. The general did what he could, but soon he was repulsed by a force far superior in numbers. Just as he had said earlier in the day: these were not a handful of skirmishers out in the hills but the main force of the sultan's army, the cream of the Seljuk fighting cavalry. Raised in the saddle and renowned for their ability to loose bolts from their composite bows with uncanny rapidity and accuracy, the Turks were massed in the hills to the south of the Byzantine position. Bryennius, after having staged a brave fighting retreat, rode back to Manzikert with two arrows lodged in his back and a wound to the shoulder.

The moonless night that followed was filled with terror for the Byzantines. Some of their Turkic mercenaries were caught by surprise outside the walls of the Manzikert citadel—as they rushed in from the Seljuk ambush, it was difficult to tell friend from foe. The blackness came alive with cries and alarums from all sides, as shadowy horsemen raced round the palisade of stakes encircling the camp, shooting flaming arrows into the huddled soldiery within. Wild rumors spread that a gate had been breached, that the citadel had fallen, that much of the Turkic mercenary force had defected. Daybreak revealed the last rumor to be true.

Shortly after dawn an embassy arrived at Romanus' tent, envoys from the Abbasid caliph himself, although Sultan Alp Arslan could not have been a stranger to their mission. After being obliged to lie facedown on the ground before the basileus, the dignitaries dusted themselves off and proposed a peace treaty with the Byzantine Empire. Romanus, demanding unacceptable concessions, turned them down. He had mustered a great army and marched all the way into Armenia, and he knew that the intriguers in Constantinople would be apopleptic if he shrank from battle when the elusive enemy was finally within reach, all in exchange for a tenuous and easily betrayed promise of a lasting truce. Whether warrior pride or political calculation made Romanus rebuff the Abbasid ambassadors can never be known. By so doing, he made the choice to take the fight to the Turks.

Mass was heard in the camp at Manzikert. The sacred icons were paraded within view of the estimated thirty thousand or so foot soldiers and horsemen readying themselves for the clash, the calls to Christian duty alternating with exhortations to crush the Seljuk hordes. Nearby, in the hills, Alp Arslan dismounted and harangued his followers. While the phrasings in the speech may be the imaginings of later Muslim chroniclers, the sentiments expressed are telling:

Either I shall be victorious and fulfill my goal or I shall be a martyr and enter Paradise. Those who desire to follow me, come with me; those who wish to go back may do so freely. There is here no Sultan commanding and no soldier being commanded. For I am today only one of you . . . When some of you who follow me and dedicate their lives to the most high God die, they will enter Paradise, and those who stay alive will acquire great riches. Eternal fire and infamy await those who desert us.

What had started as a dispute over the porous borders of Armenia had become tinged with the rhetoric of jihad, at least in the subsequent legends of the battle. Just as Christian authors transformed Roland at Roncesvalles from a straggler ambushed by the Basques into a saint slain by the Muslims, Islamic historians would effect a similar switch for Alp Arslan, making a sultan concerned primarily with protecting himself from a neighboring empire into a holy warrior bent on destroying the infidel. This does and does not matter: whatever Alp's inner life, the Islamization of Asia Minor would be his testament.

Romanus formed up his men in a long straight line probably four or five ranks deep and marched them into the plain south of Manzikert. He commanded the center; Bryennius, the left; a Cappadocian general, Alyattes, the right. Tailing them, at a considerable distance, came the private armies of the great Anatolian landowners, led by Andronicus Ducas, to function as a rear guard ready to jump into the fray should the situation call for it. Even at half strength, this huge Byzantine army, heavily armored and ably commanded, would have been a sight to make the heart quail.

And so it seemed to have done to the Turks. Throughout the morning and afternoon they fell back as the Greek bulldozer inexorably rolled forward, the retreating Turkish forces forming the shape of the crescent that they would soon bequeath to Islamic iconography. At the tips of this crescent, however, the Seljuks showed no fear. All day their horsemen displayed the nomad's virtuosity with bow and arrow, harrying the extremities of the Greek lines and luring exasperated groups to break ranks and ride out to punish their tormentors. These Turks would then flee into the lateral hills that ring the plain, peppering their retreat with a rain of arrows fired to their rear—a feat of over-the-shoulder bowmanship for which they would become famous—and thus further spurring their furious pursuers to close with them. Once away from the main body of troops and cloaked from sight by the hilly terrain, the isolated Greeks fell into the murderous ambushes that had been set for them. As detachments of cavalry on the flanks again and again took the poisonous bait and sheared off from the compact mass of the army, only to vanish for good, the advance nonetheless continued. The center of the Byzantine line, under Romanus, had barely been bloodied or even come within range of the enemy, but still it pressed on.

As the great force neared the end of the plain, where the hills rise in the south, Romanus noticed the lengthening shadows they cast. A glance west told him that the sun was dangerously low for soldiers so far from the safety of their camp. They would have to fight another day. The basileus ordered the imperial standards to be reversed, the signal for an orderly retreat.

Alp Arslan had been waiting for this moment all day. He ordered the attack. The main force of his army in the bulging belly of the Turkish crescent wheeled about and rode full tilt toward the Byzantine soldiers as they turned to make their way back across the steppe. Down from the hills poured thousands of mounted bowmen, loosing a cloud of arrows. Farther north, from their hiding places in the rough terrain on both sides of the battlefield, galloped fresh new contingents of skirmishers, racing to cut off the Byzantine route back to Manzikert. They met up and turned toward the startled Greeks, who suddenly found themselves beset on all sides.

This was the moment for the Byzantine rear guard to come to the rescue, to smash the curtain of Turks separating it from the main army. It never came. Instead Andronicus Ducas spread the word that Romanus had been slain. Such, so he said, was the significance of the reversed imperial standards. The many mercenaries in the army, not knowing any better, believed the lie. The court intrigues of the past half-century had finally found their vilest, most destructive expression on this steppe in western Armenia. As the forces of the rear guard rode back toward, then beyond Manzikert, its leaders no doubt delighted with themselves for leaving Romanus in the lurch, the surrounded Byzantine army dissolved in panic, each man determined to run for his life. In the ensuing pandemonium, the shouts of an enraged Romanus were drowned out. Attaliates, the eyewitness, described the scene:

> It was like an earthquake: the shouting, the sweat, the swift rushes of fear, the clouds of dust, and not least hordes of Turks riding all around us. Depending on his speed, resolution and strength, each man sought safety in flight. The enemy followed in pursuit, killing some, capturing others and trampling yet others under their horses' hooves. It was a tragic sight, beyond any mourning or lamenting. What indeed could be more pitiable than to see the entire imperial army in flight, defeated and pursued by cruel and inhuman barbarians; the Emperor defenceless and surrounded by more of the same; the imperial tents, symbols of military might and sovereignty, taken over by men of such a kind, the whole Roman state overturned—and knowing that the Empire itself was on the verge of collapse?

Once the bloodlust subsided, a few hundred fortunate survivors were taken prisoner and guarded throughout the night as their wounded comrades lay agonizing on the ground, awaiting the dagger stroke of scavengers in search of weapons and armor. The Byzantine camp at Manzikert, its imperial occupant missing, was stripped of all its valuables. Sometime the next morning a slave trader brought a wounded warrior into the presence of Alp Arslan, claiming that his captive was none other than the king of the Rumi himself. The sultan, disbelieving, summoned Basilacius, the cavalry commander taken prisoner after his disastrous sortie a few days earlier. Upon seeing his basileus, the Armenian cried out and fell to his knees. Then must have come a moment of realization, a moment when sultan and basileus, Turk and Greek, Muslim and Christian, looked into each other's eyes. Alp Arslan, horsetail switch in hand, ordered Romanus IV Diogenes to grovel on the ground.

⤙ ⤙ ⤚ ⤚

South and east of Manzikert's monumental Gateway to Anatolia stretches the dun-brown steppe leading to the foothills of Mount Suphan, a snow-capped volcano that towers to an altitude of 4,058 meters on the north shore of Lake Van. A few horsemen, like visitors from the past, pick their way over the upturned soil, disappearing from view behind undetected undulations in the expanse, their turbans the first to reappear as the next gentle incline is climbed. The riders trot along the crest of a ridge, their silhouettes sharp, then vanish entirely. The sky is a harsh blue, the air still, except for the occasional swirl of dust kicked up by the passage of a car.

About ten kilometers farther on to the southeast the hills begin, a great crescent shape of geological violence. Their slopes are treeless, irregular, yellow with stiff grasses unshifting in the noonday quiet. The landscape becomes a maze of hidden defiles and blind valleys—the type of terrain ideal for lying in ambush. In one crease of the land where hill meets plain is a lone Kurdish village, a huddle of cinder-block cubes topped with corrugated metal sheeting. Beside most of the twenty or so houses stand tall pyramids of dung, drying out to be used as fuel once the sting of winter arrives. The local headman scrambles uphill to find out more about the intruders standing above his village. His smile reveals gold, his weathered face creases in pleasure when informed why outsiders are on his hill gazing out over the plain of Manzikert. He speaks of amateur digs—everyone has been looking for a treasure from Alp Arslan—and of how little of much value has ever been found. He has, alas, nothing to sell. Nobody knows where the battle took place.

He is right. For all the abundant source material, we will never determine where precisely the battle occurred. The only certainty is that it happened somewhere out in the wide, flat plain below—and in the crescent of hills that closes off the expanse. With a sweep of his hand and an almost propietary pride, the Kurd villager indicates several far-off mountain ranges, some blocking the way west to the interior, others the route north to Erzurum and thence to the Black Sea. In all directions, in fact, mountains guard the horizon, mute spectators to the doings on this staging ground of history.

Somewhere near or in these hills, Romanus Diogenes stretched out on the ground before Alp Arslan; on the plain below at the same time lay the bodies of thousands, perhaps tens of thousands, of the slain. The double-headed eagles on the standards of Byzantium had been trampled into the blood-soaked dirt. Although on the day of the battle Alp Arslan had used his strengths brilliantly, deploying his mounted archers to devastating effect, in the end the brave basileus of the Byzantines was defeated by his own side. Betrayal lost Anatolia for the Greeks.

At Khilat (now called Ahlat), from which Roussel, Tarchaniotes, and their armies ran away to find safety in central Anatolia, a different narrative emerges. The small Kurdish town on the north shore of Lake Van has no monument to Alp Arslan. Instead, in an overgrown meadow on a height overlooking the lake, there is a large graveyard, filled with hundreds of headstones carved from rust-colored volcanic rock. This is a Seljuk holy place from the eleventh through fifteenth centuries, undisturbed and untended, the resting place of lords and ladies whose pieties are celebrated in delicate calligraphy that runs the length of each man-sized rectangle of stone. As a marker of a vanished civilization, the Seljuk cemetery of Ahlat is supremely evocative, its forlorn setting in what is now a backwater of Turkey adding poignancy to its grandeur. Mount Suphan stands off to the east, majestic and indifferent, its reflection caught on the surface of the lake. Of the cats that haunt the cemetery, few are of the unnerving Van variety, snowy white with one eye green, the other blue. Ahlat reminds us of the end of the Seljuks; nearby Manzikert, of their beginnings.

The new world ushered in at Manzikert had several lasting consequences. The eleventh-century heyday of the Great Seljuks—the unitary empire ruled by a lone sultan—turned out to be one of intellectual and spiritual ferment. Nizam al-Mulk, the powerful Persian grand vizier of both Alp Arslan and Malikshah, the son who succeeded him in 1072, turned his attentions to the elaboration of Islam. The conquest of Fatimid Egypt would be left to other times. Nizam established *madrasas*, "places of learning," taking care to be inclusive of the many strands of sunni thought. The madrasa, an Islamic innovation second only in importance to the mosque, would serve as an engine of piety and scholarship throughout the Middle East and form an important part of the superstructure of the Muslim state. However great his contribution to faith, Nizam is also credited with fostering the arts. The Seljuk grand vizier is thought to have been the patron of his fellow Persian Omar Khayyam, whose *Rubaiyat* (Quatrains) makes gentle mockery of the pretensions of the powerful and the pious.

Closer to the Mediterranean, the interplay between Christian and Muslim in the Turkish dominion would bear surprising fruit. Although the empire of the Great Seljuks broke up after the reign of Malikshah, victim to nomadic share-the-wealth inheritance customs, the smaller, successor states of various Turkish *atabegs* (governors) proved equally fertile ground for change. In Anatolia, where, with a toponymic tip of the turban to the Byzantines, the Sultanate of Rum (as in Rumi, or Romans) took shape, the encounter between Turkomans,

Two of hundreds of carved gravestones at the Seljuk cemetery at Ahlat (Khilat), looking north toward the hills ringing the Manzikert steppe.

Seljuks, Islamizing Greeks, and irredentist Christians left a profound impression on what would become Turkish Islam. Byzantine monasticism and the extravagant mysticism of its holy men informed the development of ecstatic Muslim brotherhoods. Persian and Turkish traditions met Greek thought and practice, and the resulting orders of dervishes, mevlevi mystics, and other Sufi sects (possibly from *suf*, the woolen garment they wore) represented a melding of beliefs characteristic of the brighter days around the medieval Mediterranean. The greatest mystic of the Sultanate—revered by Muslim and Christian alike—was the aptly named Jalaluddin Rumi, a Persian in his adoptive homeland of Greek and Turk. "Muslims, Christians, Jews, and Zoroastrians should be viewed with the same eye," Rumi declared. This message of tolerance and spirituality, preached to the heterogeneous crowds of thirteenth-century Konya, the capital of the Sultanate, was in the end as revolutionary and humane as that of his Christian contemporary, Francis of Assisi.

At the moment of Manzikert, however, Konya's days of convivencia lay in an unforeseeable future. The ashen taste of defeat was all that the Greeks knew in 1071—and it affected their judgment. In a testament to the self-destructive backstabbing of the court at Constantinople, the terms offered by a conciliatory Alp Arslan were turned down—not by Romanus, who was treated with every courtesy following his ritual abasement, but by the rivals who had betrayed him. Alp proposed to let Romanus return to his capital, in exchange for the surrender of a few border towns and the payment of a whopping annual tribute. He offered peace. Romanus, taking the sultan at his word, attempted to regain Constantinople, defeated but an emperor still.

The Ducas clan would have none of it. Andronicus, the traitor at Manzikert, brought up his armies and negotiated with the homebound Romanus—the basileus would be allowed to abdicate and live out his life, quietly and untouched, on his Cappadocian estates. Once again Romanus miscalculated the younger man's talent for treachery. On surrendering himself to Andronicus, Romanus had his eyes gouged out with such violence that death from infection was a certainty. As he lay a blinded prisoner on Prinkipo Island in the Sea of Marmara, the traditional holding pen for disgraced demigods, the shameless Michael Psellus wrote to him that his infirmity was a blessing, in that he could see only the light of his Lord Savior. Romanus died of his wounds in 1072. The terms offered by Alp Arslan died with him.

The Turkomans poured over the borders. The center of Anatolia slowly collapsed. Although the Ducas schemers had secured the throne, they could not secure the empire. After several catastrophically irreversible years, the purple was finally worn by members of a clan who knew that Byzantine losses had to be cut. The Comnenus family, to whom the chronicler Anna Comnena belonged, eventually restored a modicum of order to the demoralized and shrunken empire. They would rule for over a century, guaranteeing the survival of a rump of Anatolian Byzantium, primarily its coasts, and the entirety of its Balkan possessions. This was no meager accomplishment, given the scope of the debacle.

For the greater Mediterranean world, the accession to power of the Comneni helped spark the most famous Muslim-Christian conflagration of the Middle Ages. When the basileus Alexius I Comnenus (Anna's father) sent a letter to the Latin West in the 1090s, pleading with his estranged Christian cousins to come to the aid of a beleaguered Byzantium, their response far exceeded his expectations. Indeed, he would have reason to rue the success of his mission. In 1095, Pope Urban II preached his fiery call to arms to the assembled nobility at Clermont—and thereby ushered in the age of the Crusades and the intrusion of the Frank into the turf of Byzantine, Seljuk, and Fatimid. The Turkish victory at Manzikert had, ironically, ended in a very Greek notion: the opening of Pandora's box.

CHAPTER FIVE

PALERMO AND TOLEDO

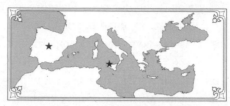

*Intellectual and cultural convivencia in the era of the Crusades;
Sicily, Castile, and the storming of Jerusalem; eleventh and
twelfth centuries*

In January 1072, an observer standing on a tall slope in the hinterland of Palermo, Sicily, would have seen a curtain of sails growing ominously large on the northern horizon. By land, off to the east, in a cloud of dust kicked up by mules bringing their loads to the siege engines in place, he could have made out the dull glint of sunlight on armor, as a horde of warriors attacked the city walls. Distracted by the bedlam of shouts and screams reaching him, he most likely would not have had the serenity to realize that lasting change was about to occur. The mountainous amphitheater ringing Palermo, as majestic as a similar stage on the steppe of western Armenia, would now witness a stunning counterpoint to the Battle of Manzikert, which had taken place just six months earlier.

As the winter sun reached its zenith, the ships gliding in from the Tyrrhenian Sea and past the city's imperious headland—soon to be rechristened Monte Pellegrino—distinguished themselves as galleys. Oars pulling in unison, they crashed through the defenses of the harbor and disgorged hundreds of fighters, their halberds and pikes slashing away at the port's terrified garrison. The forces of Robert Guiscard and his youngest brother, Roger, were launching their final assault on this keystone to their conquest of Sicily. At the same time as Christian Anatolia saw the Turks pushing ever closer to the Mediterranean, the metropolis of Sicilian Islam experienced the coming of the Normans. The Hautevilles were to succeed where the Byzantines had failed.

In Sicily all hopes of a Byzantine restoration had been dashed a generation earlier. In the early 1040s an imperial army under a ferocious giant of a

man—George Maniakes—had fought its way from the eastern port of
Messina into the center of the island. Among his commanders during those
heady days was a young Harald Hardrada, the hero of Scandinavian sagas, en
route home from a pilgrimage to Jerusalem; also present were the three elder
Hauteville brothers—William, Drogo, and Humphrey—and, in the early
stages, a youthful Roussel de Bailleul, the future adventurer of Manzikert.
Despite such formidable company Maniakes would not achieve his goal, for
this was the era of folly on the Bosporus: the great general fell victim to a
whispering campaign conducted by his enemies at court and, against all dictates of common sense, was replaced by an incompetent who promptly ran
the offensive into the ground. The Byzantines' knack for inflicting defeats
on themselves would not be imitated by the Normans.

Their chance had arisen in 1061, after a supremely short-sighted emir of Cata-
nia and Syracuse asked Guiscard and Roger to help him in his quarrel with the
Muslim leader of Palermo. It was an odd mirror image of the ninth century,
when a Byzantine rebel (the fellow enamored of the nun) had invited the Muslims to the island. A decade after the emir's mistake, the Normans were pounding at the gates of Palermo. Just months before, Robert Guiscard had captured
the last Greek holdout in Apulia—the fortress city of Bari on the Adriatic—and
annihilated Byzantine power in Italy forever. The last survivor of Magna Graecia, an echo of antiquity, had gone silent in the year of Manzikert.

Palermo fell to the Hauteville brothers in that January of 1072. Within twenty
years all of Sicily, the bustling entrepôt of the Muslim Mediterranean, returned
to the overlordship of Christian rulers, albeit with an unexpected result. When
the Norman warriors sheathed their swords to admire their prize, they saw a
civilization composed of a majority of Muslims (Arab, Berber, Persian), a great
number of Greek Christians, and substantial communities of Jews, all living in
relative amity.

Palermo was a city of some 300,000 souls and, according to the tenth-century
Iraqi traveler Ibn Hawkal (the same merchant who praised al-Andalus), of
three hundred mosques. The various springs and brooks in the hinterland conspired to make the city a garden that delighted and astonished visitors, as lush a
pleasure dome as any place in the Mediterranean world. In the fields of the Val
de Mazara, beyond Palermo's mountainous amphitheater, Arab farmers had
imported the same irrigation techniques that had done wonders in Spain, and
the Sicilian countryside yielded, among other things, cotton, hemp, papyrus,
sugarcane, oranges, lemons, and the durum wheat that would become a staple

of the Italian diet as pasta. In twelfth-century Palermo, a pasta-making factory was noted by the Arab geographer al-Idrisi, as was the work of artisans weaving homegrown Sicilian silk for export. The Normans had conquered a people who far outstripped them in sophistication and subtlety. To their everlasting credit, they recognized their shortcomings and set about creating a Christian counterpart in convivencia to the recently vanished Córdoba of the Umayyads.

Their achievement is all the more remarkable given the tenor of the times, for the Mediterranean during Palermo's ascendancy in the eleventh and twelfth centuries was undergoing, in the long encounter between Muslim and Christian, a moment of fever pitch in both word and deed. The clashes of that crusading era color our view of the relationship between the two faiths in the Middle Ages. Yet however central to any consideration of the interaction of Christianity and Islam, the Crusades should not cloud the memory of the multiconfessional culture fostered at the contemporaneous court of Palermo—and, just as impressively, at its sister-city in convivencia, Toledo, which the Castilian king, Alfonso VI, captured in 1085. In Sicily and Castile, the call to Christian holy war, even at a time when that notion had its greatest currency, was muted by the workings of curiosity and pragmatism.

⧏ ⧏   ⧐ ⧐

The scars of the modern era are impossible to miss in Palermo. On the Conca d'Oro, the once-paradisiacal conch-shaped valley lying between the city and its limestone backdrop, a dense forest of shoddy tower blocks now blights the countryside. Some of this development may be put down to the hasty rebuilding of the city following the devastation of the Second World War, but much of it dates from the last third of the twentieth century, when Palermitan civic life was cowed by gangsters and greed. In the old town, nonetheless, some past glories of the city can be discerned, down alleyways and within courtyards, in church, palazzo, and square. Together they form one of the richest urban fabrics in Europe, which, though threadbare in places, gives ample evidence of the many foreigners to have ruled the city. A list of these vanished occupiers, working backward through time, is impressive for its heterogeneity: Spanish, Austrian, Aragonese, French, German, Norman, Ifriqiyan, Byzantine, Roman, Carthaginian, and Greek. There is no shortage of memories connected to this place, which is only now being restored to stem the tide of *fatiscente,* the exquisite decrepitude so pleasing to visiting aesthetes.

The century of Norman rule over Muslim, Greek, and Jew has left some telling monuments in the city and its environs. In the midst of the nondescript Calatafimi quarter of town stands the Zisa (from *al-aʒiʒa*, "the magnificent" or "marvelous"), a summer pavilion of Norman kings that, even in its much-reduced state, attests to an extraordinary encounter of artistic traditions. The tall central arch of the three-story facade gives onto a gracious central hall that once housed a fountain in the Andalusi fashion; farther within, a warren of discreet rooms and niches is adorned with *muqarnas*, the stalactite roof vaultings seen throughout the dar al Islam.

The Christian monarchs who disported themselves here with their harems could walk out of the Zisa—or a neighboring pavilion, the Cuba (*kaaba*, cube)—and stroll through the finest garden of Latin Europe, replete with palm groves, gurgling pools, and parading peacocks. Known by the Normans as the Genoard (a corruption of *jah'nat al-ard*, "terrestial paradise"), this oasis of Islamic refinement gained such fame throughout Christendom that Boccaccio used it as a setting for a tale of star-crossed lovers on the fifth day of his *Decameron*.

The Zisa, the Islamic pleasure palace of the Norman kings of Palermo, as it appeared in the nineteenth century.

The tireless twelfth-century sephardic traveler Benjamin of Tudela, who visited Jewish communities on a journey from his native Navarre to western Asia and back, was moved to digress on seeing the Zisa and the Genoard: "In the park there is also a great palace, the walls of which are painted, and overlaid with gold and silver; the paving of the floors is of marble, picked out in gold and silver in all manner of designs. There is no building like this anywhere."

To recapture what Benjamin saw, the modern-day visitor is reduced to using his mind's eye; fortunately, other remnants of Norman Sicily require no trick of the imagination. One such place stands on a height overlooking Palermo from the south. From this viewpoint, at the village of Balhara, an observer of the siege of 1072 would have had an incomparable view of the fall of the Muslim capital. The hill, renamed Monreale (royal mountain) by the invaders, came to possess a cathedral built by order of a Norman king who hoped, through his munificence, to put the archbishop of Palermo—and his cathedral in the city—to shame. The royal pique was understandable: Palermitan bishops sided with the barons of the island in resisting kingly authority and encouraged successive popes to take a dim view of Norman complaisance with Islam.

Whatever the motive behind its creation, the abbey church of Santa Maria la Nuova at Monreale ranks as one of the most arresting sights bequeathed to us by the medieval Mediterranean, as compelling a structure as the Mezquita and the Ayasofya. Sited squarely in the middle of the inland sea, the twelfth-century complex of church and cloister shows a melding of rival cultures reminiscent of that of the Umayyad mosque in Damascus—and like that building, it escapes the traps of confessional confusion afflicting both Abd al-Rahman's mosque-turned-church in Córdoba and Justinian's church-turned-mosque in Istanbul. Santa Maria la Nuova is, and always will be, a temple of Christianity.

The walls of Santa Maria's nave and apse are blanketed in gold tesserae, nearly two acres of glittering background for the scores of biblical and devotional scenes that Greek mosaic makers executed for their Latin taskmasters. The mix of Latin, Byzantine and, in its grace notes, Islamic influences delights the eye even as it is drawn to the Judeo-Christian narrative so exuberantly depicted on the walls. In the adjoining cloister, notable for more than two hundred deftly sculpted columns and capitals framing dozens of arches of Islamic inspiration, a fountain in the southwest corner plashes quietly, although its presence fairly shouts out the heterodoxy of Norman Sicily. This fountain, surrounded by its own colonnade, contains a swirling central pillar and water basin that, in design and function, seem wholly transported from the forecourt of an Umayyad or

Fatimid mosque. The Benedictine monks who haunted the near-perfect enclosure of the cloister used the fountain as a lavabo, perfoming their ablutions as devoutly as Muslims do before prayer.

Some claim that the liturgy in many Norman Sicilian churches was performed in the vernacular of the island: that is, Arabic. Less contestable is the written evidence of the mores of the conquered influencing the conduct of the conquerors. Ibn Jubayr, a Spanish Muslim who visited Palermo a decade or so after his Jewish countryman, Benjamin of Tudela, remarked that the Christian women there were "dressed in robes of gold-embroidered silk, wrapped in elegant cloaks, concealed by coloured veils, and shod with gilt slippers. Thus they parade to their churches . . . bearing all the adornments of Muslim women, including jewellry, henna on the fingers, and perfumes." As more and more Latin immigrants arrived in Sicily from Normandy, Norman England, and the Italian peninsula, they must first have found themselves disoriented—or perhaps oriented—by what they found there.

Presiding over this interplay of faiths and customs were the Norman kings. The first, and greatest, to reign in the twelfth century was Roger II, the son of the Roger who had conquered the island and thus the nephew of Robert Guiscard. Raised to rule cosmopolitan Palermo, conversant in Greek and Arabic, Roger II strove to make his capital a rival to Constantinople and Cairo in its splendor and learning. Muslim scholars were invited to stay on the island, or to return; bilingual, sometimes trilingual, coinage was struck extolling "King Roger, powerful through the grace of Allah"; and an Arabized Greek of Syria, George of Antioch, became the king's trusted *amir al-umara* (whence our *admiral*), or emir of emirs. George would alternately contract alliances or go to war with the kingdom's Ifriqiyan neighbors, defend Roger's domain from Byzantine and Germanic encroachments, and conduct diplomacy with Amalfi, Pisa, and Genoa, the Tyrrhenian maritime republics intent on keeping the shipping lanes of the Strait of Messina open for their commerce. Whoever controlled that narrow and treacherous stretch of water, where Scylla and Charybdis had given grief to Homer's Ulysses, controlled a choke point between the eastern and western Mediterranean.

Roger, his feet firmly planted on the island and the mainland, had surpassed the Muslim emirs of Sicily in reaping the benefits of a strategic position. He would even outdo his fellow Normans. Early in his rule, he had finessed the papacy (by backing a rival contender to the throne of St. Peter) into officially

The fountain, of clear Islamic inspiration, in the cloister of the abbey church of Santa Maria la Nuova at Monreale, Sicily.

making his possession a kingdom—although neither a historical precedent nor even a flimsy genealogical pretext existed for this promotion. No matter—in typical Hauteville fashion, Roger felt no constraint on his pretensions and had himself crowned king in 1130. He ruled as "king of Sicily, of the duchy of Apulia and of the principality of Capua." The lucrative addition of all of southern Italy to his domain had been effected by crushing his cousins' claims to that region. The wily Robert Guiscard, dead for forty-odd years and thus spared seeing his lineage so cleverly dispossessed by Roger, would have been outraged.

The palace chapel Roger II commissioned for his residence at Palermo attests to the wealth of the new Norman kingdom—and, as at Monreale and the Zisa, to the playful syncretism at work in this hothouse of Mediterranean cultures. In Roger's Palatine Chapel, Byzantine mosaics shimmer above the colorful marbling of Latin pillars, which themselves stretch up to a thicket of muqarna stalactites, painted with distinctly unorthodox Islamic figurative scenes of the hunt and other pleasures. This sanctuary, as splendid a jewel box as the Sainte Chapelle in Paris, made manifest not only the fullness of the king's faith (and, not incidentally, his treasury) but also his most un-Parisian appreciation of other traditions.

To his Muslim subjects in Palermo, despite the church bells pealing ever more loudly in their city, Roger may have appeared a continuation of what their ancestors had known. True, the slipper was on the other foot: they, not the Christians, were the second-class citizens subject to higher taxation, and their main Friday mosque had been turned into Palermo's cathedral. But many of the symbols and practices of power remained rooted in the Muslim ancien régime. A ceremonial silken cloak presented to Roger around 1133 by the Muslims of the city has survived: on it a pair of ferocious lions can be seen attacking two unfortunate camels, and the central axis shows a stylized palm tree, an iconographic nod to the Arabic tree of life. On its hem a text in Kufic characters reads: "This was made in the royal factory for the good fortune, supreme honor, perfection and power, the betterment, capacity, prosperity, sublimity, glory, beauty, the increase of his security, fulfillment of his hopes, the goodness of his days and nights without end or interruption, for his power and guard, his defence and protection, good fortune, salvation, victory and excellence. In the capital of Sicily, the 528th year [of the hijra]." It was hardly the type of raiment favored by other Christian kings of the time.

Then again, by most accounts Roger was entirely unlike his fellow Latin monarchs. Supremely intelligent, scrupulous in managing his kingdom's accounts (many of which were handled by Arab civil servants), and fond of the Byzantine tactic of forestalling war through bribery, he was above all else a man of great intellectual curiosity. The superior accomplishments of Islamic arts and sciences fascinated him. "His knowledge of mathematics and applied science was boundless," wrote one admiring Muslim scholar. "He was deeply grounded in every aspect of these two disciplines, studied them comprehensively and himself made new discoveries and wonderful inventions, as no prince before him had."

On the mainland, it is thought, Roger may have opened the royal purse for the famous medical school of Salerno, founded in the ninth century under the

Mosaic depicting Roger II of Sicily being crowned by Christ in Palermo's Martorana, a church funded by the king's admiral, George of Antioch.

Lombards. Salerno translators brought the treatises on the healing arts practiced by the Muslims and Jews of the dar al Islam to the Christian west. On the island, Roger's court at Palermo shone brightly as a lamplight of the arts and of scientific inquiry, undimmed by any consideration of confessional identity. The Church of Rome was kept at arm's length by an absolutist Roger, and scholars of the Mediterranean basin were drawn to the free-flowing convergence of Arab, Greek, and Latin knowledge.

The most celebrated arrival in Palermo was Abu Abdallah Muhammad Ibn Muhammad Ibn Abdallah Ibn Idris al-Qurtubi al-Hasani, known usually under the mercifully shortened name of al-Idrisi. Although his origins are disputed, this polymath and personal favorite of Roger is thought to have studied in Córdoba before making his way to Sicily—thereby earning the status of renegade among disapproving Muslim scholars in Islamic lands. Of his many writings, the most astounding for its time is undoubtedly *The delight of he who looks to travel throughout the world*, better known as *The Book of Roger* (*al-kitab al-rujari*) in honor of its patron. The work, fifteen years in the making, is a gazetteer and atlas, containing information on Asia, Africa, and Europe culled, in part, from interviews with the sailors, merchants, and wayfarers passing through the busy ports of Sicily. A remarkable geographical compendium, it constitutes a fitting tribute to the pragmatic and avid king who collaborated with al-Idrisi in its compilation. To accompany the book and its maps, the Muslim scholar also presented Roger with a planisphere, made of solid silver and thus worthy of the regal gaze.

In one last respect Roger proved an exception among the crowned heads of Europe: he appears to have truly loved his wife. His first marriage stands out for its happiness, in an era when royal unions were sometimes honored only as long as they were useful.* When Roger's queen died, in her thirties, he went into such deep mourning that his courtiers feared for his sanity. Indeed, Roger's seclusion was so prolonged that some of his kinsmen in southern Italy, still rankled by his usurpation of their rights, dared to hope that he too had died. They rose in revolt, calling on the Germanic emperor and the pope to help them.

The lady whose untimely demise caused the commotion—Roger eventually restored order—was Elvira of Castile. By her birthright, she could not have been a better bride for a ruler of Norman Palermo, for Elvira was the daughter of Alfonso VI, the Castilian monarch who had taken Muslim Toledo and made it his

---

*His widowed mother, Adelaide, remarried a crusader king of Jerusalem, only to be discarded when it looked as if she might inherit the kingdom.

capital. The excitements of Palermo would have been familiar to Elvira, as her upbringing in Toledo was no doubt accompanied by an equally voluble babel of convivencia. Unfortunately, not much is known for certain about Roger's beloved queen, aside from her having given him five sons and one daughter in the space of ten years. Yet as a woman of Toledo, then of Palermo, Elvira must have been worldly and educated—and perhaps even a little impatient with the martial bigotry of her fellow Latins. However significant the capture of these cities in rolling back the great Arab conquests of the early Middle Ages, both places came to show that, despite their new masters, people of different faiths could still get along. In Spain, the Christians would follow the trail of tolerance blazed by the Muslims.

❄ ❄   ❄ ❄

In 1072, the moment of the Norman conquest of Palermo, other epochal stirrings occurred elsewhere in the Mediterranean world. In that same year Alfonso of León—the future Alfonso VI—spent nine months as a refugee in Toledo. He was accorded the hospitality of the urbane ruler of that city, al-Mam'un, who thus earned left-handed praise as a *caballero aunque moro* (a knight although a Moor). Although one later account has a crafty Alfonso inspecting the city's fortifications for weaknesses, in all probability he and his genial host spent their days hunting and supping together and otherwise enjoying the amenities that a pleasure-loving court has to offer. Under al-Mam'un, Toledo was a supremely civilized place, its arts and sciences developed to a degree undreamed of in Christian Spain. Known throughout al-Andalus for a wondrous clepsydra (water clock) constructed by an astronomer in a hillside pavilion opposite the city, Toledo also possessed magnificent royal gardens that were tended by the greatest agronomes of the age.

Alfonso had been driven into this sophisticated place of exile by his brother, Sancho, who had refused to respect the partitioning of the royal domain drawn up by their late father. In the eleventh century the primitive Christian kingdoms of the north had begun, at last, to coalesce into coherent entities worth squabbling over. An assassin conveniently eliminated Sancho in late 1072 as he was besieging their sister's fortress, enabling Alfonso to leave Toledo and realize the goal that had underlain the sibling rivalry: uniting under one ruler the kingdoms of León, Castile, and to the west, Galicia. (Alfonso dispossessed another brother there.) That left Navarre, Aragon, and Catalonia out of his grasp, but still Alfonso's realm encompassed half of the Christian north of the Iberian peninsula.

According to a chronicle unsympathetic to Alfonso, the king was humiliated on returning from Toledo by a vassal of the murdered Sancho. The event supposedly occurred in a church in Burgos, where the monarch was forced to swear publicly on holy relics that he had had no part in the killing of his brother. Whatever the truth of the story, the vassal in question, and his chastened king, would eventually reconcile and demonstrate in a convincing fashion that a new state of affairs obtained in the countries bordering al-Andalus. No longer were the Christian kingdoms at the mercy of an Almanzor; to the contrary, the northerners were now in a position of force.

Rodrigo Díaz de Vivar, the vassal to have supposedly needled the king's conscience in public, is better known as El Cid (from *sayyid*, "chief"). The Cid made a career of bullying local magnates out of land and money in the free-for-all that followed the final collapse of the unitary state governed from Córdoba in 1031. A minor nobleman from near Burgos, he was a superb warrior and leader of men, seldom bested on the battlefield and adept at political maneuvering. The Cid is usually thought of as personifying the *reconquista*—that is, the capture of Spain from the Muslims and, by extension, the fight for Christian supremacy in the Mediterranean world. However compelling that reputation may be, it is now recognized as fanciful, having been fabricated by latter-day churchmen and historians imbued with an ideology of Iberian Catholic predestination.

What we know of the historical Cid, primarily from a chronicle and a brilliant epic poem of the twelfth century, gives us a portrait of someone far simpler than an exalted holy warrior or a protonationalist visionary. The Cid, like Robert Guiscard, was an opportunist. A man on the make, he was one of many in eleventh-century Iberia eager to take advantage of a chaotic situation. And the confused circumstances of the time offered splendid openings for freelance employment; when the Cid had one of his frequent disputes with King Alfonso, for example, he simply switched sides, once becoming the military leader of the Muslim kingdom of Zaragoza. That he could occupy this post for five years, then return to the service of a Christian monarch, attests to the fluidity of the arrangements on the peninsula.

The disappearance of the Umayyads had created these opportunites. When the fragile edifice of the Andalusi caliphate finally came crashing down in 1031, the pieces were not put back together. Instead, a patchwork of competing city-states throughout al-Andalus came into being, each with its own ruling family vying for dynastic permanence. Known as the *taifas* (from *muluk al-tawa'if*, or "rulers of the factions"), these three dozen or so statelets were, much like the cities of the

Italian Renaissance, keen rivals in art, commerce, and war. In the arts, remnants of which are now scattered like glittering confetti in the museums of Europe and America, the eleventh-century taifas showed considerable creative brio, the surviving examples of their ivory carving, sculpture in wood and marble, ceramics, metalwork, and textiles attesting to a high tide of refinement. Just as impressive was the work of taifa poets, who continued the Cordoban celebration of fine feeling and the good life. Seville, especially, had a court led and peopled by sybarites, its successive kings of the Abbaḍid dynasty proving themselves to be

The stupendously bewhiskered monument to El Cid in Burgos, Spain.

accomplished poets. In all of the higher pursuits, the taifas strove to outdo their neighbors, and in the process they created a golden age of art and learning.

Yet these cities, as the Cid and his fellow Christian adventurers well knew, were also locked in a permanent life-or-death struggle. The perilousness of their situation ensured that few impediments were put in the way of exceptional and useful men, whatever their provenance. Hence the career of Grenada's powerful Jewish grand vizier, general, poet, and rabbi, Shmuel HaNagid, and that of a later figure, Abu al-Fadl Hasday ibn Hasday, the Jewish grand vizier of Zaragoza at the time of the Cid's employment there. Gold from trade with Africa flowed into the six biggest city-states—Granada, Seville, Badajoz, Valencia, Toledo, and Zaragoza—to pay the mercenary armies that marched out to conduct a succession of bloody campaigns for preeminence. However gossamer the sensibilities of the taifa courts, barbarity was never far away. In 1053, to cite one instance, the poet-king of Seville invited the neighboring rulers of Arcos, Jérez, Morón, and Ronda for a peace conference: as they enjoyed his hammam prior to the negotiations, their host slipped out of the building and instructed his men to lock the doors and stop up the air vents so that his guests died, suffocated and scorched, in a cloud of steam. He later celebrated the exploit in a poem, part of which reads: "How many rivals did I kill, / Steadily, one after another: / Of their heads I made a garland / Adorning the edge of the side wall!"

Such viciousness played into the hands of the Christian northerners. Although not without their own divisions, the emerging kingdoms beyond the Ebro and Duero exploited for their own profit the far greater disunity of the Muslim south. Hired initially as mercenaries by the taifas, as the eleventh century progressed the Castilians, Aragonese, and Catalans came to be enforcers of what can only be called a protection racket. In exchange for not being attacked by the Christians, the taifas paid punishing annual tributes, known as *parias*, to whoever proved the most menacing. At one point near midcentury León received protection money from Toledo, Seville, Zaragoza, and Granada, often on the order of twenty to thirty thousand gold coins per annum (from each client, no less). This torrent of Muslim gold flowed northward for the enrichment of kings, courtiers, and warriors, the construction of churches, and the endowment of monasteries as far afield as Cluny, in Burgundy—all of it extorted under threat of violence. As extra taxes had to be levied in the taifas to meet these payments—and some taxes violated long-standing Islamic practice—the Muslim, Mozarab, and Jewish inhabitants of the cities grew restive, thereby making unstable al-Andalus even more volatile. Such was the world in which Alfonso VI and the Cid operated.

The fall of Toledo came about in 1085, at the culmination of a long series of depredations in the Toledan countryside, ruinous annual payments to León, wars with Muslim Valencia, and a siege that had brought on famine. Also, Alfonso had been propping up a remarkably ineffectual and unpopular leader, the grandson of his host of 1072, as part of what appears to have been a deliberate policy to weaken the great taifa from within. Eventually the bickering town fathers bowed to the inexorable and the Christian monarch was invited in, not as a refugee but as a conqueror, after having promised to respect the different communities of the city and allow, in particular, the Muslims to keep their main Friday mosque. On May 25, 1085, the same day that the theocratic Pope Gregory VII died in Salerno, Alfonso VI entered what, almost four centuries earlier, had been the capital of Visigothic Spain. His successors, conscious of this connection to the time of the mare nostrum yet aware of the changed circumstances of the present day, each styled himself as "emperor of the three religions."

Whether Alfonso VI would have taken the title seriously is unclear—the promise about the main mosque, for one, was immediately broken. At the behest of the city's new Latin bishop, a Cluniac monk from north of the Pyrenees ill disposed to both Mozarabs and Muslims, Alfonso permitted the mosque to be transformed into a cathedral. Another monk from Cluny, Odo of Châtillon, as Pope Urban II, quickly moved to make the uncompromising bishop of Toledo the primate of the entire Iberian peninsula, charged with imposing a Latin, Catholic orthodoxy on the indigenous Christian community, many of whom had worshiped under an old Visigothic rite for centuries. The beginnings of the new convivencia, for Mozarabs much less Muslims, did not look rosy.

Paradoxically, developments in al-Andalus would foster a measure of broad-mindedness in Christian Spain. The borders of the latter had been moved significantly to the south, and the no-man's-land around such outposts as Medinaceli resettled in the wake of the successes of Alfonso. But despite his desire to extend his dominion over all of Iberia, the great king would push barely beyond the Tagus, the river that winds around the rocky eminence on which Toledo is built. The reason for this scaled-back ambition was simple: in the once-anarchic south emerged a force that could not be intimidated into paying parias or ceding territory through battle. Shortly after the fall of Toledo, the rest of al-Andalus would come under the control of a group of religious enthusiasts from Africa called the Almoravids. These desert-hardened men halted the advance of León-Castile in its tracks and put an end to the practice of systematic extortion. Alfonso could only watch, from his new citadel in Toledo, as al-Andalus became united again.

◄← ◄← →► →►

The mysterious Almoravids had risen to prominence far away from Iberia, on the southwestern fringes of the Sahara. Sometime in the 1030s, a local chieftain of the area, newly invigorated in the faith as he returned home from a pilgrimage to Mecca, had met a charismatic missionary named Abd Allah ibn Yasin. The holy man was invited to come and proselytize several tribes of heretofore diffident Muslim Berbers of the Sanhaja tribe, in what is now Mauretania. Ibn Yasin made little headway against the rough and ready Sanhaja; in the face of their hostility he was forced to flee to the Atlantic coast, where he established a fortified religious outpost, or *ribat*, somewhere near the mouth of the river Senegal. Here his luck changed, and Ibn Yasin's austere and disciplined message drew thousands of recruits to the sanctuary, so that the new force came to be known as the "people of the ribat" (*al-murabitun*, whence *almoravid*). To the south they advanced to destroy the great sub-Saharan kingdom of Ghana and establish their dominion as far as the lower reaches of the river Niger. To the north, as Andalusi influence had waned in the Maghrib in the troubled taifa times, the Almoravids moved to fill the power vacuum, conquering all of Saharan west Africa before crossing the Atlas Mountains to the fertile lands near the Strait of Gibraltar. There, they looked across the waters to Europe and were aghast at what they saw: lazy drunken voluptuaries, in their view, in thrall to the Christians and in bed with the Jews. As revivalists, they abhorred their lax coreligionists in al-Andalus and contemplated waging a holy war against them.

All of which left the taifas in a delicate position. The Christians from the north had heretofore been a nuisance, little more than organized gangs of quasi-civilized fellow Iberians to be chased away with bags of coins. But the fall of Toledo changed all that. The disappearance of that great taifa, wrote the Muslim king of Granada in his memoirs, "sent a great tremor through all al-Andalus and filled the inhabitants with fear and despair." With al-Andalus in danger of being overrun by uncouth unbelievers, the taifa rulers debated whether to call on fellow Muslims to protect it. The Christians were the devil they knew, but then again, so too were the Almoravids. To the Andalusi sophisticates, these desert fanatics were just Berber tribesmen, the age-old enemy of the landed Arab classes since the time of the immigrant Abd al-Rahman. To their north and south, then, the taifas had decidedly unsavory neighbors: with whom should they cast their lot? A decision was made, which was famously summed up by the king of Seville, al-Mu'tamid, the son of the man who had suffocated his guests in a bathhouse: "I have no desire to be branded by my descendants as the man who delivered al-Andalus as prey to the infidels . . . I would rather be a camel-driver in Morocco than a swineherd in Castile."

The Almoravids were entreated to cross the strait. In 1086, the year after the Christian capture of Toledo, the Almoravids crushed the heavy cavalry of Alfonso VI at Sagrajas, a village near the western taifa of Badajoz. The Castilians would go no further for a generation, with the reliable exception of the Cid, who captured wealthy Valencia and repulsed Almoravid attacks until his death in 1099. As for the taifas, they too would be gone, swallowed up by saviors turned usurpers, for the Almoravids elected to stay and rule in al-Andalus. In the disorder of collapse and conquest, al-Mu'tamid's widowed daughter-in-law, Zaida, escaped northward, thereby avoiding the deportation of Seville's ruling family to Africa—a removal that reduced al-Mu'tamid to poverty in Morocco, just as he had feared. Zaida, however, did not end up a swineherd: when she

The Koutoubia Mosque in Marrakesh, Morocco, begun in 1147 after the capture of the Almoravid capital by the Almohads.

arrived in Toledo, Alfonso immediately took her as his mistress and, once she had converted and christened herself Isabel, made her his wife. The king would henceforth consort with the Moor. Out of their union was born Elvira of Castile, princess of Toledo and future queen of Palermo. For a twelfth-century European, few lineages could be more evocative of convivencia.

⤙ ⤙ ⤚ ⤚

Centuries of go-it-alone Christianity have obscured the multiconfessional Toledo of Elvira's day. From the steep hillside once occupied by the clepsydra pavilion, the view of the city on the opposite bank of the Tagus looks uncannily like what El Greco painted in the sixteenth century: a stoutly fortified town on a dramatic granite eminence, its slopes a palette of brown brick and terra-cotta rising toward the turbulent sky of La Mancha. The spire of the mosque-turned-cathedral—an enormous Gothic structure from the twelfth and thirteenth centuries—pokes upward from one side of the hill; on the summit stand the four gray towers of a once-royal residence, the Alcázar, entirely rebuilt after being leveled in the Spanish Civil War.

Toledo has been many things in its long history, but only in the twelfth and thirteenth centuries did it rival the other capitals of Europe for learning and match splendid Palermo in polyglot scholarship. The present-day municipal authorities play up this shining moment of their past, billing the city as a monument to tolerance and politely ignoring its later role as exporter of inquisitors. Convivencia, not reconquista, is the memory that modern Spain has chosen to embrace, perhaps in reaction to the centuries of myth-making about the country's Christian heroes. Whatever the reason, a concerted effort has been made to celebrate the vanished communities of medieval Toledo: the Jews and the Muslims—or as the latter would soon be known, the Mudejars, Spanish Muslims under Christian rule.

What these two communities helped to do, in conjunction with the Mozarabs, was play host to a revolution in thought. Much of the heritage of the mare nostrum had been forgotten by the Christian west, but it had hardly been lost. In the splendid libraries of the Islamic world, from Córdoba to Baghdad, the philosophical and scientific works of antiquity had been preserved, translated into Arabic and commented upon by such intellectual giants as Avicenna (Ibn Sina), a tenth-century Persian, and Averroes (Ibn Rushd), a twelfth-century Andalusi. The literature was vast, wide-ranging, and intellectually intoxicating.

When Alfonso and his Castilians captured Toledo, they unwittingly cracked open a window onto the Mediterranean past, a time before the advent of the one stern god of Christianity and Islam. Far from letting in a stale blast of arcane knowledge, the Toledan window allowed in a gust of fresh air, for the concerns of ancient thinkers were as germane to the Middle Ages as they are to us today. Under twelfth-century Bishop Raymond, Toledans and visiting scholars from all over the Mediterranean and Europe set to work translating the trove of Arabic documents, rendering them into Hebrew, Latin, and the Romance vernaculars that would mature as the languages of modern Europe.

Aristotle mattered most. Prior to the literary excavations of Toledo, an extremely well-read westerner would have been familiar only with six essays on logic by Aristotle, which had been translated into Latin in the sixth century C.E. Under the supervision of the astonishingly open-minded Bishop Raymond, who saw no reason to censor or edit in the service of Christian orthodoxy, much more of Aristotle's encyclopedic output came into circulation—*Physics*, *Metaphysics*, and *On the Soul*, as well as studies of natural science and essays

An engraving depicting the gorge of the Tagus River as it approaches Toledo.
The building on the tallest eminence is the Alcázar.

on politics and ethics, all of which had been admired in Islamic capitals for centuries.

These works alighted in western Europe at the best possible time. The reawakening around the year 1000 had been followed by a burst of sustained activity. By the mid–twelfth century towns had grown in number and size, new land had been cleared and diet improved, trade and banking reestablished, pilgrimage routes secured, and massive new cathedrals begun. Among the unlettered, in response to the changed circumstances of life, arose a yearning for a more meaningful, personal god—a sincere and praiseworthy quest that would, however, give rise to persecution and pogrom in its darker hours. For the educated few, those nominally within the embrace of the Church, the impulse was similar: the twelfth century saw students congregating in Paris, Bologna, and Oxford like bees around a honey pot. In those cities, twelfth-century teachers and thinkers were laboring to find a reason behind what they had been told to believe.

Into this febrile atmosphere the manuscripts from the dar al Islam arrived as a godsend. Within a generation of the first Toledan translations in the 1130s, Aristotelian thought had entered the speculations of the scholastics. Just as Avicenna did in Persia, Averroes, in Seville, and Moses Maimonides, the greatest sephardic thinker, in Cairo, the finest minds of Christendom were forced to reconcile the observations of reason with the adumbrations of revelation. In some sense the Christians were reinventing the wheel, for the other two religions of the sea of faith had already grappled with the ramifications of ancient Greek thought. To Thomas Aquinas, whose thirteenth-century *summa* was a culmination of this process in Christendom, Aristotle was known, simply, as the Philosopher, and Averroes, whom Aquinas cited several hundred times, as the Commentator. Islamic culture, through Toledo, Palermo, and a half-dozen minor centers of translation, had brought the west an incomparable gift: self-knowledge.

The Philosopher was far from being the sole Greek to be resurrected in Toledo. Thanks to Gerard of Cremona and Adelard of Bath, the most prolific translators of the time, Euclid's *Elements of Geometry* at last reappeared in the west, as did the *Almagest*, Ptolemy's authoritative presentation of mathematical astronomy. (Gerard of Cremona translated it from the Arabic; a Greek-to-Latin translation would later be done in Palermo). That the second-century work of Ptolemy should resurface in medieval Toledo was appropriate, given the city's long-standing connection with astronomy. In the taifa days of al-Ma'mun, celestial observations and star charts had been compiled into a reference work called the *Toledan Tables*, much of it from the pen of Abu Ishaq Ibrahim ibn Yahya An-Naqqash Az-Zarqali, known in the west as Arzachel. This great astronomer and inventor—the water clock was his doing—also perfected the flat astrolabe, the instrument used to calculate, among other things, the time of day, the altitude of physical features, and the projected location of heavenly bodies. It has been called the slide rule and pocket watch of the Middle Ages. Arzachel's work with the astrolabe did not escape the notice of the translators, who ensured its subsequent fame throughout Europe. When Pierre Abélard, the French champion of Aristotelian syllogism, was given a son by his beloved Héloïse, the name they chose for the infant could well have served as an homage to Toledo, the wellspring of their new thinking. The boy was christened Astrolabe.

The story of the dissemination of Arzachel's work underlines what is often glossed over in accounts of the intellectual recovery of the west, which emphasize the ancients of Greece at the expense of contemporaneous knowledge drawn from Islamic sources. The libraries of the Muslim world that were being translated also contained works on Indian mathematics and Persian medicine, as well as those produced in the brilliant courts of al-Andalus. In a sense, the Christian kingdoms of Spain had gone from picking taifa pockets through parias to picking their brains through translation. Arabic treatises on astrology and the natural sciences—all left the study rooms by the Tagus to cross the Pyrenees and add such words as *algebra*, *algorithm*, and *alchemy* to the lexicon of the west. And in an eddy of this tide of rationalism, the abundant Arabic catalog of works on necromancy was made available to Europe. Latin practitioners of magic were adept in what was known as *ars toledana*.

The convivencia of Toledo—its role as a clearinghouse of ideas lasted two hundred years—also entailed the far less lofty business of simple people, living together. Aside from the exceptional scholar translating alongside his Mozarab or Jewish colleague, the Mudejar community is thought to have been composed chiefly of laborers and craftsmen—as well as a great number of slaves. The decorative arts of medieval Iberia attest to Mudejar influence, as does the brickwork architecture of the churches that sprang up in lands formerly under Muslim control. For as a cosmopolitan cadre of linguists pored over manuscripts in Toledo, the descendants of Alfonso VI eventually resumed the push south from the city, the drying-up of extorted Andalusi gold having given rise to an ethic of conquest. In the twelfth century, a confraternity of monk-warriors, the

Knights of Calatrava, was founded with the express purpose of extending the reach of Christian hegemony in Iberia.

Toledo's historical moment combines the two strands of the medieval Spanish experience that compete for primacy in the national memory: tolerance and conquest. The former was not of the modern, multicultural variety, however sweet that might be to imagine. The Mudejars (and the Jews) possessed fewer rights and paid higher taxes than the Christians, and the communities had separate residential areas, the market square, Plaza Zocodover (from Arabic *sük ed-dawabb*, "horse market"), serving as the principal place for mundane social intermingling. Still, for Latin Europe (Sicily excluded), this interconfessional civility was remarkable, a rare Christian mirror of what had long been the practice in the more tolerant lands of Islam. An odd coincidence had the Christians adopting the enlightened convivencia of Islam at the same time as the Almoravids were abandoning it by chasing out many of the Christians and Jews from al-Andalus. The western end of the Mediterranean world had been turned upside down, just as its eastern shore was on the verge of an even greater upheaval.

Manzikert: 1071. Palermo: 1072. Toledo: 1085. The changes had come in quick succession. In less than a generation, epochal events had occurred that would alter the confessional geography of the Mediterranean. If convivencia emerged in Palermo, Toledo, and, later, Konya (the capital of the Sultanate of Rum), the working of subsequent centuries of discrimination—and episodes of malign leadership—gradually ground down the culture of tolerance, and entire regions became militantly monoconfessional. The changes set in motion in the 1070s and 1080s are still with us: Anatolia is overwhelmingly Muslim; Sicily and Castile, Christian.

Despite the importance of these three events in the hectic close of the eleventh century, one other occurrence overshadows all others in the shared story of Islam and Christianity. In 1095, less than a decade after the fall of Toledo, the Cluniac monk Odo of Châtillon, as Pope Urban II, preached to several hundred expectant noblemen in a clearing in Clermont, France. Although the text of his sermon has been lost, later chroniclers set down its gist. Jerusalem, the pope declared, had to be taken. A scarcely human enemy—the Muslims—had for too long controlled the Holy Sepulchre, the place where the crucified Christ had been laid to rest and come back to life. Pilgrims to Jerusalem from Europe, Urban claimed, were beset by scandalous extortions and inhumane vexations, and their brothers in the faith, the Christians of the east, faced persecution and invasion from the Turks. The time had come for a new sort of pilgrimage, one that combined the martial bravery of the Christian knight with the purity of purpose of the Roman Church. All pilgrims to Jerusalem who took up arms in the service of this holy cause would be granted a remission of their sins. A war must be waged to recover Palestine: God wills it.

A week after the Cid closed his eyes for the last time in Valencia, an army of pilgrims carried out God's will. On July 15, 1099, crusading knights broke through St. Stephen's Gate of Jerusalem and went utterly berserk. On the Temple Mount, around which Caliph Umar had been escorted by Patriarch Sophronius some 450 years earlier, the exultant westerners herded people into mosque and synagogue for wholesale slaughter. "The defenders fled along the walls and through the city," wrote one eyewitness. "Our men followed them, killing and slaying even to the Temple of Solomon, where the slaughter was so great that our men waded in blood up to their ankles." The Jews of the city were herded into the main synagogue, which was then torched. A similar fate awaited those who did not subscribe to the Latin faith of the conquerors. "After a very great and cruel slaughter of Saracens, of whom 10,000 fell in that same place, they put to the sword great numbers of gentiles who were running about the quarters of the city, fleeing in all directions on account of their fear of death: they were stabbing women who had fled into palaces and dwellings; seizing infants by the soles of their feet from their mothers' laps or their cradles and dashing them against the walls and breaking their necks; they were slaughtering some with weapons, or striking them down with stones; they were sparing absolutely no gentile of any place or kind." Few natives of Jerusalem survived their city's liberation. In the following days, as the stench of victory grew unbearable, the thousands who had been butchered were carted outside the fortifications, thrown in heaps two or three stories tall, then burned. Such was the culmination of what is now known as the First Crusade.

The slaughter in Jerusalem had its precursors, and not only in the Middle East. It had taken the crusaders almost three years to reach their goal, during which time they endured unspeakable hardship and indulged in hair-raising savagery. The whole enterprise had initially been launched following a plea by the basileus Alexius Comnenus, father of the chronicler Anna and leader of the

Church of the Holy Sepulchre, Jerusalem.

capable dynasty that guided Constantinople after the debacle of Manzikert. Alexius sent a letter to Pope Urban asking for reinforcements in his struggle against the Turks, which was read out at a clerical conclave in Piacenza, Italy, in the spring of 1095. The Byzantine got in return far more than he had requested: on learning of the pope's appeal at Clermont later in the year and being prodded to action by such charismatic preachers as Peter the Hermit, tens of thousands of ordinary men and women, enthusiasts of a holy, purifying journey to Jerusalem, streamed east across Europe, warming up for their muscular pilgrimage, as it were, by massacring Jews they encountered en route. In May 1096, whole communities of Jews were killed in such places as Mainz and Worms, inaugurating a sinister western tradition that would reach its ghastly apotheosis in the Shoah of the twentieth century. Alexius, appalled when this uninvited mass of exalted peasants and monks arrived at his doorstep, had them quickly spirited across the Bosporus and into Bithynia, the region south of the Sea of Marmara. There the eighteen-year-old sultan of Rum, Kilij Arslan, a great-nephew of Alp, annihilated these first crusaders—some twenty thousand people, it is thought—at a place called Civetot, on the Marmara's Gulf of Nicomedia.

When the armored and mounted men of war—the toughened knights from northern France, Provence, Flanders, Germany, and Norman Italy—arrived in Constantinople in the wake of this debacle, they clearly constituted a force far more formidable than the lost souls of the so-called People's Crusade. Alexius was aware of their abilities—he had barely managed to turn back Robert Guiscard in the Balkans only a decade earlier. As a canny diplomat with a network of spies, the basileus also kept abreast of the rivalries that were sapping the Muslim world of its capacity to resist effectively. Beyond the central Anatolia of the Turks, who themselves excelled at civil war, lay a fractured Seljuk empire in Syria and Mesopotamia, where local atabegs and dynasts of such centers as Aleppo, Antioch, Mosul, and Damascus cordially detested each other. Syria and the al-Jazeera had, in short, their version of the taifas. In Palestine, the situation was not much better, as the allies of the Fatimids fell victim to court intrigues. Alexius, sensing strength in his unpredictable Christian allies and weakness in his familiar Muslim enemies, had the leaders of the crusade swear oaths to refrain from appropriating for themselves any Byzantine land that they might reconquer on their way to Jerusalem.

The basileus was too shrewd a man not to realize that these oaths were, in all likelihood, worthless. Religious fervor, which the crusaders had in spades, did not preclude or even hinder their worldly ambition. Faith may even have stoked it, the certainty of divine approval making the business of enriching oneself while eviscerating one's enemy a saintly enterprise. In this, these rough newcomers from the west were no different from Alp Arslan, or Caliph Muawiya, or any of a number of Mediterranean conquerors who reconciled belief with cupidity. The first proof of crusader acquisitiveness came in Edessa (Urfa, Turkey), the upper Mesopotamian town that had long sat on the border between the Seljuk and Byzantine empires.

A knight named Baldwin of Boulogne, on hearing of the difficulties of Edessa's king, an Armenian potentate with no heir, quit the main southward advance of the crusading Franks and headed inland. Baldwin offered to help the city if the king adopted him as a son. Doing so would ensure Baldwin's accession to the throne in the lamentable event of the monarch's demise. That last occurrence wasn't long in coming: shortly after a strange adoption ceremony that had the principals stripped to the waist in a public embrace, the king was hacked to death in his citadel by a mob let in by his faithless new son. Baldwin of Boulogne became count of Edessa, the ruler of the first crusader state. The commitment to return lands to Byzantine control had been forgotten.

A similar expropriation took place in the great city of Antioch, which had been taken back by the Muslims after the departure of the gigantic George Maniakes for his misadventure in Sicily. The crusader capture of Antioch was engineered by a son of Robert Guiscard. Bohemond of Taranto, born of Guiscard's first marriage, had been disowned by his stepmother, the amazon Sichelgaita.* Bohemond, a battle-hardened Norman denied his inheritance, was thus a pilgrim of an extremely hungry stripe. In 1098, after months of siege, battle, atrocity, and the opportune discovery of what the crusaders claimed to be the lance that had pierced the side of Jesus' body, the city was overrun and the requisite massacre of its inhabitants conducted. In the ensuing power struggle among the leaders of the crusade, Bohemond succeeded in brushing aside his noble rivals and setting himself up as prince of Antioch. Once again, the undertakings made at Constantinople had been flouted.

In the months and years that followed the contours of a new Latin entity took shape in the Levant. The powerful comtal family of Toulouse, the Saint-Gilles, made themselves masters of Tripoli, the greatest port on the eastern littoral

---

*She had made sure Apulia and Calabria reverted to her own son, but that patrimony, it will be recalled, was then swallowed up by King Roger II of Sicily.

since the time of the Phoenicians. The ruin of the crusader citadel, called *qal'at sinjil* after the ruling Latin clan, can still be seen in the city today. Jerusalem, despite caviling by a clergy reluctant to see it demoted from otherworldly status, became a kingdom like any other. By 1110, what was called Outremer (Beyond the Sea)—the lands controlled by the Latins from Edessa, Antioch, Tripoli, and Jerusalem—had become a force in the region, a Christian federation undreamed of only fifteen years earlier. The Byzantines, far from rejoicing at seeing Heraclius avenged, looked with unease at this new and unruly presence on their doorstep.

The Muslim view of their new neighbors was, as might not be expected, just as ambivalent. The lords of Aleppo, Damascus, and Mosul could not overcome their loathing of one another to unite in the face of a common threat. In a remarkably short time, in fact, the indigenous warrior classes came to view these strange and powerful Franks as useful bludgeons in the intra-Muslim struggle for primacy in Syria. Although endless rounds of raiding, kidnapping, and ransoming characterized the relations between Latin and Muslim, there were several instances of formal alliances between the grandees of Outremer and the atabegs of Islam. As early as 1108 the Frankish count of Edessa allied with the emir of Mosul to fight the Latin prince of Antioch and the Muslim king of Aleppo. Such strategic cooperation, the convivencia of bloodshed, was not uncommon.

Within Outremer itself, the Latins had to come to an understanding with their subjects if they were to profit from their sojourn in the promised land. No matter how many people they killed or exiled, the newcomers would always be outnumbered by the large, heterogeneous populace of the region. The Levant was a kaleidoscope of belief: in addition to a native Jewish population, Zoroastrians, Druzes, non-Latin Christians (Armenians, Greek Orthodox, Jacobites, Maronites, and Nestorians), and different communities of sunni and shia Muslims all resided there. Clearly if Outremer were to survive, the peasants had to be left on the land and the merchants in the cities, whatever their faith. This pressure to achieve a modicum of convivencia came not only from within, but also from without. The merchants of Genoa, Pisa, and Venice had negotiated their concessions on the conquered coastline, and their terms were clear: for Outremer to stay connected to the west through the services of their mariners, it had to ensure that the trade routes from the east remained open and ran, more important, directly into the cargo holds of the Italian ships at anchor off

Tripoli, Tyre, Sidon, Acre, and Ascalon. The crusaders might take a cut, but the locals were the ones who knew how to conduct this business. Few in numbers, short on the skills of peace, the Latin knights had no choice but to adopt the Muslim practice of tolerance.

Unlike that of Palermo and Toledo, the twelfth-century convivencia of Outremer was a fragile shoot. Toledo, its supply of belligerent Castilians inexhaustible, could defend itself against Almoravid incursions. Palermo, sited on a wealthy island that became a magnet for Christian immigration, had little to fear from Ifriqiyan marauders. The Latins of Outremer, however, were alone, perched at the edge of the great expanse of the dar al Islam, the sea at their back. The horrors attendant upon their arrival in the east would have been told and retold to the outraged faithful of the umma. The slaughters of Jerusalem and Antioch, while reprehensible, approached but did not go beyond the bounds of the acceptable in an extremely violent era.

However, that was not the case elsewhere. In the winter of 1097–98 an army of famished crusaders had stormed Ma'arat al-Numan, a town on the Orontes River south of Aleppo. There, according to both Christian and Muslim chroniclers, the Latin warriors killed all of the townspeople and then set about roasting and eating them. The slain children, apparently, were a delicacy. Even to medieval eyes, this was an atrocity. It could only be a matter of time before a disunited Muslim world came together for vengeance, no matter how much the barbarous Latins adapted to the mores of Middle Eastern convivencia. As it turned out, less than a century would pass before the eviction notice was served.

CHAPTER SIX

HATTIN 1187

Jihad and Crusade; the doom of Outremer

Outremer can still be seen in Syria. The Mediterranean coast south of Latakia, the main port of the Syrian Arab Republic, is a narrow strip of land bordered to the east by the forested wall of the Jebel Ansariye mountain range. On this sliver of littoral and farther south in Lebanon, the crusaders dug in their heels, erecting castle, fortified church, and isolated redoubt in the hope of retaining their new kingdoms. Inland, the alarmed Muslims did the same, bequeathing to the region one of the greatest concentrations of medieval castles to be found anywhere in the world. The swords of the warriors ceded to the winches of the stonemasons, as each piece in the Outremer puzzle sought safety behind massive walls.

One needs little imagination to enter the past in this part of Syria, despite the gimcrack resort hotels and the unsightly legions of polyethylene greenhouses lining the shore. To look landward from the seaside town of Baniyas is to stare straight up at a behemoth rising 360 meters into the sky, its windowless round towers bespeaking a time of constant peril. This sinister fortress, Marqab, first contructed in 1062, then ceded to the Latins in the early eleventh century, housed a crusader confraternity of knights, intent on keeping the pilgrimage routes open. A brooding castle of black basalt stone, Marqab nicely reflects the soured optimism of the crusaders a mere generation or two after their success in Jerusalem.

Further proof of crusader anxiety, and piety, lies a dozen kilometers to the south of Marqab, at the port of Tartus. A few blocks in from its tidy breakwater, in a large traffic island of a park, stands the Church of Our Lady of Tortosa (Tartus). The cathedral's devotional pedigree is untouchable—the site is thought to have housed, in classical times, the very first sanctuary dedicated to the Virgin Mary. In the twelfth and thirteenth centuries, Mary was eclipsed by Mars, for the building, which is the best preserved of all crusader churches in the Middle East, is as solid and defensible as any fortress. The pleasant Mediterranean garden now surrounding it cannot disguise the warlike posture of the sanctuary. Although two of its corner towers have long since been removed (to be replaced by a lone minaret), this great gray hedgehog of stone was patently built to withstand attack. Nonetheless it is of rare beauty, especially underneath the graceful tan vaulting of its nave and two aisles. Our Lady of Tortosa can be considered a crusader herself: a fortified church very much of the day in its mix of mature Romanesque and early Gothic, it seems somehow plucked out of the Île-de-France and deposited, pilgrimlike, on the eastern shore of the Mediterranean. Within it now is a dusty museum displaying Phoenician sarcophagi, friezes of Baal, and Roman mosaics—the archaeological memories of an ancient land. Compared to all those represented in the museum, the crusaders were mere passersby, their stay here lasting from 1099 to 1291.

Our Lady of Tortosa, a fortified crusader church in Tartus, Syria. The building is now an archaeological museum.

To move inland from Tartus is to quit Latin territory. North of town today, on the coastal highway, stands a large statue of the late Syrian president Hafez al-Assad, his back to the sea, his golden arms outstretched as if to embrace the cement plant opposite. At this point a narrow connecting road leads off eastward, abruptly scaling slopes dotted with the second homes of the rich and well-connected of Homs and Damascus. Beyond the crest of the ridge, hundreds of meters high, the view of the sea disappears and the rugged landscape of the Jebel Ansariye takes over. Geology has conspired, as in much of the Mediterranean, to cut the coast off from the interior. In this instance it reflects the confessional geography of the crusader day.

The road inland dips and winds through a prospect of blind cliffsides falling into bottomless ravines, the thickets of myrtle and oak scrub slashed into clearings to make way for the occasional pebble-strewn olive grove. Despite the harshness of the surroundings, villages of concrete-cube houses line the summit route, apparently inhabited in the majority by unveiled girls in track suits strolling arm in arm past groups of laughing street urchins. These settlements grow scarcer, and vanish entirely once the town of Sheikh Badr is left behind. The road dives into a gorge so deep as to be in permanent shadow, then ascends a shrub-covered slope cut by striations of white limestone made dazzling by the return of sunlight. The spine of this new ridge, windswept and scorched dry, tops a peninsular finger of land pointing into a valley sealed on three sides by cave-riddled eminences. At the very extremity of the peninsula, rising out of a forbidding outcropping of rock, are the ruins of the Qalaat al-Kahf (Castle of the Cavern), once the headquarters of Sinan ibn Salman ibn Muhammad, whom the crusaders called the Old Man of the Mountain. This tortured upland of inhospitable scrub and sudden drop was, in the twelfth and thirteenth centuries, the province of a sect known to the Christians as the Assassins.

To examine the rubble of this lair is to enter the precincts of legend. The battlements, now barely distinguishable from the scarified pile of rock, were those from which some of Sinan's devotees, so the story goes, hurled themselves to their deaths at the command of their leader, for the edification of a visiting crusader dignitary, Henry of Champagne. Horrified, Henry implored his host to desist.* Even more lurid were stories of hashish-induced glimpses of paradise (whence, it was once thought, the name *hashishi*, or Assassin): the acolyte

---

*Weirdly, given the scene he was supposed to have witnessed, Henry met his death by falling out of a window in Acre in 1197. At the time he was the king of Jerusalem.

would be led, stoned, into a grove of fleshy pleasure—a foretaste of the afterlife—then rendered unconscious, brought back to this world, and given a martyr's mission that would be zealously fulfilled so as to regain admission to that voluptuous land of limitless ambrosia and languorous maidens. These stories, embellished by westerners (Marco Polo was a great Assassin mythologizer), reflect more on the tale-teller than on the subject—but anyone clambering past the cisterns and gateways of al-Kahf cannot help but feel a twinge of excitement. The walls of one half-exposed chamber, once the castle's hammam, are covered with hennaed handprints, burnt-orange mysteries that have resisted the winds whistling in from the gorge. Murderers? Maidens? The rock does not answer.

The presence of Sinan and his Assassins in Syria lent homicidal nuance to the affairs of Outremer. The sect, which had arisen in eleventh-century Persia, believed that Islam had been waylaid by heretical impostors. The genuine authority over the umma, according to their lights, hewed faithfully to the descendants of Huseyn—Ali's son killed at Karbala in 680—until the seventh generation (to a certain Ismail), then dipped out of sight for several generations before resurfacing in the shia Fatimid caliphate of Egypt. When a legitimate heir to that throne, Nizar, was murdered by his younger brother in 1095, the Ismailis held that the mantle of imam, or spiritual guide of Islam, somehow came to be bestowed on successive leaders of the Assassin sect in their mountain hideaway of Alamut, near the Caspian Sea.

Depending on the demands of the moment, the Assassins—or more correctly, the Nizari Ismailis—could ally themselves with the unwelcome crusaders of the coast or with their unloved sunni brethren of the Orontes Valley. Or they could be discreetly hired for sensitive operations by an interested third party. During the Third Crusade (1189–92), a capable king of Jerusalem, Conrad of Montferrat, fell victim to their daggers. The identity of the contractor is a matter of speculation: perhaps it was King Richard Lionheart, jealous of Conrad's influence, or the sultan Saladin, worried about Conrad's warring abilities—or neither. Count Raymond of Tripoli met a similar fate at the hands of the Assassins, as did an heir to the Christian principality of Antioch, cut down by killers disguised as monks as he stepped out of a Christmas service held at Our Lady of Tortosa. The hideout of Qalaat al-Kahf lay only one night's stealthy ride from the crusader church. As for Marqab, it was only ten kilometers away from the Old Man of the Mountain, as the crow flies.

However unnerving that proximity must have seemed to the Latin knights, the sunni Muslims had the most to fear from this independent county of fanatics in the Jebel Ansariye. (The Assassins possessed a dozen or so castles there.) "To shed the blood of a heretic is more meritorious than to kill seventy Greek infidels," wrote an exponent of their faith. As possessors of absolute truth and authority, the Nizaris took it upon themselves to terrorize, and thus destabilize, the ruling sunni elite of Islam. Their first victim was Nizam al-Mulk, the all-powerful vizier of Alp Arslan and Malikshah, who had done so much to aid the spread of sunni orthodoxy. Scores of other dignitaries—among them two Abbasid caliphs—fell to the Nizaris of Alamut, in attacks usually carried out after Friday prayers in the courtyard of a prominent mosque, to ensure maximum publicity, horror, and, of course, instant martyrdom for the murderer, whom the enraged bystanders would waste no time in tearing to pieces.

The successful expansion of the Nizaris into Syria coincided with the arrival of the Crusaders. In a Muslim east beset by quarrels among city-states ruled by independent Turkish atabegs paying lip service to the Seljuk sultan, the terrain was ripe for interlopers to carve out kingdoms for themselves, whether they were inflamed by faith or greed, or both. The First Crusade had

The Assassin castle at Masyaf, at the foot of the Jebel Ansariye. Saladin lifted his siege of the fortress after realizing his bodyguards were themselves Assassins.

blundered into Syria at just the right time: the rulers of Aleppo and Damascus, two brothers, were at each other's throats; the Turks of Anatolia were fighting their own internecine wars; and even mighty Egypt, long ruled by the charismatic Fatimids, had lost much of its cohesion as a series of viziers wrested power from the shia caliphs. The Crusaders had stumbled across this opportunity unwittingly; the Nizaris, attuned to the discord, made their move with calculation.

Both groups of intruders coveted the wealthy cities of the Syrian interior, the same desert ports that Heraclius had been forced to give up in the seventh century. Of all these, none is more redolent of the era of Outremer than Aleppo, now a sprawling metropolis of millions but still possessed of a historic heart that would not seem unfamilar to any Assassin infiltrator or Latin ambassador. In the market streets of its souk, or bazaar, shafts of sunlight stream through cracks in the weathered stone vaults to pick out motes of dust floating above Armenian goldsmith, Kurdish pistachio merchant, and Arab butcher hoisting a freshly slaughtered calf from the back of his donkey onto a swinging meat hook. At the principal mosque of the old town, rebuilt in the twelfth century after fire had destroyed the original Umayyad structure, crowds of children skitter across the marble geometry of the courtyard while their devout parents cluster inside around the shrine of Zachariah, John the Baptist's father. Across an alley alongside the mosque, half-blocked by supplicant blind men, a doorway opens onto the Halawiye madrasa, a center of sunni learning since the time of Nizam al-Mulk. The learned sit on carpets in a domed hall and welcome the visitor with unaffected warmth, their backs to a semicircle of six pillars topped with a flamboyant jungle of acanthus leaves. This half-lit room is all that remains of the Cathedral of St. Helen, a fragment of Byzantine antiquity (Helen was Constantine's mother) that was used without hindrance by local Christians for centuries after the Muslim conquest—until the 1120s, when their crusading coreligionists rode in from Marqab and other coastal fortresses to enact the customary atrocities in the Aleppan countryside. In reprisal, the Christians of Aleppo were evicted from their remnant of a church and the scholars of the madrasa moved in, where they have been ever since.

In these places—madrasa, mosque, and souk—medieval Aleppans heard the rumors of Latin aggression and Assassin conspiracy. The Persian Nizaris, adept at converting many Syrians to their Ismaili creed, moved freely throughout the city in the confused years of the early twelfth century. One emir of Aleppo, Ridwan, a nephew of Malikshah, was believed by his suspicious subjects to be a master of black magic, so fortuitously did his enemies meet untimely ends. A partial explanation of his luck lay in his secret ties with the Assassins, whom he also used to intimidate his hated brother, Duqaq, the ruler of Damascus.

The threat from the crusaders was, by contrast, out in the open. They brazenly sought tribute and plunder in the Orontes and control of the great cities of Syria. In Aleppo their main foe was inanimate: the citadel. A masterpiece of military architecture, it glowers over the old city on a natural lozenge-shaped hill that stretches fifty-five meters into the air above an encircling ditch. The massive structure atop the hill, which protects a palatine city unto itself, proved impregnable to the crusading knights during repeated sieges. A year after a failed attempt in 1118, the Latin forces of Antioch marched out to utter rout at the hands of the Aleppans near a place called Balat, to the south of the ruins of the basilica of St. Simeon the Stylite. The Aleppo citadel would not, however, fill with illustrious prisoners to ransom: the Turkoman then leading the city, Il-Ghazi, gave no quarter. "In less than an hour," wrote a Muslim chronicler, "the Franks were all lying dead, cavalry and infantry with their horses and armour, and none escaped to bear the news." Known to the westerners as the Field of

The sole entrance to the formidable Citadel of Aleppo, a fortified height overlooking the old city.

Blood, the battle of Balat marked the first serious setback of the crusader cause. That it was not exploited by the Muslims—the road to Antioch lay open—can be put down to the indiscipline of Il-Ghazi. He distributed the booty, disbanded his army, and then returned to the citadel to indulge in a celebratory binge. When he sobered up three weeks later, the neighboring crusader states had restored the defenses of Antioch. Muslim Syria still awaited its avenger.

‹‹ ‹‹   ›› ››

The crusaders knew that keeping Syria at bay was essential to their survival. Proof of their conviction can still be seen some two hundred kilometers to the southwest of Aleppo, in a crusader fortress as awe-inspiring as that old city's citadel. The Krak des Chevaliers, the Brobdingnag of all medieval castles, dominates the southernmost slopes of the Jebel Ansariye. To the north of it was the rugged terrain of the Assassins; to the south, a valley known as the Homs Gap, a corridor of cultivation that leads from the Orontes to the Mediterranean by passing between the Ansariye range and the much taller mountainous massif of Lebanon. As the most accessible route from coast to interior in the rich segment of the Fertile Crescent stretching from Turkey to Palestine, the valley overlooked by the Krak has always been a place of great strategic importance. Indeed, as early as 1275 B.C.E., an army of the pharaohs clashed with the Hittites nearby at a place called Qadesh.

For the Muslims of the day, many of whom labored on its enlargements, the sheer size of the Hospitalers' additions to the Krak would have confirmed that these strange, powerful men from beyond the sea had every intention of staying in the Levant. (The word *Krak* derives from the name of the original small fortress on the site built in 1031: Husn al-Akrad, Fortress of the Kurds.) For nearly two hundred years under the crusaders, the castle grew stronger and bigger, as successive generations of military engineers brought in from Europe undertook to reinforce what was called "the key to Christendom." As the science of castle construction in the west became ever more developed given the endemic warfare of feudal lords, the techniques of fashioning the impregnable naturally headed east with the embattled crusaders.

The Krak's sole entrance, a tortuous ascending passageway wide enough for three heavily armored knights to ride side by side, passes through several defensive walls before giving out onto a central esplanade surrounded by battlements. Everywhere there are cyclopean constructions: great round towers rise above the line of the already-tall curtain walls; an inner wall, separated from the outer by a deep moat, encircles a cluster of buildings that house a large and stately Gothic grand hall and a 120-meter-long kitchen and refectory (and no doubt storeroom) that could feed hundreds under its cavernous vaults. The scale of the complex beggars the imagination. From without, visible from almost any part of the Homs Gap, the castle's stone appears to change colors with the shifting light of day, a monument to the permanent and the ephemeral all at the same time.

As at Marqab, its brother in gigantism, the custodians of the Krak were members of a military order of armed monks, one of several martial brotherhoods founded in the time of Outremer. The occupants of the Krak and Marqab were Hospitalers, an order originally established to tend to pilgrims who fell ill. The mother house was in Jerusalem, near the Church of the Holy Sepulchre, and was founded under Muslim rule in the 1080s by the Amalfitan merchants who then held a monopoly of trade with the Islamic east. Subsequent to the Christian capture of the city, the Hospitalers evolved from a nursing confraternity into a military organization, even if they kept hospices in most of the major centers of Outremer and in the pilgrimage embarkation ports of Europe. Also known as

The Krak des Chevaliers, the greatest of Outremer's crusader castles.

the Knights of the Hospital of St. John (their patron was John the Baptist), they figured large in events around the sea of faith until well into the sixteenth century.

The Hospitalers' counterparts—and often bitter rivals—were the Templars, whose name came from the location of their mother house on the Temple Mount of Jerusalem, their headquarters itself being the expropriated al-Aqsa Mosque. Founded in the early twelfth century, the Templars set as their original mission the protection of pilgrims from the brigands who haunted the holy sites of Palestine. In the wake of the First Crusade, more and more pilgrims poured into the Levant, perhaps unaware that the crusading armies had gone home, leaving only a skeletal contingent of knights to protect the cities and castles that had been captured. Outside the walls of these strongholds the wide-eyed western pilgrim could easily fall into an ambush and end up on the auction block in Damascus or Cairo. The Templars, at first few in number, tried to foil these abductions.

From these laudable origins, both orders developed into fearsome war machines with robust treasuries. Their monastic discipline—which included chastity, self-abnegation, and a code of silence—immediately won admiration throughout Europe, which was then experiencing an upsurge in piety typified by the rapid rise of the reforming Cistercian monks, headed by the powerful

The mailed habit of the Templars, an order of warrior-monks founded in Jerusalem
following the success of the First Crusade.

Bernard of Clairvaux. The most influential prelate of the twelfth century, Bernard used his enormous prestige to help these mail-clad ecstatics by extolling a new concept of permanent Christian belligerence in his *De laude novae militae* (*In Praise of the New Knighthood*). The violent proclivities of Europe's feudal warriors, so inimical to the salvation of their souls—and, not incidentally, to the property of the Church—could be gainfully deflected to service in the Holy Land. It was a marriage made in heaven. Bequests, donations, and benefices soon enriched the orders, and recruits flocked to the many houses they established across Europe. At the peak of their power the Templars alone had nine thousand lordships and manors in the west, and even in Bernard's time they had begun developing their most famous sideline: moneylending. Dodging the Church's ban on usury, the warrior-monks encouraged pilgrims to deposit money at their local Templar manor in exchange for a letter of credit that could be redeemed, for a fee, in Outremer. They also built a fleet to ferry paying passengers to and from the ports of Palestine and Syria, thereby stepping on the toes of the Italian merchant republics. The Templars, who in their earliest days had been known as the Poor Fellow-Soldiers of Christ, ended up staggeringly wealthy.

Hospitalers and Templars were an entirely new phenomenon, in that they were organized orders of knights answerable only to the pope. The kings of Europe, much less the king of Jerusalem, could not touch them or order them about. Their fanatic attachment to the survival of Outremer made them ideal candidates for manning isolated castles, especially after the Latin nobles realized that they would always be seriously outnumbered and were best off clustered in the coastal cities. Many of the outposts in the Outremer hinterland, like the Krak, were ceded to these men who had sworn to give no quarter, to engage in battle no matter how great the odds, and, if captured, never to allow themselves to be ransomed.

Their compatriots were another matter, especially after a few decades had passed and the Latins became acclimated to their surroundings. The lords and ladies of Outremer were, mostly, the descendants of those who had stayed on after the euphoric bloodletting of the First Crusade. They were indigenous to the region, accustomed to its climate, diet, and delights, and not at all immune to Muslim mores. In this, they were much like the Normans of Palermo. The kings of Jerusalem wore burnooses and kaffiyeh; hot water and soap held no terrors for them; dancing girls entertained them; professional mourners ululated at their funerals; and their villas, replete with colorful mosaics and a central fountain, resembled nothing so much as a typical Syrian mansion.

We owe many of these observations to Usamah ibn Munqidh, a diplomat and noble from Shayzar, a castle in the Orontes Valley located close to Assassin territory. Usamah's colorful autobiographical memoir, written in the 1180s when he was in his nineties, opens a window onto the uneasy coexistence between the Muslim Arabs of the region and these native foreigners. Usamah's sometimes hilarious testimony—he could not resist cuckold stories—nonetheless underscored what was to be a constant tension in Outremer: the divide between the indigenous Latins and those newly arrived from Europe, either on crusade or in search of adventure. For the latter, the shock of finding kinsmen who had "gone native" led to castigating them as *poulains* ("children" or "kids")—that is, epigones, or feebler descendants, of the heroes of the First Crusade. Moreover, the enthusiasm of the newcomers, just off the boat and eager to join battle with the infidel, was thwarted by the live-and-let-live policy adopted by the orientalized poulains, who knew that their wealth depended on Muslim peasants and traders and that fragile Outremer could ill afford virtuoso displays of rapine and plunder. Even the monks of the Temple and the Hospital, who in no way adapted to local customs in their life of warrior asceticism, knew that one had to pick one's fights carefully. The brash hothead, an admired figure in European warrior circles, might spark a catastrophe in Outremer, in the form of a concerted Muslim riposte to the crusader occupation.

Usamah provided an illuminating story of the difference between the poulain and the crusader in recounting a misdventure he had had in Jerusalem in about the year 1140:

Everyone who is a fresh emigrant from the Frankish lands is ruder in character than those who have become acclimatized and have held long association with the the Moslems. Here is an illustration of their rude character.

Whenever I visited Jerusalem I always entered the Aqsa Mosque, beside which stood a small mosque which the Franks had converted into a church. When I used to enter the Aqsa Mosque, which was occupied by the Templars, who were my friends, the Templars would evacuate the little adjoining mosque so that I might pray in it. One day I entered this mosque, repeated the first formula, "Allah is great," and stood up in the act of praying, upon which one of the Franks rushed on me, got hold of me and turned my face eastward saying, "This is the way thou shouldst pray!" A group of Templars hastened to him, seized him and repelled him from me. I resumed my prayer. The same man, while the others were otherwise busy, rushed once more on me and turned my face eastward, saying, "This is the way thou shouldst pray!" The Templars again came in to him and expelled him. They apologized to me, saying, "This is a stranger who has only recently arrived from the land of the Franks and he has never before seen anyone praying except eastward." Thereupon I said to myself, "I have had enough prayer." So I went out and have ever been surprised at the conduct of this devil of a man, at the change in the color of his face, his trembling and his sentiment at the sight of one praying towards the qiblah.*

However considerate Usamah's friends, to hail the native Latins as paragons of tolerance would be a gross overstatement. They were living at a time when the concept of a Christian holy war was being fully elaborated and could hardly fail to be influenced by the pervasiveness of the crusader ethos, not only by virtue of the perceived sacredness of where they lived but also precisely because of the presence in Outremer of the type of uncouth firebrand deplored by Usamah. This "devil of a man" was not a lone sociopath: the ships from the west regularly deposited armed pilgrims on the jetties of Outremer, fired up for action against the infidel. It is misleading to consider the eight upper-case Crusades outlined by traditional historiography as the sole moments of European contribution to the manpower of Outremer. In between these great mobilizations came a constant stream of unsung arrivals: private individuals, sizable contingents not large enough to be deemed an official Crusade, even families of settlers bound for adventure on the eastern frontier. Although Outremer was chronically undermanned, it was hardly understimulated.

Likewise, the conception that holy war was somehow at odds with Christianity does not square with the evolution of the faith. In its infancy a pacifist creed of persecuted underdogs, once the faith was adopted by imperial Rome, the sword entered the Church. Constantine had conquered by the sign of the cross. In his new Rome, Constantinople, the icons and the priests blessed the belligerent activities of the city's armies for almost a millennium. In the west, Augustine of Hippo, aghast at the collapse of the old order of the mare nostrum, had endorsed the concept of a just Christian war. The warring Carolingians thought themselves endowed with a sacred mission, long before the sermon given at

---

An Arab-Syrian Gentleman & Warrior in the Period of the Crusades: Memoirs of Usamah ibn-Munqidh, trans. Philip K. Hitti (New York: Columbia University Press, 2000), 163–64. The *qiblah* (or *qibla*) is the direction of Mecca.

Clermont by Urban II. One of his immediate predecessors had even called for a crusade against the Norman Robert Guiscard.

To be sure, there were voices raised in dismay at the unapologetic martial vehemence of twelfth-century Christianity. An English Cistercian of the day, Isaac of Étoile, mixed pragmatism with piety when he wrote about the new warrior monks:

This dreadful new military order that someone has rather pleasantly called the order of the fifth gospel was founded for the purpose of forcing infidels to accept the faith at the point of the sword. Its members consider that they have every right to attack anyone not confessing Christ's name, leaving him destitute, whereas if they themselves are killed while thus unjustly attacking the pagans, they are called martyrs for the faith. . . . We do not maintain that all they do is wrong, but we do insist that what they are doing can be an occasion of many future evils.

Such thoughts would not have crossed the minds of the two hundred Hospitaler knights holding down the Krak. At their silent evening meals in the massive refectory, a brother would read aloud from the Books of Joshua and the Maccabees and other appropriately fire-breathing texts of the Old Testament. Passages from Psalm 17—"And I shall beat them as small as dust against the wind: I shall bring them to nought, like the dirt in the streets"—would have tripped easily off their tongues as they rode through the Orontes Valley to encounter enemy raiding parties. If they killed, they did not sin. In his *In Praise of the New Knighthood*, Bernard of Clairvaux had concocted for them a distinction between "malecide" and homicide—that is, when they struck down an infidel, they were slaying evil, not a man. Had they known about it, the Assassins, the Krak's neighbors, would have roundly applauded the sentiment. Other churchmen, more in line with the reservations expressed by Isaac of Étoile, hastened to impress on the monastic knights that such a dispensation—the absence of sin—could be granted only if they, as agents of God's will, were themselves pure. "It is useless indeed for us to attack exterior enemies," wrote a prior of La Grande Chartreuse monastery to the Templars, "if we do not first conquer those of the interior." Had he known it, he would have realized, horrified, that he had just described the greatest threat to Outremer: jihad.

◄- ◄- ►- ►-

The idea of striving in the path of God—jihad—is enshrined in the Islamic canon. The Quran has thirty-five verses in which it is mentioned, ranging from the poetically ambiguous to the pointedly belligerent. In the dark days of his exile in Madina, Muhammad instilled in his followers a duty to be combative against the umma's foes in Mecca. "Fight the polytheists totally as they fight you totally," states verse fourteen of the ninth sura. In one of the hadiths—the sayings of the Prophet given the imprimatur of authenticity through centuries of exegetical scholarship—Muhammad declared, "A morning or an evening expedition in God's path is better than the world and what it contains, and for one of you to remain in the line of battle is better than his prayers for sixty years." Subsequent compilations of Islamic law, the sharia, elevated jihad to a sixth pillar of the faith, an equal of the hajj and alms-giving for each able-bodied member of the faithful.

The letter of the Carthusian cited above would not seem so uncannily Islamic without a further refinement in the idea of righteous struggle. The Quran and the traditions describe a second jihad, superior to the first; it involves the individual's fight to go beyond the baser instincts of his nature in order to lead a pious, upright life. This "greater jihad" is far harder to undertake, as it requires application, discipline, and humility, qualities denied the common ruck of humanity. For some scholars, one could not carry out the lesser jihad of war until one had completed the greater jihad of self-correction. In this view there could be no holy war without warriors who were holy—precisely the point the monk was making in his letter to the Templars.

In practice, finding enough saints to man an army is well-nigh impossible, and divesting war, no matter how sacred it has been deemed, of its more mundane motives is hardly any easier. The imperfections of men, however, did not diminish the power behind the idea of jihad. Given the right circumstances and messengers, jihad could be invoked to stem and reverse the demoralization of a populace. To an educated Syrian of the crusader era, the great Arab conquests of the past—Yarmuk, Egypt, al-Andalus—could be seen through the lens of jihad, and rightly so, since some participants in those distant victories no doubt felt they were doing God's work. By the time of the Abbasid ascendancy in the eighth and ninth centuries, with its stabilization of the borders between Islam and the west, jihad had taken on a more ritualistic cast, as the caliph dutifully marched out on a regular basis to skirmish with the Byzantines. Harun al-Rashid went on jihad one year, hajj the next. Similarly, the greatest caliph of Umayyad Spain, Abd al-Rahman III, annually conducted what he called jihad in harrassing the Christians of the north—and, not incidentally, dropping in on any disobedient emirs of his borderlands. A generation later, Almanzor cloaked himself in jihad on his frequent incursions into Aragon and Castile, conveniently ignoring the fact that a sizable portion of his armies were Christians.

With the fissuring of the dar al Islam, the undertaking of jihad became the initiative of local rulers rather than the caliphs. In the tenth century, a short-lived shia dynasty of Aleppo conducted repeated offensives against the Byzantines, its ardent declaration of jihad attracting volunteers—*mujahadeen* or *ghazi*—from all over the Middle East. But thereafter, the spark went out of Syrian Muslims, the fracturing of the Seljuk sultanate into backstabbing petty kingdoms hindering any collective action, beyond the merely expedient.

The coming of the Franks and the establishment of Outremer did not immediately change matters. It was a clarion call only to the religious authorities. The success of the infidel, in their view, was the result of their own neglect of both the greater and the lesser jihad. Like the Byzantines after Yarmuk, the holy men of Islam saw the taking of Jerusalem as divine punishment. At different times in the early crusader period, two revivalists—one each from Damascus and Aleppo—traveled to Baghdad to rouse the nominal Muslim leadership from its diffidence. Yet the fervor inspired by their sermons proved to be a will-o'-the-wisp once up against the hard reality of local Syrian jealousies. Ridwan, the emir of Aleppo, closed the gates of his city to an army of would-be allies dispatched from al-Jazeera, who returned the favor by laying waste to the Aleppan countryside. In 1115, an even greater army, equally primed for jihad and this time composed of the best Seljuk fighters of Iraq, arrived in Syria to find the princes of the competing cities united, for once, in defending their land—but against the Seljuks. To deepen the insult, among those gathered at Damascus for the common effort were the armored knights of King Baldwin of Jerusalem, proof that jihad mattered little to the Muslim Syrian elite. Even after the first major setback for the Franks at the hands of the Muslims, the Field of Blood in 1119, the attempts of the qadi of Aleppo—the same man who had preached in Baghdad—to inaugurate a sustained jihad came to naught. For his pains at trying to instill zeal in the struggle against Christians and heretics, he was killed by the Assassins. So too, in fact, was the Damascene revivalist in Baghdad.

In the end, military success encouraged jihad, not the other way around. By the middle of the 1120s, the cities of Mosul and Aleppo had become united into a single kingdom, awaiting only a forceful leader who could somehow improve the lot of Muslims in Syria, many of whom had been forced to recognize the suzerainty of—and therefore pay tribute to—the Christians of Outremer. The providential man was Imad al-Jahir Zengi, a hard-drinking warlord who ended his life a hero of Islam. Initially the governor of Basra (from which Sinan, the Old Man of the Mountain, hailed), Zengi had gained promotion by saving the Seljuk sultan from a palace revolt led by an Abbasid caliph unwilling to be a mere figurehead. One of the last of his family ever to attempt to reassert Arab control over the Turkish soldiery, Caliph al-Mustarshid was put back in his toothless place by Zengi in 1127, for which the grateful Seljuk sultan gave him the prize of Mosul and Aleppo. It was a fateful appointment for Outremer and Muslim Syria. In a career that spanned two decades, the merciless Zengi forged a disciplined army from his heretofore squabbling subjects and absorbed many of the smaller cities of the Orontes Valley into his dominion, all the while protecting himself from attack in Mesopotamia, which remained turbulent after al-Mustarshid's failed uprising. In one such rearguard action in 1132, at the town of Tikrit on the Tigris, Zengi's life was saved in the breach by a local Kurd, Najm al-Din Ayyub. Zengi later granted the man a fief in the Bekaa Valley of Lebanon; there, Ayyub's son, known to history as Saladin, grew up.

Zengi's exploits and atrocities came to be feared and celebrated throughout the Near East, although his greatest ambition, to become the master of Damascus, eluded him. Usamah ibn Munqidh, the bemused observer of the Franks, served as intermediary between Muslim Damascus and Christian Jerusalem. Thwarted at Damascus, Zengi turned his attentions elsewhere. Eventually, he made the move that would win him adulation: he attacked Edessa. Founded as the first crusader state in 1098 by Baldwin of Boulogne after the convenient murder of his adoptive father, Edessa fell to Zengi in 1144. For the Muslim east, the occasion caused rejoicing; for the Christian west, despair.

≺-≺- ≺-≺-   ≻-≻ ≻-≻

On learning of the loss of Edessa, Bernard of Clairvaux sprang into action. More persuasive than the preachers of Damascus and Aleppo had been in Baghdad, he deployed his great gifts of oratory to call for a new crusade. After a stirring speech Bernard delivered in Vézelay, France, the exalted enthusiasm felt fifty years earlier swept through Europe again. "The villages and towns are deserted," he wrote with a hint of self-satisfaction. "You'd have difficulty finding one man for every seven women. Everywhere there are widows whose husbands are still alive." The French and German monarchs took the cross, agreeing to lead tens of thousands of armed pilgrims to victory. In 1147 the Second Crusade got under way.

It was a fiasco. The Byzantines, then at war with Roger II of Sicily, gave little help to their Latin visitors, and even what advice they offered was disastrously ignored. Seeing cowardice in Byzantine counsels of caution about the Rum Seljuks, Emperor Conrad III of Germany brushed aside pleas to stick to the Greek-held coasts of Anatolia and struck out through the heart of the peninsula. Near Dorylaeum, halfway between Constantinople and Ankara, his army was massacred—and he barely escaped with his life, returning to the Bosporus to lick his wounds and avoid the smug glances of the Greek generals. King Louis VII of France, by contrast, had followed their advice, but his progression along the seashore became a nightmare of ambush and attrition. Louis was not the most stout-hearted of men—terrorized, he ceded command of his army to the Templars, an unprecedently public admission of regal incompetence. On the southern coast of Anatolia, his disarray had grown to such proportions that he eventually left the bulk of his men to fight their way overland by themselves. He took ship with his knights and their ladies and sailed to the safety of Antioch.

The bedraggled crusaders found no respite. At Antioch, the French monarch and the assembled poulain grandees quarreled over what to do next. To poison matters further, Eleanor of Aquitaine, the young, beautiful, and very wealthy French queen who had insisted on joining the crusade, set tongues wagging in the city with the attentions she began lavishing on her dashing uncle, Raymond of Poitiers, the prince of Antioch. Hardly immune to the lure of courtship—his father was the first troubadour—Raymond reciprocated the affections of his niece. The spirited Eleanor had taken the measure of her husband Louis in the adversity of Anatolia and disliked what she had seen; she informed him that she would seek to have their marriage annulled. Humiliated, Louis dragged Eleanor away from Antioch after the decision was taken to go not to Edessa, or even to Aleppo, which Raymond had wisely suggested they attack, but to Tyre and Jerusalem, where further parleys would be held.

The crusaders were frittering away a temporary advantage, for they had no monopoly on indignity. In 1146 Zengi had been stabbed to death in his bed by a eunuch fearful of being punished the next morning. (A drunken, half-asleep Zengi had threatened the eunuch after seeing him steal a sip from his wine goblet.) This touched off rounds of centrifugal maneuvering, as local lords tried to regain their independence in the absence of a strong leader. Zengi's second son, Nur al-Din, struggled to keep his father's accomplishment intact. In time, Mosul,

Aleppo, and Edessa came around to accept his leadership, but their allegiance was still fledgling, and thus susceptible to pressure. Raymond understood that if the crusaders could dislodge the party of Nur al-Din from one of these centers, Muslim Syria—indeed, the al-Jazeera area of upper Mesopotamia—might slide back into the chaos that served the purposes of Outremer.

Conrad sailed from Constaninople with his few remaining knights and joined Louis in the Levant. The poulains, led by Raymond of Poitiers, insisted once again that they attack Aleppo or Edessa, in order to break up the dangerous Zengid confederacy. Once again advice was ignored. The two monarchs chose instead to attack Damascus—the only great city in Syria to have allied *with* the Latin kingdoms *against* Zengi. Such colossal wrongheadedness is difficult to understand, but the city's proximity, wealth, renown, and perceived weakness may have played a role in making it a target. Dismissing doubts about the wisdom of assaulting the enemy of their enemy, the crusaders and the local Latins—who began to exhibit signs of defection from the holy cause—camped outside the eastern walls of Damascus in July 1148.

The Damascenes, for their part, knew what to fear from an army of Franks new to the east: the sack of Jerusalem and the cannibalism at Ma'arat al-Numan would not have been forgotten. After putting up tough resistance for several days, they asked Nur al-Din for help, thus burying the hatchet with Aleppo. In one stroke, Louis and Conrad had brought about what the great Zengi had labored to achieve for twenty years: the union of Aleppo and Damascus (with Mosul and Edessa thrown in for good measure). The crusaders, on hearing that a large army had set out from Aleppo to relieve Damascus, lost their composure and fled central Syria, scrambling over the volcanic plain of Yarmuk to regroup in Galilee, near the height of Hattin. Within a few months of this undignified flight, the crusade leaders had set sail for Europe, their bold banners and cross-embossed gonfalons tucked between their legs.

Not only had the debacle of the Second Crusade united Muslim Syria, it had also made a hero of a warrior who, had he been born in Europe, would have made an exemplary Templar. Nur al-Din accepted the permanent obeisance of Damascus in 1154. His name, meaning "Light of Religion," indicates that he was believed to be a servant of the greater jihad, leading an abstemious life that contrasted favorably, for the devout, with the wine-sodden mores that had been the norm in the courts of Syria. The long-scandalized religious authorities were delighted with him, especially after the new ruler allotted monies for the construction or refurbishment of mosques in the lands he controlled. Many of

Nur al-Din's bequests still stand, magnificent structures in the old quarters of Aleppo, Ma'arat al-Numan, Hama, and Homs. Although hardheaded in his dealings with Outremer—he concluded several truces with the Latins—he was careful to couch his actions in the language of jihad and undermine his critics and rivals by sending out letters designed to be read from the minbars, or pulpits, throughout the dar al Islam. He had a sure touch for propaganda: as both his reputation and the groundswell for jihad grew, Nur al-Din had an exquisite wood and ivory minbar constructed at great expense. Its intended home, he made the world know, was the al-Aqsa Mosque in Jerusalem.

◄◄ ◄◄ ►► ►►

Cairo, the city founded by the Fatimids in 973 alongside the Fustat of Amr Ibn al As, had long since enveloped the elder settlement and sprawled and agglomerated into one of the great cities of the Mediterranean world. Its al-Azhar academy, thought to be the oldest university anywhere, has turned out a steady stream of religious scholars since its foundation in the late tenth century. Through the Geniza archive, a cache of medieval Jewish trading documents discovered in 1864, we know that commercial contacts thrived between Cairene merchants and a clientele stretching from Málaga to Samarkand. By the dawn of the twelfth century, upstart Cairo had definitively supplanted all other Muslim cities as the leading metropolis of the dar al Islam.

The rulers of the city were the Fatimids, claimants to the descendance of Ali. As such, they were locked in a struggle for supremacy in Islam with the sunni Abbasids and their Seljuk masters. Just as Alp Arslan wanted to swoop south from Asia Minor to eradicate the shia, so too did the shia Fatimids dream of rolling up the Fertile Crescent and conquering sunni Baghdad. Around the year 1000 a charismatic and quite possibly mad caliph, al-Hakim, had gone so far as to transgress the injunctions of the Prophet. Not only did he arrogate for himself divine status (which lives on in the beliefs of the Druze sectaries of Islam), but he also overturned the notion that fellow monotheists, the People of the Book, should escape punishment. In the painful exception to convivencia that was al-Hakim's reign, Jews and Coptic Christians were persecuted with as much vigor as had been the practice in the old days of Heraclius and the Byzantine patriarchs. In Jerusalem, the Church of the Holy Sepulchre was razed to the ground in 1009. (The basileus Constantine IX Monomachus subsidized the church's rebuilding three decades later.)

The minbar of Nur al-Din in the al-Aqsa Mosque of Jerusalem. Installed by Saladin, it stood there until its destruction in 1969.

More humane Muslim custom prevailed after al-Hakim's death, even if the institution of the caliphate had been irredeemably weakened. Successive viziers, many of Turkish and Armenian origin, wielded effective power, but their efforts at setting up behind-the-scenes dynasties for their descendants fell foul of caliphal loyalists, officers of the *mamluk* (slave) armies and rivals at court. When the Latin knights of the First Crusade arrived in Fatimid Palestine, like meteorites from a dimly understood galaxy beyond Byzantium, the Cairene leadership was caught unprepared. Possessed of a great fleet, Fatimid Egypt was unable to influence the course of the campaign and lost its moorings, literally, along the coast of the Levant to the Latins. Jerusalem was in Fatimid hands when it fell in 1099; their last haven on the Palestinian shoreline, Ascalon, was taken by the Latins in 1144.

By the time Nur al-Din brought unity to Syria, the factionalism of the Egyptian ruling elites had become irreversible. What had not changed, however, was the country's great wealth. When a crusader embassy came calling at midcentury, "they were led past colonnades and fountains and gardens where the Court menageries and aviaries were kept, through hall after hall, heavy with hangings of silk and golden thread, studded with jewels, till at last a great golden curtain was raised to show the boy-Caliph seated veiled on his golden throne." That incomparable wealth lay there for the taking. The two enemies, Nur al-Din of Aleppo and Amalric, the new and capable king of Jerusalem, took their eyes off each other and looked at Cairo.

To be fair, both had good reasons beyond mere cupidity to venture into Egypt. For Outremer, the legacy of the Second Crusade was bad enough—its neighbor, a newly united Syria, resounded with bloodcurdling cries to jihad; yet the prospect would be darker still were Nur al-Din to corral Egypt into his domain, thereby placing the Latin kingdoms between the pincers of a great Islamic state. From the opposite perspective, the ruler of Aleppo saw the advantage in having the obnoxious Franks trapped between two claws—Syria and Egypt—ready to snap shut. Further, the spies and informants of Zengi's son would have told him of the troubles within Outremer, of its lack of manpower and its squabbling barons and warrior-monks. To let the Franks somehow tap into the gift of the Nile, thereby gaining the wherewithal to place large armies in the field, would render the sacred duty of crushing them all the more difficult. And last, in Nur al-Din's sunni view, the Fatimids were an unholy heretical sect that deserved to be wiped from the face of the earth. For Nur al-Din, striving in the path of God necessarily led to Egypt.

Thus, curiously, the lead-up to the great confrontation over Outremer occurred in neither Palestine nor Syria. Between 1163 and 1169, no fewer than three campaigns were launched in Egypt by the Syrians and the Latins. There was a strange parallel migration to these wars, the poulain knights and armed monks marching beyond Gaza and through the northern Sinai, their adversaries racing down the Jordan Valley and past the Dead Sea, then joining the southern route across the peninsula. At the outset the Latins found support in a Cairene court fearful of the Aleppan ascendancy. Long allies of the Byzantines in keeping the sea free from privateering, the Fatimid viziers practiced realpolitik and succeeded in allaying, for a time, any misgivings about treating with Christian powers. However, their diplomatic maneuvering did not survive Latin ferocity— in 1168 the army of Outremer stormed the town of Bilbays in the Nile Delta and murdered every one of its inhabitants, Copt and Muslim alike. This atrocity got Cairo off the fence. Unwilling to suffer a similar fate, the Cairenes initiated a scorched-earth policy, burning old Fustat and the surrounding suburbs in a conflagration, according to the chroniclers, that lasted two months. The Latins were no longer welcome.

The beneficiaries of this surge of ill will were the Syrians, led by Shirkuh, brother of Ayyub, the Kurd who had saved Zengi at Tikrit. As Nur al-Din's champion in Syria, Shirkuh had conducted a series of skirmishes and sieges to chip away at the Latin presence there. In 1149 during the siege of an Antiochene fortress, Shirkuh had killed Raymond of Poitiers, the overly fond uncle of Eleanor of Aquitaine. (While resting in Sicily on the voyage home from the Second Crusade, Eleanor learned the distressing news that Raymond's skull, set in a silver case, had been sent to the caliph in Baghdad.) In the Syrian conquest of Egypt, a similar tie of kinship came into play: Shirkuh's nephew, and first lieutenant, was Ayyub's son, Salah al-Din Yusuf ibn Ayyub, or Saladin.* The old warrior relied on his young nephew in conducting coordinated operations far apart, many of these dependent on the use of carrier pigeons, a technology unknown to the Latins as they blundered from one missed opportunity to the next. When, in 1169, Shirkuh finally chased them from the Nile Delta, won the submission of the Cairenes, and surveyed the limitless vistas of personal wealth before him, he died—the victim of gorging himself at a feast.

Saladin, aged thirty, succeeded his uncle as governor of Egypt. As a youth in Damascus and in Baalbek of the Bekaa Valley, a Muslim outpost in the shadow

*At the time he was known only as Yusuf, or Joseph.

of the great ruins of pagan antiquity, he had proved himself to be studious both in the arts of war and in the pursuit of piety. His strength lay in combining the warrior ability of Zengi and the pious circumspection of Nur al-Din; his weakness, in not having a drop of their blood. He was a Kurd, an outsider, neither of the Turkish ruling classes nor of the native Arab populations. His master in Aleppo soon had reason to suspect him of overreaching his station in life. On two occasions after the fall of Egypt, Nur al-Din had gone on razzias in Palestine, and both times Saladin had refused to link up with him, once turning tail and scurrying back across the Sinai after being within less than a day's ride of the Syrian's army. Although letters full of placating flatteries invariably arrived in Aleppo to explain away these and other actions that might be deemed insubordinate, Nur al-Din had increasing reason to believe that his unassuming servant had outsize ambitions.

The barons of Outremer could only watch hopefully the growing estrangement between Aleppo and Cairo. They had been beaten, soundly, on the Nile, and their plucky but defeated leader, Amalric of Jerusalem, had been succeeded on his demise from dysentery at age thirty-eight by a bright adolescent, Baldwin IV, who had the signal disadvantage of being a leper. The Latins were in no position to repel a concerted offensive. The counterbalance to Syrian jihad was definitively gone: in 1171 Saladin abolished the Fatimid caliphate and thereby extinguished the great shia dream of refashioning the Islamic umma. Worse yet, the Byzantines, the Latins' sometime allies, were permanently sidelined in 1178. After generations of careful stewardship under the Comnenan dynasty, the armies of Constantinople suffered a devastating defeat at the hands of the Rum Seljuks on a battlefield near Ankara known as Myriokephalon. The loser, Manuel Comnenus, compared the debacle to Manzikert—and this was indeed the last time the Byzantines would try to dislodge the Turks from Anatolia.

Given these great events—the end of the Fatimid counterpoise to Syria and the disappearance of the Byzantines in the east—the decade of the 1170s saw the Latins grow more and more isolated in the Levant. They knew that if Saladin and the Zengid ruler of Aleppo, Nur al-Din, could compose their differences, the Muslims would no doubt turn their attentions to Outremer. In the meantime the stonemasons got to work, strengthening the myriad fortresses of the three remaining Latin states—Jerusalem, Tripoli, Antioch—in anticipation of the coming storm.

They won a reprieve. When in 1174, at age fifty-eight, Nur al-Din expired unexpectedly from what is thought to have been angina, the discord between

Saladin and the Zengids only worsened. Squabbling immediately broke out over who should be the regent of the Aleppan heir, al-Salih, an eleven-year-old surrounded by kinsmen resentful of Saladin's presumptions. The great Kurd quit Cairo to become master of Damascus, his proximity to his rivals only exacerbating the rift. The letter-writers in Damascus and Aleppo set to work wheedling out of the caliph in Baghdad, the titular head of sunni Islam, formal approval for their masters' claims of legitimacy. In the al-Jazeera the leader of Mosul and its dependencies came out forthrightly against Saladin, viewing him as a usurper unworthy of the dominion won by Zengi and Nur al-Din. As the partisans of jihad against the infidel wrung their hands in frustration, Saladin conducted campaigns in Mesopotamia and Anatolia, far away from the running sore of impiety that was Outremer. Once again Muslim fought Muslim, while truces were negotiated with the barbaric Franks. Nothing short of the grossest provocation would turn minds back to the holy duty of jihad.

≺← ≺←   →≻ →≻

Reynaud of Châtillon was a minor nobleman who came to the Levant with the Second Crusade. At its ignominious conclusion, Reynaud chose to stay on in Outremer rather than return to France, where, as a younger brother from a small fief in the Loire Valley, he could have expected little advancement. A tall and handsome man with reddish hair and an impressive bearing, the young Reynaud eventually turned the head of the princess of Antioch, the widow of Raymond of Poitiers. The courtship shocked Outremer. The princess, Constance, was one of the grandest ladies of the land—she was the great-granddaughter of Robert Guiscard—and by rights should have considered only the highest born of men as potential mates. Strong-willed and smitten, Constance shrugged off entreaties from bishop, king, and basileus to consider other suitors—she married her low-born lover in 1153, making a crusading pauper into a prince of Outremer. It was scandalous, William of Tyre remarked in his chronicle, that "a woman so eminent, so distinguished and powerful, who had been the wife of a very illustrious man, should stoop to marry an ordinary knight."

The new prince of Antioch wasted no time in making his mark. Disregarding the claims of its suzerain, the basileus Manuel Comnenus, Reynaud decided to seize peaceable and prosperous Byzantine Cyprus. To finance this adventure, he demanded money from the Latin patriarch of Antioch, who had opposed

Constance's love match in the first place and made no secret of his contempt for
the parvenu prince. Predictably, the prelate refused to countenance the scheme.
By way of reply, Reynaud had him stripped, beaten to a pulp, covered with
honey, and exposed to the sunshine of midday, to be tormented by insects. His
mind concentrated, the patriarch opened his treasury, and soon Reynaud sailed
to Cyprus, in the company of the Christian king of Cilician Armenia.*

Once in Cyprus Reynaud showed that he was a crusader of the old style: his
army pillaged, raped, and murdered at will, unmindful of the awkward fact
that the islanders were Christian. Reynaud rounded up all the Orthodox
priests of Cyprus, cut off their noses, and then sent the mutilated men to Constantinople as a signal of defiance to the basileus. In no time he had offended
the Latins, by torturing the patriarch of Antioch, and outraged the Byzantines, by laying waste to Cyprus. The Muslims would have to wait their turn: in
1160, while out in the hinterland of Antioch rustling livestock from Syrian
Christians, Reynaud was captured by an armed detachment of Nur al-Din's
men. He was thrown into a cell in Aleppo's great citadel, to languish for sixteen
years, as no one offered to pay his ransom.

Reynaud's sojourn in the dungeons of Aleppo coincided with the Egyptian
wars of Amalric and the ascent of Saladin. As the call to jihad rose outside the
walls of his prison, Reynaud, now fluent in Arabic, would have come to know
his enemy—and how to insult and wound Muslims deeply. He was released in
1175 or 1176, in the unsettled period when the Zengids of Aleppo, following the
death of Nur al-Din, sought allies among the Latins to deflect the ambitions of
Saladin.

Reynaud's wife, Princess Constance, had died two years after his capture,
leaving Antioch to a son from her previous marriage. Reynaud therefore had to
seek a position elsewhere. Sometime in the late 1170s he wooed and won yet another powerful widow, Stephanie of Milly, heiress to Hebron and the Outre-
Jourdain, the Latin marchland south of the Dead Sea known in the Bible as
Moab. A distant corner of Outremer, it was nonetheless of crucial significance:
the main caravan routes from Syria to Egypt passed through the Outre-
Jourdain, as did, every year, thousands of pilgrims making the hajj to Mecca. Its
two castles, Kerak and Montreal, rivaled the Krak des Chevaliers and Marqab
for massive impregnability. Now Reynaud of Châtillon was master of these

*Lesser—sometimes Little—Armenia, the southern Anatolian neighbor just to the north of
the Latin states.

fortresses, perched high above a valley frequented by treasure-laden travelers. Even for someone possessing scruples, the temptation would have been great.

Ibn Jubayr, the Andalusi traveler whom we encountered earlier admiring the Christian women of Palermo, noted that despite the hostility between Outremer and Syria, the caravan trade was sacrosanct: "The Christians impose a tax on the Muslims in their land which gives them full security; and likewise the Christian merchants pay a tax upon their goods in Muslim lands. Agreement exists between them, and there is equal treatment in all cases. The soldiers engage themselves in their war, while the people are at peace." In addition, the Latin kingdoms were, for once, in concord with their Muslim neighbors: drought and incipient famine had induced the knights to agree, in 1180, to an extended truce with Saladin, who was glad of the respite so that he could deal with opponents in Mesopotamia. Despite these glimmerings of civility, the new master of Kerak could not contain himself. In 1181 Reynaud rode down a column of pilgrims on the hajj, stripping them of all their possessions and hauling many of them into captivity. This was a flagrant breach of the truce, as an angered Saladin was quick to point out, but the king of Jerusalem, the increasingly leprous Baldwin, dared not take any punitive action against his fiery vassal.

The following year Reynaud outdid himself. He launched a fleet of five ships at Eilat, on the Gulf of Aqaba. Their destination was, incredibly, Mecca. The pirate flotilla burst into the Red Sea, plundering unsuspecting merchant and pilgrim vessels, raiding both the Arabian and African shores, and making stops to rob and rape hajj pilgrims inland. This insane razzia got to within a day's ride of Madina. Eventually a fleet sent by Saladin's brother arrived from Egypt to capture the perpetrators. They were subsequently beheaded, but the mastermind of the operation, Reynaud, remained untouched in the safety of Kerak.

In the mosques and madrasas of the dar al Islam there was stupefaction: first the Franks had taken Jerusalem; now they wanted to defile the holiest of holies, the cities of the Hijaz. Saladin, aware of the wave of anger sweeping his empire, turned his attentions from Syria and the al-Jazeera and marched on Palestine in 1183. The Latin forces, following the sage advice of Raymond of Tripoli, a poulain lord of the Saint-Gilles family of Toulouse, did not engage Saladin's great army. They took up a strong and fortified position and resisted the temptation to attack, even though the hotheads in the Latin ranks bayed for blood. Frustrated, Saladin eventually had his men head south to ravage the Outre-Jourdain and lay siege to Kerak, in the hope that the great castle might yield the most hated Frank of Outremer. Reynaud, however, was too well protected in his clifftop aerie—and by the time of Saladin's siege, he was not alone. The wedding celebrations of his stepdaughter to a baron of Palestine had brought the quarrelsome nobility of Outremer under his roof. As Saladin's siege engines pounded the fortifications, the festivities continued. Even given the enmity he felt for Reynaud, Saladin showed a sensibility here, as he would elsewhere, that won him a place in the annals of gallantry. On learning of the nuptials, Saladin asked where the newlyweds were to be lodged and consequently directed the fire of his catapults away from that section of the castle. When, at last, a relieving army of Latins arrived from Jerusalem, he beat his retreat.

Decorum nothwithstanding, a larger showdown was imminent. On the Muslim side, calls to put an end to the continuing scandal of internecine war became shrilly insistent. The Assassins, driven out of the cities of Syria to the Jebel Ansariye, had been an on-again, off-again threat to the coalescing unity of the region. In the 1160s, they temporarily sidelined themselves by embracing the radical millenarianism espoused by the leader of the sect in Persia. Declaring himself to be the hidden imam announcing the end of time, Hasan, the lord of Alamut, unilaterally abrogated the laws of Islam and ordered his followers to partake of pleasures theretofore denied, as they were now in the presence of the eternal. In Syria the order was enthusiastically obeyed, and for a time, according to one local historian, "the people . . . gave way to iniquity and debauchery, and called themselves 'the Pure.' Men and women mingled in drinking sessions [and] no man abstained from his sister or daughter."

Eventually, under Sinan's whip hand, the Assassins came to their senses and resumed their holy work of spreading terror. Saladin, as the new champion of sunni Islam, was naturally a target: after barely escaping assassination in 1175 and 1176, he took to wearing armor at all times and sleeping in a bed that rested on an elevated wooden tower. Saladin is believed to have finally come to an understanding with Sinan, as evidenced by the inexpicably abrupt way he lifted his siege of Masyaf, an Assassin castle that still guards the eastern approach to the Ansariye range. Why he opted for compromise with these decidedly unorthodox sectaries is recounted in a famous tale of the thirteenth-century *Chronicle of Aleppo*. The chronicler, Kemal al-Din, relates that one day Saladin received a visitor who claimed to be in possession of a message from Sinan that had to be delivered in private. Once the stranger was searched for hidden weapons, Saladin dismissed his courtiers, save for two mamluk bodyguards. The man insisted on seeing the sultan alone; Saladin refused.

He [the messenger] said: "Why do you not send away these two as you sent away the others?" Saladin replied: "I regard these as my own sons, and they and I are one." Then the messenger turned to the two Mamluks and said: "If I ordered you in the name of my master to kill this Sultan, would you do so?" They answered yes, and drew their swords, saying: "Command us as you wish." Sultan Saladin (God have mercy on him) was astounded, and the messenger left, taking them with him. And thereupon Saladin (God have mercy on him) inclined to make peace with him [Sinan] and enter into friendly relations with him.

Whatever the truth of that chilling anecdote, by the 1180s the Assassins had switched from terrifying Saladin to harassing his foes. Moreover, the harried Zengids at last caved in to the sunni consensus that the Kurdish usurper was the man to take the fight to the Christians. On the death of Nur al-Din's son, al-Salih, Aleppo submitted to Saladin, and in 1186 so too did Mosul. The Rum Seljuks had crushed the Byzantine Christians at Myriokephalon some ten years earlier; Saladin was beseeched to do the same with the Latins of Outremer.

As the sultan of the al-Jazeera, Syria, Egypt, the Hijaz, and Yemen weighed whether to risk his hard-won peace in a decisive battle with the Franks—with whom he had signed another four-year truce—Reynaud of Châtillon forced the matter. Toward the end of 1186, an enormous caravan traveling from Cairo to Damascus passed tantalizingly by his doorstep. In spite of the truce and the practice of tolls paid for safe passage, the lord of Kerak swooped down on the lightly guarded merchants and relieved them of all their precious wares. The travelers were then thrown into the dungeons of Kerak, destined for sale in the slave markets of Outremer. When the prisoners protested their innocence, Reynaud was reported to have said, "Let your Muhammad come and deliver you!" Saladin, on learning of this latest outrage, swore to kill Reynaud with his own hands. The threshold of the intolerable had at last been crossed. The following spring, from every corner of Saladin's empire, troops were summoned for jihad. They were to meet in southwestern Syria, on the plateau near the river Yarmuk.

◄┼ ◄┼   ┼► ┼►

Galilee. The pale hills and valleys of this corner of the Promised Land present a picture of peaceful village and sun-bleached pastorale. Appearances deceive, as this region has been at the epicenter of conflict for thousands of years, the overgrown ruin of Palestinian settlements vacated in 1948 just the latest remnants of turmoil. Indeed, an archaeological site in Lower Galilee, Megiddo, gave its name to Armageddon. Farther to the north and east stretches the Bet Netofa Valley, the most ample of the region, which leads from the coastal plain near Haifa and Akko (Acre) inland toward the Sea of Galilee. It too is a picture of rural calm, which belies its past role as the scene of a decisive, violent shock between Christianity and Islam.

At a height called the Horns of Hattin, Outremer met its Armageddon. From this hillock, within sight of the sparkling waters of the Sea of Galilee, the greatest knights of the Latin kingdoms were bested by Saladin—and by thirst. They no doubt thought their god had forsaken them, for the surrounding landscape was central to their Christian faith. Almost within shouting distance of Hattin, on a ridge closing off the southern side of the valley of Bet Netofa, stands the town of Nazareth, where their savior was supposed to have grown to manhood. Nearby, in what is now a suburb of Nazareth, rise the bell towers and minarets of Cana, known to Christians as the village where Jesus performed his first miracle by changing water into wine for a wedding party. On the broiling hot day of July 4, 1187, however, the Muslims celebrated a miracle and the Christians went thirsty.

The lord of Galilee at the time was Raymond of Tripoli, a great-great-grandson of Count Raymond of Toulouse, who had stormed Jerusalem in 1099. Respected for his wisdom (he had counseled the passive strategy to foil Saladin in 1183) yet a poulain of the type detested by newcomers from Europe, Raymond was on good terms with the sultan, with whom he conversed in Arabic, and on execrable terms with his fellow Christians. In the months leading up to the clash at Hattin, Raymond and his foes among the nobility of Outremer came to the brink of civil war, at precisely the moment of greatest peril.

The contentious issue was the throne of Jerusalem. In 1185, on the death of Baldwin IV of leprosy at age twenty-four, his seven-year-old nephew, Baldwin V, won approval from the nobility as the legitimate monarch—in theory, the barons of Outremer elected the king, although the custom of primogeniture had strengthened over time. Sickly, Baldwin V expired the following year. As regent of the kingdom, Raymond of Tripoli expected everyone to respect the agreement that had been hashed out on the boy's accession to the throne: his successor would be chosen by a board of arbitration formed of the pope, the

Germanic emperor, and the kings of England and France. And surely he, Raymond, was best suited to take the reins of power. The Latins of Outremer were all alone now: the disaster of Myriokephalon had eliminated their ally of last resort, the Byzantine Empire. Also, the Byzantines' Orthodox coreligionists in the Levant, having experienced eighty years of Latin discrimination and usurpation, were unlikely to come to the aid of Outremer. These perils—Muslim unity, Byzantine impotence, Orthodox hostility—made the need for a wise leader, such as Raymond of Tripoli, all the more pressing.

Such considerations did not interest Baldwin IV's widowed sister, Sibylla, the mother of the late boy-king. Sibylla came from a long line of strong-willed women to play a role in the affairs of Outremer. Given the fact that her brother (Baldwin IV) and son (Baldwin V) had both been monarchs, Sibylla not surprisingly wanted the vacated throne for herself and her husband, Guy of Lusignan. Guy's story is instructive of the mores of Outremer: having been urged to come to the Levant by his brother, who was the lover of Sibylla's mother, the dashing minor nobleman from France duly won Sibylla's affections and wed her in 1180. Less enamored of this handsome newcomer were the native Latins of Outremer, who saw him as a weak-willed westerner bereft of the tact and flexibility needed to deal with the Muslim enemy. Despite the unpopularity of her beloved Guy, Sibylla possessed the necessary guile to have her way: while the influential Raymond of Tripoli was away in Samaria, she staged a furtive coronation ceremony in Jerusalem.

Her allies on that occasion of 1186 were a colorful lot. Proffering the crown to the couple was a corrupt priest from the Auvergne named Eraclius, who had been made Latin patriarch of Jerusalem several years earlier by virtue of sharing the bed of Sibylla's mother. (He had preceded Guy's brother as her lover.) Patriarch Eraclius had since taken up with a married lady of Nablus, known throughout the kingdom as Madame la Patriarchesse. Another of Guy's supporters, Gérard of Ridefort, the leader of the Templars, had a sizable ax to grind. On arriving in Outremer in 1173, he had gone into the service of Raymond of Tripoli, on the understanding that the count would find him a wealthy fief once a marriageable widow came on the market. Raymond, for reasons unknown, reneged on the deal, giving a certain Lucia, the widowed heiress of Botrun, in what is now Lebanon, to a Pisan merchant in exchange for a hefty payment of gold. Gérard, infuriated, joined the Templars and rose through the ranks to the office of grand master, his hatred of his former master sharpened by the insult of having been passed over for a mere merchant. When Guy of

Lusignan bowed his head to receive the regalia, Gérard averred smugly, "This crown compensates for the Botrun marriage." Applauding alongside him was the inevitable Reynaud of Châtillon. A pliant monarch—and one indebted to him for his ascent to power—was precisely the type of man the lord of Kerak sought for Jerusalem. King Guy would not dare interfere with his sponsor's campaign of anti-Muslim brigandage. The hawks of Outremer, those fired by newcomer zeal and greed, had orchestrated a coup.

Disgusted, Raymond of Tripoli watched as his fellow poulain barons hastened to Jerusalem to make obeisance to King Guy and Queen Sibylla. The great lord of Tripoli rode in the opposite direction, up the Jordan River Valley to Tiberias, the capital of his wife's fief on the Sea of Galilee. Fearful that his enemies would try to undermine him further, Raymond entered into negotiations with Saladin, with a view to forming an alliance in the event of attack from the forces of Jerusalem. This overture was, if not treasonous, certainly unusual. For Saladin, the offer came as heartening proof that his intent to fight the Franks later in the year was well timed, for obviously they were now afflicted with the same divisiveness that had plagued the Muslims for so long. Saladin replied to Raymond's peace feeler by making an equally unusual request: he asked to send an armed reconnaissance party through the count's possessions in lower Galilee, just to get a sense of the lay of the land. After mulling over the matter for a few days, Raymond gave his assent, on condition that the Muslim cavalry arrive after dawn and leave before sunset and engage in no looting or rapine. May 1, 1187, was set as the date for this peaceful razzia. Raymond's messengers rode out to the towns and castles of Galilee, warning one and all to stay indoors.

Had the hawks of Jerusalem remained true to form in shunning Raymond, the day might have passed without incident. However, Guy and Sibylla realized that reconciliation with such a powerful baron had to be attempted and to that end had dispatched a delegation of nobles northward to smooth the count's ruffled feathers. They had just entered Galilee when a messenger from Tiberias arrived bearing news of the upcoming one-day invasion and of Raymond's recommendation to lie low. For some in the Jerusalem embassy, this complaisance with the enemy proved that the Arabic-speaking, orientalized count of Tripoli was, indeed, an apostate. For others, notably Gérard of Ridefort, just hearing news of approaching Muslims was tantamount to waving a red flag before a bull. He and his counterpart, the master of the Hospitalers, summoned as many men as they could from their orders' possessions in the area. By midday of May 1, a force of about 130 armored knights lumbered north toward Nazareth, in search of their quarry.

The contingent led by Kukburi, an experienced Mesopotamian emir, is said to have numbered seven thousand mounted archers and light cavalry. Even if that figure is exaggerated, the day-trippers from Syria vastly outnumbered their would-be ambushers. True to the accord passed with Raymond, the Muslim force had forded the Jordan at dawn and gone on a long loop through Galilee, scrupulously avoiding damage to crops or property and, no doubt, reconnoitering the terrain for a future engagement. Toward the end of the afternoon, they stopped to water their horses at a spring called Cresson, just below Cana. Just then the Templars and Hospitalers crested the ridge at Nazareth and saw the size of the enemy force. The master of the Hospital suggested they exercise the better part of valor, as did another commander of the Templars, James of Mailly. Grand Master Ridefort taunted the latter, "You love your blond head too well to want to lose it!" The two sensible men were shamed into changing their minds. The knights, as suicidal as any Assassin, then charged down the hill into the mass of the Muslim cavalry. The outcome was one-sided: of the Christians, only Gérard of Ridefort and two others survived the battle to ride away to safety.

In the dying light of the day, Raymond of Tripoli, in his citadel in Tiberias, would have been gladdened to see Kukburi and his men approaching his city on their way out of Galilee, showing that the risky agreement had been honored. Relief would have then changed to consternation as he recognized the heads of dozens of Templar and Hospitaler knights affixed to the lances of the passing cavalry. News of the massacre spread quickly, spurring King Guy to call every able-bodied man of Outremer to arms. A large sum of money that had been donated to the Templars and the Hospitalers by Henry II of England—as atonement for his role in the recent murder of Thomas Becket—was used to buy armor and hire mercenaries. Raymond of Tripoli, appalled by the result of his flirtation with Saladin, made amends and joined the king in Acre, the great fortified port of the Levant that had been turned into a marshaling yard for the largest army Outremer would ever field. By late June the preparations were over. The Latins headed east into the Bet Netofa Valley, some twelve hundred armored knights, a greater number of lighter cavalry, and perhaps ten thousand foot soldiers, supplemented by crossbowmen from the Italian merchant fleet. The bishop of Acre held aloft a relic known as the True Cross, that long-cherished fragment of wood purportedly from the original timber on which Christ had been crucified. Normally this duty would have been performed by the patriarch of Jerusalem, but Eraclius had, characteristically, begged off.

On July 1, 1187, Saladin crossed the Jordan with a force superior in number to the Latins, estimated at twelve thousand cavalry and thirty thousand infantry. This too was the largest army he was ever to command, coming as it did from every corner of his empire. Kurds, Turks, Egyptians, Damascenes, Aleppans, Yemenis, Mespotamians, and thousands of exalted religious volunteers poured into Galilee, ready and eager to take the battle to the Christians. One army moved east, in from the Mediterranean; the other west, from the Sea of Galilee. The land could support this many men on the move for a few days, at most.

⤌ ⤌ ⤍ ⤍

Zippori, a ruined city from Roman and Byzantine antiquity alternately known as Sepphoris, spreads out over a southern ridge of the Bet Netofa Valley, its recently uncovered floor mosaics a tribute to pagan bacchanalia. A capital of Galilee under the Romans, Zippori was home to Anne and Joachim, the parents of Mary, and during its expansion in the last years before the birth of Christ, it is thought that the work available on its building sites induced Joseph to settle in nearby Nazareth. Later, during the rebellion of the Jerusalem Jews against Roman rule in the first century C.E., the city avoided the destructive wrath of the emperors Vespasian and Titus by its politic refusal to join the revolt. The Sanhedrin—the high court of the Jews—eventually moved to Zippori, where one of its leaders compiled the Mishnah, a compendium of oral traditions fundamental to rabbinic Judaism. By the time the Latins arrived, the city was depopulated, having been supplanted by Tiberias, twenty-five kilometers distant, as the main center of Galilee. Still, aware of the site's strategic and scriptural significance, the crusaders erected a small fort on its acropolis (using Roman sarcophagi as building blocks) as well as a modest church dedicated to Anne and Joachim, which is now a ruin attached to a convent of Italian nuns.

The site had lent itself to settlement for the usual reasons: its position on a height made it defensible, and its flowing spring made it sustainable. The same considerations led the large Latin army to pitch camp there on July 2, 1187. As long as they stayed in the shaded mulberry groves of Zippori, men and horses could rest and feed, ready to repel assault and ride out to skirmish. Any opponent stuck out on the bald valley floor fifty meters below could not last long in the heat. This, in essence, was what Raymond of Tripoli argued in the council of war held that night. Even after news arrived that the lower town of Tiberias had fallen to Saladin and that Raymond's wife, Eschiva, was trapped in that city's citadel, the count of Tripoli remained unmoved. He knew Saladin to be too honorable to visit any outrage upon his lady and that the customary payment of ransom would free her. Raymond argued that, if anything, the siege was a ploy to get them to leave the cool embrace of Zippori for the scorched earth of the valley leading to Tiberias. King Guy saw sense in Raymond's reasoning and ruled that the army would stay put, in the hope that Saladin and his men would dither ineffectually in the heat and then disperse. The council was dismissed.

Raymond's fiercest detractor among the hawks, Gérard of Ridefort, came back to the king's red tent later in the night. The Templar was having none of it. For Gérard, the count of Tripoli was no better than a traitor, his complicity with Saladin a public scandal. One hundred brave Templars and Hospitalers would have been alive to fight for Outremer had Raymond not given the infidels permission to cross his lands. The man, Gérard added, was not even willing to rescue his wife.

As a warrior, Gérard impressed upon Guy that this was not the time to shrink from the enemy; almost every able-bodied man in Outremer was there, ready for combat. As his sponsor in gaining the throne, Gérard leaned on the king even harder, threatening to withdraw the support of the Templars—the backbone of the kingdom—for Guy's exalted station in Outremer. There is no record of Reynaud of Châtillon being present, but his stout seconding of Gérard's arguments would have been no secret to either man. The king cracked under the pressure. The army that had gone to sleep thinking it would dig in at Zippori was awakened before dawn and told to march to Tiberias.

In the half-light, King Guy shouted at all who questioned his change of heart: "It is not for you to ask me by what counsel I am doing it," Guy bellowed. "I want you to mount your horses and prepare yourselves immediately to go to Tiberias." The Latin army of Outremer gathered around the spring of Zippori and formed three separate columns. Raymond, his warnings ignored, agreed to command the vanguard of the column—it was his due as their route would pass through his fiefs. King Guy and Reynaud, accompanied by the True Cross, led the bulk of the men in the center. In the rear, the most exposed position for an army on the march, came the Templars and the Hospitalers, commanded by their respective masters and a great baron, Balian of Ibelin. The foot soldiers, archers, and crossbowmen, their body armor consisting of sturdy leather doublets, formed human walls on the sides of the marching columns, protecting the heavily armed warhorses. The latter, the tanks of medieval warfare, had to be preserved for devastating, unstoppable charges. Lighter cavalry, many of them Turcopoles, or native Levantines forced to convert to Christianity, danced around the flanks, ready to counter any harassers with sudden sallies.

The army marched out into the valley, the rising sun glinting off the metal of thousands of swords. Sentinels posted by Saladin jumped onto their mounts and raced back to his camp in the hills beyond Nazareth with the news. Warfare in Outremer had heretofore been a succession of sieges won or lost and of cautious withdrawals to avoid a decisive encounter: on this day, with the odds in his favor, Saladin rolled the dice. He split his forces, ordering his able nephew Taliq al-Din to take the right wing of the army and head for the northern hills of the valley, a few miles in front of the Christian advance. Kukburi was to leave his position and stealthily prepare to get behind the rear of the Latins' column. The mass of soldiery under Saladin moved farther to the southern lip of Bet Netofa, at a place overlooking the village of Lubiya. In the distance, to the west, the cloud of dust from the marchers would have been visible from this vantage point, as the Christians slowly picked their way along the old Roman road running through the valley. Saladin knew that he would never again command such a huge force and, especially, that never again would the men of iron from beyond the sea needlessly expose themselves to such peril.

The attacks began almost at once, irregular at first, then building to a crescendo of bedlam later in the day. Kukburi's bowmen rode out of the hills to harass the rear and flanks, their arrows sailing upward in high arcs to seek the horses in the middle of the columns. Others fired into the flanking soldiers, retreating quickly once the Pisans had leveled their deadly but slow-to-load crossbows and let fly. The pace of attack and retreat heightened as the sun rose higher in the sky. The Latins gulped the last drops from their gourds and kept their heads down, many of their quilted garments sporting a bouquet of arrows that had found their mark but been stopped by leather and mail.

Toward the end of the morning the three columns came alongside, on their left, the Tauran ridge. An Arab village of the same name (which is still there) spread over the base of the limestone height, its spinney of trees giving proof that a spring gurgled nearby. The order was given to bypass Tauran, to stick to the road, to keep on marching eastward; the men could slake their ever-mounting thirst at dusk, once they had reached the shore of the freshwater Sea of Galilee. The columns moved on, toward the kinks of heat rising from the waterless plain before them. Seeing their mistake, Kukburi brought his full force into the field behind the Latins, blocking any backtracking to the lifesaving well of Tauran. The attacks intensified, the terrifying din of cymbals and drums echoing down from the hills as wave after wave of Kurdish bowmen, and the heavily armed infantry, charged the Christian rear. The valley grew hellish, the ordeal complete, the foot soldiers with the armed monks walking backward to protect the warhorses from repeated assault. From within the rear column, the knights of the Temple and the Hospital sent riders to King Guy to call a halt to the march: they would take their mounts and ride out to defeat the foe. When the sun was at its zenith, the Latins stopped. Raymond of Tripoli, in the vanguard several miles ahead, cursed the folly of his countrymen.

The counterattack came to nothing, the adversary melting away in the blinding light of midday, to leave the juggernaut of knights in search of a target. They regained the ranks and the march resumed, through a blizzard of violence as Saladin's men, their orange and yellow banners unfurled, swooped down to harry the central column. Raymond pleaded unsuccessfully with Guy to leave the infantry behind and stage a cavalry breakout; it was their only chance. Yet the faltering march continued, men falling by the wayside, horses shrieking as they went down, attackers loosing clouds of arrows and howls of victory. The afternoon dragged on, Galilee became an oven. Raymond, seeing that they would never make Tiberias, prevailed upon Guy to change their route, urging him to leave the gentler gradations of the valley and hurry down a dangerous cleft of land to the northeast, near the village of Hattin, its well the only thing standing between them and their creator. As the count gathered the knights of the vanguard, from Antioch, Tyre, and Tripoli, readying them for the charge to open the way, Taliq al-Din and his thousands dashed across the front of the Christian advance to block their path to Hattin. Saladin, the tactician on the hilltop, wanted to keep them as they were, a malevolent mass of infidels, trapped out in the open, dying from a thousand cuts, going mad from thirst.

Raymond's charge never came to pass. Balian of Ibelin, commanding the rear of the column, implored the king: the rear guard had had enough, the men were swooning in the heat; a camp had to be pitched, organized, fortified. Near the village of Lubiya, halfway between Zippori and Tiberias, King Guy gave the order. They would halt there for the night. Count Raymond, far ahead in the unharassed van, learned the news and cried out, "Ah! Lord God, the battle is over! We have been betrayed unto death! The Kingdom is finished!"

≺⊹ ≺⊹   ⊹≻ ⊹≻

The old village of Lubiya is now gone, the land around it cultivated by the Kibbutz Lavi, a cooperative founded by German and Austrian Jews who first fled to England to escape the Shoah, then settled in Galilee in 1949. The kibbutzniks tend pear, lichee, and almond orchards; grow wheat, barley, sunflower, and cotton; and, in a large workshop in the center of the residential complex, make furniture for synagogues throughout Israel. Asher Aldubi, the avuncular fellow who heads the kibbutz, knows full well the significance of the site from which his community draws sustenance. "We have tourists who come to the Horns," he says. "Muslims, mostly . . . The Christians, maybe they are ashamed?"

The part of the valley through which the crusaders passed on July 3, 1187, lies within Lavi farmland. On a nearly imperceptible rise running down the middle of the valley, fragments of the Roman road remain, a few faint traces of classical stone masked by a carpet of spiky weeds. A power line runs alongside it. The view to the north has the sturdy limestone barrier of Mount Tauran perhaps two kilometers away; at an equal distance to the south rise the hills near Nazareth. From either direction, the Muslim harassers had to ride across open country to get at their quarry.

Directly ahead on the line of the march the land dips into a hollow before rising into a lightly forested hill that signals the end of the open valley. Somewhere to the west of this hill, now crowned by the kibbutz buildings, the exhausted Guy ordered the camp to be set up. The Lavi hill is deceptive—beyond it the land does not fall off but rises gently into a prairie of dry grass and twisted chapparal. And the soil itself changes, from porous, water-catching limestone to hard, unforgiving basalt. At the end of this gradual incline stands the unmistakable silhouette of the Horns of Hattin, a low saddle-shaped hill with a pair of grassy brown eminences, resembling pommels, one at each extremity. Its height is not forbidding; approached from the west, through the grassland, a dirt track leads up the twenty meters or so to the summit ridge. There, between the horned peaks at each side, stretches a rectangular depression, no more than a half-kilometer in length. The gray volcanic soil supports a few prickly-pear bushes, cactuslike in their isolation, and gazelle droppings litter the burnt brown grass. Hoopoe birds pop around the expanse, letting out silly cries. Aside from the horns, the hill seems unremarkable, until one turns east and realizes how geology would torment the crusader.

The Horns of Hattin stand on the cusp of a great tear in the fabric of the earth. The Syro-African Rift, which stretches from the Orontes Valley at Antioch all the way to Mozambique, yawns open on the other side the hill, offering a perspective usually associated only with Romantic engravings or cockpit windows. The land falls away into a void, leaving just a view—north toward Lebanon, beyond a screen of taller and taller ranges, the snow-capped height of Mount Hermon towers on the horizon; directly east of the Horns, the great three-hundred-meter-tall bluffs of the Golan rise in tawny majesty and the plateau itself can be seen stretching out to some indeterminate desert horizon. And between the Golan and Hattin, down steeply pitched grassy slopes interrupted by rocky chevrons forming themselves into cliffs, is the floor of the rift, here occupied by the Sea of Galilee, an expanse of the deepest blue 213 meters below the level of the oceans. From the Horns, high up on the parched basalt, the Sea of Galilee is an immodest presence—not only is its color at odds with the surrounding rust and pale green of the land and its vegetation, but its enormous, inexhaustible volume of water seems a calculated insult. Water, jealously hoarded on the upland, covers the rift valley floor, and a whim of geology allows the beholder at Hattin to take in the entire, maddening, vast expanse in a single glance. The crusaders would succumb to thirst in sight of a profligate display of precisely what they needed to save themselves. The men of Outremer were, indeed, beyond the sea.

For the Latin army, the night spent west of Lubiya was agony. Under cover of darkness the Muslim forces crept into the valley to surround the encampment,

The Horns of Hattin, seen from the west. King Guy's last stand took place on the height to the right, which some identify as the site of the Sermon on the Mount.

creating an encirclement so tight, according to a chronicler, that not even a cat could slip through it. By the light of campfires visible to the Latins, Saladin's men ostentatiously poured streams of water onto the ground, to drive the thirst-crazed Christian to despair. A steady succession of camel trains from Tiberias brought the Muslim fighters goatskins filled with water along with thousands of arrows. These were loosed high into the blackness, to fall like deadly rain on the huddled mass of Latins, praying to the True Cross for some miracle to deliver them from doom the next day. The religious volunteers in Saladin's army, non-combatant mystics and jihad enthusiasts, had spent their time on the campaign collecting brushwood and dried grass. These great bundles they set alight, sending a choking pall over the Latin camp. A raging thirst, death falling randomly from the sky, a suffocating nimbus of throat-scorching smoke, and the constant shouts and singing from an enemy so close as to seem in their midst— the long hours of the sleepless night, alive with terrors, gradually sapped the fighting spirit of the thousands of men who had marched smartly out of Zippori the preceding day.

July 4, 1187, dawned hot and airless. Saladin's men had pulled back, allowing a gap through which the foe could proceed, vainly, toward Tiberias. The Latins marched eastward, the sun rising over the Horns of Hattin to shine directly in their faces. Smoke from the brush fires blanketed the route ahead. When the heat of the day had settled once again over the land, the Muslims increased their attacks on the rear and the flanks of the Christian columns, this time with unrelenting ferocity. King Guy and his men struggled over the Lubiya hill to the arid upland of Hattin, not so much running as stumbling through a gauntlet. The foot soldiers, exposed and protecting an ever-dwindling number of horses, could take no more. First singly, then in wild, disordered groups, they ran headlong from the columns, seeking a way out through the broiling heat and the eye-stinging haze to water and to safety. The only route open led to the Horns. They clambered up and away from the din of the battle to the summit ridge. From there, the Sea of Galilee glinted cruelly below them, but the perilous slope down to it was blocked by Saladin's army. A messenger from King Guy ordered his mutinous subjects back to the plain; instead they lay down on the ground, inert and helpless. One of their number explained, "We are not coming down because we are dying of thirst and we will not fight."

Raymond of Tripoli exhorted the knights in the center to hold fast. He would smash through the Kurds on the left and create an opening in the gorge that runs near the northern horn down to the village of Hattin. His charge met no

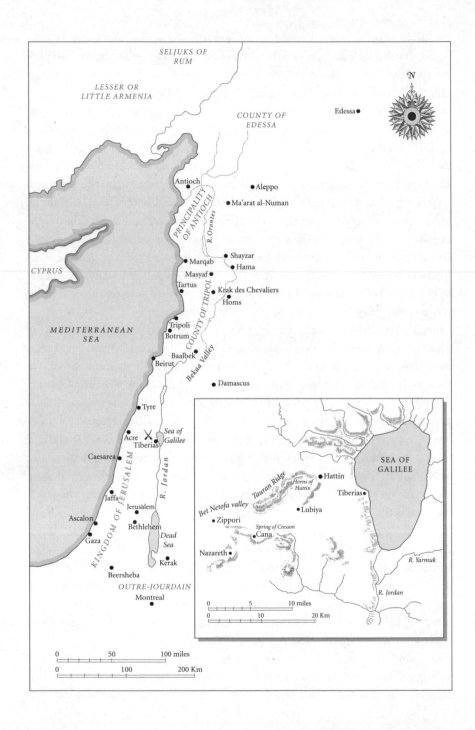

SELJUKS OF
RUM

LESSER OR
LITTLE ARMENIA

COUNTY OF
EDESSA

Edessa●

𝒩

Antioch●

●Aleppo

●Ma'arat al-Numan

PRINCIPALITY
OF ANTIOCH

R. Orontes

●Shayzar
●Hama

Marqab●

Masyaf●
●Krak des Chevaliers

COUNTY OF TRIPOL

Tartus●

●Homs

CYPRUS

MEDITERRANEAN
SEA

Tripoli●
Botrum●

Baalbek●

Bekaa Valley

Beirut●

●Damascus

Tyre●

Acre● ✕ Sea of
Tiberias● Galilee

Caesarea●

R. Jordan

KINGDOM OF JERUSALEM

Jaffa●

Jerusalem●

Ascalon●

Bethlehem●

Dead
Sea

Gaza●

Kerak●

Beersheba●

OUTRE-JOURDAIN

Montreal●

0   50   100 miles

0   100   200 Km

SEA OF
GALILEE

Tauran Ridge

Hattin●
Horns of
Hattin

Tiberias●

Bet Netofa valley

●Lubiya

Zippori●

Spring of Cresson
Cana●

Nazareth●

R. Yarmuk

R. Jordan

0   5   10 miles

0   10   20 Km

resistance; the disciplined formations of Taliq al-Din parted to let the desperate
knights hurtle on through, then closed up behind them. Raymond and his men
thundered down the steep cleft, unable to turn back and help their comrades.
They were safe but dishonored; they spurred their mounts and picked their way
through the highlands to the north back toward the Mediterranean. Before the
year was out Raymond would be dead—of shame, said his enemies.

Up on the plain, the knights were beset on all sides. Guy had set up his tent as
a rallying point on the Horns. Repeatedly the Latins made desperate charges
into the mass of their attackers, trying somehow to cleave a path through to Saladin himself. Taliq's horsemen lunged into the melee, smashing a way to the
True Cross reliquary held aloft by the bishop of Acre. He died defending it, and
Taliq carried it away in triumph. Saladin's fifteen-year-old son, al-Afdal, was at
his father's side in these climactic moments:

The Frankish king had retreated to the hill with his own band and from there
he led a furious charge against the Moslems facing him, forcing them back
upon my father. I saw that he was ashen pale and distraught, and he tugged
at his beard as he went forward, crying: "Away with the Devil's lie." The
Moslems turned to counterattack and drove the Franks back up the hill.
When I saw the Franks retreating before the Moslems I cried out for joy:
"We have beaten them!" But they returned to the charge with redoubled ar-
dour and drove our army back towards my father. His response was the same
as before, and the Franks retired back to the hill. Again I cried: "We have
beaten them!" but my father turned to me and said: "Be silent; we shall not
have beaten them until that tent falls!" As he spoke the royal tent fell and the
Sultan dismounted and prostrated himself in thanks to God, weeping for joy.

King Guy and his men collapsed from exhaustion. Saladin's envoys found
them on the ground, panting from thirst, unable to go on, utterly spent. The great
nobles of Outremer were helped to their feet and led down the slope covered
with the dead and the dying. Saladin welcomed them into his tent. He extended
a goblet of rose water, chilled by snow from Mount Hermon, to the king of
Jerusalem. Guy took a long gulp, then passed the cup to Reynaud of Châtillon.
The sultan peremptorily noted that he had not offered the drink to Reynaud.
Custom held that hospitality implied clemency, and Saladin had made a vow
about the raider of the Holy Places. He berated Reynaud for repeatedly breaking truces and offered to spare him if he converted to Islam. The old knight

refused, truculent to the last. Saladin raised his sword and brought it down deep
into Reynaud's shoulder. A bodyguard then lopped off his head. Guy fell to his
knees, terrified, as the corpse was dragged out. Saladin reassured him, saying,
"A king does not kill a king."

  All of the lay nobles were spared by a gracious Saladin. They would eventually be freed in exchange for great sums of money. One group—the warrior-
monks—had no mercy shown to it. The Templars and Hospitalers ranked as
the sultan's most redoubtable enemies, dedicated to permanent war against the
Muslims. Past experience had shown that they refused to be ransomed and, if
sold, made rebellious slaves. Alive and in captivity, the knights of the Temple
and the Hospital would have been a burden. Saladin handed over the two hundred or so monks to their Muslim counterparts, at least in religious fervor—the
noncombatant volunteers of his army who had answered the call to jihad. One
by one the entire contingent of Templars and Hospitalers was beheaded, in
killings often gruesomely botched by the amateur swordsmen from the
mosques. Only Gérard of Ridefort, in many ways the architect of the disaster at
Hattin, was allowed to live, in deference to his rank and with a view to using
him as a bargaining chip in future campaigns. As for the thousands of ordinary
soldiers on the losing side, they too kept their heads, but were henceforth condemned to a life of servitude. Shackled together, the men of Outremer were led
out of Galilee in a long and sorrowful column destined for the slave markets of
Damascus. Their numbers soon caused a glut in the trade, triggering a sharp fall
in prices. One man, it was said, was sold for a pair of sandals.

⤛ ⤛   ⤜ ⤜

The Kibbutz Lavi has not erected a monument to the battle—the hill called the
Horns of Hattin, untouched and instantly recognizable, is monument enough.
Down the cleft of land where Raymond of Tripoli charged, in the shadow
of the northern horn, stands a large Druze seminary, brilliantly white, built
around what is believed to be the tomb of Jethro, Moses' father-in-law. Beat-up
old cars fill the parking lot, boys and girls run around the tables of a makeshift
café. On the grassy flank of the southern horn, a promising stela turns out to be
Christian, but unrelated to Outremer. On its face is a passage from the Gospel
of Mark (3:13), in which Jesus calls the faithful to a mountain. The inscription
shows that the parishioners of the Church of God of Prophecy, of Cleveland,
Tennessee, believe Hattin to be the setting of the Sermon on the Mount. It is

thus the Mount of Beatitudes. Still a minority view, the Horns have yet to supplant a height near Capharnum, on the north shore of the Sea of Galilee, as the Beatitudes bus stop for Christian pilgrims. Irony would be served if at Hattin the phrase "Blessed are the peacemakers" had first been uttered.

If the mantle of peacemaker could be given to anyone connected to the abattoir of Hattin, the Muslim leader most deserved it. Saladin's actions immediately after his victory were remarkably conciliatory, his reputation for magnaminity growing so bright that some western bards later imagined a Christian mother or grandmother lurking somewhere in his genealogy. In the months following the battle, Saladin preferred accepting peaceful surrender to laying prolonged siege, and he scrupulously honored agreements of safe passage for those willing to quit their strongholds. Much of their Latin soldiery in slavery and their Jewish, Orthodox, and Muslim populations ready to revolt, the port cities of Outremer gave up with barely a whimper. Ascalon, Jaffa, Acre, and Sidon were quickly conquered, leaving only Tripoli and Tyre in Latin hands. Inland, in the Jebel Ansariye, the Hospitaler centers of Marqab and the Krak des Chevaliers were judged to be still too belligerent—no warrior-monk would place himself at Saladin's mercy after Hattin—to be taken without a lengthy and costly assault, although the citadel at Tartus and the Church of Our Lady of Tortosa came under attack.

The eternal prize, the siren of jihad and crusade, fell after a brief siege in the closing days of September 1187. On Friday, October 2, or the twenty-seventh day of Rahab—the anniversary of the Prophet's Night Journey into the heavens—Saladin entered Jerusalem. The al-Haram al-Sharif was reclaimed for the faith, the large cross torn down from the roof of the Dome of the Rock and Nur al-Din's minbar installed within the al-Aqsa Mosque (where it would stand until August 21, 1969, when an insane Australian destroyed it with an incendiary bomb). The Christian impedimenta of Jerusalem were joyously dismantled.

To the Latin populace cowering in fear of Muslim revenge for the atrocity of the First Crusade, Saladin proved notably indulgent, scoring a propaganda victory that still impresses. Under the terms of agreement negotiated by Balian of Ibelin (who had escaped Hattin), each Latin could ransom himself for a small payment, then take all his worldly possessions to Tyre, unmolested. For those too indigent to make the payment, the sultan and his brother opened their purses. Although Saladin's treasurers protested when they saw Eraclius and Madame la Patriarchesse, after paying their pittance, leave in wagons laden with sumptuous vestments and precious vessels, the sultan insisted that the bargain be kept.

(He later gave Eraclius' palace to the Sufis.) Saladin invited the Orthodox Christians to remain in Jerusalem, handing over to them the Church of the Holy Sepulchre, from which they had been evicted by the Latins in 1099. The sanctuary, derisively called the Church of Refuse (based on an Arabic pun that changes "resurrection," *al-qiyama*, into "refuse," *al-qumama*), was deemed pointless to destroy, as Christians would always strive to visit the site, church or no church. The sultan also resettled Jews in Jerusalem, to which they had been barred after the local Jewish population had all perished in the First Crusade's sack of the city.

For Outremer, Saladin's capture of Jerusalem and its kingdom compounded the catastrophe of Hattin. The Latin presence in the Levant was reduced to toeholds on the coast and a few isolated fortresses, almost entirely dependent on Europe for survival. The complex jigsaw of Outremer in Syria and Palestine had been shattered, the inland estates of the poulain aristocracy reverting to Muslim control. Armies assembled in France, Britain, and Germany would periodically take ship for the Levant, but their presence, and their occasional victories, proved ephemeral. King Richard Lionheart, in the storied Third Crusade against Saladin in the wake of Hattin, won back several Levantine ports but signally failed to capture Jerusalem. Less than a century later, the crusader king of France, Louis IX (later St. Louis), failed even more spectacularly in Egypt and then in Tunisia, dying in a futile attack on the Ifriqiyan coastline. In 1291, after generations of attrition, the last mainland holding of Outremer, Akko (St. Jean d'Acre), was abandoned following a ferocious siege. The crusaders of the Levant were gone, but not, by any means, the idea of crusading.

As the victor at Hattin, Saladin gained a lasting place in the history of the sea of faith. Even so, the dynasty he founded—the Ayyubids (after *ibn Ayyub*, or "son of Job")—barely lasted eighty years, his brothers and nephews quickly transforming his empire into a quarrelsome patchwork that would have been familiar to Zengi. In Jerusalem today, the sultan's memory is muted. Near the pools of Bethesda, he makes a fleeting appearance at the crusader Church of St. Anne—yet another spot, like Zippori, said to be the home of Joachim and Anne, the parents of the Mary. The overrestored old chuch bears a twelfth-century inscription over its main portal proclaiming Saladin's conversion of the sanctuary into a madrasa. The vagaries of history have canceled that bequest; in the nineteenth century the Ottoman Turks gave it back to the French, their ally in the Crimean War. More lasting, and far noisier, is East Jerusalem's ever-busy Saladin Street, a Palestinian commercial thoroughfare that leaves the northern walls of the Old City from the Damascus Gate.

The modern equestrian monument to Saladin in front of the Citadel of Damascus.

It is in Damascus, the city of Straight Street, where Saladin is best remembered. Just outside the Umayyad Mosque stands the funerary pavilion dedicated
to the great Kurd. He died in Damascus in 1193, a sultan but almost penniless,
his fortune spent on good works. His medieval resting place—a richly sculpted
wooden bier—now stands under glass, replaced by a marble sarcophagus donated by Germany, to coincide with the visit in 1898 of Kaiser Wilhelm II, then
one among many vultures circling around the collapsing Ottoman dominion.
Saladin thus has two graves, befitting his ambiguous place in historical memory;
in a curiosity of posterity, he was long remembered more in the west than he
was in Islamic countries. For the crusading period, Muslim literature and folk-
tales preferred to celebrate the pious Nur al-Din as well as the scourge of later
Levant Latins, Sultan Baybars of Egypt. European lionizing of Saladin as a
paragon of chivalry—in Walter Scott's *The Talisman*, for example—gradually
seeped into Muslim Arab memory, principally in the colonial period. Only then
was he reclaimed as a Levantine Simon Bolívar, his role as liberator dovetailing
nicely with nascent nationalisms.

More recently, the morass of confessional politics in Israel and Palestine has
given a further fillip to the cult of Saladin. His latest incarnation stands outside
the walls of the old city's citadel, its weathered stones a testament to the successive civilizational layering that is characteristic of the Mediterranean world.
There, in 1992, a Syrian sculptor, Abdallah al-Sayed, unveiled an oversize
equestrian statue of Saladin, to mark the eight hundredth anniversary of his
death in the city. On either side of the stern-faced sultan stand a Sufi swordsman
and a spear-wielding infantryman. Sitting morosely near the animal's rear end
are two saddened crusaders: King Guy holds a bag of money for his ransom;
Reynaud of Châtillon stares at the ground, doomed. Saladin himself, astride a
great mount charging forward, looks eerily like Charlemagne, as depicted before Paris's Notre Dame Cathedral. The sultan is riding west, toward the Golan.
Modern Damascene sweethearts have their pictures taken in front of him.

CHAPTER SEVEN

LAS NAVAS DE TOLOSA 1212

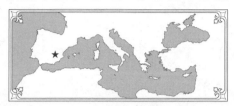

The deathblow to al-Andalus

The Giralda of Seville nicely illustrates the fickleness of confessional allegiances around the medieval Mediterranean. A stately brick and tile minaret completed in the 1180s as proof of the permanence of Muslim rule in al-Andalus, it became, barely sixty years later, the bell tower of a Christian cathedral. In the sixteenth century a weathervane was placed atop the structure, crowned by a statue (*giraldillo*) to spin in the warm breezes blowing off the Guadalquivir. That adornment makes it the superior even of the Mezquita and the Ayasofya in evoking the encounter between Christianity and Islam. Not only does the Giralda display the displacement of one faith by another, but it suggests, thanks to its statue, the workings of chance in deciding which creed would come out a winner.

The Giralda and its giradillo weathervane should be kept in mind when the temptation beckons to view history as a juggernaut, slowly but surely rolling toward a predetermined destination. Neither the Byzantines at Yarmuk and at Manzikert nor the defenders of Muslim Palermo and Toledo thought they were pitching themselves down the maw of the preordained. What, at a distance of several centuries, seems self-evident—the Christian loss of Jerusalem, for example—had nothing of the inevitable about it. Feared by all generals, the breezes of contingency can yield far-reaching results, all the more so when the outcome of battle ends up touching the most profound beliefs of a people—how they see themselves in this world and, especially, in the next.

For the eastern Mediterranean of the time, one can argue that the Latin defeat

The Almohad Giralda of Seville, transformed into a bell tower for the reconquista-era cathedral, the largest Gothic church in the world.

at Hattin quashed an experiment that had been doomed at the outset by the sheer force of numbers. In the west, the events of the early thirteenth century are devoid of such calculations—there was no disparity in forces that would guarantee an outcome. The raids and battles that raged up and down the Iberian peninsula in those years, as cruel and calculating as any in the Levant, were just as much a struggle to fashion the spiritual landscape of a people, but, in contrast to Outremer, the combatants were evenly matched. The stake for the Iberians was the culture in which their descendants would live. In both cases, the memory of what was lost in these years—Outremer and al-Andalus—remains a source of resentment or pride to this day.

In Spain, the bias of the victors comes through in referring to the struggle as the reconquest, *la reconquista*, of the peninsula by the Christians. That label implies they were recovering something that was rightfully theirs in the first place, rather than conquering, plain and simple. Historians of another time, imbued with a certain religiosity, dutifully repeated the term, which was taken up, naturally enough, by pietistic Spanish nationalists who saw the hand of God directing events. The present day is still not immune to the idea of the conquest of al-Andalus as a struggle pitting the native against the foreign: in 1998 one popular historian could write of a twelfth-century Christian effort "to free most of the soil of Spain from its alien invaders." This opinion skirts the awkward fact that by the year 1200 Islam had been installed in Iberia for half a millennium—about the same period of time as it had been present in Syria, and four full centuries longer than it had existed in the Muslim country we now know as Turkey (or, if one prefers, the same length of time Africans and Europeans have been in the Americas). Despite the vicissitudes in its fortunes after the fall of the Umayyads, al-Andalus was a Muslim country of long standing, a venerable constituent of the dar al-Islam. If its leaders in the 1100s and 1200s were, in some ways, "alien" to Spain (Moroccan Almoravids, then Almohads), the bulk of their armies and their subjects were nonetheless Andalusis, as Iberian and indigenous as the Cid himself. A more apt term for the reconquista might be the Medieval Spanish Civil War.

The undercurrent of Iberian convivencia added piquancy to the conflict. Alliances of convenience were often formed between Muslim and Christian chieftains in Spain, many of whom were related through the exertions of their concubines. In Toledo, a remarkable meeting of minds was also taking place. Translators pounced on the works of the philosopher Averroes even as their rulers attacked the cities—Seville, Córdoba, Granada—that were the font of the new knowledge. An odd state of permanent war and heightened cultural intercourse obtained in Spain, as in nowhere else around the Mediterranean. The language later to mature as Castilian Spanish attests to this promiscuity through its adoption of thousands of Arabic words, a wholesale borrowing—estimated at about ten percent of the lexicon—unique among the Romance languages of the Mediterranean. The absorption of al-Andalus into Christendom still echoes wherever Spanish is spoken.

⫷ ⫷   ⫸ ⫸

The years leading up to the watershed of 1212 resemble the long, confused road to successful jihad in Syria and Outremer. Instability and backstabbing prevailed on both sides of the Iberian battle line. Among the Christians the principal divisions were dynastic. In León-Castile, Alfonso VI, the victor at Toledo in 1085 and the vanquished at Sagrajas in 1086, forged a union of north and central Spain, but his descendants wasted little time in tearing it apart. In the early twelfth century a French adventurer given Alfonso's daughter in marriage carved out a separate kingdom for himself, thereby ensuring Portugal an existence independent of the rest of Iberia. In a sideshow there to the disastrous Second Crusade, which failed before Damascus, several boatloads of English, Flemish, and German crusaders bound for Outremer in 1147 were induced to disembark on the Atlantic coast and wrest the town of Lisbon from Islam, their success being the only net Christian gain of that whole sorry enterprise. Elsewhere at the same time Alfonso's grandson, Alfonso VII, conducted a series of merciless raids deep into al-Andalus, but those proved only temporary victories: he had the misguided idea of splitting his inheritance between his sons and thus guaranteed a debilitating power struggle between León and Castile after his death.

The other kingdoms of Christian Spain kept their autonomy, although Navarre, in Basque country, was usually beholden in one way or another to its larger neighbors. Around the time the detoured crusaders took Lisbon, a marriage between the ruling families of Aragon and Barcelona brought those two regions under one lordship. The Crown of Aragon (as the heterogeneous union of inland, feudal Aragon and maritime, merchant Catalonia was known) provided a counterweight to the mounting power of Castile. It conducted its own campaigns against the Muslims during the twelfth century. One Aragonese king, yet another Alfonso, was known as the *Batallador* ("Battler" or "Fighter") for his devotion to warring on the Muslims. Of the twenty-nine battles he won against them—some employing Crusaders returning from Outremer—Alfonso's capture of the great city of Zaragoza in 1118 was the most significant and was rightly seen in al-Andalus as a disaster on the scale of Toledo some thirty years earlier. The Battler subsequently launched a spectacular campaign to the southern extremity of the Iberian peninsula and returned with ten thousand Christians of Granada to settle the valley of the Ebro. The Almoravid emir, urged on by the grandfather of Averroes (who was an official of Córdoba), then took reprisal by expelling many of the remaining Mozarabs to Morocco, to languish in a land that had never known convivencia.

Although the actions undertaken by Christian monarchs against al-Andalus at the time were uncoordinated, the destructive raiding slowly chipped away at the Muslim dominion. The line of the Ebro and the Duero had been breached, the threshold of Medinaceli long since overrun. From their forward position along the Tagus—the river of Toledo and Lisbon—the Christians attacked and repelled attack. Motives, as usual, were mixed. The sophisticated cities of al-Andalus were a mouthwatering prize for the rustic northerners, as were the wide grazing lands of La Mancha and, beyond, the fertile valleys of the Guadiana and the Guadalquivir. Some monarchs managed to combine the earthly and the heavenly better than others. In his will, the childless and quite possibly impotent Alfonso the Battler of Aragon left his entire kingdom to the Templars and other warrior orders, enjoining them to continue his holy fight. Alarmed nobles of the realm weighed in against this bequest, and Aragon narrowly avoided becoming a nation ruled by monks in mail. Instead, Alfonso's brother—an ordinary, pacific monk—was hustled out of his monastery and made a layman and then a monarch in short order.

Still, the Templars and other such orders came to play a greater role in the conduct of the conquest of al-Andalus. Homegrown warrior monasteries sprang up in the twelfth century, the most powerful being the knightly orders of Santiago and Calatrava. The Latin motto of the former, *Rubet ensis sanguine Arabum* (May the sword be red with Arab blood), gives an idea of what their goals entailed. Ironically, the lands around Calatrava, in the dangerous march between La Mancha and al-Andalus, came into Christian hands as part of the dowry of Zaida, Alfonso VI's Sevillan wife and mother of Elvira of Castile, queen of Palermo. In endowering Zaida with this necklace of fortresses, her father-in-law (he of the camel-driver/swineherd comment) had unwittingly given militant Christian knights a redoubt—a ribat, in fact—in which to foster their single-minded devotion to aggression. The castle at Calatrava would fall, be recaptured, be rebuilt, then fall again, but it remained a symbol and a rallying cry for those engaged in expanding Christendom, a Krak des Chevaliers on the *meseta* of Spain. When, as often happened in the struggle for primacy on the peninsula, the Christian monarchs attacked one another rather than the infidel, the friars of Santiago and Calatrava had to defend the marchland alone. Fortunately for them, for much of the twelfth century the Muslims were as divided as the Christians.

◄◄ ◄◄   ►► ►►

The Almoravids, whose empire stretched from the river Niger to La Mancha and from the Algarve to Libya, disappeared from Spain in the middle years of the twelfth century. The hot flame of religious fervor that had animated these Berbers of the ribat had guttered once it came in contact with the refined air of al-Andalus. The Almoravid monarchs, if not their foot soldiers, became as worldly as the latter taifa kings. On doctrinal matters, a literalist, legalistic reading of the Quran—as taught by Almoravid clerics—did not sit well with the native Andalusis; nor did, especially, the ethnic humiliation entailed in being ruled from Marrakesh by Berbers. As early as the 1120s, revolts in the Guadalquivir Valley had become commonplace.

However dangerous such Andalusi irredentism, the fatal blow was delivered in Africa: the Almoravids had to face a rival Berber federation centered on the Masmuda clan of the Atlas Mountains of Morocco. Begun—as had the Almoravid movement—by a holy man returning from an initiatory trip to the east, this new force would eventually crush the Almoravids. Ibn Tumart, the Masmuda visionary, preached such a radical monotheism that his supporters were known as the Unitarians, or *al-muwahhidun* (whence the western word *Almohad*). The Almohads detested the Almoravids, claiming that their pedestrian approach to Revelation had led them into the heresy of ascribing anthropomorphic attributes to the unknowable essence of God. The Quran, the Almohads argued, should be interpreted collectively by the sages leading the community of the faithful. Ibn Tumart, as shrewd and ruthless as the Prophet had been in cementing the umma behind him, allowed himself to be declared a *mahdi*—an infallible emissary of God sent to purify Islam. Armed with this ferocious certitude, the Almohads roared out of the Atlas to eliminate the Almoravids. By the 1150s the Almohad caliph—Ibn Tumart's successor—was ensconced in the palaces of Marrakesh.

The transfer of power in Spain took rather longer, as Iberia was not central to the concerns of the new Berber dynasts. The Almohads first wanted to consolidate their hold on the Maghrib and Ifriqiya—their armies drove the Norman Sicilians of King Roger from the coastline of Tunisia. As these conquests unfolded, in al-Andalus the decades following the midcentury mark saw a period of confusion, a second era of taifas, as Almohad emissaries and Almoravid loyalists waged war from rival cities, all the while trying to counter Andalusi rebels eager to compose with the Christian northerners, their fellow Iberians.

The rebels' greatest figure was one Ibn Mardanish, called King Lobo (Wolf) by the Christians, an accomplished juggler of alliances who successfully parried repeated attacks on his eastern kingdom of Valencia and Murcia. On his death in 1172, however, his sons submitted to the Almohads. Although many Andalusis of Lobo's generation were willing to become vassals of either Castile or the Crown of Aragon in exchange for a measure of self-rule, the Almohads eventually turned the situation to their own advantage, relying on the confessional zeal of volunteer mujahadeen and on the hardening of religious atttitudes among the Muslim Andalusis. Allying with the Christians to fight fellow Muslims was no longer conscionable.

Allying with Christians to fight Christians was another matter. Caliph Abu Yusuf Yaqub, the builder of the Giralda, brilliantly exploited the jealousies and ambitions of rival rulers in the north. Coordinating his actions with those of the kings of Navarre and León, the Almohad leader slipped across the Despeñaperros Pass, the main threshold through the Sierra Morena mountains between Andalusia and La Mancha, and inflicted a severe defeat on the Castilians at the frontier fortress of Alarcos, in 1195. The rout—from which King Alfonso VIII of Castile barely escaped with forty of his knights—horrified Christendom, which was still reeling from the recent disaster of Hattin and the failure of the Third Crusade to recapture Jerusalem. The gains made in Spain by the armies of Christ during a century of intermittent warfare looked to be imperiled; worse yet, the shortsightedness of competing Spanish monarchs was the root cause of the disarray. Excommunications and interdicts flew out of Rome, to little effect. Alone and assailed by its enemies throughout central Spain, Castile barely held on to Toledo in the Almohad onslaught.

Unexpectedly, the Almoravids came to the rescue. Although chased from the Iberian mainland, they had hung on to power on the Balearic Islands. Quick to adopt the piratical mores for which those islands are admirably suited, the Almoravids of Majorca did not limit themselves to spreading seaborne misery—their hatred of the Almohad usurpers ran much deeper. As Caliph Abu Yusuf Yaqub warred in the middle of Spain, the Almoravids harassed his empire. Ten years earlier they had fanned the discontent of subject peoples in Ifriqiya, and their continued campaigns were judged a threat to the Almohad commonwealth. When the caliph died in 1199, his successor— Muhammad al-Nasir—directed his attentions away from Iberia to the conquest of the Balearics. Also, most of the Almohad armies retired across the Strait of Gibraltar to deal with various rebellions, allowing the battered Castile of Alfonso VIII to get back on its feet. However devastating the defeat at Alarcos, the Almohads did not exploit it. A truce was signed between Muslim and Christian in Iberia, giving the northern kingdoms of Spain the opportunity to regroup and, with the passage of time, to resolve their differences. What was needed for a great offensive against Islam was a spirit of collective crusade. It was at this juncture that the most powerful pope of the Middle Ages ascended the throne of St. Peter.

◄┼ ◄┼   ┼► ┼►

In 1198, Lotario dei Conti di Segni, a thirty-seven-year-old Roman nobleman, became the pontiff of Latin Christendom. He took the name Innocent III. Not since Gregory VII, the man who had launched the eleventh-century reform of the Church and freed it from subservience to secular rulers, had such a brilliant and energetic leader worn the papal tiara. To Innocent's mind, he had been awarded "not only the universal church but the whole world to govern." Not surprisingly, given this view, his pontificate proved dangerous to anyone who disagreed with him.

Like many of his predecessors, Innocent wanted to make over the world through crusade; unlike them, he possessed the intellectual, diplomatic, and organizational strengths to give it a try. His reign, from 1198 to 1216, sparked off a series of tumultuous events around the Mediterranean, many of them yielding unwonted results—what today is termed collateral damage. The most resounding, in the encounter between Christianity and Islam, was the fatal weakening of the Byzantine Empire. Innocent's Fourth Crusade, preached enthusiastically at the outset of his pontificate, achieved what for centuries Muslim, Norman, and barbarian armies had not once succeeded in doing: taking and sacking Constantinople. Even for an age of impulsive, often harebrained violence, the event defied all norms.

The catastrophe came about when the northern Europeans of Innocent's

Fourth Crusade, faced with extortionate fees demanded by Venetian mariners for the voyage to Outremer, reluctantly agreed to a novel barter arrangement: in exchange for eventual sea passage, they would do the bidding of Enrico Dandolo, the doge of Venice. After Dandolo—wily, blind, and well into his eighties—had them besiege and destroy a Christian city on the Dalmatian coast that was a rival to Venice, he spirited the Crusaders to the Bosporus, home to his city's other main competitor for maritime traffic in the eastern Mediterranean. Intrigues with a pretender to the mantle of the basileus, long-standing Latin hostility to the Greeks, and a frustrating wait outside the walls of Constantinople, a wealthy city the like of which did not exist in the west—all of these eventually coalesced into a toxic medieval soup of greed and warrior fury.

When the Latins burst through the gates on April 12, 1204, mayhem ensued. It lasted three days, as a world capital uncaptured since its founding in antiquity was stripped of its treasures. Amid scenes of mass murder, whores cavorted on the altar of the Hagia Sophia; monasteries, churches, palaces, and libraries were

Pope Innocent III, as depicted in a fresco in Subiaco, Italy.

looted; and the statuary of classical times, gathered by Constantine for his new capital in the fourth century, was either melted down or carted off as swag. Notoriously, the Hippodrome's bronze equestrian group believed to have been fashioned by Lysippos, the court sculptor of Alexander the Great, made its way to Venice, to become the Horses of St. Mark in that city's cathedral. The crusading Latin bishops particularly prized the holy relics contained in Constantinople, as their transferral to distant European monasteries and churches ensured a steady stream of visitors, blessings—and revenues. A partial inventory of the haul: the Crown of Thorns, a finger of the Apostle Thomas, parts of the True Cross, Jesus' funeral shroud, a vial of Jesus' blood, a vial of the Virgin Mary's milk, and the heads of St. Stephen, the Apostle Thomas, St. John the Baptist, and James (Jesus' brother). The relics contained in Constantinople were so coveted that forty years later the Sainte Chapelle in Paris was constructed to house some of the sacred objects stolen from the Byzantine capital and subsequently bought by King Louis IX of France. The relics were said to cost more than the building.

Innocent, professing chagrin that his armed pilgrims never reached the Levant, nonetheless saw opportunity in the sordid event. The Great Schism of 1054 could be undone, and the independence of the Orthodox Church finally squelched. The pope installed an Italian, Thomas Morosoni, as patriarch of Constantinople, to dispense the Latin rite in the east. Baldwin of Flanders, a leader of the crusade, was crowned Latin emperor of Constantinople. The Greeks were appalled—the survivors of the court moved to Nicaea (Iznik), in Bithynia near the Sea of Marmara, where a Byzantium-in-exile was established under the guidance of the Lascaris family.

Undeterred, Innocent continued his work promoting the faith to the world at large. Under his stewardship the Teutonic Knights, a military order modeled along the lines of the Templars, were encouraged to keep up their raids around the Baltic and deep into eastern Europe, as part of a campaign of armed proselytism. For those already within the bounds of Christendom, Innocent proved even more zealous. Several sects of dissident Christians—heretics, to the Church—had bubbled up in the cultural effervescence of twelfth-century Europe, only to be suppressed with difficulty. With Innocent in charge, the hunt for heretics intensified.

The pope's ire came to be focused on the region of Languedoc, a patchwork of cities and towns whose leaders owed allegiance to France, the Crown of Aragon, and various lesser entities. The greatest nobleman of the area, Count Raymond VI of Toulouse, was of the same Saint-Gilles family that had stormed Jerusalem and, more recently, in the person of Raymond of Tripoli, had unsuccessfully counseled caution at the spring of Zippori on the eve of Hattin. This crusading lineage failed to impress the pontiff, who bewailed the "foxes in the vineyard of the Lord" being sheltered by Raymond of Toulouse and his kinsmen.

Those foxes were the Cathars, or Albigensians, believers in an austere, pacifist form of Christianity. They held the worldly trappings of Innocent and his clergy and the cult of relics to be heretical abominations that proved the message of Jesus had been hijacked by Roman worshipers of an evil, material god. As with the Almoravids and the Almohads on the other shore of the Mediterranean, the enmity between the two sides of the same coin was profound. Innocent dispatched a Castilian preacher of genius, Domingo de Guzmán, the eponym and founder of the Dominican order of friars, to the Midi in the hope of coaxing the Cathars back into the fold. When he failed, and his successor, a Cistercian papal legate, was murdered in 1208, Innocent finally had the pretext to goad the northern nobility of France into a full-scale assault on Languedoc. Known to history as the Albigensian Crusade, the campaign raged intermittently for twenty years, reducing a once-wealthy region to a smoking ruin and consigning thousands to death in battle, captivity, or the flames of giant bonfires in which scores, sometimes hundreds, of unrepentant Cathars were burned alive while their cowled executioners sang hymns to the glory of God. Such was Innocent's response to dissent.

Even without the active promotion of the pope, the era was capable of generating similarly arresting spectacles of piety. In 1212, as the Albigensian Crusade was in full swing, a strange, unsanctioned mass movement took place in northern Europe. A peasant named Stephen in France, and one named Nicolas in the Rhineland, exhorted young men and women to leave their humble occupations in the fields and go marching to Jerusalem, to prove that the poor could succeed where the great lords and ladies of the Second, Third, and Fourth Crusades had so abysmally failed. Long embellished in folklore as the "Children's Crusade,"* this mysterious, spontaneous procession, numbering in the thousands, begged its way down the Rhône and through the passes of the Alps to the ports of the Mediterranean. Although trustworthy contemporary sources are scarce, on arriving at the shore they apparently expected the sea to part to allow them to continue their march. When this did not happen, the movement broke up in confusion. The mariners of Genoa and Marseille no doubt offered passage to

---

*From taking the Latin word used by the chroniclers, *puer*, to mean, literally, "boy" rather than "young fellow" or "landless youth."

Outremer at prices reminiscent of those the Venetians demanded in the Fourth
Crusade. The fate of these starry-eyed youths remains unknown—though
some may well have been lured aboard ships with the promise of free passage,
then been sold on the high seas to Almohad slavers out of Algeria.

The youngsters of 1212, whoever they were, had picked the wrong crusade.
Pope Innocent had chosen that year to turn his attentions to Spain. Truces had expired and the once-quarrelsome Christian kings, hectored by the clergy, were
close to burying the hatchet. Further concentrating minds was a change in their
opponents: having tired of Castilian and Aragonese raids into al-Andalus
following the end of the truce, the Almohad caliph Muhammad al-Nasir finally
acquiesced in calls for jihad from his own clergy and resumed large-scale operations in Iberia. In 1211 an Almohad army had crossed the Sierra Morena and,
after a lengthy siege, taken Salvatierra, a castle manned by the Knights of Calatrava. An outpost of the Spanish warrior-monks in the southern swath of La Mancha held by the Almohads, Salvatierra had long been a bothersome anomaly to the
Muslims. The castle's fall—news of which was trumpeted mournfully from the
pulpits of Europe—occurred too late in the campaign season to follow up with
further offensives. Muhammad retired to Seville, ready to resume the following
year. Clearly, both sides were ready to abandon raiding for waging all-out war.

Innocent thus gave his blessing to yet another crusade. His other initiative,
against the Cathars, was proving a ghastly success: in 1211 his emissaries had
performed the largest auto da fé of the Middle Ages by burning four hundred
Cathars together in a small Languedoc town. Notwithstanding this intra-
Christian violence and that visited upon the Orthodox of Constantinople in
1204, in Spain the pope threatened to excommunicate anyone who engaged in
hostilities against his fellow Christians. He announced a remission of sins to all
who mustered for crusade in Toledo in the spring of 1212. There, King Alfonso
VIII awaited, eager to cleanse the stain of his defeat at Alarcos some seventeen
years earlier. His wife's brother, the late Richard Lionheart, had been a respected crusader; Alfonso aimed to establish an even more glorious legacy.
With Innocent's blessing, the formidable archbishop of Toledo, Rodrigo
Jiménez de Rada, patron of the translators but implacable foe of Islam, agreed
to part with half of the Castilian Church's revenues to finance the crusade.

King and archbishop were doubtless pleased to see the response to Innocent's
summons. Throughout May and June, thousands of soldiers and knights arrived in Toledo and camped out in the Huerta del Rey, the same royal garden
tended by eminent Arab botanists in the day, 150 years previously, when the

monarch's great-great-grandfather, Alfonso VI, had fled León for the hospitality of the taifa king al-Mam'un. The sloping green became a blanket of tents. The citizen militias of most Castilian towns had heeded the call, with Madrid, Ávila, Segovia, Medina del Campo, Cuenca, Huete, Uclés, Valladolid, and Soria furnishing both horse and foot warriors. Also present with his feudal levy was one other powerful Spanish king: Pedro II of Aragon. Still chary of the Castilians, the monarchs of Portugal, León, and Navarre had remained at home, although many of their barons had been permitted to come.

A great number of foreigners were also in the encampment, mostly from France, ever the land of enthusiasts for crusading ventures. Among them with his knights was a vassal of the Aragonese, Arnold Amaury, archbishop of Narbonne. A Cistercian who led the Albigensian crusade in its first few years, Arnold was later credited with having said, in response to a question about distinguishing Cathar from Catholic, "Kill them all, God will know his own." True to their reputation and crusader tradition, the French at Toledo immediately set about despoiling and murdering the Jews of the city, only to be forcibly restrained by the Castilians and Aragonese. Convivencia had never been particularly strong north of the Pyrenees.

Hundreds of kilometers to the south, near Seville, Caliph Muhammad gathered his armies in the same months of 1212. Volunteers for the jihad had streamed first into Marrakesh, then were shipped across the Strait of Gibraltar. An army was assembled from among the cities of al-Andalus, and smaller contingents of Berbers—the crack troops of the force—had also gathered. The treasury had been opened to mercenaries—Turkish mounted bowmen from Anatolia and Arab bedouin irregulars, the latter usually an enemy of the Berber elite. As with the crusade, jihad had momentarily trumped local resentments. Muhammad, a thirty-year-old whose red hair and penetrating blue eyes may have been inherited from his mother, Zahar, a Christian concubine, reviewed his troops down by the Guadalquivir from behind a line of black African bodyguards. The Muslims may have numbered as many as thirty thousand; the Christians, slightly fewer. In June, both armies set out, one heading north, the other, south.

◄◄ ◄◄   ►► ►►

The armies would contend across a terrain of spectacular natural barriers that is the Iberian peninsula's gift to the landscape painter and curse to the empire builder. The demarcation of geological change is unmissable between La Mancha and Andalusia. The gray-green heights of the Sierra Morena—which are not brown (*morena*)—rise at the southernmost edge of the central meseta of Spain, a note of drama closing off a vast expanse of grazing land and waving grains to the north. On the other side of the mountain range the land becomes unruly, folding and crumpling as it leads southward to the valley of the Guadalquivir, every summit, slope, and dale soon covered in a seemingly infinite grid of olive groves. The Manchegan side of the Morena exhibits monotony but no pattern; the Andalusian, the opposite.

Getting from one landscape to another is difficult, as the mountains form a solid pine-covered wall stretching hundreds of meters tall. Here and there, a denuded gray outcropping can be seen, the rock like the pipes of an organ, hinting

The Despeñaperros, the defile through the Sierra Morena that links Andalusia to La Mancha.

at a defile that might somehow lead the way through the barrier. The surest path is the Despeñaperros* gorge, the best natural gap to wind through the maze of rock and tree. Travelers racing along the main Madrid-Seville highway toward the gap must slow once it is reached, for the twists and turns of the road, and the view of the surrounding wilderness, command attention.

At the foot of the descent, in Andalusia, is the village of Santa Elena, a tidy, white settlement with a church to which is affixed an eighteenth-century commemorative plaque to the Battle of Las Navas de Tolosa. The shrine set up in the vicinity by Alfonso VIII has long since vanished. The *navas* themselves— or flats—lie just to the west of the village in a plain studded by hills. The Arabs, by contrast, name the battle after these hills—al-Ikab (mound)—rather than the flat land in between them. The only man-made attraction in the area is an ecological highway rest stop, the Puerta del Andalucía, set up to inform northern Europeans barreling south to the Costa del Sol of the threshold of flora and fauna they have just crossed. No mention is made in the displays of the epochal battle that occurred nearby, but a dirt road leads from the center into the national park of Despeñaperros. There, a kilometer or two farther on, at a site unvisited and unmarked, two armies decided the future of Spain.

◄┼ ◄┼ ┼► ┼►

The progress of the Christian army was chronicled through letters written by Alfonso VIII, Arnold Amaury, and Rodrigo Jiménez de Rada. The crusading force left Toledo in three separate detachments in the days around June 20, 1212, heading south toward the hot plain of La Mancha. Far ahead in the van were the French, led by a Castilian noble, Diego López de Haro. Whether they received the honor of going first because the Toledans desired to see their backs is not addressed in the testimonies.

The army crossed the Christian-held regions south of Toledo, a hilly open range for livestock, without incident. There, in the past few generations the warrior-knights of Calatrava and Santiago, as lords of this marchland, had pioneered the herding and rustling techniques that their descendants in husbandry, cowboys and gauchos, would practice in the New World. Eventually, the expanse that the crusaders traversed would come to be known as New

---

*Politically dubious etymology holds that *despeñaperros*—roughly, "throw the dogs from cliff"—was what the victorious Christians did to the defeated Muslims in 1212.

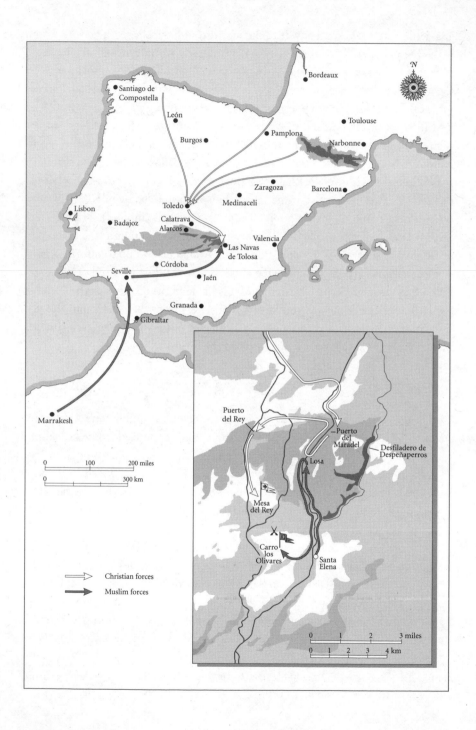

Christian forces

Muslim forces

Castile—like Old Castile in the north, a land named after its surfeit of defensive castles.

At Malagón, a fortress just north of the present-day city of Ciudad Real, the French entered Almohad territory. They besieged the castle without waiting for the arrival of the Castilians or Aragonese. Many of them veterans of warfare in Outremer or Languedoc, they made short work of the defenses of the small fortress town. When the Muslim inhabitants surrendered in the expectation of being shown mercy, they found out that they had been disastrously mistaken. All but three—the lord and his two sons—were put to the sword. By the time Alfonso VIII arrived, the French had appropriated most of the town's booty for themselves.

The crusaders pushed on, picking their way across streams that had been booby-trapped with iron spikes to lame the horses. At Calatrava, a site on the Guadiana River of inestimable significance for the warrior-monks, a halt was called. The friars of the Calatrava order, who had originally taken possession of the castle in 1158 from Templars unwilling to hold it against the Almohad advance, wanted their mother house back, for they, in turn, had lost the fortress after the debacle at Alarcos in 1195. Alfonso, judging the castle likely to occasion a lengthy siege that his massive army could ill afford in the mounting heat of the summer, offered generous terms to the Muslim garrison and townspeople. They could leave, unharmed but empty-handed. Yusuf Ibn Qadis, the Andalusi governor of the castle admired for his comportment in the frontier wars, gladly agreed to Alfonso's generous terms. The governor, according to a chronicler, wanted to save lives.

To the French crusaders, this was the ultimate betrayal. First the Jews of Toledo, now the Muslims of Calatrava—the enemies of their faith were being allowed to go about their business with impunity. The loot from Calatrava could not placate them, even after Alfonso, denying his Castilians their share, split the abundant take in food and weapons between the Aragonese and the French. It was to no avail: the northerners, declaring that the sun had become unbearable, had already decided that these feckless Spanish kings lacked sufficient ardor. They spurred their horses northward, to retrace their route to the Pyrenees and beyond; only Archbishop Arnold Amaury and his 150 knights, vassals of Pedro of Aragon, remained. As the retreating French crusaders passed by the walls of Toledo—which prudently shut its gates to them—they were pelted with refuse.

The caliph, whose spies were at work in the crusader army, must have been

delighted. He ordered his large and unwieldy force to move away from the protective walls of Jaén, the principal city south of the Sierra Morena. He too had
his problems—victualing the great host he had assembled was proving difficult.
Two intendants had been decapitated on his order in early June, and his rough
treatment of the native peasants may have disconcerted his Andalusi troops.
Worse yet for morale was his treatment of Ibn Qadis, the commander who had
surrendered Calatrava. Two Arab chroniclers relate that this great lord, under
whom many of the Andalusi militias had willingly served, was summarily beheaded for giving up the fortress. If news of the French defection—perhaps a
third of the Christians' best heavy cavalry—pleased the Muslim army, the execution of Ibn Qadis could only have sown discord.

The Muslims advanced north to the rough country just below the Despeñaperros Pass. The Almohad leader set up camp near what is now the village of Santa Elena. At this stage he could have moved his army up beyond the
Sierra Morena and deployed it on the wide meseta, but his strategic intention
lay elsewhere. He would have his men block the passageways through the mountains, leaving the Christians stranded in the unforgiving sun of the plateau of
La Mancha. Their propensity for internecine feuding would do the rest. Once a
demoralized, thirsty crusader army had split up in acrimony, Caliph Muhammad, presumably, planned to take the offensive.

For Alfonso and Pedro, the departure of the French may have seemed a
calamity, but the absence of that querulous, headstrong contingent was not
without its benefits. The Spaniards, despite their diverse origins, were united in
purpose, and thus more likely to avoid the pitfalls of indiscipline when the decisive moment arrived. Morale was further raised when King Sancho VII of
Navarre and his knights galloped into view to join the march southward. The
Navarrese monarch had put aside his quarrels with both Aragon and Castile and
decided, not a moment too soon, to participate in a collective effort against al-
Andalus. The threats and blandishments of Pope Innocent had had their desired
effect: three Spanish monarchs had come together, at last, to take on the enemy
as one.

The Christians made their way through Almohad La Mancha, reducing as
many fortresses as they could without getting bogged down in long engagements. Fortunately for Alfonso's pride, the castle of Alarcos, the scene of his
humiliation in 1195, fell quickly. Several lesser strongholds were captured as
well, but another symbol of Almohad triumph—Salvatierra—presented a
dilemma. To lay siege to the great castle would have expended precious time

and effort, and the French, despite their treachery, had been right—the heat was growing stifling. Ten months earlier, the knights of Calatrava had surrendered this island in a sea of Muslim castles. Alfonso proposed attacking it but was dissuaded by Pedro and Sancho, who feared the onset of high summer and the resulting strain on the army's stores. Further dissension arose when news reached the camp of the actions of the king of León. Immune to the threats of excommunication issued by Innocent earlier in the year, the Leonese monarch had taken advantage of the absence of his rivals to launch an attack on northern Castile. Alfonso, arguing that the large army gathered at Salvatierra would never be equaled in power, advocated heading back up north to confront his treacherous neighbor. The Almohads were as good as beaten, Alfonso maintained—their army had failed to show up for a fight. Sancho of Navarre was not amused and reminded the Castilian that he had joined forces with him to fight Muslims, not Christians. In the end, the Spaniards staged a great parade before Salvatierra, marching past its fortifications with banners flying and reliquaries held high. The ceremony took place less to impress the Muslim garrison than to reassure themselves.

⤙ ⤙ ⤚ ⤚

The wall of the Sierra Morena now stood before them. Knowing the Despeñaperros to be stoppered tight by enemy forces, Alfonso asked his able deputy, Diego López de Haro, the Castilian noble who had chaperoned the obstreperous French through La Mancha, to scout for another pass over the mountains. Don Diego led a small detachment up to a height to the west of Despeñaperros called the Puerto Muradal. The Muslims lay in wait, but the Castilians had the better of the day. They gained a small but serviceable plateau atop the sierra—and the following day, the rest of the army joined them. From there they could see, a few kilometers distant in the haze, the Muslim forces massed in the low hills to the south. A red silk tent signaled the presence of the Miramamolín, the melodious Spanish corruption of *amir al-muminin*, the commander of the faithful, or caliph. The foe was in sight, but there remained the problem of getting to grips with him. Don Diego once again went scouting. The most direct way down to the valley, through a narrow canyon known as the Losa, was a death trap. Muslim archers waited in ambush. "A thousand men," Alfonso later wrote the pope about the Losa, "could hold it against all the men there are under heaven." Nearby, other defiles carved by the annual runoff of winter rains were bone dry, overgrown, and impossibly steep. After a few deadly skirmishes, Diego's men found that even these egresses were alive with hidden defenders. They were stuck on the Puerto Muradal, their only option retreat.

What happened next, as recounted in the letters of Alfonso and the archbishop of Toledo, strains verisimilitude, but the fact remains that somehow the Spaniards managed to get off the arid mountaintop safely. According to these accounts, after a somber, inconclusive meeting of the monarchs, the nobles, and the friars, a bedraggled villein was brought into the presence of Alfonso, later identified by legend as St. Isidoro, the patron of Madrid. The man, a shepherd, offered to show another route leading down the southern face of the sierra. He claimed the Muslims did not suspect its existence. Given the army's parlous situation, Alfonso ordered Diego to go off with the stranger and see if what he said was true.

It was. A kilometer or two farther west, a small declivity on the summit, called the Puerto del Rey, led to a *cañada*, or sheep run, that wound down to the south. At daybreak on July 14, the vigilant Muslims may have believed that their strategy had paid dividends: the height of the Muradal, on which they had stranded the crusaders, was empty. The Christians, they thought, had given up and gone away. What the Muslims could not see was that very early in the morning of that day, the entire crusader army had picked its way laterally to the west, high up the northern slope of the Morena, just below the summit ridge and thus out of sight to anyone peering upward from Andalusia. Eventually they reached the Puerto del Rey and hurried across it—in full view of the Muslim sentinels below. The alarm was sounded and skirmishers headed to the hills to impede the Christians toiling down the narrow path below the pass. The Muslims loosed arrows, threw spears and rocks, trying to stem the flow of man and beast pouring down the mountain, but to no avail. At the bottom, about a mile south of the Morena, rose a flat-topped hill called the Mesa del Rey. The Spaniards, outnumbering the hastily assembled defenders, fought their way to the top of the eminence. By late morning, thousands of men and horses covered the mesa, tents had been erected and standards bearing the cross raised around the encampment.

The caliph's commanders tried to engage with the enemy immediately. They moved their forces the few kilometers west from the original encampment near the foot of Despeñaperros to a position facing the Christians, most likely to the hill, or *al-ikab*, now called Olivares. It was an axiom of medieval warfare that an army just arrived from a long march was at its most vulnerable—and these Christians were hardly fresh, having crossed New Castile and La Mancha for three weeks in the scorching heat, spent two days marooned on a mountaintop, then guided horses and pack animals down the steep slopes of the Sierra Morena that very morning. The great kettledrums rolled, and the caliph's army advanced into the plain between the Olivares and the Mesa del Rey, arrayed for battle.

The Christians did not move. The quarrels of their crossbows chased away those foolhardy enough to come too close to their encampment. Safe atop their slightly wooded mesa, impervious to attack, on a naturally fortified position, they could choose the moment of battle. By late afternoon, the Muslim commanders realized the futility of their stance and moved back to their camp at the Olivares. The caliph's tent was pitched on its summit, and the Turks, Arabs, Berbers, and Andalusis settled down around this new emplacement.

The following day was a Sunday. The tired armies of the three Spanish kings took their day of rest. When the Almohad forces formed their battle lines once again, they were confronted with the same passive response. By noon, everyone was back at camp, surveying the other side, playing dice, praying, waiting for the next day. The decisive battle would take place on Monday, July 16, 1212.

The Christian battle order was quite simple. The three kings and the various mailed bishops and their vassals occupied the rear guard, Alfonso in the middle, Pedro on the left, and Sancho on the right. An intermediate contingent, composed of a mix of citizen militias and warrior-monks, stood in front of each sovereign. In the vanguard, dead in the center, were the shock troops of the Christian army, the vassal knights and kinsmen of Diego López de Haro. An anecdote holds that his son, born of a mother who had deserted the family, tried to stoke his father's belligerence by saying that he never wanted to be known as "the son of a coward," to which Diego replied, "They'll call you the son of a whore, not the son of a coward."

This vanguard began the encounter. Racing down the Mesa del Rey, Diego and his men plowed into the slowly advancing center of the caliph's men, composed of religious volunteers, many of whom had never seen battle or were past the age of putting up a good fight. The Castilian knights mowed them down, hacking their lines to pieces in a horrific one-sided encounter.

Once they had finished butchering the volunteers, Don Diego and his men began the ascent of the Olivares, which was crowned by their goal, the red tent of the Miramamolín. Between them and it stood the regular contingents of the

Almohad army, shields planted in the ground, Berber horsemen ready to dart out between foot soldiers, spears, lances, and scimitars at the ready. The Castilian knights struggled up the slope and attempted to pierce the Almohad line, but it was too strong. Don Diego's men faltered, began to fall back, losing ground and momentum as the Berbers let out war cries and counterattacked.

The second corps of the Christian center advanced, over the carnage of the Muslim volunteers, toward the melee that was now backing down into the plain. Diego's embattled vanguard, forced rearward by the Berbers, came crashing into this second line of combatants, the Spaniards a confused mass beset on all sides. The day seemed to be going for the caliph. Battle standards wavered in the dust and shouting, as the Christians desperately tried to hold their ground but seemed poised to desert en masse. From his vantage point atop the Mesa del Rey, King Alfonso is supposed to have turned away from the disheartening spectacle and said to Rodrigo Jiménez de Rada, "Archbishop, let us die here, you and I."

Although there is no shortage of accounts of the battle, many of them at this point turn to miracles for an explanation of the ensuing action. A cross appeared in the sky; a pennant carried into the thick of the fighting remained unsullied; various saints appeared to slay the infidel. What can be stated with a degree of rationality is that the kings in the rear guard, sometime in the late morning, gave the order to charge. A fresh wave of armored knights rolled off the Mesa del Rey and smashed into the fray. For reasons that cannot be adequately explained, the Muslims then collapsed. One source speaks of the Andalusis on the wings of the formation running away without ever having fought. Others say that the soldiery's discontent over pay arrears and mistreatment ran so deep that even the smallest reversal of fortune was enough to spark off a generalized retreat. Whatever the reasons, the giralda of contingency spun to favor the Christians. The battle became a rout. The caliph leaped onto a fast steed and galloped back to Jaén, and thence all the way to Seville. His followers were not so lucky—in the hills and hollows south of the battlefield a great throng of distraught, disorganized men fled in panic, to be hunted down for the rest of the day and night and slain by the thousands. Alfonso, Sancho, and Pedro had won an unimaginable victory. They followed it up in the ensuing days by attacking Baeza and Ubeda, well into al-Andalus. These Muslim cities fell to the medieval conquistadors, and all of their inhabitants were either slaughtered or sold into slavery. Innocent, on learning of his crusade's great triumph, had church bells peal across the length and breadth of Christendom. The impiety that was al-Andalus still stood, but the day of Las Navas de Tolosa had doomed it.

⤝ ⤝   ⤞ ⤞

The poet Abu al-Baqa al-Rundi, from Ronda, summed up the feeling of sad bewilderment felt through the dar al Islam at the events of the half-century following Las Navas de Tolosa:

> Therefore ask Valencia what is the state of Murcia; and where is Játiva, and where is Jaén?
> Where is Córdoba, the home of the sciences, and many a scholar whose rank was once lofty in it?
> Where is Seville and the pleasures it contains, as well as its sweet river overflowing and brimming full?
> [They are] capitals which were the pillars of the land, yet when the pillars are gone, it may no longer endure!
> The tap of the white ablution fount weeps in despair, like a passionate lover weeping at the departure of the beloved,
> Over dwellings emptied of Islam that were first vacated and are now inhabited by unbelief;
> In which the mosques have become churches wherein only bells and crosses may be found.
> Even the mirhabs weep though they are solid; even the pulpits mourn though they are wooden!

In the end, the actors of the battle, save the fighting archbishop of Toledo, did not live to see the further triumphs of Christian Spain. Caliph Muhammad al-Nasir died in 1213—of drink, it is thought—in Marrakesh. He was succeeded by an incompetent. In the same year Pedro II of Aragon met a paradoxical end, this time fighting *against* a crusade: that of Innocent's French eviscerators of the Cathars in Languedoc. Alfonso VIII passed the following year, his work to be left up to his grandson, Fernando III. Canonized in the seventeenth century, Fernando was a man of great piety and martial skill, a Nur al-Din of Christendom. As the Almohads plunged into a swift and irreversible decline in Morocco and the rest of the Maghrib, the Castilian monarch doggedly campaigned to carve up their Iberian possessions: Jaén fell to him in 1246, Seville in 1248. When Córdoba was taken, Archbishop Rodrigo Jiménez de Rada wrote of the capture of Abd al-Rahman's exquisite Mezquita: "Once the filth of Muhammad had been eliminated and holy water had been sprinkled, they transformed it into a church, erected an altar in honor of the Blessed Virgin and solemnly celebrated mass." Fernando shipped Almanzor's bells-turned-lamps back to the pilgrimage site of Santiago de Compostela. Only the kingdom of Granada held out, through diplomacy and the strength of its arms. It would survive the Battle of Las Navas de Tolosa for an unlikely 280 years and mark its passage indelibly by building the Alhambra.

Today the battlefield lies unvisited, except by hunters and their prey, in a national park. The Mesa del Rey is clearly distinguishable, a great wooded hill in the shape of a capsized rowboat. Local archaeologists have discovered the iron detritus of medieval battle everywhere in the area. Finding the passageway that the shepherd showed Don Diego is more problematic. The paths of the sierra wind back and forth through the scrub, the only true route being, as always, an old Roman road of the mare nostrum, its paving stones instantly recognizable. The village of Las Navas de Tolosa lies a good ten kilometers from the site and is now a suburb of the busy market town of La Carolina, named for the king (Carlos III) who invited central European peasants to found a settlement there in the seventeenth century as a means of pacifying an area then infested with bandits. In La Carolina stands a stern monument to the battle, in a scruffy park orphaned by an expressway. Erected in the Franco era, it shows a group of kings and clergy standing behind shields, their white figures elongated, their faces stern. Behind them rise two slim walls of concrete, between which hovers a cross in a nod to one of the miracle stories. The overall effect is mournful, especially given the monument's placement in a spot best driven by at great speed.

To be sure, monuments to the battle are scattered throughout Spain. In Jaén, the administrative capital of the province in which the clash took place, a tall, elegant column commemorating the victory stands at the intersection of two busy boulevards. In Vilches, a hilltop town near Santa Elena, a banner said to have been carried by the Christians into battle hangs in the darkness of the town's main church; at the convent of Las Huelgas, founded by Alfonso VIII in the northern city of Burgos, an enormous swath of cloth advertised as the personal standard of the Miramamolín adorns a wall. However touching the sympathetic magic once attributed to these objects, the most important monument to Las Navas de Tolosa and its pivotal role in history will always be intangible.

The monument to Las Navas de Tolosa at La Carolina. The figures depicted are three Spanish kings and the archbishop of Toledo.

In this respect, Spain is one of the most interesting places of memory around the sea of faith, as it partakes of a shared recollection. Al-Andalus remains a presence in Arab-language lore and literature, its loss keenly felt. Any comparison with Latin melancholy over the collapse of Outremer is far-fetched—for those present-day westerners who do not subscribe to the newly revived idea of a militant Christianity, the Crusades are an era to lament, not for passing, but for having occurred in the first place. Not so al-Andalus: in the memory of Muslims—and of Jews, who would suffer greatly as a result of the regained Christian ascendancy—the era resembles a golden age, the polyglot poets and superb craftsmen overshadowing, in recollection, the cruelties and wars that were a hallmark of the age.

As for the descendants of the victors, the time of unquestioning acceptance of the narrative of king and bishop is most definitively over. The Spaniards, alive to their history in a way not seen in other western European countries, are in the process of reclaiming their memory from pious legend. A historiographical struggle has been joined. In the Spanish province of Andalusia, the scene of so much reconquista lore, the authorities have laid out tourist routes celebrating the Islamic past. Impeccably maintained secondary roads have been branded with colorful iconography indicating the Route of the Caliphs, or the Route of the Nasrids (Granada's last taifa dynasty). The pendulum of memory is swinging toward a reconciliation of many different traditions. In the summer of 2004, the provincial government of Jaén announced it was budgeting one million euros for the construction of a museum on the site of the battle of 1212. One suspects that it will commemorate both al-Ikab and Las Navas de Tolosa.

CHAPTER EIGHT

THE SEA OF FAITH

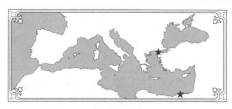

*Missionaries, merchants and monarchs, a convivencia of
contradictions; the thirteenth and fourteenth centuries; the rise of
the Ottomans*

Damietta (Dumyat, Egypt). Saladin's nephew, Malik al-Kamil, the Ayyubid sultan, must have been bemused when his mamluks hauled a gray-
robed, sandal-shod Frank into his presence. The year was 1219. A day's ride to
the north of the sultan's encampment, the knights of the Fifth Crusade were
massed in the Nile Delta, where they had been trying to take the town of Damietta. Despite the perils of the hour, the visitor would not have troubled the sultan overmuch, for the family of al-Kamil had a long history of dealing with
invading Franks. Al-Kamil's father, at the bidding of his brother, Saladin, had
gone on repeated missions of mediation to the camp of the Franks during the
Third Crusade in the 1190s. So taken was King Richard Lionheart with al-
Kamil's father that he briefly floated the idea of giving him his sister. The
woman in question, Joanna of England, became "furious with indignation and
wrath" at the thought of wedding and bedding an infidel—although her eventual mate, Raymond of Toulouse, the protector of the Languedoc Cathars,
would scarcely be any more pleasing in the eyes of Catholic orthodoxy.

Sultan al-Kamil's visitor on that day of 1219 was not a heretic, but neither was
he an ordinary Christian. Disheveled, dirt poor, and—like so many spiritual
rabble-rousers of the age—charismatic, Francis of Assisi had been spared from
excommunication several years earlier by Innocent III, who, so the story goes,
saw in a dream that the tatterdemalion piety of the Franciscans would reinvigorate the Church. Innocent, who died in 1216, four years to the day after Las
Navas de Tolosa, would never know of his protégé's Egyptian exploit: Francis

had slipped out of the crusader camp before Damietta and made the risky journey across hostile territory, animated by a simple, if herculean, goal—to convert Sultan al-Kamil's subjects to Christianity. Failing that, perhaps someone
would make him a martyr.

The ruler of Cairo, a worldly Muslim accustomed to the excesses of his Sufis,
gave the man a polite hearing. According to the hagiographers of Francis, the
sultan came away so impressed with the saint's pious harangues that he tried to
load him down with gifts, all of which the holy ascetic refused—thereby re-
doubling al-Kamil's admiration for him. What actually transpired during this
peculiar interview will forever remain unknown, save that Saladin's nephew allowed Francis to talk—and to live. And that each man kept worshiping his own
god. Dante Alighieri wrote in Canto XI of his *Paradise*:

> Then in the haughty presence of the Sultan,
> urged by a burning thirst for martyrdom,
> he preached Christ and his blessèd followers,
> but, finding no one ripe for harvest there,
> and loath to waste his labors, he returned
> to reap a crop in the Italian fields.

The sultan's meeting with the ecstatic genius of Assisi can be seen as emblematic
of the next two centuries around the Mediterranean. There would be more to the
relationship between Christian and Muslim than merely the sword or the study
room. On that occasion in Damietta, a steely-eyed realist came up against a foot-
in-the-other-world fanatic. Others like them would meet in many places of the
Mediterranean of the time, an era when medieval convivencia took on its broadest
meaning. Muslim and Christian were no longer strangers anywhere around the
inland sea; their commingling, centuries old, had gone beyond sibling rivalry to
become acrimonious and accommodating all at once. This was the fullest sense of
convivencia, where strife and friction went hand in hand with acceptance of the
other. In a time of crusade and reconquista, it was not, however, a synonym for
conviviality. The stalemate of the thirteenth century around much of the Mediterranean would lead to the drama of the fourteenth, when a powerful new force
emerged in the east that would soon rock all the boats on the sea of faith.

⤛ ⤛   ⤜ ⤜

There are two types of people:
Those with brains and no religion,
And those with religion and no brains.

This observation by an eleventh-century Syrian poet, pithy and perhaps unfair, points to a truth about degrees of piety. The same thirteenth-century Mediterranean that bred a Francis of Assisi, whose life was devoted to imitating Jesus's apostles, could also give rise to a merchant of Genoa, or Venice, who was as at home in the great Islamic entrepôts of Alexandria or Cairo as any of his Muslim hosts. On both sides of the confessional divide were those more than willing to consort with their opposite numbers, their religious allegiance less important than the business of life—and those who despaired of such promiscuity.

For the devout of Islam, the blows of Las Navas de Tolosa and other successes of the Spanish Christians had landed hard. In some regions taken by the Crown of Aragon, Jews and Mudejar Muslims were herded into churches for compulsory lectures on the superiority of Christianity. God had previously beamed on the Muslims—in the wake of the Arab conquests a worthy of Syria had remarked to a Christian monk, "It is a sign of God's love for us and pleasure with our faith that he has given us dominion over all regions and all peoples." Now events in Spain and elsewhere seemed to be proving the opposite.

In 1258 Baghdad was overrun by a ferocious invader from easternmost Asia: the armies of the Mongol khan. The great city on the Tigris was long past its heyday, but its sack profoundly shocked the Muslim world—just as the fifth-century Visigothic capture of Rome had shocked the Christians of the mare nostrum. The last Abbasid caliph of Baghdad, the symbol of Qurayshi continuity, was rolled up in a carpet and then stomped to death by Mongol warhorses. It is believed that the victorious general, Hulegu, influenced by two of his Nestorian Christian wives, ordered only Muslims and Jews to be killed in the ensuing massacre. The Christians of the city were spared. If true, the catastrophe smacked uncomfortably of divine retribution.

To explain Islam's reversal of fortune, people of the time had no shortage of culprits at which to point fingers. The umma had become a fractured family of warring dynasts, its divisiveness at odds with the message of brotherhood preached by the Prophet. If its leaders would but adhere to the tenets of Islam, the message came thundering from the minbars, then the faith would not suffer such devastating losses. Even Saladin's lineage, the Ayyubids, broke his kingdom up into squabbling principalities immediately after his death. As a result, the weakened Ayyubids lasted no longer than three generations in power—their Turkish slave soldiers, the Mamluks, took over from them. In Anatolia, the descendants of the Seljuks engaged in incessant internecine wars. North Africa presented a similarly dismal spectacle.

Some went beyond simply lamenting the chronic instability of Islam and praying for a change in men's hearts. In the fourteenth century, a historian of genius, Ibn Khaldun, looked for a reason behind the fratricide that characterized much of Muslim past, taking as his subjects the Almoravids and Almohads of his native Morocco. For Ibn Khaldun, religious faith may have been an important impetus behind empire-building, but also present were the virtues and vices of *asabiyya*—that is, the ties of loyalty that bind kinship groups and extended clans and that aid in the capture and maintenance of power. A sympathetic observer of the misfortunes to have befallen Islam, Ibn Khaldun saw asabiyya seconding religion as a source of the success of the faith. This partly sociological view of events, revolutionary in a time when the hand of the divine was a palpable presence in men's affairs, held that the ties of kinship inevitably weakened once an empire was established and that the ruling elite separated itself from its fellows. This disintegration of asabiyya guaranteed decline, which was thus not entirely the result of wrongdoing or of God's displeasure—or, indeed, of external enemies. Laying Muslim woes at the doorstep of Christianity would not have occurred to Ibn Khaldun.

In this, he was joined by most other apologists of Islam, which is important to underscore, given attitudes on the other side. The knights invading al-Andalus and the Near East were certainly the enemy of Islam, but their religion was less so—an ambivalence that lies at the heart of Islam's relationship with Christianity in the Middle Ages, and even today. To a pious Muslim, the Christians had somehow deviated from the true message of Jesus, and it was only through the Prophet's teachings that a correct reading of Jesus' life was possible. The holiness of the Virgin Mary, the overarching influence of Jesus—all of this was undisputed in Muslim doctrine. What was disputed were his divinity, the triune nature of God, the idea that God could have a son-God born of a woman, and that this God could die. Jesus was a great man, in this view, but his rising from the dead had to be nothing more than a mere fable. In the Dome of the Rock, commissioned in the infancy of Islam, the inscription on its southeast wall could not be plainer: "O you People of the Book, overstep not bounds in your religion, and of God speak only the truth. The Messiah, Jesus, son of Mary, is only an apostle of God, and his Word which he conveyed unto Mary, and a Spirit proceeding from him. Believe therefore in God and his apostles, and say not Three. It will be better for you. God is only one God. Far be it from his glory that he should have a son." More offensive, for polemicists, was the symbolic cannibalism at the heart of the Christian Eucharist, as well as the elements of pagan idolatry in the reverence lavished on icons, crucifixes, and the like. Christendom's warriors might give the dar al Islam many sorrows, but their faith, though a corruption of Quranic teachings about Jesus, merited a measure of respect.

◄← ◄←   →► →►

For many in the other camp during this period around the Mediterranean, respect could not possibly play a role in acceptance of the status quo. Despite the successes in Spain and in the islands of the western Mediterranean, where the Catalans and the Genoese swept all before them, the failure of the crusades to Palestine, as well as other expeditions throughout the Mediterranean, still rankled. As the thirteenth and fourteenth centuries progressed, successive misadventures in north Africa and the Holy Land took their toll on crusader zeal, and the string of ports that constituted the reduced Outremer coastline became subject to bickering and bloodshed among merchants, noblemen, and warrior-monks. For Christians, then, the period looked bleak as well, but—in an important distinction—the continuing existence of Islam represented a slap in the face.

Unlike Muslim ambivalence toward Christianity, the pious Christian could not countenance the other faith, as it constituted an outright denial of revealed truth. Christianity held that Jesus had no successor in the line of prophets, as Islam outrageously posited. The Messiah had come. Thus, for Christian thinkers, the Quran was not so much a corrupted scripture as a corrupt fraud. The two landmark translations of the Quran done in Toledo in the twelfth and thirteenth centuries—the first for the head of Cluny, the second for Archbishop Rodrigo Jiménez de Rada—were undertaken not to study or understand Islam but to ridicule and denigrate it.

This fundamental hostility accounts for the lush forest of medieval Christian polemic concerning Islam. The first dhimmis, in conquered Syria and Spain, had shrugged off the newcomers as passing irritants attached to a Christological curiosity. Once Islam's staying power sank in and the faith won over millions of theretofore fervent Christians, the invective from a defensive Church flowed freely. Muslims were idolaters, their shrine at Mecca the scene of bloodthirsty orgy and incestuous filth. The standard calumnies about religious deviants from classical times—much of it originally aimed at Christians—were repeated and embroidered upon, to paint a repulsive portrait of Arabian paganism.

As familiarity with Islam grew through centuries of commingling around the inner sea, the charge of paganism could no longer be sustained. In its place came the widely accepted notion of Islam as a virulent heresy, akin in noxiousness to the creed preached by the Cathars. The heresiarch, Muhammad, received especial attention, the purveyors of polemic rising to new heights of inventiveness in producing hostile biographies of him as early as the tenth century. Not only was Muhammad a false prophet, he was a charlatan who faked miracles and passed off his epileptic fits as moments of divine inspiration. He concocted his postseizure revelations on the advice of Jews and the supposedly heretical Christian monk who had recognized his potential in Bosra, Syria. On Muhammad's death, the Prophet's body was left outside in the expectation of his resurrection; dogs—or pigs—feasted on the unusually foul-stinking corpse until nothing was left but his feet. Chagrined, his followers had his few remains placed in a metal box, which they suspended in midair through the use of concealed magnets so as to fool the credulous. Such was the content of the Kaaba, the boxlike building draped in black, of Mecca.

That sampler of vituperation pales in comparison to the stories circulated about the Prophet's personal life. Scholars of the subject underline that much of the slandering of Muhammad revolved around his supposedly insatiable carnal desires. This line of thought was perhaps inevitable, for the study of a happy polygamist by celibate, misogynist clerics could hardly fail to bear strange fruit. The incorrigibly lascivious Muhammad was said to have partaken of all of his warriors' comely wives, to have forced himself on the young of both sexes, and even to have boasted that he would, on entering Paradise, deflower the Virgin Mary. These, and other stories of this nature, gained currency in many quarters of Christendom, which by the thirteenth century was prepared to be titillated by similarly unedifying tales of heretics and Jews. As the Church grew more repressive—these years saw the founding of papal inquisitions—the faintest whiff of subversiveness toward the prevailing view of Christian superiority became suspect. A thirteenth-century chronicler of León, aware of the attainments of the Andalusi civilization that his Christian lords were conquering, claimed that Islam's impressive catalog of speculative philosophy arose from a theft of Christian thinking hundreds of years earlier. A great cache of stolen Visigothic treatises had eventually made its way to none other than Avicenna, who hauled it off to Baghdad for translation into Arabic. The translations made, the Christian originals were then consigned to the flames by the Muslim copycats. We can only guess at whether this tall tale betrays ambivalence or embarrassment about the transmission of knowledge still under way in Toledo and Palermo.

There were many other strains of polemic regarding Islam, one of the most important seeing Muhammad as the Antichrist—or, alternately, the six-hundred-year perdurance of Islam as prelude to the End Days prophesied in the Book of Revelation. Ingenious calculations about the age of the earth and the corresponding eras of mankind were commonplace in medieval millenarian writing. Pope Innocent III had crunched the numbers when he evoked the approaching apocalypse as justification for calling a Fifth Crusade—the one on which Francis of Assisi had taken ship. Some of Innocent's successors would see the sudden advent of the Mongols, who devastated not only the dar al Islam but also parts of Russia and eastern Europe, as the coming of the armies of Gog and Magog, yet another event foretold by John of Patmos in his New Testament apocalypse. In this grand view, the Muslims became lumped in with the Jews—instruments for the fulfillment of Christian prophecy.

That still left the problem of what to do with them. For the supremely assertive Church of the thirteenth century, passivity in the face of the unfolding eschatological plan was unacceptable—action was necessary, which would help bring about the realization of the divine design. As Christendom bore down on its own dissidents and minorities through persecution and inquisition, many of its most militant believers quit Europe to travel through the dar al Islam on proselytizing missions. Francis of Assisi may have met with no success, but his followers soon hit upon the tactic practiced hundreds of years earlier by the martyrs of Córdoba: goad Islamic authorities into killing them. Thus martyred, the missionaries' sanctified remains would work miracles and thereby effect wholescale conversion of the infidel.

Armed with this logic, Franciscan friars took to the streets of north Africa and, to the acute discomfort of local Christian minorities, loudly insulted the Prophet and all his works. Unlike the martyrs of Córdoba, these Franciscans were not working at home—they had crossed the sea to give offense in an alien culture. Like their predecessors, however, many of the Franciscans suffered the indignity of leniency from the qadis who wanted no communal trouble in their cities. Eventually, the more persistent got their wish: five friars were executed in Marrakesh (1220); six, in Ceuta (1227); two, in Valencia (1228); five, again in Marrakesh (1232); one, in Fez (1246); and seven, in Tripoli (1289). St. Bonaventure, the scholar leading the Franciscan order from 1250 to 1274, wrote that "to long for death for Christ, to expose oneself to death for Christ, and to delight in the agony of death is an act of perfect love." This danse macabre of the Franciscans was one extreme of Christian reaction to Islam.

⤛ ⤛   ⤜ ⤜

Of the people the Syrian poet called "those with brains and no religion," there is no better exemplar than Frederick II, the Holy Roman Emperor in the first half of the twelfth century. Known in his day as Stupor Mundi—the Wonder of the World—Frederick was a polyglot artist and autocrat who, through a latticework of royal marriages, had inherited the Norman kingdom of Sicily as his birthright. He lies today with King Roger in the Palermo cathedral, both larger-than-life monarchs ensconced in fittingly oversize porphyry sarcophagi. Their chapel, also fittingly, is the farthest from the altar.

Frederick represented convivencia in all its contradictions. A brutal tyrant in the Byzantine mold, he so alienated Muslim peasants and barons of Sicily that repeated revolts against his rule occurred—leading him to deport the majority of them from the island and extinguish the presence of Islam there. Yet at the same time Frederick showed himself an adept at oriental panache, traveling to overawe his vassals on the Italian mainland in the company of a menagerie of exotic birds; an escort of elephants, camels, and tigers; and a personal body-guard composed of Muslim swordsmen. His contribution to literature—a manual on falconry, the Islamic princely pastime par excellence—remained unsurpassed in accuracy and erudition for centuries.

Frederick cared little for the pretensions of the papacy—he was a multiple excommunicate—yet his own were quite breathtaking. A student of the history of the mare nostrum, Frederick saw himself as a philosopher-emperor, in the model of a Marcus Aurelius; others, always on the lookout for the End Time, saw in him the Antichrist, or a new form of demon. His intellectual curiosity left him open for such invidious accusations. The so-called "Sicilian Questions" formulated by Frederick—on the eternity of matter and the immortality of the soul, among other things—were circulated widely, especially in the lands he thought most likely to come up with a satisfactory answer to them: the dar al Islam. Among the enemies of Islam, there was dismay when the Ayyubid sultan of Egypt, Malik al-Kamil—the interlocutor of Francis of Assisi—sent to Frederick's court scholars and theologians to discuss his questions at length.

When the time came for Frederick to go on crusade, a promise he had vouchsafed

to his childhood guardian, Innocent III, the result was predictably eccentric. In
1229 Frederick, excommunicated for delaying his expedition to Outremer, and
his friend al-Kamil, threatened by rivals in Syria and marauders from Iraq,
struck a deal: on the promise of nonbelligerence, the payment of a large sum,
and an undertaking not to repair Jerusalem's defensive walls, Frederick II could
crown himself king of the holy city. The Christians would, in effect, be tenants
of the Ayyubids in Jerusalem, allowed a renewable lease of ten years. Bethlehem and Nazareth were thrown in for good measure.

*The sarcophagus of Frederick II, Stupor Mundi, in Palermo's cathedral. To the rear is the
canopy above a similar tomb for Roger II.*

Religious authorities in the Islamic world were horrified by this amiable horse trading between sultan and emperor over the holy city. Christian opinion was no less scandalized by the excommunicate's bizarre crusade. Not only had no infidel blood been spilled, but Frederick's comportment on his pilgrimage to Jerusalem verged on the incomprehensible. Much of his time had been spent on the Temple Mount—the al-Haram al-Sharif—chatting away in Arabic with Islamic scholars there. He had even chided them for silencing the muezzins on the mistaken assumption that his royal ears would be offended by the call to prayer—Frederick complained that he had been looking forward to waking in Jerusalem to the sonorous chants of Islam. Although this tourist-crusader did not stay long in the Levant—the pope used his absence to encourage attacks on Frederick's Italian possessions—his behavior hinted at a new nonideological approach to the dar al Islam.

Frederick's aesthetic and intellectual appreciation of the Islamic east—he may well have been the first Orientalist—was complemented by the wholly pragmatic acceptance of the Muslim Mediterranean by a growing force in the Christian west. The Italian maritime republics, particularly Genoa and Venice, had shoved aside Jewish and Greek traders in the eastern Mediterranean and come to monopolize commerce in the region. They had no quarrel with Islam; indeed, the Italians may be said to have had brains and no scruples, so intelligently did they flout repeated pleas from the pope to desist from trading with the infidel. The merchants knew that Christendom was changing and that demand for the spices and luxuries of the east would continue growing. No longer was sumptuary dress and ostentatious display the preserve of a few families of lords and ladies; in the prosperous thirteenth century, during which western Europe was spared major convulsive wars, an emerging class of townsmen—and their wives—sought to emulate the splendor of their social betters. *Stadtluft macht frei*—town air makes men free—ran the medieval axiom; it also made them free-spending.

From their timorous beginnings around the year 1000, these merchant navies of Italy—and of Catalonia—now boldly sailed to all points of the Tyrrhenian, Adriatic, Aegean, and Black seas and to all the ports of the Middle East. Adventurers such as Marco Polo retraced the spice route all the way east to the court of the Mongol khan. Their success had been greatly abetted by the crusaders, whose opening up of the Palestinian and Lebanese coastline had given the merchants a base from which to weave a network of commercial contacts in Muslim

Aleppo and Damascus and beyond. After a time, it became clear that trade was possible no matter what the confessional complexion of a city, and that the Christian merchants in Acre and other ports of Outremer would not be drawn into another bloody debacle in the Galilean wilderness for the sake of some otherworldly ideal. Jerusalem was the city on the hill, but not the water: Frederick's reappropriation of the city lasted barely fifteen years, as the wealthy coastal communities of Outremer turned their backs on it. That, and incessant internecine strife, made it easy prey for recapture by the Muslims in 1244.

In ports they did not control, the Italians and Catalans were given their own trading counters—called *funduqs*—that also included living quarters, warehouses, baths, and chapels. Under the Ayyubids, especially the broad-minded al-Kamil, few hindrances were put in the way of Latin traders working in Alexandria, Damietta, and Cairo. The successor dynasty in Egypt, the Mamluks, proved just as hospitable, reaping considerable profits from directing the trade of the Indian Ocean up the Red Sea and into their souks, where the Europeans paid stiff tariffs for merchandise. Venice, a commercial oligarchy, created the forerunner of the modern diplomatic corps in these years, its resident merchants championing the interests of their state and reporting back on the developments in their host city. The Pisans, thanks to the mathematician Leonardo Fibonacci, the son of a funduq ambassador in Bougie (Bejaia, Algeria), introduced Arabic numerals into the lengthening account ledgers of the westerners. And the Catalans, eager to get at the gold from sub-Saharan Africa, descended on the coast of the Maghrib as traders rather than warriors. The Romance lexicon of commerce came to be enriched with such borrowings from the Arab funduq as *cheque, tariff, baʐaar, traffic,* and *arsenal*. If at times their Muslim partners punished these merchants for supplying logistical help for various crusading efforts against Ifriqiya and Egypt, the later Middle Ages nonetheless witnessed a steady increase in trade. For Muslim and Christian alike, God's business sometimes came a distant second to one's own.

This commercial convivencia did not, however, shut down the imperative of war. The Mamluks, congenial though they were to the Italians, pursued a campaign of belligerence in the Levant. Under Sultan Baybars, a brilliant and merciless general, the Mamluks succeeded in stopping the Mongols at the battle of Ayn Jalut in the Jordan Valley. Following that epochal triumph in 1260, Baybars and his successors turned their ferocious attentions on the Latins. The Krak des Chevaliers fell, as did Marqab, Tortosa, and all the other outposts of the Christian Levant. The great city of Antioch, one of the five sees of Christianity, was so comprehensively sacked by Baybars that it never recovered. In 1291 the last holdout, Acre, was stormed amid scenes of dreadful massacre—the Mamluks were not led by a magnanimous Saladin. The merchants, deprived of their footing in Palestine, moved their operations to Cyprus, where the descendants of Guy de Lusignan, the loser at Hattin, had established a kingdom. From there, they resumed trading with their titular enemies, as if, incredibly, nothing had happened.

Attitudes around the sea of faith were slowly being transformed, the age-old enmities whittled away by the workings of economic intercourse. The struggle between the two faiths for primacy was far from over, but both the aristocratic Frederick II and the bourgeois merchants pointed to a future in which curiosity and self-interest might check the reflex of bigotry, or at least the demonizing bred of incomprehension. From Majorca at the close of the thirteenth century, a lone voice spoke wistfully of a dream of nonviolence. Although the Franciscan Ramon Llull ended his life plumping for bloody crusade, the call to unity he wrote in his youth would have been unthinkable a hundred years earlier:

Ah! What a great good fortune it would be if . . . we could all—every man on earth—be under one religion and belief, so that there would be no more rancor and ill will among men, who hate each other because of diversity and contrariness of beliefs and of sects! And just as there is only one God, Father, Creator, and Lord of everything that exists, so all peoples could unite and become one people, and that people be on the path to salvation, under one faith and one religion, giving glory and praise to our Lord God.

That pious hope remained unrealizable. What Llull could not anticipate was that a new era of rancor and diversity was about to begin, coming not from his native Majorca, but from lands far to the east.

⤙⤙   ⤚⤚

Gallipoli. The small town, now called Gelibolu, overlooks one end of a sixty-kilometer-long strait known in antiquity as the Hellespont, in the Middle Ages as St. George's Arm, and in the present day as the Dardanelles. Here Asia meets Europe. To the southwest of Gallipoli, a peninsula of the same name—a storied battleground of the First World War—stretches to the Aegean and forms the wooded European shore of the strait. To the east, the Dardanelles opens up into

the expanse of the Sea of Marmara, which in turn narrows at Istanbul to form
the strait of the Bosporus, leading to the Black Sea. Medieval kings and sultans
knew that if ever Islam were to take hold in Europe, it would somehow have to
find a way across this watery frontier—just as it had done centuries earlier at the
western edge of the Mediterranean, when Tariq and his Berbers rowed across
the Strait of Gibraltar. The eastern crossing was eventually made at Gallipoli,
thanks to an act of God.

On March 2, 1354, an earthquake flattened the fortress town. For its Greek inhabitants, survivors of the Black Death pandemic less than a decade earlier, the
quake was one calamity too many. They deserted their ruined town and clambered aboard their ships in search of safer havens, leaving a site of strategic importance unguarded and empty, there for the taking. It was not long before their
Turkish neighbors on the Asian side noticed their absence. By the time the heat of
the summer had settled on the land, the Turks had occupied and refortified Gallipoli, the first of their stepping-stones to a European empire. With that, the final
era of the sea of faith had begun. The monotheisms used to justify medieval colli-
sions of armies would eventually be replaced, under the multinational state soon
to be formed, by arguments of self-interest. Religion was still present in sanction-
ing and sanctifying aggression, but it would take a backseat to the realities of
commerce and the dictates of naked imperialism. If the merchants of Genoa and
Venice had been the harbingers of this change, the Turks brought it about.

The settlers of Gallipoli were the Ottomans, a heretofore obscure Turkish
clan of seminomads whose achievements would far eclipse those of their settled
forebears, the Seljuks of Rum. In Asia Minor, what had begun at Manzikert
would be finished by the Ottomans—their rule saw the definitive disappearance
of Hellenism from the heartland of Byzantium. In Europe, their role was to be
more nuanced, for in founding a multiethnic and multiconfessional empire they
would, despite the terror and atrocity attendant upon their initial conquests,
create as enduring a moment of convivencia as that of Umayyad al-Andalus.
This facet of the Ottoman ascendancy is sometimes overlooked. Through the
lens of nineteenth-century Balkan nationalists, when the Ottoman Empire was,
as has been nicely put, "a prodigy of decay," the early days of Turkey in Europe
came also to be seen as the wellspring of all evil, a dead hand impeding the
progress of man. In fact, the Ottomans in their first centuries created a vibrant
amalgam of conflict and coexistence, one that was worthy of the rich variety of
cultures to have arisen around the Mediterranean. If the Ottomans, like many
in their time, were practitioners of acts nowadays decried as "medieval" in their

cruelty, they nonetheless helped bridge the gap to the modern—and their opportunistic crossing of the strait at Gallipoli set in motion the change.

They had been on the doorstep of Europe for years. Originally a minor clan
of the Seljuk confederacy that had been left in tatters by Mongol depredations, the Ottomans, or Osmanlis, first rode into view under their eponymous
leader, Osman, at the start of the fourteenth century. Granted a *beylik*—a
petty prinicipality—in the northwestern extremity of Anatolia, Osman set
about snapping up the remnants of Constantinople's holdings in Asia. From
Bursa, their capital south of the Marmara, the Ottoman ghazis—warriors of
the faith—waged a relentless campaign of territorial expansion. They were
fortunate in having three long-lived and extremely capable warlords during
this time: Osman, who reigned from 1300 to 1326; Orhan (1326–60); and Murad I (1360–89). Born generals and, like all the early Ottomans, raised in the
saddle, these leaders enthusiastically attacked Christian and Muslim alike. As
the number of rival Turkish princelings in Anatolia steadily dwindled under
their assault, the rough and ready of every stripe—Turkoman nomads, Christian adventurers—flocked to the Ottoman banners. By the time Orhan gazed
across the Dardanelles, he had a formidable force behind him.

The Ottomans were also fortunate in that the Europe they beheld in the middle
of the fourteenth century was every bit as muddled as Anatolia. The collapse of
Byzantine rule in Europe following the Fourth Crusade's sack of Constantinople
had never been repaired. A coup d'état engineered by Genoa regained Constantinople for the Greeks in 1261—in exchange for supplanting Venice in Levantine
trade—and a competent dynasty, the Palaeologi, came to power, but never again
would the Byzantines exercise control over their once-vast European territories.
They were left with a pitiful rump of an empire that comprised parts of the
Peloponnese, the city of Thessalonica, the Thracian hinterland around the city
of Adrianople, and the capital itself. Everything else was in play: by the sea, the
ports of the Greek and Balkan mainland and the islands of the Aegean saw repeated wars by the rapacious Italian maritime republics; inland, the forested
highlands of the Balkans witnessed the rise and fall of ephemeral empires and
evanescent baronies. The sole kingdom to come close to duplicating Byzantine
glory in the Balkans, the Serbian empire of Stephen Dushan, would fall apart
into squabbling principalities on his death in 1355.

For the Balkans of these years, the sole unifying factor was cultural, the Slavs
adopting the trappings and titles of their former Greek masters and, in the case

of the Serbs and Bulgars, establishing their own independent patriarchates, an act of imitation and originality all at the same time. As the Ottomans contemplated their move into Europe, what has been called a "Byzantine commonwealth" of religious and cultural expression was alive and thriving in the Balkans. However sublime, a civilization gazing toward the monks of Mount Athos for guidance was unsuited to repel a pragmatic invader—especially one that cared not a whit if that cultural commonwealth prospered or withered. For the Ottomans, power mattered, not faith or language. When they looked to Europe, they saw not the beauty of Slavic Christendom but a fissiparous feudal maze. The formidable unitary empire of the Byzantines was gone—Europe was, in practice, Anatolia all over again.

And again fortune smiled on the Turks. Prior to establishing their permanent bridgehead at Gallipoli, the Ottomans had been invited into Europe—paid handsomely, in effect, to conduct an exploratory razzia. The occasion was a Byzantine civil war over the Palaeologi succession at midcentury. The result of the Turkish reconnaissance can hardly be overstated—the hungry Ottomans acquired a firsthand knowledge of the strengths and weaknesses of the Christian forces and, just as crucially, saw the pastureland of Thrace and heard of the mineral riches beyond the mountains in the verdant interior. Orhan also had a good look at basileus John VI Cantacuzenus' three beautiful daughters, one of whom, Theodora, he demanded—and got—in marriage. He was, by many accounts, deeply smitten.

Once Orhan took Gallipoli, he no longer needed permission to visit. The years that followed saw an almost uninterrupted series of Ottoman victories. Thrace was overrun, Thessaly threatened. The town of Adrianople, notorious for the death of Emperor Valens at the hands of the Visigoths a millennium earlier, became the capital of the Ottoman world under the name of Edirne. The Bulgars and even the Byzantines became tribute-paying vassals to the triumphant sultan. In 1371, the chimera of a south Slav empire, one that reached all the way to the warm waters of the Mediterranean, was smashed forever. At the Marica River, to the west of Edirne, the Ottomans routed the Serbs, who were forced to retreat permanently behind the mountainous walls of Macedonia. Marica, the most important battle in subduing the region, was soon followed by other Ottoman feats of arms. In 1389 Sultan Murad I assembled his forces and marched far inland to the crossroads of the southern Balkans, near the watershed of the Aegean and

Black seas. There, on a desolate upland called the Field of the Blackbirds, or Kosovo Polje, the Ottomans and their Christian allies met a combined Serb and Bosnian army supplemented by Hungarians and Albanians.

The battle of Kosovo, not the far more decisive encounter at Marica, has lived on in the folk memory of the Balkans. An elaborate congeries of religious and nationalistic myth similar to the fog surrounding Las Navas de Tolosa, Kosovo became an allegory for the martyrdom of the Serbs at the hands of the Turks. For all the prose and poetry connected to the battle—much of it composed centuries afterward—we can be certain only that the principal leader of the Serbian armies, Prince Lazar Hrebeljanovic, was killed sometime in the clash, and that Sultan Murad, too, met his end there, perhaps assassinated. Otherwise, the battle may even have been a draw rather than an outright Ottoman victory.

The many monuments and chapels dedicated to Kosovo tell a fuller story, of which there are three main narrative strands: the beheading of a defiant Prince Lazar by the Turks; the treacherous desertion of one Vuk Brankovic and his men, whose actions absolved the Serbs of responsibility for the defeat; and, above all else, the bravery of the hero-assassin of the sultan, Milos Kobilic, who wormed his way to the great Ottoman's side by pretending to be a traitor. This last personage, whom some historians unkindly believe to be a total fabrication, is an especially powerful element of the Kosovo myth, epitomizing love of coun-

The monument to the battle of 1389 at Kosovo Polje.

try grandly sweeping away any petty concern of personal survival. In 1914 it was thought providential that Serbia's most famous assassin, Gavrilo Princip, shot the archduke in Sarajevo on a June 28, the day celebrated as the anniversary of Kobilic's deed. Whatever the truth behind the Kosovo story, it remains one of the most protean legacies that the struggle between medieval Muslim and Christian armies has bequeathed to the present day, an argument for faith, self-sacrifice, resistance to tyranny, and national solidarity. Even those figures with a far greater supranational resonance in collective memory—Martel at Poitiers or Saladin at Hattin—cannot match Kosovo's Shakespearean cocktail of betrayal, martyrdom, and murder.

For the Turks of the time, the battle was a milestone for entirely different reasons. The killing of Murad represented an unprecedented stumble in the Ottoman march to empire, deplored in subsequent Turkish chronicles. That misstep was only partially rectified by his son and successor, Beyazit I, also known as Yilderim (Thunderbolt) for his mercurial temperament and actions—on learning of his father's death, to take but one example, he promptly gouged out the eyes of his elder brother. Eager to consolidate power gained through this deed, Beyazit quickly made peace with the Serbs after Kosovo and cultivated the friendship of their leaders. Stefan Lazarevic, the son of the slain Lazar, became a faithful vassal of the Turks and participated in many of Beyazit's campaigns in Europe and Asia. Stefan's sister, Olivera, wed the Ottoman sultan, thereby cementing the bonds between Turk and Serb. Given the tales that grew up around this moment of Balkan history, it is ironic that Kosovo, in reality, ushered in close to a century of alliance between the two peoples.

Nor were the Ottomans completely unwelcome in other parts of the Balkans. In the territories conquered outright by the Turks, many of the peasants who had fled began returning to the land once the customary horrors of ghazi raiding and slaving had subsided and the sultan's governance taken control. The new dispensation was seen to have its advantages, principally in the easing of the common man's feudal burden, as the Ottoman system of landholding demanded far fewer compulsory days of work on the lord's manor. Moreover, not all churches became mosques, and provided the new punitive taxes were paid, the commonwealth of priest and archimandrite could still guide its flocks, with the blessing and encouragement of the sultan. A tentative convivencia, in short, had settled on the lands.

Still, the harshness of conquest should not be washed away in rose water. Where the Ottomans did innovate in a malevolent way was in the establishment of the *yeni ceri* (new troops), or Janissaries. These were Christian youngsters

taken from their families, in what became a regular cull of the Balkans, to learn
the techniques of war in the Ottoman capital and serve as the sultan's praetorian regiments. This boy tribute, the cause of boundless heartbreak over the
centuries in the fastnesses of the Balkans, became a pillar propping up the Ottoman state, arguably as important as Islam itself. Forcibly converted and forbidden to marry, the Janissary youths formed the first permanent standing army
of the mare nostrum since the Roman Empire and provided an institutional
counterpoint to the ghazis of the early Ottoman ascendancy. The nomadic
ghazis, distressed at the settling down brought on by success, pined for the simpler days of border raiding and rapine. The uprooted Janissaries would anchor
the empire; the rootless ghazis, provide it with its ethos of constant expansion.

≪ ≪   ≫ ≫

Anadolu Hisari. The streams known as the Sweet Waters of Asia meet the
Bosporus nine kilometers north of the great city on the Golden Horn, toward the
other end of the watery frontier separating Europe and Asia. Here, at the narrowest point of the Bosporus, on the Asian side, Sultan Beyazit built the Anatolian Fortress, the Anadolu Hisari, a mean-looking castle dedicated to harassing
maritime traffic. Today, in the small park enclosed by its crumbling crenella-
tions, a rickety swingset echoes with the squeals of uniformed schoolchildren

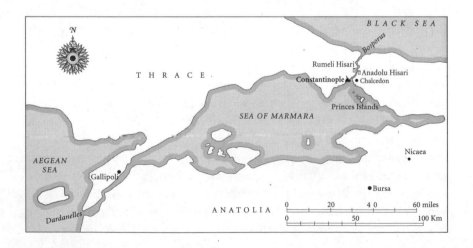

under the gaze of their nannies, and of Ataturk. A bust of the great man rests on a plinth, the inscription on its base his paean to the sheer felicity of being born a Turk: "How Happy Is He Who Can Say He Is a Turk."

Ataturk's Turcophilia is fitting, given the significance of the Anadolu Hisari. The construction of the fortress marked the second stage of the sea change initiated at Gallipoli. When Beyazit completed the fort at the dawn of the fifteenth century, the old city's final days as a Christian capital appearted to have begun, for the Ottomans clearly wanted to make Constantinople their own. In the decade following Kosovo, Beyazit had battled unceasingly in Anatolia, doubling the size of the empire his father had left to him there, so that the Ottomans grandly bestrode Europe and Asia, their territories remarkably similar in extent to the long-vanished embrace of the Byzantine imperium. The only thing missing was the center, the cynosure—Constantinople, the "Red Apple" of temptation in Turkish lore. The Prophet, in a hadith, had said, "They shall conquer Qostantinya, glory be to the prince and to the army that shall achieve it."

Beyazit's idea was simple: wear the city down. At the same time as he was laying siege before the great land walls of Constantinople, he would attempt to place a tourniquet on the Bosporus. From Anadolu Hisari his raiders would hinder the transports gliding through the dark waters in from the Black Sea,

Rendering of the Anadolu Hisari as it might have looked in Beyazit's time. Beyond it are the hills of the Asian shore of the Bosporus.

laden with the grains and minerals of the Trebizond, the carpets and silks of Persia and Armenia, and the shackled masses of Circassians bound for sexual or military slavery throughout the Mediterranean world. Destined first for the Genoese trading city of Galata on the northern shore of the Golden Horn across from Constantinople, these ships were the source of wealth for much of the Christian east. Starve the Byzantine capital on land; cripple its Latin suburb on the water—he assumed that in only a matter of time the city would be his.

This calculation did not take into account the reaction of his adversaries. In duplicating the old empire ruled from the Bosporus, Beyazit also inherited its problems. Just like the Byzantines prior to Manzikert, the sultan was soon faced with two threats, one from the east, the other from the west. The latter emerged first, in the form of the greatest international crusade to be launched in more than a century. The powers of western Christendom finally took note of the Ottoman menace—the capture by Beyazit and his generals of Bulgaria and much of Greece and Hungary had sounded the alarm. Accordingly, in July 1396, an immense host of warriors from Wallachia, France, Germany, Poland, Italy, Spain, and England mustered at Buda, then marched down the Danube under the command of the Hungarian king, Sigismund. The crusaders, thought to number as many as one hundred thousand, aimed to crush the Turkish infidel.

Alarmed, Beyazit summoned all the men at his command, lifting the siege of Constantinople and instructing his vassals to strike out north into the Balkans to thwart the holy warriors of Christendom. On September 25, 1396, at Nicopolis, the Danubian town now known as Nikopol, Bulgaria, the collision of the two huge forces took place, the outcome having been decided before the westerners even realized that Beyazit's great army was in the vicinity. Unfamiliar with Turkish tactics of deception, thousands of Burgundian knights, eager to emulate the heroics celebrated in the *chansons de geste*, charged a small contingent of Ottoman outriders seen trotting on a hilltop; when the knights crested the hill in pursuit of their fleeing quarry, they found themselves riding at full tilt into the midst of the main Ottoman army, tens of thousands strong, deployed behind the concealing hill. Massacre ensued. Riderless horses came cantering back to the encampment of the Christian army before Nicopolis, and foreboding gave way to panic once the great Turkish host at last emerged from its hiding place and roared down the same slope over which the headstrong Burgundians had just disappeared. It was said that the exultant Beyazit had more than ten thousand captives beheaded on that September day—until his own men begged him for a respite. The defeat, a catastrophe of such magnitude that early reports of it were not believed in the capitals of the west, seemed certain to spell the doom of Christianity's eastern capital. Beyazit's besiegers once again appeared in the Thracian plain outside the land walls of Constantinople, and the skirmishers of the Anadolu Hisari took to the waters of the Bosporus. Nothing short of an unimaginably powerful bolt from the blue seemed able to counter Yilderim the Thunderbolt.

It came from the east. There was one force fiercer than the Ottoman sultan: a warlord of Samarkand known as Tamerlane, or Timur Leng (Timur the Lame). His fourteenth-century Mongol armies mixed the inhuman toughness of the steppe nomad with an exalted belief in jihad—even against fellow Muslims—and exceeded all of their predecessors in the pursuit of atrocity. Not only did they brutally sack many of the great cities of Islam—Isfahan, Baghdad, Mosul, Aleppo, Damascus—they also made a point of constructing tall pyramids with the heads of their victims, the macabre monuments often containing tens of thousands of skulls. The wives and daughters of those so arrayed were stripped and hauled from the sanctuary of the Muslim home to the shame of the public square or the nomad tent. In central and west Asia in the last decades of the fourteenth century, millions were killed or enslaved.

Around 1400 Timur came west to devastate Syria, causing its immediate neighbors to fear, quite rightly, the spread of the Mongol contagion. In a meeting as unusual as that between Francis of Assisi and Sultan al-Kamil, the great scholar Ibn Khaldun was enlisted by the Mamluks of Egypt to treat with the dread Timur. The two men, despite the chasm separating their pursuits, had several long conversations, and Ibn Khaldun came away impressed with Timur's thoughtfulness—perhaps he saw in him the vector of asabiyya, the kinship system central to building an Islamic empire. The contemplative interlude did not last, for Timur, in his late sixties but possessed of an indomitable thirst for war, was bent on punishing all those who ignored his demands for submission. Conspicuously defiant had been the Ottomans. He sent messengers to Beyazit ordering him to return all the lands of Anatolia to the Byzantines and to the various Turkish emirs the Ottomans had despoiled.

Enraged and no doubt exasperated at having to lift the siege of Constantinople yet again, Beyazit summoned his troops and raced into Anatolia, this time to inflict punishment in the east. The decisive encounter occurred near Ankara on July 28, 1402. Although no horrific one-sided massacre occurred, the Ottomans were soundly beaten. Stefan Lazarevic and his Serbs, who had fought alongside the Turks at Nicopolis, resisted best the Mongol onslaught and managed to rescue some of the sultan's kinsmen from capture. The Thunderbolt was not as lucky—taken prisoner, he was carted around in a litter, which later legend made into a cage, as Timur sacked the cities of northwestern Turkey that the sultan's ancestors, Osman and Orhan, had conquered. Apparently, during this campaign Beyazit's lovely Serbian bride, Olivera, was relieved of her clothes and forced to serve, stark naked, at the table of the great Mongol. Beyazit, dejected and humiliated, died the following year.

The Christians of Constantinople could scarcely believe their luck. Their hopes had been dashed at Nicopolis, only to revive at Ankara. The Ottomans were now divided and sullen, their empire on shaky footing, their soldiery huddled around the walls of the Anadolu Hisari, not to harass Christian shipping but to shelter from the wrath of Timur's marauding Mongols. As if to prove that the good fortune was heaven sent, Timur's dangerous armies left as quickly as they had come—the astounding old warrior decided to turn around and march across the world to conquer China instead. Beyazit was no more, and a civil war broke out among the Ottomans over his succession. Constantinople, the new Rome of the mare nostrum, had been saved—for the moment.

CHAPTER NINE

CONSTANTINOPLE 1453 AND KOSTANTINIYYE

The fall of the new Rome; the rise of the new convivencia

By definition a reprieve is temporary. In the fifty years following Timur's eleventh-hour rescue of Constantinople from Beyazit, there was reason to hope that the capital of eastern Christendom might defy the lexicon of defeat. The Ottomans ineffectually besieged Constantinople in 1422, but dynastic quarrels at the time hampered their ability to mete out sustained grief to their Greek neighbors. Restoration of purpose and of glory occurred under a long-lived and capable sultan, Murad II, who, for all his warrior prowess, confounded expectations by preferring the life of the mind to the tent of the campaigner. He and his statesmanlike vizier, Chandarli Halil Pasha, seemed satisfied with an uneasy peace. The sea of faith, at least in its eastern reaches, looked as if it might just settle into placid convivencia.

Twice, however, Murad was summoned out of the early retirement he had accorded himself to face down threats in the north, from which the great Transylvanian lord and regent of Hungary, John Hunyadi, led invading armies intent on smashing Ottoman power. The sultan annihilated a Christian host at Varna, Bulgaria, in 1444 and again at Kosovo's already-notorious Field of the Blackbirds, in 1448. This second battle of Kosovo was a close-run affair—had the armies of George Skanderbeg, a truly redoubtable Albanian warlord, managed to rendezvous with Hunyadi's forces before the sultan got to them, the outcome could have been entirely different. As it was, Skanderbeg failed to show in time, and Hunyadi had to fight the Turks alone. Like the Serbs before them, the once-mighty Hungarians were decisively knocked out of contention for the remnants of the Byzantine Empire.

Despite the double disaster, Christians praying that Timur's reprieve would last could still discern a silver lining. Murad's recent triumphs were defensive in nature—the Hungarians had violated the truces—and throughout his career the sultan had left his non-Muslim subjects to their own pursuits, with the notable exception of the boy-tribute for the Janissary corps. And while the Ottomans had harassed or reduced to vassalhood most of the sovereign cities and statelets of eastern Europe, Halil Pasha was on excellent terms with his Greek counterparts—so much so that some whispered he was no stranger to the largesse of Constantinople's treasury. A facilitator and a diplomat, in the mold of the Ayyubid sultan al-Kamil who had given St. Francis a hearing and the Stupor Mundi the keys to Jerusalem two centuries earlier, the immensely powerful grand vizier—his father and grandfather had been viziers before him—was seen as the guarantor of good governance and sensible coexistence. With Halil Pasha in charge, some thought hopefully, the person wearing the sultan's turban barely mattered.

The optimists' theory was put to the test in 1451, at the death of Murad II. His nineteen-year-old son, Mehmet (Muhammad) II, took the throne—after prudently having his infant stepbrother drowned in the bath—and promised ambassadors from all and sundry the maintenance of the status quo. The Europeans were gladdened by this undertaking and, in some cases, emboldened to stir up trouble for the Turks in Thrace. This same Mehmet, while barely an adolescent, had briefly taken command of the Ottoman Empire on his father's self-imposed retirement prior to Varna and Kosovo, and he had proved to be putty in Halil Pasha's hands—and unpopular with the rank and file of the Turkish armies. Surely the young man, now sultan for the foreseeable future, would persist in his career of perfect incompetence.

Alas, for the Europeans, he would not. Rarely, in fact, did the acquisition of power and the onset of maturity forge a leader as outstanding as the new sultan. At the court in Edirne (Adrianople), the primacy of Halil Pasha suffered incremental but steady abrasion as his pacific counsels were ignored and a new generation of pashas and generals came to the fore. Many of Mehmet's coterie were renegades, capable Christian adventurers who had "turned Turk" in the pursuit of advancement and wealth. Such men were seldom peace-lovers. Mehmet, conversant in Turkish, Greek, Hebrew, Arabic, Persian, and Latin, welcomed individuals of great ability regardless of their origins and possessed a breadth of knowledge that precluded clannish small-mindedness. After mealtimes, as he reclined with the women and boys to enjoy his favor, he had biographies of Alexander the Great read to him in the original Greek. His interest in Graeco-Roman antiquity went far beyond avocation, for this fleshy-lipped, starry-eyed scion of the Ottomans saw himself not only as the sultan of the Turks, but also as emperor of the Romans. With Mehmet, the mare nostrum had come full circle—Islam was less the lucky beneficiary of the legacy of antiquity than its rightful and legitimate continuator, in much the same way as the Quran had made obsolete the revelations of the Christians and the Jews. The Byzantine Greeks, in this view, had outlived their role as the torch-bearers of Alexander. The great basileus Heraclius—and indeed the Prophet himself—would have been dumbfounded at this turn of the wheel; for Mehmet, it was as natural as the absolute power he held over millions of lives. His mission was to become what Turks call him to this very day: Fatih, "Conqueror."

Mehmet II, conqueror of Constantinople, in middle age.

During the first few months of his reign, knowledge of the scope of his ambition remained in the sole possession of his inner circle. Yet rumors began to fly—the courts of the Christian kingdoms and the Ottoman sultanate had too intimate a history of intermarriage and intermingling for confidences to be kept for very long. So it was that by the spring of 1452 those Christians formerly sanguine about the new sultan's incompetence and irresoluteness had to admit the truth: they had been clutching at straws. In May, after perfunctorily informing the authorities of Constantinople of his intentions, Mehmet arrived on the European shore of the Bosporus at the head of an army bearing a tactical component of hundreds of stonemasons. As their warrior comrades stood guard, in the unlikely event of an attack from the skeletal army of the Greeks, the masons set to work, spending four feverish months just upstream from the Byzantine capital. Three of Mehmet's pashas, including Halil, were each given a portion of the project to complete, thus ensuring that rivalry would spur them to prodigies of speed. The arrangement worked its desired effect: at the end of August 1452, the gigantic Rumeli Hisari was finished.

Still today a stone cascade of turrets and curtain walls spilling down a steep slope to the Bosporus at its narrowest point, the Rumeli Hisari—the Rumelian (European) Castle—dwarfs its sister seven hundred meters opposite on the Asian shore, Beyazit's Anadolu (Anatolian) Hisari. In Mehmet's day the two fortresses formed what the Turks called *bogaz kesen*, the strait-cutter: henceforth no one would be allowed passage from the Black Sea to Constantinople without the sultan's say-so. With no Timur to burst onto the scene and create havoc, young Mehmet intended to succeed where Beyazit had failed.

At the Rumeli Hisari of today there is no playground, as there is at the Anadolu. Instead, within its massive embrace, scores of old cannons molder in the mist that drifts in from the dark waters of the strait. Although loud groups of schoolchildren clamber over them as if they were intended for play, the cannons serve more appositely as a sharp reminder of Mehmet's martial genius. However much he was a dreamer of the heroics of past campaigns, the young sultan recognized the hard outlines of future warfare: on hearing that the Greeks had spurned the talents of a Hungarian cannon-founder named Urban, he engaged the man to construct a ballistic device capable of keeping the promise implied by *bogaz kesen*. Unlike Callinichus, the Syrian who had saved Byzantium from Muawiya with his invention of Greek fire, Urban brought to bear a technological innovation that would hasten its destruction.

By the fall Urban had delivered. His ballistic behemoth was installed at the Rumeli Hisari. Warnings were issued, the wait began. In early November two Venetian merchant galleys ran before a strong wind below the walls of the fortress. The cannon roared; its payload splashed harmlessly into the Bosporus. The daredevil sailors were greeted joyfully in the Venetian quarter of the capital, on the southern shores of the Golden Horn. Mehmet's artillery sergeants corrected their range and adjusted the trajectory. Two weeks later, emboldened by the success of its sister, another Venetian ship tried running the gauntlet. Urban's cannon blew it out of the water. The crew was fished out of the waves and beheaded; the ship's captain, Antonio Rizzo, was brought to the sultan near Edirne, who promptly had him impaled. The builder of the Rumeli Hisari had given notice that he would countenance no further impertinence. Satisfied with his summer project, the sultan spent the winter months assembling the soldiery required for the next phase of his plan. The stonemasons were dismissed.

❮❮ ❮❮ ❯❯ ❯❯

The Rumeli Hisari today, looking north toward the Bosporus as it approaches the Black Sea.

The last Christmas of Byzantine Constantinople was celebrated amid much trepidation. News had been filtering back from spies in Edirne of unprecedented activity around the sultan's headquarters. Troops were assembling there from all points of the compass; even such Christian vassals as the Serbs had promised to contribute hefty contingents to bring down the new Rome. The city of Constantine, alone and encircled by the Ottoman Empire, was in desperate need of men to defend itself. All eyes turned to the Marmara and thence to the Aegean—surely the Latin powers of western Christendom would launch great fleets to succor their beleaguered brethren. But as the new year dawned and the cold winds snapped the banners atop the sea walls of the city, no sails appeared. The order was given to melt down the silver monstrances of the churches in order to buy stores and hire mercenaries. Byzantine galleys braved the storm-swept Aegean in search of men. A pitiful few—from Crete and the Dodecanese—answered the call.

The inaction of the west in this, Constantinople's direst crisis, cannot be put down to mere ignorance. Despite the sirens of optimism during the fifty-year reprieve, many in Constantinople had read the calligraphy on the wall and raced west to sound the alarm. Different wearers of the imperial regalia visited European capitals—one went as far afield as Paris and London—to impress upon their Latin counterparts that a fight to the death was looming. Yet there would be no repeat of Urban's sermon at Clermont, no reopening of Pandora's box: ever since the disaster at Nicopolis in 1396, enthusiasm for adventures in the east had dampened, and a succession of homegrown troubles (the most notorious being the destructive Hundred Years War between England and France) had tied the hands of many monarchs.

More eloquent than any official plea for assistance was the human tide of scholars quitting Byzantium. The Byzantine Empire had for more than a millennium maintained a level of artistic and intellectual sophistication that towered above the other Christian civilizations of the medieval Mediterranean; with that empire shrunk to the sole city of Constantinople and an autonomous Peloponnesian province, Morea, the learned desperately sought out patrons for their scholarship and gave clear evidence, by their wholesale flight to foreign climes, of the coming collapse. The city-states of Italy, alive with the rediscovery of antiquity that we now term the Renaissance, welcomed the exiles with open arms, dazzled by the newcomers' easy familiarity with the writings of the ancients. In a great irony the Byzantine emigrants would unwittingly have their revenge on Islam, for their highly vaunted role in the elaboration of Renaissance thought would dispatch to oblivion, in western memory, the part played by earlier scholars of Baghdad, Córdoba, Toledo, and Palermo in safeguarding the heritage of the mare nostrum. Less worth gloating over, however, was the parallel tradition then inaugurated: the tendency of western scholars to admire the Greeks of yesteryear to the detriment of the Greeks of their own day.

Among those willing to deal with their contemporaries of the fifteenth century, foremost were the popes in Rome—and for good reason. They had their schismatic Orthodox counterparts over a barrel; if the arbiter of western Christendom were to rally help on their behalf, the Greeks would have to undo the split formalized by the events of 1054 and fall into line with the doctrine of papal supremacy. This, at least, was the calculation. In truth, powerful popes such as Innocent III were a thing of the past. Rome had lost much of its influence as the national monarchies of Europe rose to eminence in the later Middle Ages, and in any event many Orthodox churchmen were unwilling to give in to the loathsome Latins. The filioque irritant, the Great Schism, the sack of 1204, the Latin emperors—too many slights, great and small, had been inflicted to be forgiven.

Although several monarchs of Constantinople had flirted, for political reasons, with reunifying the churches, the large number of vocal dissidents on the Orthodox side made a mockery of successive conclaves that ringingly announced the rift to be at an end. In the cheerless December of 1452 in Constantinople, the populace widely disparaged a ceremony of formal union held under the dome of the Hagia Sophia: if their lives were in danger from the Turks, ran the reasoning, why endanger their souls as well through an opportunistic embrace of the Latin heresiarchs? A great nobleman of the city, Lucas Notaras, was not even sure of the first half of that proposition—after all, the vast majority of Greek Orthodox Christians—in the Balkans, Anatolia, and elsewhere—were living peacefully under Ottoman rule. Notaras is credited with saying of the choice faced by the Greeks: "Better a sultan's turban than a cardinal's hat." This remark might at first seem similar to the quip about swineherds and camel-drivers, but Notaras was not advocating solidarity with his coreligionists as the king of Seville had done four centuries earlier. To the contrary, the sea of faith had seen long periods of convivencia, and no longer was religious allegiance a cause for reflexive alliance. Some Greeks of Constantinople, in other words, saw salvation in Ottoman rule.

Still, no one doubted, in the winter of 1452–53, that before any accommodation was reached, much blood would have to be shed. The last basileus of Byzantium prepared his city for a long siege. By poetic coincidence, he was a Constantine, born of a Helena, as had been the first emperor of Constantinople. A capable

ruler in the prime of life, Constantine XI Dragases worked tirelessly to lift spirits in the frightened city. He tried wooing volunteers on the opposite shore of the
Golden Horn, in the Genoese trading suburb of Galata (also called Pera), whose
neutrality in the coming clash had been declared but whose denizens might not
all be immune to a call to bear arms for Christ. The Venetians, installed in Constantinople proper by the southern waters of the Horn, were similarly entreated.
All, in any case, were forbidden to leave the city and its environs for the duration.

On January 26, 1453, sentinels on the Marmara sea walls at last espied the long-
awaited sails. Three Genoese galleys under the command of a nobleman from a
distinguished family rounded the headland of the city and lowered their anchors
in the Golden Horn. Giovanni Giustiniani Longo and his seven hundred heavily
armored men had arrived to take up their posts. Although commerce-minded
Genoa—like Venice—did not want to provoke the Ottoman sultan by openly sid-
ing with the Byzantines and thus risk losing lucrative colonies in the Black and
Aegean seas, the city did not discourage its bravest men from rushing to the defense of eastern Christendom on their own initiative. Such a man was Giustiniani Longo, an expert in siege warfare spoiling for a fight. The capital went into
raptures—even the antiunion Greeks and the Venetian *frères ennemis* of the Genoese gave the famous warrior a hero's welcome. Giustiniani asked for, and was
immediately granted by the elated basileus, command of the land walls of the city
facing the Thracian countryside. Were there any weaknesses in this already formidable defense, the Genoan would detect them and see to their repair.

The boost to morale came none too soon, for the rumors from Edirne had
grown scarcely credible. Engineers were working on the old Roman road linking the Ottoman capital to Constantinople, leveling its grades and reinforcing
its paving stones. There was dark talk of Urban the cannon-founder and a
hideous new weapon he was constructing. Closer to home, the observers on the
land walls could see detachments of the Turkish forces digging ditches and
preparing the ground for what promised to be an enormous host of besiegers.
From Anatolia came news that a huge Ottoman army was approaching the
Asian side of the Bosporus. As the winter wore on, nerves frayed. On February
26, a month after the arrival of the Genoese volunteers, a Venetian galley and
six Cretan merchant vessels, almost listing from the weight of their many desperate passengers, stole out of the Golden Horn in the dead of night and sailed
through the Dardanelles to safety. The basileus might sputter in anger at having
his edict so egregiously flouted, but he could do nothing about it.

The following month brought a nastier surprise. The mariners of Constantinople and the merchant seamen of Genoa and Venice all knew that the Turks possessed no navy. For more than a century, the Latins had made their fortune carrying the trade of the Ottoman Empire and, on occasion, ferrying the sultan's armies around the eastern Mediterranean. Yet in late March the unthinkable appeared: an Ottoman fleet of more than one hundred ships glided regally through the Marmara and past the city to dock at a harbor on the Bosporus just downstream from the Rumeli Hisari. Sultan Mehmet was indeed a student of history, and, like Muawiya before him, he had realized that the Christians could not be allowed mastery of the seas if he were to further his conquests. During the previous summer, as all eyes had watched with dread the erection of the Rumeli Hisari, the sultan's shipwrights had worked unnoticed in the port of Gallipoli, the site of the first Ottoman foothold in Europe. Under the guidance of a Bulgarian renegade, ships had been bought, built, or refitted. Although few vessels of this instant fleet rode as high above the waves as the Italian and Catalan galleys, they were still men-of-war, capable of inflicting damage and moving soldiers, horses, and munitions across the Bosporus. Appalled, the basileus ordered the capital's last line of maritime defense to be deployed: a great chain, supported by floating booms, was stretched across the mouth of the Golden Horn from the headland of Constantinople to the point of Galata. The Christian fleet—twenty-six vessels—moored in the Horn was, for the moment, safe behind the immense chain, part of which today lies coiled in a corner of the city's Naval Museum—itself located on the cove where that first astonishing Ottoman fleet dropped anchor.

The threat of the Turkish fleet, however, seemed trivial in comparison to what was approaching by land. In the first week of April the Ottoman armies and their allies appeared within sight of the walls. Scholarly consensus holds that they numbered approximately eighty thousand troops, to which could be added twenty thousand *bashi-bazouks,* irregular soldiers and adventurers of diverse origins with nothing to lose but their lives. As this flood of malevolent humanity came ever closer to the city over the plain of Thrace, the basileus Constantine asked George Phrantzes, his secretary and one of the most reliable sources for the events of these months, to make a census of the forces at his disposition. The tally was dispiriting: a mere 4,900 Greeks and 2,000 Latins were available to man the perimeter land and sea walls that ran for twenty kilometers around the capital. They were outnumbered more than ten to one. Sensibly, Constantine ordered Phrantzes to keep the figures to himself.

To Giustiniani and his commanders in the front line of the defenses, the size of the attacking force was not necessarily a problem, given the stoutness of the

walls. What worried the Genoese on the ramparts, rather, was what they saw
being laboriously hauled over the improved road from Edirne. Urban the Hungarian had been busy over the winter. A stupefyingly big cannon, pulled by
sixty oxen and kept lashed to its carriage by a trained corps of two hundred
men, lumbered toward its emplacement opposite the land walls. Eight meters
long, it was more than twice the size of the monster at Rumeli Hisari.

Mehmet at last arrived and ordered Constantine to surrender his city peacefully or be responsible for its siege, capture, and sack. To drive home the point,
the Ottomans captured two small Byzantine forts outside the walls and impaled
their defenders. Constantine, unmoved, turned Mehmet down.

On April 6, 1453, Urban's cannon thundered into action. A missile weighing
more than half a ton screamed across the ditches and moats separating the armies
and crashed with a telluric thud into the fortifications. Brick and mortar were pul-
verized, tumbling earthward in a nimbus of debris. The reprieve was over.

⤛ ⤛   ⤜ ⤜

The besieged city, originally founded as Byzantium in the seventh century
B.C.E., had been coveted long before the advent of Mehmet II but had proved remarkably resistant to attack. Shaped somewhat like a pudgy thumb stretched
outward from the landmass of Europe, the prominence that would become
Constantinople is bounded by watery moats on two sides: the Sea of Marmara
to the south, and the Golden Horn to the north. The latter is an inlet seven kilometers long fed by streams known as the Sweet Waters of Europe—their Asian
counterparts flow near the Anadolu Hisari. A grand sickle of placid blue-gray,
the Golden Horn offers secure moorings no matter how wild the weather and,
as every visitor past and present has realized, unexpected scenes of maritime
beauty from the slopes of the city's seven steep hills.

However arresting its seaside situation, the might of Constantinople is best appreciated along what was, paradoxically, the scene of its downfall: the six-
kilometer-long line of fortifications that ran from the Marmara to the Horn,
closing off the roughly triangular form into which the capital grew and, more
important, protecting the city on its vulnerable landward side against invaders
from Thrace. For more than a thousand years these land walls had held fast—
the crusaders of 1204 gained access near the sea walls of the Golden Horn—
and they still stand defiant in the midst of what is now Europe's most populous
megalopolis. Despite a skein of choked roadways, the eyesore of immense mar-

shaling yards, and a huge mausoleum for a modern-day Turkish prime minister, the cyclopean construction dominates the rolling cityscape, its watchtowers rising five or six stories tall, its bands of rust-red brick relieving the stolid mass of stone put in place by an army of slave laborers in the fourth century C.E. for Emperor Theodosius II. The Theodosian wall on view today is the tallest and the innermost of what were three lines of walls, their gradations in height punctuated by 192 towers, deep moats, labyrinthine passageways, postern gates, and subterranean aqueducts. Given this superb stone buckler, the decision made by Constantine XI and Giustiniani Longo to defy the disparity in numbers between attacker and defender seems a reasonable risk to have run. Besides, every Greek then alive knew that surrender would mean the end of a world.

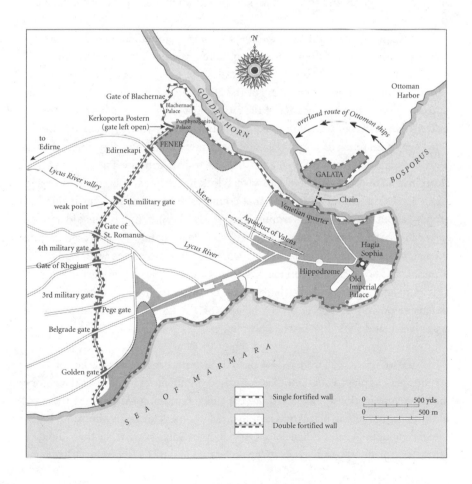

By the Marmara, near where the land walls meet the sea, a grand reminder of that vanished world still stretches up into the sky. The Golden Gate was the archway through which great leaders of eastern Christendom—Heraclius, Basil the Bulgar-Slayer, Alexius Comnenus—passed after triumph in the field or acclamation as basileus by their armies. Today, its glittering cover of gold plate is long gone and the archway itself is bricked up—so as not to tempt fate, according to the lore of the vanquished, and leave the city open to a Byzantine restoration led by some as-yet-unrevealed Greek mahdi. In point of fact, the Golden Gate was similarly blocked in Giustiniani's day, not only because there had been no Byzantine triumphs to celebrate for centuries, but, quite simply, as a defensive measure. The magnificent structure was incorporated into the land walls, and the maze of courtyards and towers that had sprung up about it made it the linchpin of the fortifications.

Far more problematic for Constantine's Genoan commander was the other extremity of the wall, by the Golden Horn. This was the quarter of the Blachernae, the imperial residence ever since a basileus of the crusading era had quit the old palace in the crowded precincts of the Hippodrome to seek more salubrious surroundings in a distant corner of the city. The wall of the Blachernae was several meters thick but was unprotected by a bulwark of further walls beyond it. This new wall, much of it constructed by Manuel Comnenus, the vanquished at Myriokephalon in the twelfth century, met the fourth-century Theodosian fortification at an awkward right angle, a weak link in the linear march of tower and moat across the countryside. And that countryside was not without its natural traps—about two kilometers from the perpendicular junction of the old and the new ran the stream of the Lycus, a watercourse leading into the city that, despite its insignificance, had carved a dangerous valley into which the walls had to descend. By sighting cannons on the lips of this valley, near the modern-day mausoleum and opposite, Turkish gunners could fire directly down into the defensive positions. There, on the heights of the Lycus, Urban's masterpiece was placed, and the sultan pitched his tent.

Thus, the stretch of wall from the Lycus to the Blachernae is where the fate of Constantinople was played out. Few places are more momentous for historical memory and more ostentatiously neglected. Perhaps the continuing existence of the wall, although crumbling in places and cannibalized in others for Gypsy housing, is testament enough. At the Edirnekapi (Adrianople Gate) pedestrian threshhold, a large stone plaque was affixed in 1953 to celebrate Mehmet's feat of arms five hundred years earlier. The plaque is now a grime-covered affair under which, on a recent visit, amiable vagrants offered to share what appeared to be raki or vodka straight out of the bottle. The neighboring Blachernae is a ruin, the yawning well of its underground dungeons a reminder that the civilization destined to disappear was not entirely benign. A small playground adorns an anonymous courtyard of the palace. Nearby, at the right-angle turn of the walls, a brother Byzantine residence—the Palace of the Porphyrogenitus—has better weathered the insults of time, the white marble and red brick of its three-story facade displaying the intricate geometry of master craftsmanship. Although inside an empty husk, the Porphyrogenitus—Tekfursarayi, in Turkish, or "Palace of the Sovereign"—has an ample and evocative forecourt, rare in the warren of its run-down neighborhood; on the day of the merry derelicts at the Edirnekapi, a television crew had assembled at the Porphyrogenitus to tape a tryst for an episode of a Turkish soap opera. Aside from these present-day incongruities, this stretch of the wall is graced by several cypress-ringed cemeteries—Turkish, Greek, Armenian—that pay indirect homage, through their dignity, to the importance of the site.

Another evocative marker of the momentous events of 1453 lies a short way upstream from the Blachernae on a curve of the Golden Horn. According to the lore of the victors, on arriving from Edirne that year Mehmet's men miraculously discovered there the remains of one Eyup Ensari, a friend of the Prophet and a standard-bearer of Islam who had met his death in old age at Muawiya's

The meeting point of the Theodosian and Blachernae land walls of Constantinople. The tallest building is the Palace of the Porphyrogenitus.

failed siege of Constantinople. Fired by faith, Mehmet built the Companion a worthy tomb—now a graceful mosque surrounded by the mausoleums of Ottoman grandees—and thus guaranteed the success of his venture. The lore, like that concerning the Golden Gate, may be somewhat fanciful—a shrine was known to be there in Byzantine times—but that detail in no way diminishes the cult surrounding the Eyup Sultan Mosque, which is now the holiest spot of Turkish Islam, or the role Mehmet played in bringing it to prominence. In addition, the young sultan, in his devotional magnanimity to Eyup, may have unknowingly tipped the scale in his favor. Eyup is the Turkish form of Ayyub, or Job, a name regularly linked to Islam's greatest triumphs in the eastern Mediterranean. From Dar Ayyub, the grave of Job, Khalid ibn al Walid had dashed to victory at Yarmuk; and at Hattin Saladin, the son of a Job and the founder of the Ayyubids, had crushed the Latins of Outremer. In that spring of 1453, Mehmet could hardly have picked a better patron saint than the Job of the Turks.

⤙ ⤙ ⤚ ⤚

The deafening cannonade of early April was relentless. Although Urban's great weapon could be fired only once every three hours or so, dozens of other guns pounded the land walls day and night, for weeks on end. The city did not sleep. Giustiniani ordered work details out into the maelstrom, to shore up the shattered stretches of the outer defenses. Men rushed through the lists between the walls to these breaches, trundling barrels filled with stones to be hoisted atop the makeshift berms that spade-wielding navvies desperately labored to complete before the next salvo struck. Giustiniani seemed to be everywhere at once, from the Marmara to the Horn. Even the Venetians obeyed him. The Genoan herded the volunteers to where they were needed; Phrantzes' census had tallied only able-bodied warriors, but with their life, their honor, and their city in peril, women and youths pitched in as well. Yet they too were few in number—a metropolis of perhaps a half-million in the twelfth century, the capital now counted around fifty thousand souls, the great walls of the city actually enclosing a series of village clusters separated by fields dotted with vestiges of imperial grandeur. The decline of the centuries had never been reversed, and Constantinople had become that most dangerous of things—an idea. Its conquest, to Mehmet, would mean continuity; its loss, to Constantine, extinction.

To the common soldiery besieging the city, it would mean riches. On repeated occasions in the firestorm of April, thousands of bashi-bazouks rushed headlong

to the Lycus-Blachernae fortification once a cloud of dust had settled to reveal a
gap, their shrill cries mixing with barked imprecations from the defenders. Each
time the attackers were repulsed, their onslaught impeded by the confusion of
hundreds of men jostling together to gain access to the same sliver of precious
daylight beyond the wall. The Christians brought withering fire to bear on them
from atop the undamaged section of the walls; down below, any narrow gap
could be plugged with a relatively small number of determined men. In addition,
armor had improved immeasurably since the time of the crusades, and the Genoese and Greeks wore light curved breastplates to deflect sword blows and
sturdy metal helmets that had nothing in common with the heavy stovepipes
donned by knights of an earlier day. The poorly armored irregulars of the Turks
were no match for the well-protected Latins and Byzantines, who were equally
light on their feet.

Within the walls, the days passed in a ceaseless round of prayers and invoca-
tions. In that exceptionally rainy spring, icons were paraded through the mud
from church to monastery, the dull roar of the bombardment a sinister counterpoint to the chanted liturgies. On the morning of April 20, atop the sea walls of
the Marmara near the Golden Gate, monks impressed into service as sentinels
interrupted the dirge of battle with a clarion of joy. Once again three Genoese
sails appeared on the horizon, this time as escort to a huge grain ship dispatched
by the pope to provision the besieged, whose lifeline to the Black Sea had been
strangled by the strait-cutter. The Ottoman fleet, moored near the Rumeli Hisari, weighed anchor and rowed mightily against the wind to intercept the great
galleys. Mehmet, on hearing of the convoy, quit the Lycus Valley, crossed the
Horn near Eyup's shrine, and then rode over the hill of the Galata to the
Bosporus shore. According to many accounts, his impatience was such that he
spurred his mount into the water, shouting instructions to his Bulgarian renegade admiral. The Turks, however, could do nothing against the wind—the tall
Italian ships barreled onward, nearing the headland of the city. The ecstatic defenders prepared to lower the chain protecting the Golden Horn.

Then the wind died. The Bulgarian quickly closed on the becalmed ships, their
great sails limp. What followed was a deadly daylong scrum watched by thousands on the nearby shores, as dozens of small Turkish warships surrounded the
Genoese flotilla, their sailors hurling grappling hooks and attempting to board.
The Latins lashed their ships together, to form a floating fortress. In the hours of
hand-to-hand fighting the defenders had the advantage—from the tall decks of
their great vessels they occupied the higher ground and could slash down at will at

the swarms of Turks desperately hanging on to the hulls. Mehmet watched with mounting dismay as the oars of the small Turkish galleys milling about the fight became entangled and as the shot from their light guns whistled harmlessly above the waterline of the Christian ships. Worst of all, as the sun sank lower over the plain of Thrace, the wind picked up once again. The Genoese sails billowed, the chain was lowered, and two Venetian war galleys rushed out of the Horn to give them cover. Within minutes, all were behind the boom, safe and victorious.

It was a very public defeat for the Ottoman Alexander. Disgusted, Mehmet berated his admiral and ordered his immediate execution. The unfortunate man's officers bravely intervened, imploring the sultan to show clemency in view of his personal valor throughout the entire engagement. Uncharacteristically, Mehmet relented; he simply condemned the Bulgarian to a bastinado—flogging the soles of the feet to a pulp—and exile as a dispossessed beggar. Justice having been served, the sting of conspicuous humiliation still remained to be assuaged; within days Mehmet had speeded a scheme to restore morale in his camp and to crush it in the Christians'. If the Turkish fleet could not sail into the Golden Horn, then it would ride in, overland.

A newly installed battery of guns—which, according to some military historians, were placed pointing skyward, at Mehmet's suggestion, and thereby inaugurated the era of the mortar—roared into action on Sunday, April 22, from the hilltop above the Genoese settlement of Galata. The bombardment surprised the sailors moored opposite in the waters before Constantinople, as well as its defenders on the sea battlements. Heretofore the firepower of the Ottomans had been centered on the land walls. As the Greeks and the Venetian, Catalan, and Cretan volunteers cowered in their shelters, a spectacle worthy of the ancients took place on the sudden slopes behind the Latin suburb. A road, paved with greased wooden planks, had been carved up and down the seventy-to-eighty-meter-tall ridge separating the Bosporus from the Golden Horn. Hundreds of men and oxen strained to haul the Ottoman ships over the height, as the cannons shielded their ungainly progress with a punishing barrage. By day's end most of the Ottoman fleet was in the Golden Horn, opposite Eyup, a few kilometers upstream from the Christian fleet huddled near the now-obsolete chain. A Latin plan to launch fireships against the intruders failed—mainly through delay caused by bickering between the Genoese and the Venetians—and by the end of April the Horn was no longer a safe haven. Constantinople was now well and truly surrounded.

‹‹ ‹‹   ›› ››

Where, in God's name, was the help from the west? The questioning became sharper. What had been the point of stifling objections and accepting the union of the churches in the past winter, if there was to be no quid pro quo? Rumors had flown of a Venetian and even a papal fleet approaching to raise the siege, but they had proved chimeras of wishful thinking. What the Greeks could not know was that the Latins were being dilatory and disputatious to the last. Well aware of the dangers of backlash on its Ottoman trade, Venice was proceeding cautiously, gathering ships at a snail's pace to launch a rescue mission sometime in the summer. This undertaking was, in the event, better than that of Genoa— which abstained altogether from any grand enterprise—and those of western European monarchs, who had issued hot blasts of air condemning the siege, but nothing more. The remarkable absence of urgency may have stemmed from seeing Constantinople, albeit in a manner different from Mehmet and Constantine, as an idea—or an ideal. To Christendom, it had always been there, like the polestar, inextinguishable and permanent; a Mediterranean world without it was unthinkable.

What the Latins could not know, or perhaps even imagine, was that by mid-May that sempiternal light was flickering. The ceaseless bombardment of the land walls had pummeled into shapeless rubble much of the breastwork in the Lycus Valley. Mehmet had also summoned tunnelers from Novo Brodo, the silver mines near Kosovo, to join their Serbian brethren opposite the Blachernae. The sappers sought to mine the fortification there, digging long passageways from their camp to the underpinnings of the wall. Fortunately, for the besieged, a Latin volunteer named Johannes Grant came to the fore at this moment; a German or perhaps a Scot, Grant had a mole's nose for the subterranean darkness, and within days the Serbs had been driven back through flooding, countermining, and vicious hand-to-hand fighting underground.

That small but important victory could not, however, dispel the gathering gloom. The time of illusions had come to an end. Earlier in May a dozen valorous sailors of the city, disguised as Turks and flying a tricked-up Ottoman banner for the occasion, had brazenly sailed past Mehmet's ships and made for the Dardanelles—they had volunteered to find out if any Latin war fleet was tacking across the Aegean to put an end to the misery of the siege. They spent two weeks looking, questioning the inhabitants of various island colonies, scanning the horizon; loyal to the end, they returned to the city they now knew to be doomed and informed Constantine that no help was on the way. His advisers begged him to flee while there was still time and to set up a government-in-exile, perhaps in the Peloponnese. Constantine demurred. He would not be basileus anywhere but in the city that bore his name.

On the Turkish side, there was no cause for complacency. The Ottomans had been encamped in the mud before the great walls for nearly two months yet had won no decisive victory. The exploit of the Golden Horn, however heartening, had not brought about the capitulation of the city. Assaults had been checked, siege towers had had no effect, their army had suffered grievously. Halil Pasha argued for lifting the siege, before the blow to Ottoman prestige became too devastating. Constantinople was supremely useful as a hostage, a pawn to be deployed in wringing concessions from the Christian powers; it would be dangerous as a lightning rod for Christian resistance to the sultan's empire. Mehmet listened to his father's confidant one last time, but again rejected his advice. He and the other pashas decided to gamble on a massive assault.

In Constantinople's final week of existence as a Christian capital, the elements combined to give it an eerie send-off. We know this from several eyewitness accounts, including those by penned by George Phrantzes, Nicolo Barbaro—a level-headed Venetian surgeon—and several other chroniclers, Turkish and western. Already aware of the divine disfavor that the unusually wretched spring suggested, the last of the Byzantines watched in dismay on the night of May 24, 1453, as the full moon above them disappeared. A lunar eclipse plunged the city into blackness for three full hours, the only bright light in the sky coming from the flash of the cannonade beyond the walls. Stricken by this awful sight, the people of Constantinople gathered the next morning to form a procession behind the city's holiest icon of the Virgin Mary, hoping she would perform a miracle and save them. As they moved through the streets, rain began to fall. The icon slipped and fell into the mud; no hand seemed able to lift it back into place. The sky then opened with a deafening crash and a hailstorm of titanic ferocity whipped earthward, scattering the terrified worshipers and causing torrents of water to run through the streets and nearly carry off the children. The procession was over, the miracle left unperformed.

Further portents followed, without precedent in living memory. The next day, the seven hills and the desolate remnants of imperial Constantinople were blanketed with impenetrable fog, unheard of for that time of year. When it lifted the following evening, the great dome of the Hagia Sophia came alive with some strange incandescence, a purplish-pink glow that shimmered and threw off an unearthly light. To this day the phenomenon has never been adequately explained. Even Mehmet, far away beyond the walls, saw the uncanny spectacle; his Sufis told him not to worry, that it was a sign the city was about to be possessed by the light of Islam—"the light of Heaven and Earth . . . not that which shines through glass or gleams in the morning star or glows in the firebrand," as the inscription on the dome now reads.

The following day, May 28, dawned utterly silent: no storm, no fog, no strange light—and no bombardment. Giustiniani Longo's watchmen peered over the battlements and saw the Turkish armies moving closer to the wall. The great attack was imminent. Processions formed within the city, the church bells rang, icons were lifted skyward. Constantine addressed a large gathering of defenders near the walls. The basileus gave them four reasons to fight to the death—for one's faith, one's country, one's family, and one's sovereign. On the morrow the people of Constantinople would have not one but all of those reasons to show their courage.

That evening, the last great Christian service in the Hagia Sophia took place. Everyone came—Greek, Latin, noble, merchant, commoner, slave, man, woman, child. The sanctity of union between Latin and Orthodox churches was no longer a shibboleth—all prayed as one for deliverance, their eyes glistening in the light thrown off from the mosaics. As darkness fell, Constantine and Phrantzes left the great church and rode along the Mese, the main artery of the old capital, until they reached the land walls. At the Blachernae, the basileus bade farewell to his staff and servants, asking them to forgive him any injustice he had ever done them. He went out onto a terrace and looked out over the sea of campfires in the Thracian plain. He took his leave of Phrantzes—for the last time—strapped on his armor, and headed to the Lycus to see if everyone was at the ready.

At the same time, barely two hundred meters away, Mehmet and his generals rode up and down the line of attack, encouraging their men, telling them that God expected nothing less than victory. Glory was within reach, if not in this life then in the next—all those who died a martyr's death in the approaching moment of battle would instantly savor the joys of paradise.

Midnight tolled. On the battlements the Christians fingered their crosses and amulets; in the fields below, a deep groundswell of prayer rose heavenward, as tens of thousands prostrated themselves.

In the end, men turned to God in their hour of fear. Constantinople may have been an idea, an ideal, or even just a feather in the cap of a great man bent on conquest, but to all it also remained the citadel of the sea of faith.

‹‹ ‹‹ ›› ››

In the very early hours of Tuesday, May 29, 1453, the night was shattered. On every side of Constantinople a volcano of bedlam erupted. Hundreds of cannons spat their fire, kettledrums sounded, horns blared, fifes whistled, horses and mules shrieked in terror, cries and curses rent the air. On the Horn, ships throwing incendiary devices neared the walls; on the Marmara, guns boomed from indistinct shapes out at sea. And before the whole length of the land walls, a great wave surged forward, torches aloft, voices raised, oblivious to the cannonballs whistling overhead and crashing into the ancient stone. The defenders saw that no place was to be spared attack, that Mehmet had thrown the full force of his armies against them, that few Christians could be spared to join their comrades where the fighting would be fiercest—at the Lycus-Blachernae.

There, in the crumbling mess left by six weeks of bombardment, the main event occurred. All else, however deadly, was distraction. From their vantage point atop the walls of the Lycus, Constantine and Giustiniani watched a huge cohort of bashi-bazouks come screaming out of the darkness, a wild rabble of warriors clambering up the makeshift slopes of the outer defenses. The Latins and Greeks were there to meet them, in a hellish melee of sword and halberd. From the walls, arquebuses popped, arrows sang, crossbolts let fly. The Turks fell by the hundreds, littering the earthen slope. More appeared, to meet the same wall of death, then more still. The hours passed; the fighting knew no letup. At a sign a new mass of men hurtled forward—the Anatolian regular troops, more disciplined than the bashi-bazouks. The same clutch of desperate defenders, a thousand at the very most, held off this fresh, raging sea of constant, murderous assault as the missiles from Mehmet's cannons tore through the mass of humanity to bring down more of the fortifications. The fight became centered on the rubble of the middle walls, where a horrific game of king of the castle was played out in the darkness as each side tried to hold the summits. Not for nothing do playgrounds seem to be the ornament of choice for old battlefields.

The Janissaries came on, exhorted by Mehmet, "Go on my falcons, march on my lions!" Magnificent physical specimens—the biggest and strongest males from the Balkans—they moved quickly and silently up to the walls, their flowing white uniforms in the predawn light making them seem like an army of gigantic wraiths. Legend has the largest of them all, an Anatolian colossus named Hasan, scaling the wall and taking out dozens of Christians single-handedly before finally being overwhelmed, Gulliver-like, by the force of numbers. Yet collective discipline, not individual heroics, made the Janissaries so fearsome: before the Lycus walls they crashed like breakers on the shore, each bloodied wave retiring in good order to let a new onslaught rush forward. The Christians, exhausted from fighting for hours without respite, were faced with a continuous battering from fresh and ferocious soldiery. The defenders wavered, backing down into the moat before the last, inner wall.

Atop that wall, a missile pierced the armor of Giustiniani Longo, mortally wounding him. Knowing his end to be at hand, the Genoan had his men lift him into a stretcher to be carried to a ship waiting in the Golden Horn. The basileus pleaded with him to remain at his post, so as not to demoralize the increasingly

Janissary foot soldier in the early days of firearms.

desperate defenders. Giustiniani refused. As the cortege set off, the Genoese in the moat saw it and lost heart. They ran back into the city, leaving their Greek comrades to be massacred by the swarming Janissaries.

At this moment, an Ottoman banner was seen flying atop the wall near the Palace of the Porphyrogenitus. At the vulnerable right angle of fortifications, a postern gate had apparently been left open in the confusion; a squad of attackers had spotted it and rushed through. Soon they were joined by more and more Turks, overwhelming the Venetians defending the Blachernae quarter.

The end had come. Constantine XI Dragases, the eighty-ninth and last emperor of Byzantium, tried rallying his men to turn back what was now an unstoppable tide. In all likelihood, he and his faithful courtiers rushed to the breach of the Lycus, and died there, fighting for their world. The rest of the defenders on those walls met the same fate, as the armies of Mehmet poured into the city. The Red Apple was theirs.

Sometime in the midafternoon, Mehmet II, now Fatih the Conqueror, rode slowly through the Edirnekapi into Constantinople. His horse picked its way along the same Mese down which Constantine and Phrantzes had traveled the night before. Fatih had promised his men a three-day sack of the city—the customary fate of any town taken by force—and they had been vigorously looting, raping, killing, and enslaving since daybreak. Smoke hung in the air; bodies lay sprawled in the streets.

At last Fatih reached the Hagia Sophia. He dismounted, crouched briefly on the ground, and then sprinkled a handful of dirt over his turban in a gesture of humility. The congregants, who had gathered there in the morning to pray for an angel to appear and smite the Muslim invaders, were all gone—shackled and herded into groups to be sold, ransomed, or ravished. Pious legend has the priests disappearing into the very walls of the church, destined to reemerge and continue their service once Christ returned to Constantinople.

Fatih entered the sanctuary, which was empty save for a few tardy treasure-hunters squabbling over the slim pickings left by the thorough looting of the morning. The sultan sharply ordered one man to desist from prying a marble slab from the floor. Fatih looked upward at the great dome, just as Justinian had done nine hundred years earlier when he boasted of surpassing Solomon. The Hagia Sophia would henceforth be a mosque.

The conqueror climbed up onto the dome of the Ayasofya. From this dizzying vantage point he could see nearby the old palace of the Byzantine emperors, by then a mournful ruin, neglected for centuries in favor of the Blachernae and the

Porphyrogenitus. The musty grandeur of the building moved Fatih to melancholy. On this, the day of his greatest triumph, the twenty-one-year-old showed a largeness of soul uncommon in men of action three times his age. On beholding the desolate panorama spread out below, Fatih recited an old Persian couplet about kings long dead and the fate to which they—and we—are all condemned, no matter how great their works:

The spider serves as gatekeeper in the halls of Chosroes
The owl calls the watches in the palace of Afrasiyab.

⤙ ⤙ ⤚ ⤚

The Edirnekapi, through which Mehmet II rode to take possession of Constantinople. To the right is the commemorative plaque affixed in 1953.

The miracle awaited by the Greeks did not happen. Somehow, the angel on duty in 1453 had neglected to swoop down from heaven to drive back the infidel berserks. What had begun at Manzikert was now complete—the Byzantine Empire was gone. Yet for all the loud lamentations that this occasioned in the capitals of Christendom, a miracle did indeed occur: Constantinople was born anew.

For Fatih, the collection of scattered villages that was the Constantinople of May 29, 1453—their churches in disrepair, their hedgerows shored up by fragments of forgotten statuary, their inhabitants murdered or enslaved by his soldiers—could hardly have resembled the prize he had coveted. If, from his perch atop the newest and grandest mosque of the dar al Islam, his mind's eye conjured up the ghosts of vanished monarchs, he could still see very well stretched out beneath him what had made this city such a marvel. Its location remained peerless. The steady flow of the Bosporus, the expanse of the Marmara, the haven of the Golden Horn, the land and sea walls, the forested hills, the meeting of Europe and Asia, the passage from Black to White (Mediterranean) seas—despite the devastation, these assets endured. In classical days, the inhabitants of Byzantium used to joke that their cousins in Chalcedon (Kadikoy) had to be blind: how else could they have foolishly installed their *polis* on the Asian side, a generation before the eponymous Byzas came across what was obviously the finest place in the world to found a city?

The sultan was not blind. Although the lovely Ottoman capital of Edirne lay invitingly between forest and river to the northwest, Fatih saw that its seductions paled in comparison to those of Constantinople. For a conqueror with pretensions that spanned two continents and centuries of history, a sleepy, verdant headquarters, no matter how excellent the hunting, was out of the question. He ordered an evacuation. Edirne was abandoned by its courtiers and concubines, and the Topkapi Palace began rising atop the acropolis overlooking the Golden Horn and the Sea of Marmara. Henceforth, Kostantiniyye (as both Turkish and Arabic rendered the city's name) was Fatih's capital.

The phoenix city would reflect his extraordinary personality: polyglot, cultured, libidinous, and ruthless. As the medieval millennium drew to a close in the Mediterranean, this final flowering of convivencia was about to begin, a long moment of coexistence that would conclude only during the insecurity of the modern era, when the Ottoman Empire became what was known as the Sick Man of Europe. But that rendezvous with provincialism and nationalism lay far in the future. In its first century or so as their capital, the Kostantiniyye of the

Ottomans would outdo the Córdoba of the Umayyads in its cosmopolitan embrace. Under Fatih, the line linking the Mezquita to the Ayasofya was never clearer.

The first thing the conqueror needed was people; therefore, in the renascent Kostantiniyye, everyone was invited into the city. According to debatable popular etymology, "into the city" in Greek (*ees ten polin*) would eventually slide off Turkish tongues as "Istanbul," the nickname that would eventually be decreed the city's official tag in modern times. In many instances, Fatih's invitation was coercive—thousands of Anatolian families were told to move to Kostantiniyye on pain of death. Artisans and skilled workers received special attention from the dragooning servants of the sultan. Fatih was a man in a hurry to build his capital, and his acquaintance with restraint was as glancing as one might expect from an absolute despot. In moving populations around his possessions—under the Ottomans most land belonged to the sultan—he caused tremendous human suffering, but the refurbishment of a has-been capital would have been nowhere near as rapid otherwise. And his willingness to look beyond the talent pool of Islam made the transformation even faster.

News came to the sultan in the autumn of 1453 of a remarkably learned old Greek held in slavery in Edirne. His owner, who had picked up a job lot of captive Byzantines in the buyer's market immediately after the fall of the city, recognized in his purchase an individual of extraordinary quality. The old fellow was treated reverentially, allowed to study and pray and drink wine like any self-respecting Christian holy man. Inquiries were made, and soon Fatih himself arrived to coax George Scholarius into returning to the city on the Golden Horn. Scholarius, or, as he is better known, Gennadios, was the most prominent of the Orthodox churchmen who, until the very last, had held out against any plan of unity with the Latin westerners in embattled Constantinople. Fatih promised Gennadios a restored see in Kostantiniyye—that is, an Orthodox patriarchate that would function independently of the Latins under the protection of an Islamic ruler. Although he would not give the Greeks back the Hagia Sophia, they were free to use another great church as their headquarters, and a handful of other Christian sanctuaries in the city would be ruled out of bounds to imams in search of ready-made mosques.

The overture, unprecedented for the era, was accepted. By way of contrast, the sophisticated Venice of the time collapsed into civil anarchy when the doge proposed allowing a lone mosque to be built in the city for visiting Muslim merchants.* Fatih was rumored to harbor a curiosity about Christianity—he is even said to have ventured incognito into a Franciscan church one Sunday to observe the goings-on. He had Gennadios write him a treatise explaining Christian doctrine. He commissioned a Greek sycophant of talent to write what would now be called an authorized biography. In it Fatih's dedication to Kostantiniyye produced an ecumenical lovefest, whereby the sultan took people "from all parts of Asia and Europe, and he transferred them with all possible care and speed, people of all nations, but more especially of Christians."

Whatever the affinities lying behind his motives, the result of Fatih's initiatives was enlightened. The natives of the city—those who had eluded slavery or been ransomed—returned. Although the brain drain of Byzantine scholars to the Italian peninsula accelerated, a large Greek community took root once again on the shores of the Bosporus. Soon the wharves of the Golden Horn once again rang with the shouts of Greek merchantmen. In due time the Armenians, permitted to establish their own patriarchate for their ancient monophysite version of Christianity, also returned in force, bringing with them their formidable knack for craftsmanship and commerce.

As for the Latins, their presence was at once more straightforward and more complicated. The trading concessions granted to them by Byzantine emperors were renewed by the Ottomans, and many were extended under the name of "capitulations." The Genoese of Galata became fast friends with the denizens of the Topkapi. These local Genoese—as opposed to Giustiniani and his men— had remained neutral during the siege of 1453, a politically astute posture that had not gone unnoticed. The capitulations granted the Genoese went practically untouched until modern times. The Venetians, after concluding a war with Fatih shortly after the fall of Constantinople over the rump of the Byzantine Empire in southern Greece, also set up shop in Galata, as did their rivals in Mediterranean trade, the Florentines and the Catalans.

The Levantines—the name later given to these Bosporus Latins—grew in number and influence in Fatih's effervescent city, the women famous for the dazzle of their come-hither clothing and demeanor, the men known for their

*One needn't look so far back for such counterexamples: just prior to the Athens Olympic Games of 2004 a vocal faction in the Orthodox Church opposed the erection of a mosque near the city's airport, claiming it would confuse inbound tourists about the religious identity of Greece.

acumen in business and their penchant for poisoning anyone who hindered their accumulation of wealth. (The Venetians attempted to bribe Fatih's Jewish physician into poisoning him in 1471.) Governed by their own mayors—the *podestà* for the Genoans, the *bailo* for the Venetians—and regulated by their own courts of law, the Latins of Kostantiniyye achieved a measure of autonomy and freedom that left many Muslim Turks scratching their heads. "If you wish to stand in high honor on the Sultan's threshold," wrote one, "you must either be a Jew, a Persian or a Frank." But the sultan, who reaped a tax windfall from his non-Muslim subjects under the time-honored dhimmi system, had no such qualms about his resident infidels, who in 1500 numbered an astonishing one half of Kostantiniyye's population. His agents, who tried to keep the fractious Greek and Latin Christians away from each other's throats, also made sure that the clangorous bells of their churches did not drown out the muezzins' call to prayer. If Kostantiniyye could not look like a Muslim city, at least it could sound like one.

Even more unusual was the composition of Fatih's court and household. Just as he had compelled Muslims into the city, so too were the Christians of the hinterlands forced to bend to the sultan's will. In the years following the conquest, Fatih expanded the heartless *devshirme* or "gathering" system, whereby young Christians were abducted and moved to the capital. In effect, he took the Janissary recruiting method and broadened it to what we would call the state civil service. Once every few years roving Ottoman talent scouts, accompanied by soldiers, descended on the villages of the Balkans and Anatolia and culled the most promising peasant boys from their playmates and siblings. In some instances families consented to—even encouraged—this boy tribute, hoping to see their sons get ahead in the world. In others, no doubt the majority, only sorrow and hatred ensued.

Separated from their kin, the boys were quickly circumcised and converted to Islam, then were educated in austere academies devoted to turning out the elite who would run the empire. A section was reserved for good-looking youths who would become the ruler's personal attendants. Cruel though this boy tribute may have been, it did have the signal advantage of inculcating among its victims unswerving loyalty to the sultan—brainwashing and the lure of material gain have that effect—and ensuring a formidable cohesion at the top. These formerly Christian youths became, in their adulthood, the backbone of the Ottoman state, a cohort of carefully molded men with no past or dynastic attachments. Under this system the sultans avoided the bane of European monarchs—there was no native aristocracy to challenge the authority of the ruler, hence no Magna Carta or *fronde*. Many a great pasha began life as an illiterate Balkan goatherd, and the office of grand vizier, one of the most perilous in the execution-happy courtyards of the Topkapi, was often held by a former Christian. This arrangement is reminiscent of Shmuel HaNagid's exalted position in the Granadan court, save for one notable difference: Grand Vizier HaNagid was not obliged to renounce his Judaism in order to serve his sovereign; Fatih's ministers, on the other hand, had all been forcibly converted to Islam. The mores of conviviencia had varied over the centuries, and even Kostantiniyye could go only so far in its easygoing cosmopolitanism.

❮❮ ❮❮   ❯❯ ❯❯

In Spain, the land where convivencia first shone, the idea of a multiconfessional society was a thing of the past, and developments there, famously, would make Fatih's boomtown even livelier. Across the twilight of the Moors, which had begun on a summer day at Las Navas de Tolosa, darkness finally fell. On January 2, 1492, the armies of *los reyes catolicos* (the Catholic monarchs) took possession of Granada, the capital of the last remaining taifa state. The Christian rejoiced; the Muslim mourned. Granada's last Muslim ruler, Boabdil, paused while crossing a snowy pass in the Sierra Nevada, to look back, through tears, on the Alhambra palace in his dream city. His aged mother is supposed to have said to him in reproach, "You may well weep like a woman for what you could not defend like a man."

Henceforth Islam was homeless in Iberia. The great rock of Gibraltar loomed impassive on the horizon as the Granadans sailed past it on their way to exile in the Maghrib, 781 years after Tariq had gone the other way to defeat the Visigoths. Many of the exiled Iberian Muslims fanned out over the Islamic world; naturally some made their way to the Golden Horn, where a Christian church of Galata was transformed into what is still called the Arap Camii (the Arab Mosque).

Queen Isabella and King Ferdinand, who through marriage had at last united Castile and Aragon, were intent on creating a monolith of faith in Iberia. Under the Catholic monarchs and their like-minded successors, the homeland of convivencia became its burial ground: the memory of King Alfonso's Toledo of the translators was immured in the archives; the Córdoba of the Umayyads was dredged up solely for its episode of Christian martyrdom. Cosmetic surgery was performed on the Mezquita, only to be defeated by the greatness of the original. The story of Rodrigo Díaz became clouded in incense, the legend of the Cid brilliantly making a talented adventurer into a devout paladin of Catholicism. For the rulers of Spain, the past had become an embarrassment, a skeleton of confessional promiscuity to be locked away in a closet of the sacristy.

   This new, single-minded Spain had no room for Jews. That epochal year of 1492 thus saw the expulsion of Spain's Jews, one of the most wanton acts of self-sabotage ever performed by sane rulers. Millennium-old ties of Mediterranean trade and trust, as evidenced in the trove of Cairo's Geniza documents, were denied the Spanish crown. Although many Jews accepted to convert to Christianity, only to be later persecuted by the Inquisition for having done so, many others fled across the Mediterranean. Great numbers of the Sephardim found a home in the lands of the Ottomans, particularly in Thessalonica— which in effect became a Spanish Jewish city—and in Kostantiniyye. The sultans were delighted to admit more dhimmi; aside from the corresponding increase in revenue, the influx of commercial skill, master craftsmanship, and linguistic acumen that the Jews brought could only add luster to the Ottoman work-in-progress on the Bosporus. "They say Ferdinand is a wise monarch," Fatih's son, Beyazit II, is supposed to have exclaimed to his courtiers. "How could he be, he who impoverishes his country to enrich mine!"

The jigsaw was almost complete with the arrival of the Iberian Muslims and Jews. In 1517 Ottoman armies rolled over much of the Middle East and the Arabian peninsula, toppling the long-tottering Mamluks of Cairo and installing in their place pashas answerable to the Topkapi. The Hashemites, descendants of the Prophet and *sharifs* (guardians) of Madina and Mecca, became mere subjects of the Ottomans. With this demotion came the necessity for them to put in an appearance on the Bosporus, adding yet another exotic bird to the city's menagerie of nationalities. The sultan was now the equivalent of a caliph, his home the keystone of Islam. Yet it was more than that: by the opening of the reign of Fatih's great-grandson, Suleyman the Magnificent in 1520, the Conqueror's ambition for his city had been realized.

   The view from the hills of Kostantiniyye during Suleyman's time would have gladdened the hearts of the disconsolate Byzantines of the previous century. In the Golden Horn an ever-moving waltz of masts and riggings signaled the

bustle of maritime traffic docking at the warehouses, taverns, markets, ham-
mams, barracks, and shipyards that lined both sides of the waterway. The car-
racks of the Venetians, the lateen sails of the Egyptians, the galleys of the
Genoese, the slim golden lighter of the sultan, rowed by two hundred men—all
slipped past Seraglio Point, the headland of Kostantiniyye, on errands of commerce and pleasure. The constant babel of the Golden Horn's business and
intrigue contrasted with the quieter shores of the Bosporus, enlivened by multi-
colored palaces, where wealthy grandees from Europe and Asia, from cross and
crescent, met for decorous entertainments away from the heat of the city. One
of the most lavish hosts was Joseph Nasi, a Lisbon-born Jew whose business
empire and influence stretched into the heart of Christendom. Ennobled by the
sultan and given the duchy of Naxos in the Aegean, Nasi held court in his mansion on the Bosporus, the persecutions suffered by his coreligionists in
sixteenth-century Europe an unthinkable barbarity in the Ottoman capital. Indeed, Nasi often remonstrated with his Latin counterparts, combining flattery
with threats, to have the authorities in their home countries cease harassing
the Jews.

  Under Suleyman the Magnificent a paroxysm of organizing took place in this
sprawling mosaic of cultures and creeds. His flattering sobriquet is used only by
westerners; for Turks, he is the Lawgiver. His codification of law, the largest
such undertaking since Justinian had done likewise a thousand years before on
the same acropolis, brought a semblance of order to the ad hoc elaboration of
Ottoman customs. As befitted an exceptional leader, Suleyman was also a
builder. His principal architect, Sinan, a product of the boy tribute and believed
to be of Anatolian Christian stock, undertook several prestigious projects for
the sultan, the largest and most awe-inspiring being the Suleymaniye Mosque,
a thicket of minarets and domes rising on the height near an aqueduct constructed for the Roman emperor Valens in the fourth century.* In the generations immediately following Fatih's conquest, the great Islamic sanctuaries of

---

*Valens was slain at the battle of Adrianople (Edirne) in 376 by the Visigoths, an event
deemed crucial in the fall of the Roman Empire. Thus the aqueduct evokes several strands
of our story: the disappearance of the mare nostrum; the Visigoths, who were vanquished
by the Franks near Poitiers (507) and by the Muslims in Iberia; and the early Ottoman capital of Edirne, from which Fatih marched to topple the new Rome (Constantinople). Appropriately, nowadays a boulevard named for Ataturk, the man who ushered out the
Ottomans, runs beneath the structure.

Kostantiniyye, designed to rival if not surpass the Ayasofya, rose over the ruins of Constantine's new Rome. The citadel of the sea of faith had been replaced by its last and greatest palimpsest.

In the Istanbul of today are vestiges of the centuries of convivencia begun by the events of 1453. In what was Galata, now Beyoglu, a clutch of Latin churches and western embassies and schools attests to the time, which stretched from the medieval to the modern, when this Islamic capital played host to scores of nationalities, who, if they did not lock arms, at least rubbed elbows. Much of the city's subsequent, postmedieval development had more to do with European power politics and a stagnant Ottoman sultanate than any considerations of faith. In the twentieth century the rise of Turkish nationalism in the wake of Ottoman collapse put the final nail in the coffin of the old cosmopolitanism, even if a new and vibrant Istanbul has since emerged in our own time. To the careless

The Suleymaniye Mosque complex, Sinan's masterpiece in Istanbul. In the upper left of the photograph stands the Aqueduct of Valens.

traveler, all that old Kostantiniyye evokes is not the remarkable convivencia of the fifteenth through seventeenth centuries but a sort of lingering titillation about the harem of the Topkapi, a legacy of overwrought European travel writing. At Ataturk International Airport, those departing the city can still buy a jar of fig mush labeled, in French of course, *L'Aphrodisiaque des Sultans*—a kitsch reminder of the tens of thousands of girls, many of them Slavs, abducted, purchased, or received as gifts for the sultan's seraglio, the courts of the pashas, and the brothels of Galata. This "girl tribute"—along with stories of Sudanese eunuchs ruling the harem roost—has overshadowed, in the popular imagination, the world beyond the walls of Topkapi. While hardly a multicultural Arcadia, the Kostantiniyye of convivencia was, for three centuries, the largest, most variegated city in Europe.

In its Fener district, not far from the fateful walls of the Blachernae and the Lycus, stands the church of St. Mary of the Mongols, so named for a Byzantine princess who funded it after coming home, happy to be widowed, from the court of a Mongol khan. It is the only preconquest church of Constantinople still in use as a Christian sanctuary. Indeed, many of the latter-day churches of the district are deserted—sectarian riots of 1955 forced most Greek Istanbullus into exile. The church of the present-day patriarch, also hidden in Fener, is a model of discretion, one whose low profile would no doubt shock even Gennadios.

Discretion is one thing; invisibility, another. On a recent visit to the maze of Fener, St. Mary of the Mongols was nowhere to be found. Enlightenment came

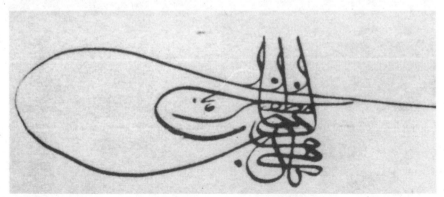

The tughra, or sultan's official monogram, of Mehmet II. It is displayed prominently on a decree of inalienability in the Church of St. Mary of the Mongols, Istanbul.

in the form of a little boy, on his way home for lunch from a Quranic school. Yes, he knew where the mosque of the Rumi was; and after winding through crowded streets, he helpfully waited outside while his charges inspected the old icons within and the framed *firman*—the decree of the sultan—guaranteeing freedom of worship and perpetual ownership of the building. The Conqueror's signature flowed across the old parchment.

Back in the sunlight, thanks were expressed and farewells exchanged. As the boy walked away, someone thought to ask his name.

He looked back over his shoulder, not breaking stride, and said, "Fatih."

CHAPTER TEN

MALTA 1565

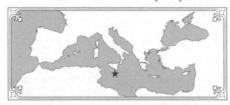

The failure of the Ottomans; the end of the
medieval sea of faith

Sometime before daybreak on June 24, 1565, a flotilla of rafts gingerly eased into the waters of the Grand Harbor of Malta. The harbor's main peninsula, now occupied by the city of Valletta, was still wreathed in the plumes from spent cannonshot when the five small craft began their journey southward. Their destination lay two hundred meters across a cove, where two smaller peninsulas, perpendicular to the main one, were crowded with hundreds of men in armor. Above them, from halyards attached to the battlements, flew the banners of their allegiance. The flags bore the eight-point cross that signified the Knights of the Order of the Hospital of St. John of Jerusalem.

The men holding the arquebuses and muskets atop the fortresses on Birgu and Senglea, the two spits of land sticking out into the Grand Harbor, were of the same breed of warrior-monks who had come to grief at Hattin some four centuries earlier; in 1565 their final hideout on the island of Malta, a speck of sandstone between Sicily and Libya, seemed imperiled as well. Where once, on the tip of the main peninsula, stood the star-shaped Fort St. Elmo, defended for more than a month by several hundred fellow knights against a huge besieging army, there was now only smoke and silence, and the remains of some eight thousand Turkish soldiers, killed in trying to overcome the fanatical defense put up by the Christians. In its final weeks, the great stone mass of St. Elmo had rocked, almost danced, through a punishing artillery barrage. From the fort's peninsula of death the mysterious waterborne offering floated into the darkness. As the sun rose on the feast day of John the Baptist, the patron saint of their order, the watching knights on the peninsulas of Birgu and Senglea realized that they were to receive, apparently, a gift from their attackers.

At a word from Jean Parisot de la Valette, the grand master of the order after whom Valletta would later be named, some local men of Malta plunged into the water to intercept the flotilla. The Maltese commoners, lorded over by French, Spanish, and German knights, performed the dirty work for their rulers, who had arrived on the island just thirty-five years earlier in the latest stop of their Mediterranean itinerary. First quartered in Jerusalem and in such places as the Krak des Chevaliers,* the Knights of St. John were evicted by Saladin and his successors, then driven out of Outremer altogether when Acre fell in 1291. After a brief stay on Cyprus, they set themselves up on Rhodes, whence for two full centuries their galleys disrupted Muslim shipping and raided the lands of Islam with impunity. In those settled years the order, which had been founded to comfort sick pilgrims en route to Jerusalem, took on its definitive late-medieval form: a confraternity of aristocratic Christian corsairs.

After the Ottoman capture of Constantinople in 1453, the piratical knights in Rhodes pointedly refused to pay homage or even respectful lip-service to Fatih. The young sultan let the insult pass for several years but eventually, in 1480, had his armies lay siege to the island. The knights could not be dislodged. Fatih's great-grandson, Suleyman the Magnificent, finally lanced the Christian boil in the eastern Mediterranean in 1522, when Rhodes surrendered, and the youthful sultan, moved to magnanimity by the suicidal bravery of the knights, renounced his right to massacre and let the Hospitalers go free. Seven years of undignified indigence followed, as these scions of the great families of Europe wandered the continent badgering their crowned cousins for a permanent land grant. The order needed a base in the Mediterranean from which to resume launching its marauding galleys. In the end the Habsburg court, correctly foreseeing the knights' usefulness in guarding the approaches to its precious possession of Sicily, bestowed the stony haven of Malta on the order in 1530. Every November 1 the knights, as a rent payment, had to hand over to the Spanish king (who was also the Holy Roman Emperor) one Maltese falcon. The place was hardly the garden of delight they had known in Rhodes, but it was a base all the same. The Maltese, of course, were not consulted. Henceforth they were to be pawns in the knights' dangerous game of baiting the Ottomans.

Thus on a June morning in 1565 a handful of Maltese men found themselves

*The Krak fell to the Mamluk warrior Baybars in 1271.

compelled to take a terrifying early-morning swim. The headlands of their superb natural harbor had become a firing range; scores of primed cannons were trained on them as they performed their task. The centrality of their predicament was fitting. Natives of what has been termed the navel of the Mediterranean, the Maltese, long before the arrival of the knights, had had more than a passing acquaintance with foreign perils: almost every wave of Mediterranean conquest—pagan, Christian, Muslim—had engulfed their island home. Speakers of a Semitic language, the Maltese claim ancestry from the Phoenicians who had colonized neighboring Carthage in the centuries prior to the establishment of the mare nostrum. Local lore explains their long-standing Christianity by having none other than St. Paul himself washing up on a Maltese beach and soddenly converting the entire population in about 59 C.E. Whatever the truth about their somewhat dimly understoood past, the one indisputable trait of the Maltese is that they they were, and still are, at home in the sea. It is supremely appropriate that these people, living square in the middle of the Mediterranean, should participate in the last drama of the medieval sea of faith.

The swimmers reached the flotilla. Cries of horror shattered the expectant quiet: lashed to each of the bobbing rafts was the decapitated body of a defender of Fort St. Elmo. Some of the torsos were nailed to their floats in an attitude of crucifixion. Such was the gift to the Knights of St. John on the holiest day of their year. The Turks on the far shore had sent them a clear message: expect no mercy, no honor, no respect, alive or dead.

Did the Muslims who had contrived this ingenious outrage know the significance of the feast day? They would certainly have known the fate of John the Baptist, beheaded at Salome's behest, and the Turkish commanders, especially those from cosmopolitan Kostantiniyye, were no strangers to the beliefs of their foes. Thousands of Christian slaves—and converts to Islam—were in their forces; indeed, the admiral of the Turkish fleet had been born a Hungarian Christian. Moreover the Order of St. John, which had spent generations in Rhodes attacking the Anatolian coast, was an enemy with whom the Turks were on terms approaching intimacy. The magnitude of the insult, the perfect barbarity of its timing and manner of execution, was anything but accidental.

The bodies were hauled ashore, and the knights sadly identified their mutilated comrades. Grand Master Valette immediately ordered the dungeons of the forts on Birgu and Senglea—the two remaining Christian-held peninsulas of the Grand Harbor—to be emptied of their prisoners. The captives were Muslims, taken either in skirmishes during the month of fighting prior to the fall of St. Elmo or in raids effected by the order's galleys in previous years. Scores of men were brought out, blinking, into the unforgiving sunshine. It was midsummer. The executioner's ax fell.

In the late morning, the victorious Janissaries picking over the remnants of Fort St. Elmo on the main peninsula leaped for cover as a cannonade erupted from Birgu and Senglea. The missiles sailed over Malta's Grand Harbor, the same narrows the hideous flotilla had traversed in the dead of night, and landed with a muffled concussion in the muck of the fallen fortress. There was no shrapnel, no exploding shot. Aghast, the Turks saw the reason—the cannonballs were heads. The artillery of the knights fired another round, then another and another, until the heads of all their prisoners had been lofted back across the Grand Harbor. The reasoning behind this sickening spectacle has not been recorded, but its inhuman one-upmanship would later give pause even to the most ardent admirers of the knights. The Muslims, after all, had decapitated dead defenders; the Christians, defenseless prisoners. In the heat and blood of the Maltese summer of 1565, however, no time remained for scruples. Indeed, the knights had precious little time even to savor trumping their enemy in bloodiness; they were called from the ramparts to assemble in the main church of Birgu, the sole village on the eastern spit of land sticking into the Grand Harbor, for the solemn mass in honor of their patron, St. John the Baptist. The dictates of holiness were not to be neglected.

D. H. Lawrence observed of Malta that "all the world might come here to sharpen its knives." Seen from a tour boat plying the island's coves and creeks, the city of Valletta confirms his judgment resoundingly. In addition to its hinterland's exposed bedrock, barren and unforgiving in the summer sun, a centuries-long tradition of fortress building in the capital has created a curtain of brooding stone. Massive crenellated walls tower over the shores of most of Valletta's many promontories, paid for by wealthy knights and, much later, by British governments. (In 1800 the Royal Navy took Malta from Napoleon, who had preemptively captured it from the knights two years earlier.) As the boat nears the rebuilt Fort St. Elmo, a behemoth of gray blocks, one cannot help thinking that this small island might rival the Strategic Air Command's mountain in Colorado as the most fortified place on earth. Certainly, no other port of the Mediterranean can have been so ostentatiously outfitted for siege warfare. As a final martial meeting place between the standard-bearers of two faiths, few settings could be more cinematic. The sea, the stake in the great medieval showdown, stretches out all around a city proudly standing behind mammoth ramparts. And here, the custodians of memory appear to be firmly in charge. This is no ironic Poitiers or half-forgotten Manzikert—Malta takes its memorializing seriously.

Valletta, a city planned and constructed just after the siege of 1565, has no choice but to revel in its past. Impeccably restored following the depredations of the Second World War, the Maltese capital seems like a visitor just off the boat from the Baroque era. Its attachment to the past is innate: Valletta's builders, the knights, were backward-looking by nature, even in the era in which they lived. By the end of the sixteenth century, their attachment to faith-based adventurism had gradually made the order an anachronism in the affairs of the continent. Belatedness, in fact, seems key to the Maltese experience. Even at the moment of the island's greatest glory, standing firm in the face of Ottoman might, the tides of

The Grand Harbor of Malta. In the foreground, Senglea; beyond it, Fort St. Angelo on Birgu. To the left is the point of Valletta near Fort St. Elmo.

western cupidity and curiosity had already shifted away, making the contest for Mediterranean supremacy a sideshow in the affairs of Europe. Eyes turned to riches and rivalries on the Atlantic instead. The Genoan Giustiniani Longo had rushed east to defend Constantinople and an old world, whereas a generation later the Genoan Columbus went west, to serve the Spanish kings in the quest for a lucrative new one. The gold and silver of the Americas came to fill the coffers of the nascent nation-states in western Europe, and the sea route to the east, around the Cape of Good Hope, had been opened for business. No longer did the conveyors of spices, slaves, and silks necessarily pass through the dar al Islam to reach the West—Arab caravans were being replaced by Portuguese caravels.

Crucially, then, the conflation of belief in another world and self-interest in this one, which was the leitmotiv of the encounter between Christian and Muslim in the Mediterranean, was to be a spur to action elsewhere, for the sea had slipped from its age-old centrality. This took time—the early modern period would witness violent clashes in the Mediterranean—but the process had begun. Even the rationale of belief was no longer a reflexive explanation for success or failure. Not that the spirit failed to move—indeed, Europe was about to plunge into the religious wars between Catholic and Protestant that would shatter its fragile medieval polity forever. Yet already in the fourteenth century, Ibn Khaldun had gingerly suggested that the inevitable rise and fall of empire might lie outside the confines of confessional thought or divinely guided destiny. For the thinkers of the Renaissance, whether a dark Machiavelli or a sunny Erasmus, the certainties of the crusaders had long ago crumbled into dust. The changes wrought by Renaissance and Reformation in the west, and by the consolidation of Ottoman power in the east, were clear enough in outline that far-seeing genius like Ibn Khaldun's was no longer required to realize that one's god might not necessarily take an interest in the doings of caliph and king. Indeed, Catholic France, its enmity toward the encircling Habsburgs of Spain and central Europe as cold as steel, went so far as to make a defensive alliance with the Muslim sovereign of Kostantiniyye. In the sixteenth century, Turkish fleets dropped anchor in Toulon. St. Louis, the thirteenth-century crusader king, would have been shocked at the confessional complaisance of his issue—but the sea of faith he had sailed was no more.

And yet Valletta stands as testament that history is not lived, or even remembered, as postscript. The city's eponym, Jean Parisot de la Valette, couched his argument for defense of the island thus: "It is the great battle of the Cross and the Koran, which is now to be fought. A formidable army of infidels are on the point of investing our island. We, for our part, are the chosen soldiers of the Cross, and if Heaven requires the sacrifice of our lives, there can be no better occasion than this. Let us hasten then, my brothers, to the sacred altar." A scion of the great—and greatly conflicted—families of Toulouse, who had slaughtered infidels in the First Crusade and defended heretics in its Albigensian variant, Valette had no doubt whatsoever that he was fighting for Christ. As for the Turks, the convivencia of their capital did not translate into religious relativism—a slain attacker was found bearing a bracelet inscribed with the words "I do not come to Malta for wealth or honour, but to save my soul." These are not the sentiments of people conscious of being superannuated.

Valletta, of course, is a monument to the Christian viewpoint, even if it was constructed after the last decisive clash of the Mediterranean encounter between the two faiths. The knights on Malta left their valedictory in stone; and, like Justinian and Abd al-Rahman, they lavished special attention on a sanctuary. In Valletta it is the astounding cathedral of St. John, the church of the order.

To understand the cathedral's message is to know that the knights were organized into *langues*—that is, "tongues," or national academies—that took specific responsibilities in the various campaigns of raiding and slaving conducted by the order. In the order's latter—and fatter—days, the langues stayed closer to home, preferring to compete with one another in memorializing themselves. Evidently there was a contest to construct the most elaborate mansion in the city—this was won by the Langue of Castile and León, whose residence, or *auberge*, is an eighteenth-century gem unrivaled anywhere else in Valletta. In the cathedral, however, it is difficult to say which langue outpaced the others. Indeed, the sanctuary of St. John is so stupendously excessive in its decoration that one almost needs sunglasses to survive a visit unblinded. Sculpted galley slaves, altars disguised as clouds, stone effigies recumbent on sarcophagi, coats of arms borne by caryatids, even a gory Caravaggio canvas that aptly takes as its subject the beheading of John the Baptist—all is here in abundance. The church's floor, every square foot of which is covered in a kaleidoscope of marble tombstones carved for dignitaries of the order, beggars the eyes. An overawed Walter Scott proclaimed it to be "the most striking interior I have ever seen." What is at work, behind the supernova of vanity, is a desire to bask in reflected glory.

That glory dates to the moment of 1565, when the island's doughty resistance made it the darling of Christian Europe. That year takes the lead in Malta's theater of memory. In the center of Valletta's grid of auberges and churches,

beside a national library displaying musty *lettres de marque* and antique testimo-
nials, present-day entertainment engineers have constructed an audiovisual
labyrinth that splashily evokes the island's travails of 1565. It, along with much
of the historical literature devoted to the knights, takes the view that pointy-
bearded and incorrigibly wicked Turks suddenly decided to descend on the
saintly Hospitaler knights in a fit of un-Christian aggression. The charge of aggression is certainly true—in their prime the Ottomans relied on conquest to
feed the voracious maw of court and capital—but without doubt Sultan Suleyman had been sorely provoked.

Out on the tour boat, as Fort St. Elmo comes up on starboard, a pincerlike outcropping shelters the entrance of the bay to port. This is Dragut Point. Its name
evokes the reason for war.

⋖ ⋖   ⋗ ⋗

Dragut Rais was a pirate. In the sixteenth century such an occupation was not a
noble calling, but neither was it irredeemably sociopathic. Piracy had its uses.
In the Mediterranean of Dragut's day two great dynasties vied for primacy, the
Habsburgs in the west (who controlled Spain, Sicily, southern Italy, Lombardy,
the Low Countries, Germany, and Austria) and the Ottomans in the east (who
controlled Turkey, Greece, the Balkans, Egypt, Libya, the Maghrib, Palestine,
Syria, Arabia, and Iraq). Each of these enormously powerful families relied on
the lawless to harass the fleet and commerce of the other.

For the Turks, the corsairs of north Africa's Barbary Coast fulfilled this function admirably. Prior to Dragut the pride of Muslim piracy was a pair of brothers originally from the Aegean island of Mytilene, the offspring of a retired
Janissary and an Orthodox priest's widow. The younger and longer-lived of the
siblings is known to history as Barbarossa (Red Beard). In Istanbul today, a
commuter ferry landing on the Bosporus bears his name—proof that even the
most ferocious reputations can be domesticated over time, for Barbarossa, a sea-
man of exceptional ability, was cruel, rapacious, and terrifying, a figure whose
raids on the Christian coastal lands of the Mediterranean led to the erection of
even more of the watchtowers that still stand guard over the sea. From the
Balearic Islands in the west to Crete in the east, Barbarossa wrought havoc.

Barbarossa began his rise to prominence by wresting from the Spanish the toeholds they had gained on what are now the Algerian and Moroccan coastlines. The
already obstreperous region—over the centuries Greeks, Carthaginians, Romans,

Vandals, Byzantines, Arabs, and Turks had all had problems asserting authority
there over the Berbers—was made even more volatile by the arrival of the resentful Iberian Muslims, many of whom had been chased from their ancestral homes
when Granada fell. Resentment, ability, and opportunity came together when Barbarossa made himself the ruler of Algiers, a wide-open port for every adventurer
and cutthroat in the Mediterranean world, the paradigm of a den of thieves.

The Barbarossa brothers, Muslim pirates of the sixteenth-century Mediterranean.

The Christian Spaniards could not possibly come to an understanding with these Muslim corsairs; for the Turks, there was no such barrier. Ibrahim Pasha, the canny Greek who was Suleyman's grand vizier, looked at the murderous maritime rabble and saw opportunity. Much as the Crown of England would later do with Francis Drake, Ibrahim sought to bring a buccaneer into the fold, all in the service of harassing Spain. Barbarossa was offered the official Ottoman governorship of the Barbary Coast, the use of the sultan's treasury in building more ships, and a place of honor at the Sublime Porte, as the governing council was then styled. Barbarossa personally supervised the construction and training of the Turkish navy in the Golden Horn and conducted stunning seaborne commando operations throughout the Mediterranean, at the head of a fleet of galleys filled with Janissaries and his own piratical mates. A particularly nasty shock to Christian complacency, one that had the pope himself running for cover, came in the 1530s, when Barbarossa devastated the coast of southern Italy, burning villages and abducting thousands for slave markets and harems. He even tried to bag the noblewoman Julia Gonzaga, reputedly the greatest beauty of the age, by laying siege to her castle—she got away in her nightgown, although the horseman she clung to while escaping was later executed, at her request, for having had too good a look at the cause of the commotion.

Dragut Rais was Barbarossa's protégé—as the older man mellowed, the younger grew bolder. Born a Christian in Anatolia, Dragut distinguished

A galley of the Order of St. John, for use in Christian piracy.

himself in his youth in the service of the sultan's army before turning freeboot-ing mariner. He took part in the battle of Preveza, where Barbarossa and his gal-leys, in the same expanse of the Ionian Sea that had witnessed the defeat of Mark Antony and Cleopatra in 31 B.C.E., confronted a Spanish fleet com-manded by the great Genoese admiral Andrea Doria. Genoa, its empire prov-ing ephemeral in the face of Ottoman naval might, was reduced to providing sailors for hire to the court of Spain (yet another reason behind the employment history of Christopher Columbus). At Preveza in 1538, the normally adroit Do-ria found himself outmaneuvered by Barbarossa, and the Christian armada, though superior in numbers, was badly mauled. The victorious Barbarossa is supposed to have said of the fearless boarding tactics of his young lieutenant, "Dragut is a lion, he is a braver man than me."

Courage aside, Dragut is more emblematic of the age than Barbarossa. His Christian antecedents—he may have been a product of the boy tribute—underscore the most arresting feature of this era of Mediterranean piracy: many of the best Muslim buccaneers were, in fact, former Christians. Vilified by the clergy and severely punished by the Inquisition if captured, such slippery con-verts had ample reason to let the Christian scales fall from their eyes. Certainly some sought only glory and wealth—both of which would be denied them by the accident of lowly birth in Europe. Others, held captive in the lands of Islam, were forced to convert, although many thousands did so willingly, their new identity as Muslims providing them a chance at freedom and at advance-ment in the ruthlessly meritocratic milieu of the Barbary Coast. Conversion held other advantages as well: no priests consigning souls to hellfire and no no-bles needing their boots licked—only a shot at lucre in this life and paradise in the next, the exploits of brigandage encouraged by a florid wink from the sul-tan in Kostantiniyye. Add to these inducements the attractions of an adopted religion free of clergy, class, and the constraints of monogamy, and the leap of faith required to become a renegade began looking like a very small step. Dragut and his fellow mariners, slavers, and thieves prospered in the embrace of a loosely understood Islam.

Their Christian opponents were no less intrepid. The Habsburg monarch and his admiral, Andrea Doria, raided north Africa repeatedly and on several occa-sions came close to finishing off Dragut. (At Jerba, off the coast of Tunisia, the Muslim pirate eluded Doria by dragging his blockaded ships across the island in the middle of the night.) The Christian fleets of Spain patrolled the western reaches of the Mediterranean to engage the Barbary corsairs, while the galleys of the knights on Malta went on what were called "caravans"—long-haul campaigns of piracy against Ottoman shipping, usually in the eastern basin of the sea. The spies of the Order of St. John kept a close watch on the dockyards of the major ports around the Mediterranean to determine the juiciest targets for the knights' attentions.

The locomotive power for all of this mayhem was the muscle of slavery. At any given time during the sailing season in the sixteenth-century Mediterranean, tens of thousands of naked wretches sat chained to benches on the high seas, forced to live in their own filth as they pulled on the great oars of the galleys. A keen nose could detect the approach of these vessels of human misery long before they were sighted on the horizon. To survive a year or two as a galley slave—frequent ransomings and exchanges of notable prisoners were concluded between Muslim and Christian—was testament to possessing an incredibly robust constitution. After setbacks at various times in their careers, both Dragut and Grand Master Valette had done their time on the galley bench, as had many other knights and renegades. These then were hard men, survivors who knew no other world than that of constant combat and physical effort. Even as they grew old, the mixture of greed, spite, and confessional fervor animating the fighters on both sides ensured that the murderous game would continue unabated.

In late June 1565, immediately after the fall of Fort St. Elmo, as the Turks swarmed the inlets of the Grand Harbor to take up their positions around Birgu and Senglea for the final assault, some among the defenders might well have regretted the actions that had brought things to this perilous pass. In the previous year, Grand Master Valette had commanded the knight Romegas, the only Christian buccaneer to rival Dragut and Barbarossa in piratical panache, to board, capture, and loot a large trading ship bound for Kostantiniyye. Valette's informants would have told him beforehand that the vessel's precious cargo had been underwritten by the chief eunuch of the seraglio, a powerful figure who was a close ally of an even more powerful Ottoman princess. The latter, the daughter given to Suleyman by his beloved Roxelane, a Ukrainian beauty by then deceased, had her widowed father's ear—and the loss of the ship and her investment in it was a splendid pretext to raise her voice. Further, her childhood nurse had been captured and enslaved by these infidels.

With this action, Valette went too far. In his youth he—along with the rest of the order—had been allowed to leave Rhodes unharmed by a gracious Suleyman, an act of compassion that the knights would never recognize or repay. Forty-three years later the sultan rued the day he had shown leniency to these Christian ingrates. Suleyman, the conqueror of Aden, Algiers, Baghdad, Belgrade, Budapest, Nakshivan, Rhodes, and Tabriz, decided at last to put an end to these fanatical crusading corsairs. In his long career he had been foiled only on rare occasions, the most notorious being his failure before Vienna in 1529. But that was long before; in the summer of 1565, an army of some forty thousand soldiers and a fleet of 180 ships, commanded by his most trusted confidants, would show that no one could trifle with the "caesar," as he called himself, who had dedicated his life to the expansion of the dar al Islam: the fate of Malta would show the world the future of the Mediterranean.

◄ ◄   ► ►

The final contest all came down to two thin fingers of rock poking into the salt waters of the Grand Harbor of Malta. Senglea, the more western, was barely inhabited, its perimeter ringed with fortifications and its tip crowned by a star-shaped fortress. It is, at most, one kilometer in length. Birgu, similarly diminutive, housed a small city of Maltese, the hostelries of the different national langues of the order, and the hospital that was the distant descendant of the knights' original establishment in Jerusalem. Birgu was the headquarters of the corsair operation—its shores were rounded with thick walls; its point crowned by a formidable castle, Fort St. Angelo; its landward side protected by great triangular bastions jutting into the rocky hinterland. Between Birgu and Senglea lay Galley Creek, a narrow stretch of water no more than 150 meters wide; across its mouth a chain had been stretched, in much the same manner as the Byzantines had blocked access to the Golden Horn a century earlier.

Valette had readied his positions for this moment—he had ample supplies of food, water, gunpowder, and cannonshot, and a pontoon bridge had been thrown across Galley Creek to allow rapid movement of soldiers from the center of one peninsula to the other. The only thing he really needed, and needed desperately, was men: under his command, after the fall of St. Elmo on the main uninhabited peninsula of the harbor, were a mere seven hundred knights and eight thousand Maltese, as well as a swollen population of women and children from the evacuated villages inland, along with the usual mass of slaves.

With overwhelming and entirely reasonable confidence in victory, tens of thousands of Turks and newly arrived north Africans busied themselves in the

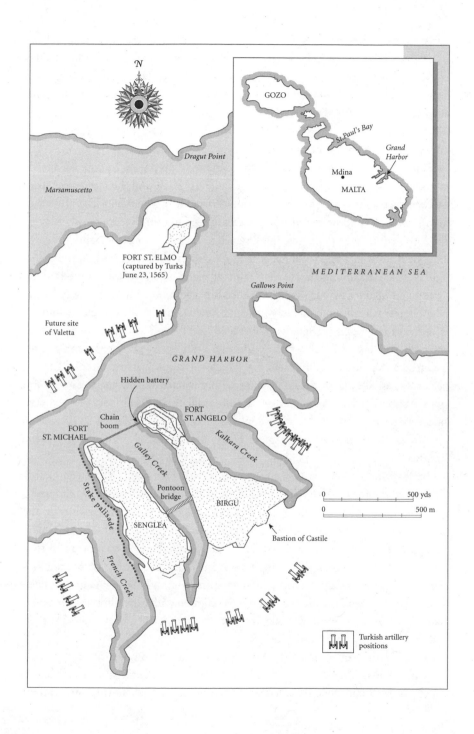

N

Dragut Point

Marsamuscetto

GOZO

St. Paul's Bay

Grand Harbor

Mdina

MALTA

MEDITERRANEAN SEA

FORT ST. ELMO
(captured by Turks
June 23, 1565)

Gallows Point

Future site
of Valetta

GRAND HARBOR

Hidden battery

Chain
boom

FORT
ST. ANGELO

FORT
ST. MICHAEL

Kalkara Creek

Galley Creek

Pontoon
bridge

BIRGU

Stake palisade

SENGLEA

Bastion of Castile

French Creek

0   500 yds

0   500 m

Turkish artillery
positions

early days of July in erecting artillery batteries and constructing siege towers. They blockaded the mouth of the Grand Harbor and, once again, hauled ships overland, this time to the rear of the harbor in order to make sure that Birgu and Senglea were entirely surrounded by land and by sea. The only sour note for the attackers was the disappearance of Dragut. The redoubtable eighty-year-old pirate had been felled by shrapnel and had died on the day the headless corpses had been floated from Fort St. Elmo.

Although it was obvious that the Ottomans were preparing to unleash a ferocious attack—gunnery had improved since Fatih's day, and the Janissaries were by then expert musketeers—the question of precisely where and when the fearsome assault would be mounted nagged at the watchful defenders. Because of the lopsided balance of forces, intelligence was crucial to the knights. In early July, help came in a theatrical fashion, as Christian sentinels spied on the opposite shore a Turkish officer waving wildly at them. The man was spotted too by Ottoman lookouts who rushed to capture him; he jumped into the Grand Harbor, his arms thrashing helplessly in an attempt to stay afloat. Maltese swimmers dived into the water at Senglea and raced surely and strongly to his rescue through a volley of musket shot; within an hour he was before Grand Master Valette and had identified himself as a Greek—but not just any Greek. The deserter was a Lascaris, of the family that had intermarried with the Comneni and placed several of its members on the imperial throne following its exile to Nicaea after the sack of Constantinople in 1204. The defection of so illustrious an officer from the Ottomans gave heart, and precious information, to the knights.

The main target was to be Senglea, on its western side, away from Galley Creek and the formidable Fort St. Angelo on Birgu. Valette promptly ordered a strange, half-submerged palisade to be constructed in the waters outside the western wall of Senglea; festooned with iron hoops, spikes, and the great spars of timber from the masts of the order's galleys, the barrier was meant to stop any seaborne attacker from nearing the fortifications and setting up scaling ladders. The Ottomans sent out their best swimmers at night to dismantle the construction; they were met by the Maltese, small men with gleaming daggers, who had known this harbor and its depths since boyhood. The dark waters turned red, the palisade remained in place.

Still, the Ottoman commander, Mustapha Pasha, could not prolong the wait. The Algerians, Moroccans, and Libyans, led by Dragut's son-in-law and a renegade who had once been a Dominican friar, were chafing to attack their longtime foes and, in the process, show up the Turkish regulars who had wasted a full month in taking the small fortress of St. Elmo. At dawn on July 15, after a deadly artillery barrage, they attacked Senglea. By sea a flotilla of ships pulled toward the peninsula from the rear of the Grand Harbor, their Barbary and Ottoman officers in full finery. "Even the rank and file wore scarlet robes," wrote an eyewitness on Senglea, "and there were many in cloth of gold, and of silver, and of crimson damask. Armed with the fine muskets of Fez, the scimitars of Alexandria and Damascus, and magnificent bows, they all wore splendid turbans." The admiring defender, a Spanish soldier whose memoir of the siege is our best source, nonetheless remarked, "They certainly made a fine sight—almost beautiful, if it had not been so dangerous." By land a corps of similarly splendid Algerians poured down the hillside to the land walls of Senglea.

The firefight lasted most of the morning. The determined Africans, despite the

Jean Parisot de la Valette in middle age.

best efforts of the Maltese, managed to pierce the improvised defense of the palisade and clamber up the walls where desperate hand-to-hand fighting took place. At the neck of Senglea the defenders threw down incendiary wooden hoops onto the massed Algerians, causing their billowing uniforms to catch fire. Into this pandemonium of flame and steel came a sudden explosive shock: a powder magazine in Senglea's fort blew up, creating a gaping hole in the fortifications and, worse, the beginnings of panic. The dispirited defenders fell back. Seeing the situation to be critical, Valette sent a detachment of knights, the manpower he so carefully husbanded on Birgu, charging across the pontoon bridge to join the melee. The defense held, barely—but Mustapha then played his ace.

As expectant eyes on both sides turned to the raging free-for-all on the ramparts, ten ships, each crammed with one hundred Janissaries, silently rowed around the point of Senglea to Galley Creek. The intention was not to force the chain drawn across its mouth, but to stage a surprise landing at the foot of Senglea's fortress and take the defenders from the rear. The thousand-man force was the cream of Ottoman soldiery, a commando unit that Mustapha assumed to be unstoppable. And so it would have been, but for one heretofore insignificant feature of the defense set up by Valette.

Just before the arrival of the Turkish fleet and army in May, the grand master had placed a concealed artillery battery below Fort St. Angelo near the tip of Birgu, at water level, facing Senglea. It was a precaution against any enemy ships that might try damaging the chain between the two peninsulas and forcing an entry into the creek. Wisely, the Ottomans had resisted such a risky gambit; hence Valette's battery had been silent for the entire siege, never firing a single shot to betray its existence. Now, some one hundred meters directly opposite its big guns, ten ships bobbed together in a group, like so many sitting ducks, jammed with men steeling themselves to storm ashore. Their backs were to Birgu. An excited order was whispered, and the cannons roared. Eight hundred Janissaries were killed outright; nine of the ten ships were sent to the bottom. The disaster was complete, the day turned. By sundown the waters around Senglea were clogged with bloated bodies—the attackers had suffered three thousand dead, the defenders, 250. Enraged, Mustapha had his scores of cannon open up on Birgu and Senglea. Every hill and height around the peninsulas hurled hot metal down on the defenders in a foretaste of the attacks to come.

There was now no question of either side negotiating, much less giving up. An old Greek slave from the Turkish encampment was sent to Birgu to deliver an ultimatum from Mustapha; Valette had the fellow blindfolded and prodded to the edge of an abyss atop a wall, at which point the blind was removed and the terrified man promptly soiled himself. Satisfied, Valette told him that the yawning ditch beneath them was where his master's troops would soon find themselves piled up as corpses.

The defenders' determination had some desperation to it. If the Turks were to capture Malta, they might use it as a stepping-stone to the old Islamic land of Sicily and beyond. If they were repulsed, their aura of invincibility would be gone, and the chronically querulous Christians of Europe might come together to thwart them in the Mediterranean. For defender and attacker alike, it mattered little that the battle lines of faith had grown fuzzy, that the future lay on the Atlantic, that their masters had long ago become partners in the acquisition of wealth and the perpetuation of power. In the end, what was at stake, unbeknownst to its protagonists, was one last attempt at changing the confessional geography of the lands ringing the ancient sea. The waters of the Mediterranean would not be calm in the modern era, but that period's concerns of empire and capital differed from the medieval fascination with faith. On Birgu and Senglea, the last drama of a vanishing world became melodrama.

The island was a furnace as July turned to August. Man abetted nature in rendering Malta unbearable, for the first week of the new month passed in an incessant firestorm. Mustapha Pasha had moved his artillery closer to the peninsulas, resighting the great guns to cause the maximum damage to the fortifications. Valette, in Birgu, sent out slaves to build barricades in the city streets, in the event a breach was made and the Turks poured through the walls. The unfortunate laborers working on these barriers died by the hundreds as the Ottoman artillery sent deadly missiles sailing into their midst. The bombardment of early August continued for six days and nights, of an earth-shaking intensity not yet witnessed on the island. In Syracuse, some 150 kilometers distant on Sicily, the broiling summer days echoed faintly with the cannonade, a strange rolling thunder under cloudless skies.

If the sinister rumble made the Sicilians think of Malta, their island was, in fact, uppermost in the minds of the belligerents at Birgu and Senglea. For the knights, their hopes of salvation lay in Sicily: the powerful Habsburg viceroy there had repeatedly promised since the beginning of the siege to send reinforcements to turn the Turkish tide, yet like the Latins in 1453 he had stubbornly failed to deliver. For the Turks, the arrival of a strong relief force from Sicily would further endanger an enterprise that grew more difficult as the weeks and months passed.

The passage of time eventually became a problem for Sicily's viceroy. As tales of the heroic defense spread, tiny Malta rose to the status of cause célèbre throughout Europe. Even the Protestant queen of England, Elizabeth, would write of this dreadful Catholic affray, "If the Turks should prevail against the isle of Malta, it is uncertain what further peril might follow to the rest of Christendom." For the Habsburg envoy, prevarication became less politic as indignation built, even if the choice facing him remained the same as it had been throughout the spring and summer: risk stripping the defenses of Sicily by sending an army south to an uncertain fate, or play it safe by keeping men and ships ready to repulse any assault on his island. It was better to lose Malta than Sicily. Despite the many voices pressing him to take action, the viceroy continued to delay as the summer drew on. On August 7 the distant thunder fell silent; listeners in Sicily wondered if Malta had finally been taken.

At Birgu and Senglea the silence meant only one thing: the knights clambered through the rubble-strewn streets and raced to the ramparts. Through the swirling smoke and dust and flames came the whizzing of musketry and the cries of thousands of men hurtling toward them. Mustapha had ordered an attack everywhere, all at once. On the landward side of Birgu, a massive outer wall of a bastion known as the Post of Castile had been breached. The Turks were streaming through. At the neck of Senglea the attackers swarmed the walls. No longer could reinforcements be sent across the pontoon bridge to one or the other of the peninsulas; both were utterly beset. Mustapha, at age seventy, drew his sword and led a charge of Janissaries into Senglea. The knights fell back, overwhelmed, straining in their armor to fend off the scimitars flashing in the sunlight. From Birgu, where a desperate standoff was taking place, Valette could see that Senglea would soon fall. Mustapha pressed on, farther and farther along the length of the promontory, the banners of the Ottomans advancing inexorably.

Suddenly Turkish trumpets onshore sounded a retreat. Puzzled, Mustapha and his men paused. Messengers reached him with the terrifying news that Christian reinforcements had landed and were at the main Turkish encampment several kilometers inland. The bloodied knights watched, amazed, as their assailants, on the verge of victory, re-formed and rushed rearward, away from Senglea. The attack was over.

Fearing the worst, Mustapha sent out scouting parties in search of the dread Sicilian expeditionary force. They scoured the island but came across no Habsburg levy of soldiers, only the customary sun-bleached emptiness. Their camp,

however, was a ruin: it lay littered with the bodies of hundreds of injured soldiers, summarily slain in their sick tents. Even the cooks had been murdered.

When Mustapha discovered the explanation for this latest atrocity, he swore to
kill every knight of the order. The end of the cannonade earlier in the day had
been noted not only by noncombatant listeners in far-off Sicily. In the center of
Malta stood the modest city of Mdina, untouched by the events of the siege and
garrisoned by a small detachment of knights and their men-at-arms. The ferocity of the week-long bombardment, followed by its sudden cessation, had led
them to suspect that an unprecedented assault was under way in the Grand Harbor, one that might draw all available manpower away from the Turks' camp. A
band of horsemen left the protective walls of Mdina and advanced through a
countryside usually thick with thousands of the foe. They met no one, until arriving at the undefended camp crowded with the weak and the wounded. The
knights from Mdina quickly set to work massacring and burning, but not before
they told those whom they judged fit enough to run away and spread the news
that they were the advance guard of a huge Sicilian army. By the time Mustapha
returned, they had vanished. A savagely brilliant ruse had saved Senglea.

The madness continued. Mustapha no longer cared about Senglea; Birgu, the
vile head and heart of the monstrous order, had to be crushed. A great siege
tower was built, covered with soaking hides, and rolled up toward the sagging
walls of the Post of Castile. The men atop the tower fired flaming arrows and
threw incendiary devices down on the defenders. Valette had foreseen the peril:
large casks of seawater stood at regular distances on the ramparts, so that his
soldiers could douse their flaming limbs and continue the fight. He had even
found a solution to the dangerous siege engine: unbeknownst to the Turks, yet
another artillery battery had been set up, hidden behind movable blocks at the
base of the bastion. When the tower finally reached the wall, the blocks were pulled
away and a tremendous salvo of shot and chain tore into the props of the structure from point-blank range. It tottered, then fell over into the ditch.

Mustapha mined, Valette countermined. Mustapha executed prisoners in
sight of the walls, Valette hanged his from the ramparts. Mustapha feigned an
attack on Senglea, then set off a tremendous charge that brought down both
the outer and inner walls of the Post of Castile. The Turks ran into Birgu
proper. Now it was Valette's turn—at seventy-one, he ran through town to the
breach, staunching the flow of his panicked men and forcing them to turn and
hold back the Turks. The Maltese civilians pelted the attackers with stones, the

knights charged, and men from rooftops threw down burning brands and iron hoops. Birgu was saved.

Throughout it all the cannons blasted away. There was no more room in the hospital. Any man who could stand was not considered wounded. They crouched on the ramparts, small children bringing them sponges soaked with wine. Women brought up the last of the munitions. In the Turkish camp, dysentery set in and news came of supply ships being hijacked on the high seas. Mustapha learned that he had less than three weeks' worth of grain to feed his great host.

Meanwhile Valette's senior commanders urged a retreat of all men, women, and children into Fort St. Angelo at the tip of Birgu. Senglea could no longer hold, they argued; neither could the town of Birgu. They would stand a fighting chance within the embrace of the fortress. Valette alone disagreed: it was better to keep the Turks occupied with many targets, even if it meant greater loss of life. To cede an inch would be to cede the battle; the attackers, he reasoned, could not know how desperate the defenders were.

On August 20 eight thousand Ottoman troops volunteered to storm Birgu or die in the attempt. Most of them fulfilled the second proposition, for the counterfire of the defenders remained withering, even from the shapeless piles of stone that had once been the proud bastions. The attack fizzled and collapsed, the Turks' morale sinking even lower than the physical condition of the defenders. Both sides were exhausted.

Only Valette knew that, a week earlier, the viceroy of Sicily had managed to get a message through to him promising to send a relieving army of sixteen thousand soldiers. The grand master had known better than to share the information or to believe in it. Yet in early September as the Turkish guns once again battered the peninsulas and another great massed attack faltered, out at sea beyond the Grand Harbor the unimaginable at last made an appearance. A line of Habsburg ships brazenly sailed into view and fired off a triple gun salute. The Turkish admiral, realizing their significance, did not give chase.

The siege of Malta was lifted on September 6, 1565. Mustapha Pasha, ever the brave commander, had his men stage a fierce fighting retreat from Birgu and Senglea all the way to the north side of the island. He remained on the beach almost to the very end, battling the Sicilian skirmishers who galloped into the surf in an effort to prevent the embarkation of the tired army. Mustapha prevented the annihilation of what remained of his great force: on the eighth the Ottomans finally weighed anchor—in the same bay where St. Paul was supposed to have landed—and made haste back to the safety of faraway Kostantiniyye. The armada of Islam had failed, against a fanatical clan of corsairs who viewed themselves as crusaders. The valediction was nearly complete. In 1565 Valette had been seventy-one; Mustapha, seventy; Dragut, eighty; and Suleyman the Magnificent, seventy-one, with just one more year to live. True to their faith, the old men had ushered out an old era in the most sanguinary style possible.

◄┼ ◄┼   ┼► ┼►

Birgu is now known, quite reasonably in view of 1565, as Vittoriosa. It is a sleepy place, its dusty streets having nothing in common with the dazzling cathedral and the audiovisual maze across the waters of the Grand Harbor in Valletta. Senglea is more industrious, a home to dockworkers and stevedores. On the side of Senglea where the watery palisade was erected during the siege is a great dockyard, a hospital of sorts for what seems to be every ailing car ferry and tramp steamer of the Mediterranean. On a recent visit the letters on the stern of one terminally rusted vessel showed its home port, ISTANBUL, and its name, DRAGUT.

In Galley Creek, now Dockyard Creek, are a yacht club, a marina and, under construction, a casino. Wandering the streets of Birgu, one comes across the different auberges of the national leagues of the knights—they are now either museums or properties purchased by the wealthy. These are different from the great Baroque mansions in Valletta, which are the product of profligate endowments and the revenues of Malta, in the seventeenth and eighteenth centuries, as the largest slave market in Europe. On Birgu, which was left neglected after the successful resistance to the siege, the buildings are modest, consonant with the order's first few decades of piracy on the island. To move landward on the peninsula is to the see the notorious Post of Castile, scrupulously rebuilt and improved over the centuries, as well as other fortifications—jauntily called cavaliers—marking Birgu off from the once-threatening interior.

For all the urban promiscuity of the peninsulas and the built-up shores of the Grand Harbor, the visitor there is unquestionably adrift in the middle of the Mediterranean. Our sea, their sea, everyone's sea—the mare nostrum—surrounds. In the improbable course of human events, the improbably successful defense of Malta in 1565 punctured, once and for all, the idea of an inexorable Turkish tide. It was a galvanizing moment, as powerful in its repercussions, if not in its site, as Alaric in Rome or the Mongols in Baghdad. Six years after the Turkish failure here, the fleets of a fractious and soon to be imploded Christendom momentarily united and met the Ottoman navy at Lepanto, once again near the Ionian locale of Mark Antony and Cleopatra. There erstwhile rivals with mixed motives—Venetians and Habsurgs—combined for one brief historical instant to deal a devastating blow to the Turkish fleet. Their temporary union was called, with a solemn face, the "Holy Alliance"—leading to a commonplace in western histories that places Lepanto as the closing of a parenthesis opened at Poitiers. Yet Lepanto was not possible, not imaginable, not even probable, without Malta. The siege of Malta marked the end of the age of Turkish supremacy in the Mediterranean; Lepanto, the halting beginnings of an early modern maritime donnybrook over whose fleet or whose pirates would gain the upper hand in slaving and looting. To students of the soul, Lepanto's prime importance lies in the survival of its most important combatant, Cervantes, who almost met his death there.

There is a sort of insane point to walking the shore of Birgu at midday, alone in August, in a moment fit only for mad dogs and Englishmen. The daze induced by the heat may be the only constant in this sea of change. Notwithstanding fixations over Palestine and Jerusalem past and present, the most important actors in the struggle over who would believe what hailed from other places of the Mediterranean, what we now call Spain and Turkey. From the days of Constantinople facing threats at Yarmuk and Manzikert to those of the Iberian Muslims at Poitiers and Las Navas de Tolosa, the most fertile ground for conflict and convivencia lay at opposite corners of the inland sea. This is a surprise. Elsewhere there were other moments, other struggles, and other long-standing periods of confessional complicity, but the greatest players were, and perhaps remain, embodied in the Mezquita and the Ayasofya. They represent the ambivalence of the Mediterranean after the collapse of antiquity. To realize this is to shake off a blinkered view of confessional history during the Middle Ages and beyond. More unexpected yet, those two countries—Spain and Turkey—are nowadays the most culturally expansive in outlook toward the worlds still labeled, by some, Christian and Muslim.

And yet the final battle was fought in the middle, in Malta, where today one still sweats in the airless embrace of Africa while the quaint Angelus of Europe sounds from a dozen unseen churches. Fort St. Angelo, a block of granite wavering in the kinks of heat, still flies the eight-pointed flag—or rather it would, were there a breath of wind. In the few shadowed recesses of the fortress, workmen have fallen asleep in their trucks. Toward the center of Birgu, in a square sized for no more than a dozen small cars or horses, a few lunatic remnants of British colonial days loudly advertise lunchtime menus of bangers and mash on their unshaded ter- races. In other places around the square are churches and chapels of exemplary discretion. One knocks, pounds, calls neighbors to get a peek inside. In the Ora- tory of St. Joseph the cool mustiness of the small sanctuary comes as a relief. A glass case lined with a garish red fabric displays a sword that belonged to Jean Parisot de la Valette. Beside the sword, tattered and appropriately headless, is his hat, a simple broad-brimmed, black felt affair, hanging there as proof that even holy warriors must one day retire.

EPILOGUE

The medieval sea of faith crashed loudest on the shores of Anatolia and Iberia, but its waters were troubled all around the Mediterranean basin. Few places were spared the clamor of armies or the sight of enemy fleets, few peoples left alone to tend their own gods. Over time Islam and Christianity have softened behavior in benign ways, but their past role as the willing accomplice of belligerence cannot be wished away, and neither can their sometimes vicious rivalry. This dual legacy disturbs, and darkens the bright moments of understanding and tolerance that also characterized the sea of faith. True, the Templar knight and the white-robed Janissary cut more dashing figures than the Mozarab scribe and the Cairene merchant, but all deserve equal seating in the gallery of collective memory. Perhaps the Córdoba and Palermo of convivencia will one day take their proper place alongside the bloodshed of the crusades and Poitiers as conversational commonplaces to describe the relationship between Muslim and Christian in the Middle Ages.

But perhaps not, for the conflict and suffering bred of that relationship have scorched memory more indelibly. Fear of the Turk, that spectral presence in western folk culture, today haunts many of the reactions to Turkey's candidacy for membership in the European Union. The phantasm of confessional peril has been resurrected in panicked predictions of a Muslim tide from Anatolia engulfing what is still described in some quarters as Christian Europe. Secular Europeans, however much they deplore or snicker at such anachronisms, cannot deny their atavistic pull. Faced with the threatening or the unfamiliar, the children of the Enlightenment may yet come to resemble the creatures of the sea of faith. In the Balkans in recent years, modern nationalism turned even more murderous than usual when admixed with religious resentment. If the geography of belief once again becomes subject to discussion, then this book, rather than highlighting a shared memory worth recovering, will be merely the first installment in a series that picks up the action in the present day and ranges far beyond the Mediterranean. Religion, for all its solace, will always be a ready-made grenade to be hurled by those seeking to inspire terror or wage war.

Nowhere is the volatile interplay of past and present experienced more powerfully than in the reality of contemporary Jerusalem. In one sense this is only to be expected, as the city remains the wellspring of the fantastic stories *behind* the

The Temple Mount, Jerusalem, 2004. In the foreground, the Western (Wailing) Wall;
beyond it, the Dome of the Rock.

stories in this work: on one of its hills, a man rose from the dead; from another, a man rode a horse to heaven and back; nearby, a temple once stood that housed a covenant linking God to man. Beyond the Mount of Olives stretches the unearthly Judean wilderness, a hinterland so operatic as to compel tale-tellers to practice their craft with supernatural brio. If classical Athens, then Rome, gave rise to the idea of a mare nostrum, Jerusalem—not Damascus or Constantinople—gave voice to the preeminent narratives of the sea of faith.

Yet, in another sense, the great old city provides an altogether new reminder of the changeling essence of confessional rivalry. Although medieval Jerusalem spurred generations to violent ecstasy, by the time of Ottoman rule it had slipped into a provincial slumber, the only real bickering occurring within rather than between its resident faiths, as evidenced by the glorious and eclectic mess that is the Church of the Holy Sepulchre. A charged atmosphere of convivencia enveloped the place, the capital of monotheism fitfully celebrating its god in different ways.

Today, however, the city does not slumber so peacefully. Approaching the Wailing Wall or the Dome of the Rock is akin to negotiating an airport, so thoroughly are possessions checked and the wand of metal detectors waved about unpleasantly. The tension, palpable and electric, might well have been borrowed whole from some of the sadder moments in the millennial chronicle stretching from Yarmuk to Malta. Wounds are fresh, changed circumstances undigested, boundaries still fluid. One can only wish, piously perhaps, that the day will come when the story of modern Jerusalem can be accepted dispassionately by everyone and that a new and more exemplary convivencia will take hold there. True, these are troubled times, and not only in Jerusalem—the language of jihad, even crusade, no longer seems so comfortingly archaic. Yet Valette's hat hangs motionless in Malta, Saladin sits forever on horseback in Damascus, and children jump on the chessboard of Poitiers and leap lightly over the cannons of Istanbul, in vivid demonstration of past chaos rendered innocuous through the curative workings of time. Awestruck crowds shuffle through the dim light of the Mezquita and the Ayasofya, relieved and gladdened, one suspects, that in at least these two sanctuaries the matter has been settled, magnificently.

GLOSSARY

Abbasids: caliphal dynasty, ruling from Baghdad (749–1258)

al-Jazeera: "island"; upper Iraqi Mesopotamia between the Tigris and Euphrates

amsar: early Muslim settlement, often at the edge of the desert near a preexisting city

Arianism: a belief holding that Jesus was a creation of God the Father

asabiyya: group solidarity, often through kinship, that aids in the capture and expansion of power; important concept in the work of Ibn Khaldun

ashura: shia festival mourning the death of Huseyn in 680

atabeg: regent of local Seljuk prince wielding effective power

basileus: Greek term for king or emperor; leader of the Byzantine Empire

bashi-bazouk: Ottoman irregular infantryman; perhaps related to modern Turkish's *basibozuk*, meaning unruly and rebellious and usually applied to youth

caliph: successor of Muhammad charged with ruling the faithful

convivencia: intelligent coexistence of different communities of faith within the same state

dar al Islam: the totality of countries under Muslim rule

devshirme: Ottoman system of enforced removal, conversion, and education of Christian boys to serve the state

dhimmi: protected non-Muslim monotheistic communities in the dar al Islam subject to certain restrictions

emir: governor

Fatimids: shia caliphal dynasty of Cairo (909–1171)

filioque: controversy over the origin of the Holy Spirit within the Trinity

funduq: trading center, often with lodgings, for merchants; called a khan in the Ottoman world

ghazi: frontier warrior fighting for the faith

hadith: a non-Quranic story of Muhammad's life or sayings checked for authenticity through scholarship

hajj: pilgrimage to Mecca

hammam: bathhouse

haram: sacred enclosure where bloodshed is forbidden; in pre-Islamic Arabia, the dwelling place of the gods

henotheism: belief system holding that there is a supreme god and several lesser gods

hijra: Muhammad's flight from Mecca to Madina in 622, the Year One of the Muslim calendar

imam: prayer leader at a mosque; in a larger sense, the spiritual leader and guide of Islam

Janissary: elite regiment of the Ottomans composed of former Christians

jihad: to strive in the way of God, either through self-purification or war to extend the dominion of Islam

littoral: shoreline

madrasa: boarding school run on an endowment for study of Quran, law, hadith, etc.; not necessarily attached to a mosque

mahdi: envoy of the divine sent to purify Islam, often with an eschatological mission to usher in the final days

mamluk: military slave; later the name of a Cairene dynasty founded by such men (1250–1517)

mawali: non-Arabian "clients" or affiliates of Arabian Muslim clans, converts to Islam

mihrab: niche in mosque indicating direction of Mecca

minaret: tower adjoining mosque

minbar: pulpit used for sermon during Friday prayers

monophysitism: belief holding that Jesus had but one nature (usually divine)

monotheism: religious belief system based on the premise that there is but one god

monothelitism: compromise belief holding that Jesus possessed two natures but only one will

Mozarab: Iberian Christian living under Muslim rule

Mudejar: Iberian Muslim living under Christian rule

muezzin: cleric who calls the faithful to prayer from a minaret

mujahadeen: fighter, usually a volunteer, in a jihad war

Nestorianism: belief holding that Jesus was two distinct persons, one human, one divine

parias: payments made by Spanish Muslim rulers to their Christian counterparts

pasha: Ottoman viceroy or, more generally, grandee

polytheism: religious belief system positing the existence of several gods

poulain: a native Latin of Outremer; criticized for adopting local customs

qadi: a magistrate charged with interpreting Islamic law and adjudicating disputes in a Muslim city; trained in a madrasa

qibla: the direction of Mecca

razzia: raid, often over a long distance

Rum Seljuks: Turkish dynasty ruling Anatolia from Konya (1077–1307)

sayyid: overlord; also, descendant of the Prophet

Seljuks: Turkic dynasty in Iran and Iraq (1038–1194)

Sephardim: Jews of al-Andalus; later, their descendants

sharia: law and code of ethical conduct based on the Quran and the hadith

sharif: descendant of the Prophet; guardian of Mecca

shia: partisans of a caliphal genealogy that passes through Ali and Huseyn

souk: bazaar or commercial district

Sufi: practitioner of a form of Islamic mysticism

sultan: deputy of caliph, effective ruler of the state

sunni: partisans of an acceptance of the usages and leadership of Islam as developed over time, with special attention given to precepts derived from Muhammad's habitual behavior

sura: chapter of the Quran

taifa: Muslim city-state of Spain after the fall of the Córdoba caliphate

Umayyads: caliphal dynasty ruling from Damascus (661–750); Iberian branch ruled from Córdoba (756–1031)

umma: the community of Muslim believers

vizier: first minister of Islamic state

wadi: seasonal stream

PEOPLE OF THE SEA OF FAITH

Dates of death, where appropriate, are given in parentheses at the end of an entry. (Many birth years are conjectural and irrelevant.) Names are given as they are habitually spelled in the narrative. Many other variant spellings exist. Emphasis is given only to those accomplishments germane to the events described.

Abd Allah ibn Yasin: founder of the Almoravid movement in Africa (1059)

Abd al-Malik: powerful Umayyad caliph who suppressed Islam's centrifugal strife; built the Dome of the Rock (705)

Abd al-Rahman al-Ghafiqi: emir of al-Andalus; defeated and slain at Poitiers (732)

Abd al-Rahman I: first Umayyad emir of al-Andalus; escaped slaughter in Syria; commissioned the Mezquita (788)

Abd al-Rahman II: Umayyad emir of al-Andalus in ninth century; patron of Ziryab (852)

Abd al-Rahman III: Umayyad caliph of al-Andalus at its apogee; constructed Madinat az-Zahra (961)

Abélard, Pierre: influential French Aristotelian schoolman (1142)

Abu Bekr: first caliph of Islam; second or third convert to the faith; father of Aisha (634)

Abu Sufyan: rich Quraysh merchant reluctant to accept Islam; fought Muslims at Badr; fought Byzantines at Yarmuk; father of Muawiya, the first Umayyad caliph (641?)

Abu Yusuf Yaqub: Almohad caliph; victor at Alarcos in 1195 (1199)

Adelard of Bath: translator of twelfth-century Toledo; early English scientist (1160)

Afsin: Turcoman brigand in Anatolia (1098)

Aisha: child-bride of Muhammad; daughter of first caliph (Abu Bekr); vanquished at the Battle of the Camel (678?)

Alexius I Comnenus: capable Byzantine basileus (reigned 1081–1118) whose call for help against the Turks precipitated the First Crusade

Alfonso I Batallador (the Battler): Aragonese king; captured Muslim Zaragoza in 1118 (1134)

Alfonso VI: Leonese king; captured Toledo in 1085 (1109)

Alfonso VIII: Castilian king; victor at Las Navas de Tolosa in 1212 (1214)

Ali (Ibn Abu Talib): fourth caliph; cousin, son-in-law, and adopted son of Muhammad; married Fatima, the Prophet's daughter; murdered in 661

Almanzor: absolute ruler of Umayyad al-Andalus; usurper (1002)

Alp Arslan: Seljuk sultan; victor at Manzikert in 1071 (1072)

Amalric: king of Jerusalem; defeated in Egypt (1174)

Amr Ibn al As: victor at Dathin; Muslim conqueror of Egypt and much of north Africa; fought for the Umayyads in first civil war (663)

Aquinas, Thomas: foremost Aristotelian scholastic of the west (1274)

Arnold Amaury: Cistercian monk; leader of Albigensian Crusade; archbishop of Narbonne; fought at Las Navas de Tolosa in 1212

Arzachel (Az-Zarqali): astronomer; mathematician; astrolabe and clepsydra engineer of Toledo (1087)

Attaliates, Michael: Byzantine chronicler and statesman; eyewitness at Manzikert in 1071

Averroes (Ibn Rushd): Andalusi physician, philosopher, commentator of Aristotle (1198)

Avicenna (Ibn Sina): Persian physican, scientist, philosopher, polymath (1037)

Baldwin IV: leper king of Jerusalem (1185)

Baldwin of Boulogne: first Latin count of Edessa; subsquently king of Jerusalem (1118)

Barbarossa: Muslim pirate; ruler of Algiers; later in charge of Ottoman navy (1547)

Basil II Bulgaroctonus (Bulgar-Slayer): longest-reigning Byzantine emperor (976–1025); expanded and consolidated empire

Basilacius: Armenian commander at Manzikert in 1071

Baybars: Mamluk sultan; victor over the Mongols of Ayn Jalut; hastened the disappearance of Outremer (1277)

Belisarius: brilliant Byzantine general; fought Ostrogoths and Vandals; reestablished Byzantine control in parts of Italy and Africa (565)

Bernard of Clairvaux: greatest churchman of twelfth century; promoter of Templars and Hospitalers; preacher of the Second Crusade (1153)

Beyazit I ("Yilderim" or Thunderbolt): Ottoman sultan; victor over crusaders at Nicopolis; vanquished by Mongols at Ankara (1402)

Bohemond of Taranto: first Latin prince of Antioch; son of Robert Guiscard (1111)

Brankovic, Vuk: combatant, charged with treason by posterity, at the first battle of Kosovo in 1389

Bryennius, Nicephorus: Byzantine general at Manzikert in 1071

Callinichus: Greek Syrian inventor of Greek fire, seventh century

Charles Martel: uniter of the Franks; victor at Poitiers in 732 (741)

Chosroes II: Persian shah; attacked and occupied, for a time, much of Byzantine Near East (628)

Comnena, Anna: Byzantine princess; memoirist of the life of her father (Alexius I Comnenus) and the crusading period in the *Alexiad* (1153)

Conrad III: German monarch of the Second Crusade (1152)

Constance of Antioch: child-widow of Raymond of Poitiers; remarried, amid much scandal, to Reynaud of Châtillon (1163)

Constans II: Byzantine emperor; moved capital to Syracuse (668)

Constantine I the Great: Roman emperor; founder of Constantinople; legitimized Christianity in the empire (337)

Constantine IV: Byzantine emperor; successfully defended Constantinople from attack by Caliph Muawiya (685)

Constantine VII Porphyrogenitus (Born in the Purple): Byzantine emperor renowned for his scholarship (959)

Constantine IX Monomachus: Byzantine emperor; patron of scholarship; failed to prevent the Great Schism in 1054 (1055)

Constantine X Ducas: unpopular Byzantine emperor; lost much of southern Italy to the Normans; failed to stem the Seljuk advance (1067)

Constantine XI Dragases: last Byzantine emperor; failed to repulse the Ottoman Turks at the siege of Constantinople (1453)

Cyrus of Alexandria: Orthodox patriarch of Egypt during the Arab conquest in the seventh century

Dandolo, Enrico: doge of Venice; diverted Fourth Crusade to sack Constantinople in 1204 (1205)

Doria, Andrea: Genoese statesman and admiral; employed to combat Ottomans and Muslim pirates by Habsburg monarch Charles V (1560)

Dragut Rais: intrepid Muslim corsair; died at the siege of Malta (1565)

Ducas, Andronicus: of a Byzantine noble family; enemy of Romanus IV Diogenes; thought to have been the agent of betrayal at Manzikert

Duqaq: early-twelfth-century atabeg of Damascus; enemy of his brother Ridwan of Aleppo, both of the descendance of Alp Arslan

El Cid (Rodrigo Díaz de Vivar): minor nobleman of Burgos; hired warrior of Castile and Muslim Zaragoza; conqueror of taifa state of Valencia (1099)

Eleanor of Aquitaine: one of the most powerful women of the Middle Ages; queen of France, then of England; companion of the Second Crusade along with her then-husband Louis VII of France; patroness of troubadours (1204)

Elvira of Castile: daughter of Alfonso VI and Zaida (Isabella); queen of Norman Sicily (1135)

Eraclius (of Caesarea): notorious Latin patriarch of Jerusalem in the time of Saladin (1199)

Eudo of Aquitaine: partner of Charles Martel in the victory over the Muslims at Poitiers in 732 (736?)

Eudoxia: first wife of Heraclius (612)

Eudoxia Macrembolitissa: Byzantine empress; niece of Cerularius, patriarch of the Great Schism; widow of Constantine X Ducas; through subterfuge wed Romanus IV Diogenes (1096)

Fatima: daughter of Muhammad; wed to Ali (632)

Fernando III: Castilian king of the reconquista, later canonized; captured most remaining cities of al-Andalus, save Granada (1253)

Fibonacci, Leonardo: Pisan mathematician (1250)

Francis of Assisi: founder of the Franciscan order of friars; canonized; attempted to convert Muslims of Egypt during the Fifth Crusade (1226)

Frederick II: king of Sicily and Holy Roman Emperor; polyglot scholar and tyrant known as Stupor Mundi (1250)

George of Antioch: twelfth-century adventurer; first in the employ of the Ifriqiyans, then admiral for Roger II of Sicily

Gerard of Cremona: foremost translator of Toledo (1187)

Gérard of Ridefort: tenth master of the Templars; credited with hotheaded advice leading to the Latin defeat at Hattin in 1187 (1189)

Gibbon, Edward: Enlightenment historian of the decline and fall of the Roman Empire (1794)

Giustiniani Longo, Giovanni: Genoese siege expert; commander of the land walls during the siege of Constantinople (1453)

Gregory (of Carthage): patrician Byzantine rebel against Constans II; slain by Arabs during conquest of north Africa (647)

Guiscard, Robert: Norman adventurer; threatened Byzantine Empire; conquered much of southern Italy (1185)

Guy of Lusignan: king of Jerusalem; vanquished at Hattin in 1187 (1194)

Hakam II, al-: Umayyad caliph of al-Andalus; eldest son of Abd al-Rahman III; famed for his learning and bookishness (976)

Halil Pasha, Chandarli: principal adviser of Ottoman sultan Murad II; advocate of peace with the Greeks; executed by Mehmet II (1454)

Hamza: uncle of the Prophet; killed at battle of Uhud; body mutilated by Meccans (625)

Harun al-Rashid: Abbasid caliph at apogee of Baghdadi power (reigned 789–806)

Hasday ibn Shaprut: Jewish physician-vizier-diplomat of Andalusi caliph Abd al-Rahman III (970)

Henry of Champagne: king of Jerusalem; ambassador to Assassins (1197)

Heraclius: Byzantine emperor; wrested Near East back from Persians only to lose it to the Muslims (641)

Hind: wife of Abu Sufyan; desecrator of Hamza's body; Meccan skeptic; participant in the Battle of Yarmuk in 636

Hisham II, al-: Umayyad caliph of al-Andalus; son of al-Hakam II; kept under house arrest in the Madinat az-Zahra by Almanzor (1013)

Hulegu: Mongol destroyer of Baghdad in 1258 (1265)

Huseyn: son of Ali; grandson of the Prophet; killed at Karbala (680)

Ibn Hawkal: Iraqi traveler and writer (990)

Ibn Hazm: Cordoban theologian and man of letters during the fall of the Umayyad caliphate (1063)

Ibn Jubayr: Andalusi traveler and writer (1217)

Ibn Khaldun: greatest historian of the Middle Ages; Moroccan scholar exiled to Mamluk Egypt (1406)

Ibn Tumart: Berber founder of the Almohads; mahdi (1130)

Idrisi, al-: scientist and geographer in twelfth-century Norman Palermo (1166)

Il-Ghazi: Turcoman ruler of Aleppo; victor at the Field of Blood (1122)

Jiménez de la Rada, Rodrigo: archbishop of Toledo; chronicler and reconquista historian (1247)

Julian of Ceuta: quasi-legendary eighth-century Byzantine governor; abetted Muslim invasion of Spain

Justinian: Byzantine emperor; lawgiver; builder of the Hagia Sophia (565)

Kahina: Berber prophetess and queen; leader of resistance to Arab conquest of the Maghrib (704?)

Khadija: widow who married Muhammad; Islam's first convert (619)

Khalid Ibn al Walid: victorious general in 636 at Yarmuk (642)

Kilij Arslan: Seljuk Rum sultan; slaughtered People's Crusade in Bithynia; lost to First Crusade at Dorylaeum in 1097 (1107)

Kobilic, Milos: shadowy historical figure; supposed assassin of Sultan Murad I at the first battle of Kosovo in 1389

Kukburi: emir of Harran and Edessa; general of Saladin at Hattin in 1187

Lazar (Hrebeljanovic): Serbian prince slain at the first battle of Kosovo in 1389

Lazarevic, Stefan: son of Prince Lazar Hrebeljanovic; vassal-ally of Ottoman sultan Beyazit I; later quasi-independent despot of Serbia (1427)

Leo III: iconoclast Byzantine emperor; repelled enormous Muslim fleet before Constantinople (741)

Llull, Ramon: Franciscan; Majorcan polyglot theologian and thinker (1316)

López de Haro, Diego: Castilian nobleman; effective commander of the army at Las Navas de Tolosa in 1212 (1214)

Louis VII: French monarch; leader of the Second Crusade; briefly husband of Eleanor of Aquitaine (1180)

Malik al-Kamil: Ayyubid sultan; Saladin's nephew; parried Fifth Crusade; agreed to lease on Jerusalem in the Sixth Crusade (1238)

Malikshah: successor of Alp Arslan to Seljuk sultanate; long friction with Vizier Nizam al-Mulk (1092)

Mam'un, al-: eleventh-century taifa king of Toledo; patron of the arts and sciences (1075)

Maniakes, George: colossus; Byzantine general; conqueror of Antioch and Edessa; frustrated general in the reconquest of Sicily; failed rebel (1043)

Manuel I Comnenus: Byzantine emperor; loser at Myriokephalon; builder of Blachernae fortifications (1180)

Martina: niece and wife of Heraclius (642)

Mehmet II (Fatih the Conqueror): Ottoman sultan; took Constantinople in 1453 (1481)

Moses Maimonides: Sephardic Cordoban; philosopher; rabbi; compiler of Jewish law; physician to Saladin's family in Cairo (1204)

Muawiya: first Umayyad caliph; son of Abu Sufyan; victor over Ali (680)

Muhammad al-Nasir: Almohad caliph; defeated at Las Navas de Tolosa in 1212 (1213)

Muhammad Ibn Abdallah: Prophet of Islam (632)

Muhammad Ibn Ishaq: first biographer of Muhammad (767)

Murad I: Ottoman sultan killed at the first battle of Kosovo (1389)

Murad II: Ottoman sultan; victor at Varna and the second battle of Kosovo (1451)

Musa ibn Nusayr: governor of Ifriqiya; authorized conquest of Visigothic Spain (716)

Mustapha Pasha: commander of Ottoman army defeated before Malta in 1565

Mustarshid, al-: Abbasid caliph; tried to regain authority from the Turkish sultanate in twelfth century (1135)

Mu'tamid, al-: last poet-king of taifa Seville; deposed by Almoravids (1095)

Najm al-Din Ayyub: Kurdish chieftain of Tikrit; governor of Baalbek; father of Saladin (1173)

Nizam al-Mulk: powerful Persian vizier of Alp Arslan and Malikshah; patron of madrasas; killed by Assassins (1092)

Nur al-Din: son and successor of Zengi; uniter of Damascus and Aleppo (1174)

Orhan: second Ottoman sultan; began Turkish move into Balkans (1360)

Osman: founder of Ottoman (also called Osmanli) dynasty (1326)

Pedro II: king of Aragon; participant at Las Navas de Tolosa (1213)

Phocas: Byzantine emperor noted for cruelty; deposed and executed by Heraclius (610)

Phrantzes, George: Byzantine statesman and historian; eyewitness at the siege of Constantinople in 1453 (1478)

Psellus, Michael: Byzantine courtier and kingmaker; memoirist (1078)

Raymond of Poitiers: prince of Antioch; suspected of dallying with his niece, Eleanor of Aquitaine; reluctant participant in the Second Crusade (1149)

Raymond of Toledo: broad-minded archbishop; great patron of the translators (1187)

Raymond of Tripoli: great baron of Outremer of the Saint-Gilles family; advice rejected prior to the Battle of Hattin in 1187 (1188)

Reynaud of Châtillon: obstreperous adventurer of Outremer; prince of Antioch, then lord of Outre-Jourdain; executed on Saladin's order at Hattin (1187)

Richard Lionheart: King Richard I of England; leader of the Third Crusade; nemesis of Saladin (1199)

Ridwan: Seljuk ruler of Aleppo; friend of Assassins (1113)

Rodrigo (Roderic): last Visigothic king of Spain; lost to Muslims at Guadalete (711)

Roger II: greatest Norman king of Sicily; patron of learning; nephew of Robert Guiscard (1154)

Romanus IV Diogenes: Byzantine emperor defeated at Manzikert in 1071 (1072)

Roussel of Bailleul: Norman adventurer; fought with George Maniakes in Sicily; deserted Romanus IV at Manzikert; later carved out ephemeral kingdom in Anatolia (1078)

Saladin (Salah al-Din Yusuf ibn Ayyub): Kurdish founder of Ayyubid dynasty; victor at Hattin; conqueror of Jerusalem (1193)

Sancho VII: king of Navarre who fought at Las Navas de Tolosa in 1212; surnamed *el Fuerte*, the Strong (1229)

Seljuk: eponymous leader who brought Seljuk Turks into Afghanistan and Persia in the early eleventh century

Shahrbaraz: Persian general of Chosroes II; took Damascus and Jerusalem from Byzantines; shahanshah for three months before being assassinated (630)

Shirkuh: brother of Najm al-Din Ayyub and uncle of Saladin; general for Zengi and Nur al-Din; conqueror of Fatimid Egypt (1169)

Shmuel HaNagid: rabbi; poet, general, and vizier of taifa Granada (1055)

Sibylla: queen of Jerusalem; sister of leper-king Baldwin IV; wed to Guy of Lusignan (1190)

Sichelgaita: second wife of Robert Guiscard; eleventh-century Lombard princess reputed to be fearsome warrior; gave Robert three sons and seven daughters

Simeon Stylites: sainted hermit of Byzantine Syria who lived more than three decades atop a pillar (459)

Sinan ibn Salman ibn Muhammad (The Old Man of the Mountain): leader of the Assassin sect in the Jebel Ansariye mountain range of Syria (1192)

Sophronius: monk and theologian opposed to monothelitism; later Byzantine patriarch of Jerusalem at the time of the Arab conquest (638)

Stephen Dushan: king, later czar of Serbia; created ephemeral Slav Balkan empire (1355)

Subh: Basque beauty and powerful concubine of Andalusi Umayyad caliph al-Hakam II; mother of al-Hisham II; lover of Almanzor (1012)

Suleyman I the Magnifcent: Ottoman sultan at the apogee of empire; a lawgiver and conqueror of much of the Balkans and central Asia; patron of the arts and especially architecture through his master builder, Sinan (1566)

Taliq al-Din: Saladin's nephew; general at Hattin

Tarchaniotes, Joseph: Byzantine general who deserted at Manzikert

Tariq ibn Ziyad: governor of Tangier; leader of the Muslim conquest of Spain (720)

Timur Leng: Mongol warlord of Samarkand; conqueror of much of central Asia; victor over the Ottomans at the battle of Ankara in 1402 (1405)

Tughril Bey: Seljuk Turk leader; conqueror of Baghdad; first Seljuk sultan under the Abbasids (1063)

Ukba ibn Nafi: founder of Kairouan (670); leader of a famous razzia the entire length of the Maghrib; killed on the return journey (683)

Umar (bin al-Khattab): second caliph of Islam; ruler at the time of Yarmuk and capture of Jerusalem; the Dome of the Rock is also called the Mosque of Umar (644)

Urban: Hungarian cannon-founder whose weapons greatly aided the Ottoman capture of Constantinople in 1453

Urban II: pope who preached the First Crusade at Clermont; advocate of reforms initiated by Gregory VII (1099)

Usamah ibn Munqidh: Syrian nobleman from Shayzar, near the Jebel Ansariye; author of a colorful memoir (1188)

Uthman ibn Affan: third calilph of Islam; generally credited with spurring the compilation of the Quran; his murder sparked off first Muslim civil war (656)

Vahan: Armenian commander; leader of Byzantine center at Yarmuk (636?)

Valette, Jean Parisot de la: forty-eighth grand master of the Knights of the Hospital of St. John; commander of the defense of Malta; eponym of Valletta (1568)

William of Tyre: archbishop of Tyre; chancellor of the kingdom of Jerusalem; author of an authoritative history of Outremer to 1184 (1190?)

Xiphilinus, John: Byzantine patriarch; historian; victim of Eudoxia Macrembolitissa's dissembling about her marriage plans (1075)

Zahar: favorite concubine of Abd al-Rahman III; reputedly the eponym of Madinat az-Zahara

Zaida: Muslim lady of Seville; lover then wife of Alfonso VI, conqueror of Toledo; convert to Christianity (1107)

Zarrar ibn al Azwar: warrior who distinguished himself at Ajnadayn and Yarmuk

Zengi: ruler of Aleppo and Mosul; initiator of Muslim resistance to Outremer; captured Edessa in 1144, thus sparking the Second Crusade (1146)

Ziryab: Baghdadi musician; ninth-century arbiter of cultural taste in Umayyad Córdoba under sponsorship of Abd al-Rahman II

SELECT TIMELINE

800   Charlemagne crowned emperor of the west

827   Muslim conquest of Sicily begins

846   Muslim raid on Rome

854   Christian martyrs of Córdoba

862   Byzantine mission sent to convert the Slavs

910   Rise of shia Fatimid caliphs in north Africa

910   Foundation of Cluny monastic movement

929   Abd al-Rahman III declares himself caliph in Córdoba

962   Otto the Great founds Holy Roman Empire

973   Foundation of Cairo

1000   Conversion to Christianity of Scandinavians and Hungarians

1002   Death of Almanzor

1009   Fatimid caliph al-Hakim razes Church of Holy Sepulchre

1025   Death of Basil the Bulgar-Slayer; start of Byzantine decline

1031   End of Umayyad caliphate in Córdoba

1046   Robert Guiscard arrives in Italy

1054   Great Schism between Latin and Orthodox Christianity

1055   Seljuk Turks take Baghdad

1071   Battle of Manzikert

1072   Norman conquest of Palermo

1073   Pontificate of Gregory VII begins (d. 1085)

1085   Castilian capture of Toledo

1086   Almoravids arrive in Spain

1095   Council of Clermont launches crusading movement

1099   Death of El Cid

1099   First Crusade takes Jerusalem

1146   Death of Zengi; rise of Nur al-Din

1148   Failure of Second Crusade before Damascus

1154   Almohads supplant Almoravids in Spain

1167   Construction of Monreale cathedral

1171   Saladin abolishes Fatimid caliphate

1174   Death of Nur al-Din

1178   Battle of Myriokephalon

1183   Construction of the Giralda

1187   Battle of Hattin

1187   Saladin enters Jerusalem

1189–92   Third Crusade fails to recapture Jerusalem

1195   Almohad capture of Alarcos

1198   Pontificate of Innocent III begins (d. 1216)

1204   Fourth Crusade sacks Constantinople

1209   Albigensian Crusade begins

1212   Battle of Las Navas de Tolosa

1219   Francis of Assisi at Damietta

1229 Frederick II negotiates Christian lease of Jerusalem
1236 Christians capture Córdoba
1244 Muslims recapture Jerusalem
1258 Mongols sack Baghdad
1260 Mamluk sultan Baybars defeats Mongols at Ayn Jalut
1261 Byzantine restoration in Constantinople
1291 Acre falls; end of Outremer
1305 Papacy moved from Rome to Avignon
1347 Black Death pandemic reaches the Mediterranean
1354 Ottomans occupy Gallipoli
1367 Papacy returns to Rome
1371 Battle of Marica (Maritsa)
1389 First battle of Kosovo
1396 Battle of Nicopolis
1402 Battle of Ankara
1444 Battle of Varna
1448 Second battle of Kosovo
1453 Siege of Constantinople
1469 Marriage of Ferdinand of Aragon and Isabella of Castile
1492 Fall of Granada
1492 Expulsion of Jews from Spain
1517 Fall of the Mamluks
1521 Ottomans take Belgrade
1522 Siege of Rhodes
1529 Suleyman the Magnificent fails before Vienna
1538 Battle of Preveza
1565 Siege of Malta
1571 Battle of Lepanto

NOTES

These notes include information—digressions, anecdotes, names, explanations, prose from other authors—that I judged better left out of the main narrative. On the whole, I do not flag information about which there is a consensus among the sources, whether secondary or primary, as doing so would require an encyclopedic notes section. The observant will note that I do not use *ibid.* or *op. cit.*; rather, I give the full bibliographical details of a book the first time it is mentioned in the notes (for each chapter), then use a shortened version of the author's name and title thereafter. Sometimes a particularly long entry entails a discussion on the principal volumes I used in reconstructing a battle. However, for a full list of the works consulted, see the Bibliography. Nonetheless, the Notes are the place where the curious should look.

INTRODUCTION

2 The peekaboo succession of spaces: The mosque has astonished visitors for more than a millennium, epecially those with a trained eye. In Jerrilynn D. Dodds, ed., *Al-Andalus: The Art of Islamic Spain* (New York: Metropolitan Museum of Art, 1992), we read in Dodds's "The Great Mosque of Córdoba": "This carnivalesque solution converts a basic building type that is repetitious and somewhat monotonous into a wild three-dimensional maze, a hall of mirrors in which the constant echo of arches and the unruly staccato of colors confuse the viewer, presenting a challenge to unravel the complexities these refinements impose upon the mosque's space" (12).

2 he had been forced to flee his native Syria: For Abd al-Rahman's remarkable story, see Chapter 3.

3 Almanzor, a ruthless vizier: As I stated in "Notes on Usage," I have opted, wherever reasonable, to use the Latinized form of Arabic and Turkish names, in the interest of making the roll call of names and historical figures less daunting for the reader. It is particularly useful in this case, for al-Mansur, the vizier's sobriquet as transliterated properly from Arabic, was used by many figures in Islamic history. It means "the Conqueror" or "the Victorious." Almanzor's story is told in Chapter 3.

3 Santiago Matamoros: In the early ninth century, in obscure circumstances, a body was discovered in Compostela, which was quickly claimed to be that of James the Apostle, "miraculously transported across the sea to the north-west coast of Spain. James was traditionally credited with the conversion of the Iberian peninsula. The discovery of his relics gave a patriarchal status to the Church in the kingdom of the Asturias (because it was 'founded' by an Apostle), and a primal quality which allowed it to compete with other great Christian centres such as

Rome, Alexandria, Antioch or Constantinople. . . . The pilgrimage to Santiago rapidly assumed a warlike aspect: early in its course, the route of the *Camino* circumnavigated an area that was in places quite close to the 'no-man's land' dividing Christians from Muslims. It was claimed that during the battle of Clavijo in 844 James the Apostle appeared in dazzling robes, on the back of a snow-white charger, and guided the Christians as they fought the enemy: he was thenceforth called the 'Moor Slayer', *Matamoros.*" Franco Cardini, *Europe and Islam*, trans. Caroline Beamish (Oxford: Blackwell, 2001), 37, 38–39.

4 When the monarch who authorized the church: Charles V (1500–58), king of Spain, king of Aragon (and its Italian possessions), duke of Burgundy, and Holy Roman emperor. This monarch, the greatest of the Habsburgs, was rivaled only by Suleyman the Magnificent, the Ottoman emperor who ruled from Kostantiniyye. See Chapter 10.

4 "You have built here . . .": Richard Fletcher, *Moorish Spain* (Berkeley: University of California, 1993), 3.

4 "a great blister of tiresomeness": Michel Butor, *The Spirit of Mediterranean Places*, trans. Lydia Davis (Evanston, Ill.: Marlboro/Northwestern, 1997), 11. The notion of a Christian carbuncle recurs in other writings on the cathedral.

4 "Solomon, I have surpassed thee": John Julius Norwich, *A Short History of Byzantium* (New York: Vintage, 1997), 66.

7 "In the name of God the Merciful and Pitiful; God is the light of Heaven and Earth . . .": John Freely, *Istanbul* (London: A&C Black, 2000), 88.

7 "clouds pinned down by the enormous needles of their minarets": John Ash, *A Byzantine Journey* (New York: Random House, 1995), 28.

7 the idea of an inevitable civilizational clash: In response to Samuel P. Huntington's *The Clash of Civilizations and the Remaking of World Order* (New York: Touchstone, 1996) and other books with a pessimistically binary view, a few works of recent scholarship have emerged to rebut or at least refine the crusader-vs.-jihadist view of contemporary Christian-Muslim relationships. To my mind, the best of the lot is Richard W. Bulliett's *The Case for Islamo-Christian Civilization* (New York: Columbia University, 2004), a short, lively, and provocative book that underlines one of this present work's central tenets: that Christianity and Islam are in fact siblings, with all the complicity and rivalry that such an idea entails. Those wishing to link what they take from *Sea of Faith* to present-day problems would be well advised to read Bulliett.

9 "Simply looking at the Mediterranean . . .": Fernand Braudel, *Memory and the Mediterranean*, trans. Siân Reynolds (New York: Vintage, 2001), 3.

12 Akdeniz: Not all Turks agree on calling the sea white or even on considering Istanbul a Mediterranean city. Orhan Pamuk, "The White Sea Is Azure," *Istanbul, Many Worlds, Mediterraneans* 10 (Winter 1997–98), 487–91.

13 Monophysitism, Arianism, Nestorianism: Briefly, monophysitism is the belief that Jesus had one nature and that it was divine. Arianism, named after the Libyan-Egyptian cleric Arius, held that within the Holy Trinity the Son (Jesus) was a creation of the Father; thus Jesus was a supernatural being but not the creator of the universe. Nestorianism, thus called after the Antiochene bishop Nestorius, held that Jesus was two distinct persons. Adherents of this belief were persecuted, and many fled to Mesopotamia.

14 "Everywhere, in humble homes . . .": Gregory of Nyssa, cited in René Guerdan, *Byzantium: Its Triumphs and Tragedy*, trans. D.L.B. Hartley (New York: G.P. Putnam's Sons, 1957). I have seen many translations of this famous passage; the one I selected seemed to me the most congenial to modern ears.

14 "No wild beasts . . .": Quoted in G. W. Bowersock, "Seeing the Voice of the Lord," *New York Times Book Review*, April 6, 2003, p. 22.

15 "I believe in God . . .": The opening of the Apostles' Creed.

16 "when modern man ceased to accord first place to religion . . .": Bernard Lewis, *The Assassins: A Radical Sect in Islam* (New York: Basic, 2003), 136.

CHAPTER 1: YARMUK 636

21 "after ten centuries, at one stroke of the Arab scimitar . . .": This stirring passage is quoted, unsourced, in Fernand Braudel, *Memory and the Mediterranean*, trans. Siân Reynolds (New York: Vintage, 2001), Evanston, 250. The critique leveled at such sentiments was crystallized in Edward Said, *Orientalism* (New York: Vintage, 1979), the must-read text for any westerner venturing east.

23 "Is it thus, O wretch . . .": Quoted in Walter E. Kaegi, *Heraclius: Emperor of Byzantium* (Cambridge: Cambridge University Press, 2003), 50.

23 October 5, 610: Heraclius arrived in the Golden Horn on October 3. Two days passed before the terrified Phocas was brought before him.

23 each district being known as a *theme*: Kaegi, in *Heraclius*, argues that Heraclius did not undertake this reorganization before taking the field against Chosroes. This assertion flies in the face of the standard assumption made in most histories of the Byzantine Empire. I am not qualified to adjudicate the disagreement—I mention the theme system primarily because its later dismantling prior to Manzikert (see Chapter 4) proved to be so disastrous.

24 "[Iran] is the navel [of the world], because our land lies in the midst of other lands . . .": *The Letter of Tansar*, ca. sixth century c.e. (trans. Mary Boyce), in Bernard Lewis, ed., *A Middle Eastern Mosaic: Fragments of Life, Letters and History* (New York: Modern Library, 2001), 7.

25 "Noblest of the Gods . . .": Quoted in John Julius Norwich, *Byzantium: The Early Centuries* (New York: Alfred A. Knopf, 1989), 284. The correspondence was reported by the Armenian chronicler Sebeos.

25 At Jerusalem, Shahrbaraz torched the Church of the Holy Sepulchre: This occurred in 614. The Persian general, Shahrbaraz, massacred all the Christians of the city and destroyed all its Christian shrines. In addition to the True Cross, the Holy Lance and Sponge were spirited away into captivity.

25 Accordingly, in 622: The first great victory of the Byzantines over the Persians occurred at an unidentified site either in Cappadocia or Bithynia, both provinces of Anatolia.

25 Ganzak: George Ostrogorsky, *History of the Byzantine State*, trans. Joan Hussey (Oxford: Blackwell, 1968), 91.

25 In September of that year: As calculated by the old Julian calendar, the hijra began around September 20, 622. Muhammad is thought to have arrived in Yathrib on September 24. An error

is to date his movements to July 16, 622, which is indeed the very first day of the Muslim calendar. But the Muslim era begins not on the precise day of the hijra but on the first day of the lunar (Islamic) year in which Muhammad emigrated.

25 the oasis town now known to us as Madina: Maxime Rodinson, *Muhammad*, trans. Anne Carter (New York: New Press, 2002), offers a surprising etymology of the city's name change: "The Jewish name for Yathrib was the Aramaic *medinta*, which simply means 'the city'; this became in Arabic *al-madina*, from which we get Medina. That the Koran itself calls it by this name is proof that Yathrib did not, as has often been claimed, take its second name from the phrase *madinat an-nabi*, 'the city of the Prophet' " (p. 139). For this section I have relied extensively on Rodinson as well as on F. Buhl, "Muhammad," *Encyclopedia of Islam* (Leiden: Brill, 1993), 7:360–76, for a discussion of the historical Muhammad.

26 the mortal portion of it that everyone can concede as having occurred: Not quite everyone: see jesusneverexisted.com.

26 the Quran . . . was compiled within a generation or two of his death in 632: This statement can be construed as presumptuous, since more than a billion people believe that the Quran, as the word of God, is an uncreated book that has existed in the presence of God for all eternity. In the interests of harmony, the phrase here—and the ones to follow concerning the Quran's composition—may be taken as referring to its mundane diffusion following the lifetime of Muhammad.

26 a benevolent uncle: Abu Talib was an important figure because Muhammad, once wealthy, adopted Abu Talib's son Ali. Later Ali married Muhammad's daughter Fatima. It is this Ali, who was to be the fourth caliph, that the shia claim as the one true inheritor of Muhammad's mantle of spiritual leadership. His descendants, not the Umayyads, in their view, should have been rulers of the umma. Hence the schism that endures to the present day.

26 The Prophet's first biographer: Muhammad Ibn Ishaq's eighth-century *The Life of the Messenger of God* was edited in the ninth century by Abd al-Malik Ibn Hisham. It remains an influential book, even if scholars of the hadith (traditions, or stories told about the Prophet and his life) reject many of its stories. The Bosra incident has a certain Bahira, who could have been a monophysite monk, recognizing the "seal of prophethood" between Muhammad's shoulder blades. This story does not appear in the Quran. The legend might have been given currency to show Christian recognition of the Prophet. Contrariwise, Christian polemicists, starting as early as the time of John of Damascus (eighth century) and continuing well into the medieval period, used the Bosra story to *discredit* Muhammad; they claimed that the monk Bahira was a heretic who fed the Prophet the dogmatic misinformation that was later to be articulated in Islam. I mention the story in this chapter because it is still widely accepted in some quarters—and because of Bosra's connection to Khalid Ibn al Walid and the Battle of Yarmuk.

27 four daughters: None of Muhammad's sons, by any of his wives, would survive into adulthood. Were it not for the constraints of nonfiction, the parlor game of "what if" would here be irresistible.

27 "Recite: in the name of thy Lord . . .": This passage occurs at the beginning of the ninety-sixth of the Quran's 114 suras. Although it is undoubtedly the first of the Prophet's revelations, its placement is a result of the Quran's nonchronological organization. The suras appear according to length (the longest is first; the shortest, last); each is composed of *ayas*, or verses. Thus

Quranic notation for this passage is 96:1–4. I have used A. J. Arberry's translation of the Quran, *The Koran Interpreted* (London: Allen & Unwin, 1955).

27 Allah: Lest a fundamental misapprehension be allowed to persist, it should be pointed out that *Allah* is simply a contraction of the Arabic word *al-ilah*, which means "the god." It is not uniquely a Muslim term; Arabic-speaking Christians and Jews use it as well. Arabians of pre-Islamic times used it. The Allah of Muhammad is most definitely *not* a new, different god. He (for *god* is construed as masculine) is the god that the other faiths worship, the god of creation.

27 attention is usually lavished on the five pillars of Islam: Some lavishing is nonetheless in order. The first pillar is *shahada*, or Islam's admirably concise profession of faith: "There is no God but God and Muhammad is the Prophet of God." This phrase—*la ilaha ill'Allah, Muhammad rasul Allah*—should be a believer's incantatory reflex, from cradle to grave. The second pillar, *salat*, concerns the performance of ritual prayer, five times daily—at dawn, midday, late afternoon, sunset, and nighttime. These prayers, involving ablutions and repeated prostrations, may be performed anywhere that is clean. *Zakat*, the third pillar, is the obligation to give of one's surplus wealth to charity. This is one of the most arresting features of Muhammad's message—its emphasis on alms-giving. Over time percentages have varied, as has the definition of surplus wealth, but charity, discreetly doled out, is a religious obligation. Also, beyond the canonically determined handout, voluntary giving—*sadaqa*—is encouraged. The fourth pillar is the fast, *sawm*, during the daylight hours of Ramadan, the ninth month of the lunar calendar. From daybreak to nightfall, Muslim adults must abstain from food, drink, and sexual intercourse. The restrictions are lifted at night. The fifth pillar concerns a pilgrimage. At least once a lifetime the Muslim, if sound of body and purse, is enjoined to perform the *hajj* to Mecca, a ritual visit to that city that must be undertaken in the second week of the twelfth month (*Dhu l-hijja*) of the lunar year. (A less important pilgrimage to Mecca, the *umra*, can be performed at any time.) Islam is often compared to a house—these five pillars rest on the solid foundation of the Quran. For a clear and brief discussion, see Neal Robinson, *Islam: A Concise Introduction* (Richmond, Surrey: Curzon, 1999), 96–148.

27 Muhammad was the conduit of a god: Of course, Muhammad was more than just a loud-speaker. He was God's greatest messenger, and in time Islamic tradition saw him as the ideal man. But he most emphatically was *not* a god. Christian writers labored for well over a millennium under the misapprehension that Muhammad is to Islam what Christ is to Christianity. Hence the use of the term "Mohammedism" to describe Islam and "Mohammedan" for Moslem or Muslim. These terms should be trimmed from any lexicon, unless the writer is striving for archaic effect or is still wearing a pith helmet.

28 "satanic verses": Notwithstanding the worldwide notoriety given this phrase by the furor over Salman Rushdie's novel of the same name, the words have always been used in describing the relevant ayas of sura 22. The idea is that Muhammad referred to the goddesses thus: "These are high-flying ones [literally, cranes] / whose intercession is to be hoped for." The henotheists were delighted and prostrated themselves with the Muslims, until Gabriel arrived from heaven to clear up the mistake. See Buhl, "Muhammad," 365, and for more on this vexed subject, F. E. Peters, *A Reader on Classical Islam* (Princeton, N.J.: Princeton University Press, 1994), 177.

29 some of the Quraysh finally had their fill of this monotheist innovator: For more on the merchants' dismay at their loss of revenue, see Buhl, "Muhammad," 364.

29 two pagan tribes of Madina: They were the Aws and Khazraj, composed of eight clans altogether. They were said to be of Yemeni origin.

29 converting the Madinans wholesale: There was some resistance, quickly overcome by force. A poet, Asma bint Marwan, derided her fellow clansmen (the proper names in the text) for accepting Muhammad:

> Fucked men of Malik and of Nabit
> And of Awf, fucked men of Khasraj:
> You obey a stranger who does not belong among you,
> Who is not of Murad, nor of Madh'hij [Yemenite tribes].
> Do you, when your own chiefs have been murdered, put your hope in him
> Like men greedy for meal soup when it is cooking?
> Is there no man of honor who will take advantage of an unguarded moment
> And cut off the gulls' hopes?

The poem comes from Ibn Ishaq's biography of Muhammad, as quoted in Rodinson, *Muhammad*, 157–58.

29 Helpers: There are several distinctions in the names given the earliest Muslims. *Ansar* (Helpers) describes the Madinans who sheltered and supported the Prophet. They were not Qurayshi. The Qurayshi who made the hijra with Muhammad from Mecca to Madina, in many ways the elite of the umma, were known as *muhajirun*, or Emigrants. I have opted for the vaguer Companions to indicate all those Muslims who actually saw or knew the Prophet. Pecking orders are important, perhaps inevitable, but they slow narratives.

29 three Jewish Arabian clans of Madina: They were the Qurayza, Nadhir, and Qaynuqa. The fate of the first two is discussed in the text. The last, a clan of goldsmiths, were the first to be ejected from Madina, but only after Muhammad had been dissuaded from executing them. There had been a quarrel over a young girl's honor in which a Muslim had been killed. The Qaynuqa's considerable wealth was confiscated. See Rodinson, *Muhammad*, 172–73.

30 eating . . . the liver: This custom would have to have been a remnant of a pre-Islamic, if not prehisoric, animism. The liver was chewed, then spat out on the ground. In this instance, an Ethiopian slave was promised his freedom by his Meccan master if he succeeded in killing Muhammad's fearsome uncle, Hamza, a big burly man and formerly a heavy drinker. This the Ethiopian did with a well-aimed javelin; then he left the battlefield, unconcerned about the outcome, a free man. This battle of 625, a reverse for the Muslims, took place just outside of Madina, on the slopes of Mount Uhud. The details are found in Ibn Ishaq.

30 Hind, the liver-eater, is supposed to have heckled him: Hind is not remembered fondly in Islamic traditions, so the heckling story might just be another way of slighting her. F. Buhl, "Hind Bit Utba," *Encylopedia of Islam* (Leiden: Brill, 1973), 3:455.

31 the body of a defeated and defunct general to be packed in salt: Norwich, *Early Centuries*, 294.

31 fierce punishment was meted out to all who had sided with the Persians: This included a massacre of Jews in Galilee and Jerusalem. Walter E. Kaegi, *Byzantium and the Early Islamic Conquests* (Cambridge: Cambridge University, 1995), 117. This is the most thoroughgoing and authoritative of modern scholarly examinations of Yarmuk.

31 A Muslim tradition . . . holds that Muhammad actually wrote letters to Heraclius and Chosroes: There are several accounts of this tradition, all of which are examined in detail by Nadia Maria el Sheikh in her *Byzantium Viewed by the Arabs* (Cambridge, Mass.: Harvard University Press, 2004), 39–54. El Sheikh convincingly argues that the different reception given the letters by basileus and shahanshah influenced later Muslim thinking toward their old enemies. The Sassanids, whose leader had torn up the Prophet's letter, were thought to have been deserving of extinction, while the Byzantines, because Heraclius had shown deference to the letter, were treated with indulgence and respect.

32 a conspicuous latecomer to the cause of the Prophet: Khalid was one of the most famously late Muslims, having commanded the Meccan armies at Uhud (the Muslim defeat in which Hamza was slain and mutilated). P. Crone, "Khalid b. Al-Walid," *Encyclopedia of Islam* (Leiden: Brill, 1978), 4:928.

33 Dathin was hardly more than a skirmish: Theophanes speaks of three hundred or so Byzantine dead. Cited in Kaegi, *Byzantium*, 91.

33 "diabolic savagery": Cited in David Nicolle, *Yarmuk 636 A.D.: The Muslim Conquest of Syria* (Oxford: Osprey, 1994), 50. Nicolle, a military historian, incorporates many of the Arab historians and traditions into his account. Unsourced, these accounts nonetheless give a different dimension to traditional western accounts of the battle, which usually do not mention the legends that have been passed on. Nicolle's work is a reminder of the importance of perceptions.

34 The ride has entered legend: A patient examination of all the problems associated with Khalid's dash through the desert (when? where?) is given in Fred McGraw Donner, *The Early Islamic Conquests* (Princeton, N.J.: Princeton University, 1981), 120–23.

34 "I am the death of the Pale Faces . . .": Quoted in Nicolle, *Yarmuk*, 48–49.

35 Banu Nadhir: Kaegi, *Byzantium*, 116–17.

35 this world-altering event: Francesco Gabrieli, *Muhammad and the Conquests of Islam*, trans. Virginia Luling and Rosamund Linell (New York: McGraw-Hill, 1968), 150: "The battle of Yarmuk had, without doubt, more important consequences than almost any other in world history."

36 sudden sandstorm blinded the Byzantines: This story, repeated in many standard histories, originated in the *Chronographia* of Theophanes (trans. Harry Turtledove), in *The Chronicle of Theophanes: An English Translation of Anni Mundi 6095–6305 (A.D. 602–813)*, (Philadelphia: University of Pennsylvania Press, 1982), and in the Armenian *History* of Sebeos. Kaegi, *Byzantium*, dismisses the story thus: "Some Christian sources speak of sand or quicksand at the battle of the Yarmuk. It is quite possible that there was a severe duststorm at the time of the battle. Dust devils are a common occurrence throughout modern Jordan and southern Syria. But the putative area of the battle is not desert and it is not covered with deep sand. There is soil, and it can be very dry in the month of August. But one should be cautious about chroniclers' claims that the Byzantine forces were overcome by sand. The terrain is just not that type. The chroniclers may simply be imagining what kind of territory Arabs might prefer for battle, or they may have heard stories from defeated Byzantines who were trying to explain away their defeat by blaming the nature of the terrain and local conditions" (137). My visit to the area in November 2003 confirmed Kaegi's description. The countryside was stony, grassy, and now intensively cultivated but was by no means of the type associated with blinding sandstorms. Moreover, in the

seventh century the Ghassanids used the area around Jabila and Nawa for pasturage, and parts of this region might have been more heavily wooded than they are today. Thus it seems the sandstorm theory, while not beyond the realm of the possible, should be acknowledged as improbable.

36 Armenian perfidy: There is no reason to believe a story that, if true, would have figured prominently in all accounts. A mutiny of such a scale would hardly have passed unnoticed. The story originated with Theophanes, in *Chronographia*, and was repeated by Nicephorus, the patriach of Constantinople. See his *Short History*, trans. and ed. C. Mango (Washington: Dumbarton Oaks, 1990). Both authors sought to deflect blame from Heraclius and his command decisions.

36 near Yaqusah: This is Kaegi's (*Byzantium and the Early Islamic Conquests*) assertion. His account of the battle is generally supported by other scholars of his stature. Hugh Kennedy, in *The Armies of the Caliphs: Military and Society in the Early Islamic State* (London: Routledge, 2001), writes: "The most detailed reconstruction we have on one of the major battles of the conquests is Kaegi's account, which is itself based on Caetani's account [*Annali dell'Islam*, 10 vols. U. Hoepli, Milan, 1905–26]. It benefits from the fact that the battlefield was visited both by Caetani and Kaegi and that the topography is clear and marked by definable features, notably the steep-sided valley of the Yarmuk itself. . . . The reconstruction is ingenious and may well be correct in its broad outlines, but the Arabic texts need to be used selectively to give so clear a picture" (5–6). An example of the chronic disagreement over Yarmuk concerns Yaqusah as the site of the encampment. In Antonio Santosousso, *Barbarians, Marauders, and Infidels: The Ways of Medieval Warfare* (Boulder, Colo.: Westview Press, 2004), we read: "It is likely that at this stage the Byzantines established their camp near Jabiya or across the right side of the upper Wadi Ruqqad between the wadi and the old Roman road" (93–94). The Jabiya hypothesis, following Donner, *Early Islamic Conquests*, makes the ultimate debacle less explicable: i.e., that of troops falling into the Yarmuk gorge, as Jabiya is near Nawa and thus far to the north of that river. In most details, I follow Kaegi.

36 armed-to-the-teeth Kibbutz Meizar: I visited this locale, given current tensions, in an entirely separate trip, which took place several months after I toured the Syrian side. A small kibbutz with a brave little bunker system facing east, Meizar offered a view of a battlefield that was tantalizingly out of reach. The locales I visited a few months earlier were plainly visible. Wadi Ruqqad, moreover, was out of bounds, fenced off as part of the security system. When we asked the leader of the kibbutz where precisely the village of Yaqusah had been located, he smiled and said, "You're standing on it!"

36 Khalid had been deprived of overall command: The overall commander was Abu Ubaida, a pious grandee who in all probability deferred in matters military to Khalid. Caliph Umar may well have been wary of Khalid's growing fame.

36 Niketas . . . was the epitome of an enemy turned collaborator: Kaegi, *Byzantium*, 118.

37 He is even thought to have organized a night raid on a Byzantine camp: Mansur, the Christian Arab governor of Damascus, is a somewhat enigmatic figure, although there is no doubt he had little patience with the demands of the Byzantine armies in his bailiwick. According to the contemporaneous Christian Arab historian Eutychius, the raid in question was a clever ploy using cymbals, drums, and shouting in the middle of the night (i.e., imitating the Muslim army) to scare the Byzantines away from the vicinity of Damascus. See Kaegi, *Byzantium*, 124–25. Interestingly, Mansur's son, Sergius, became an important Damascene official for the Umayyad

caliph—and his grandson, who first started his career in the civil service, became known as John of Damascus, a Doctor of the Church, enemy of the iconoclasts, and one of the first known polemicists against Islam. See Richard Fletcher, *The Cross and the Crescent: Christianity and Islam from Muhammad to the Reformation* (London: Penguin, 2003), 23–26.

37 the colors of Arabia: Neither green nor the crescent was then indissolubly linked to Islam. The Turks would do much to bring the crescent into Islamic iconography. Historically, black was associated with the Abbasids, green with the shia, white with the Umayyads and Fatimids, red with the Ottomans. David Nicolle, *Medieval Warfare Source Book: Christian Europe and Its Neighbours* (London: Brockhampton, 1998), 281–82.

39 The redoubtable and by now inevitable Hind: For the story and song, see Nicolle, *Yarmuk*, 72. Donner, *Early Islamic Conquests*, gives a nod to these striking stories of female intervention (135n). In an entirely different context, the stories of the heroism of the women at Yarmuk came to inspire Muslim women of Spain. During the War of Alpujarras, a sixteenth-century revolt of the Moriscos (Muslims forcibly converted to Christianity after the fall of Granada), the combatant rebel women were apparently inspired by an old tale known as the Battle of the Valley of the Yarmuk. See Mary Elizabeth Perry, *The Handless Maiden: Moriscos and the Politics of Religion in Early Modern Spain* (Princeton, N.J.: Princeton University, 2005), 90–92.

40 *Strategikon*: Written by Emperor Maurice, who was beheaded to make way for Phocas.

40 The foremost historian of Yarmuk thinks: Kaegi, *Byzantium*, 121.

40 Its commander may have been Zarrar Ibn al Zawar: This is unclear. Nicolle (*Yarmuk*, 76) believes Zarrar to have been the leader of this detachment. Other historians prefer to leave this open and even question the idea of a small detachment lurking as a secret weapon.

43 the raiders of Ayn Dhakar had ridden under cover of night to Yaqusah: Nicolle, *Yarmuk*, 77. There is, as with most events of the battle, some dispute about when the camp was captured and by whom. (We have seen earlier that there is disagreement over *where* the camp was.) If we follow Nicolle and his sources from among the Arab historians and traditions, then Zarrar would have been the likeliest candidate to press on after his capture of the bridge at Ayn Dhakar. The capture of the bridge and the camp is attributed in other histories to Khalid Ibn al Walid. The result, however, was the same.

43 Some just sat down where they were and awaited their fate: Citing Arab chroniclers al-Tabari and Baladhuri, the main Muslim sources for the period, Kaegi, *Byzantium*, 135–36.

43 Vahan and his remaining troops were overtaken and slain: A lone source, the Christian Arab chronicler Eutychius, has him escaping to Sinai and retiring to a monastery. See Kaegi, *Byzantium*, 278.

46 "Dispute not with the People of the Book . . .": Quran, 29:45 (trans. A. J. Arberry).

46 Isa (Jesus) was important to his faith: Many Christians, even today, do not fully appreciate this. See Kenneth Cragg, *Jesus and the Muslim: An Exploration* (Oxford: Oneworld, 1999).

46 He had somehow developed a morbid fear of water: The tale comes from the *Chronographia* of Theophanes. Warren Treadgold, *A History of the Byzantine State and Society* (Stanford, Calif.: Stanford University Press, 1997) p. 304. Norwich, *Early Centuries*, tells the story of the pontoon bridge but avers that it might be fanciful; given the width of the strait, a boat with tall sides might have been more practicable (308). Ostrogorsky, *Byzantine State*, plumps for a boat with "sand and foliage" (100–01).

CHAPTER 2: POITIERS 732

48 "A victorious line of march . . .": Edward Gibbon, *The Decline and Fall of the Roman Empire* (New York: Random House, 2003), 964.

49 The snide genius of Voltaire: Quoted in Elisabeth Carpentier, *Les Batailles de Poitiers: Charles Martel et les Arabes* (La Crèche: Geste, 2000), 36.

49 nineteenth-century tableaux of swarthy Moors being felled in the presence of under-dressed Amazons: Puvis de Chavannes's canvas hangs in the Hôtel de Ville of Poitiers; that of Charles Steuben, in the Musée de Versailles.

49 Poitiers remains a touchstone: A recent example of the tenacity of the Poitiers image occurred in an amusing article by Alain Badiou that appeared in *Le Monde* on February 22, 2004, called "Derrière la Loi foulardière, la peur" (Behind the Scarf Law: Fear): "Oui, la France a enfin trouvé un problème à sa mesure: le foulard sur la tête de quelques filles. On peut le dire, la décadence de ce pays est stoppée. L'invasion musulmane, depuis longtemps diagnostiquée par Le Pen, aujourd'hui confirmée par des intellectuels indubitables, a trouvé à qui parler. La bataille de Poitiers n'était que de la petite bière, Charles Martel un second couteau. Chirac, les socialistes, les féministes et les intellectuels des Lumières atteints d'islamophobie gagneront la bataille du foulard. De Poitiers au foulard, la conséquence est bonne, et le progrès considérable" (13). (Yes, France has finally found a problem worthy of its talents: the scarf on the heads of little girls. We can say it now—our national decadence is over. The Muslim invasion, so long foreseen by Le Pen and today confirmed by indubitable intellectuals, now has found an adversary. The Battle of Poitiers was small potatoes in comparison, Charles Martel a small fry. Chirac, the socialists, the feminists and the Enlightenment intellectuals stricken with Islamophobia will win the Battle of the Scarf. From Poitiers to the scarf, the result is good, our progress considerable.)

50 eight thousand pounds of gold: Peter Brown, *The Rise of Western Christendom* (Oxford: Blackwell, 1996), 113.

50 seven million bushels of grain: To be paid promptly before October 10 each year. See Thierry Bianquis, "L'Egypte depuis la conquête arabe jusqu'à la fin de l'Empire fatimide (1171)," *L'Histoire générale de l'Afrique* (Paris: UNESCO, 1990), 3:190. Bianquis gives the metric measurement of two and half million hectoliters, which unfortunately is meaningless to me; hence the conversion.

50 an expeditionary force of four thousand horsemen: V. Christides, "Misr," *Encylopedia of Islam* (Leiden: Brill, 1993), 7:153. *Misr* is Arabic for "Egypt."

51 whose name, *Copt*, is a variant of the word *Egypt*: "Most of Egypt's Christians belong to the Coptic Orthodox Church—whose name, like Egypt's, stems from the old name for Memphis, Hikaptah, House of the Ka of Ptah." See Max Rodenbeck, *Cairo: The City Victorious* (New York, Vintage, 2000), 17n.

51 monothelitism: It came to be adopted by the Maronites, who for their pains were eventually driven as heretics into the mountains of Lebanon. See William Dalrymple, *From the Holy Mountain: A Journey in the Shadow of Byzantium* (London: Flamingo, 1998), 197. The Maronites dropped monothelitism in the twelfth century when, as their land was occupied by Latin crusaders, they became associated with Roman Catholicism.

51 Cyrus, the Orthodox patriarch: This Cyrus of Alexandria should not be confused with Cyril of Alexandria, a bishop of the early fifth century who was a famed monophysite. See

Leonard George, "Monophysitism," in *The Encylopedia of Heresies and Heretics* (London: Robson, 1995), 213–14.

52 the former with her tongue cut out, the latter with his nose slit open: See John Julius Norwich, *A Short History of Byzantium* (New York: Vintage, 1999), 98. Norwich explains: "The slitting—effectively the amputation—of the nose was an ancient oriental practice, introduced for the first time in Byzantium by Heraclius. Its purpose was to invalidate the victim's claim to the throne since the Byzantines maintained that their Emperor must be free of all obvious physical imperfections." Nonetheless, less than a century later the basileus Justinian II, who had had his nose cut off and been sent into exile, returned to rule in Constantinople for six bloody years (705–11) after his disfigurement.

52 the brother of the city's monophysite bishop tied up in a sack: The unfortunate fellow was a certain Menas, brother of the monophysite bishop Benjamin.

52 a city of some 600,000 people: Bianquis, "L'Egypte depuis la conquête arabe," 191.

52 that tale has been debunked by impartial scholarship: See Bernard Lewis, *The Arabs in History* (Oxford: Oxford University, 1993), 53.

52 "Everyone knows that the defeat of the Greeks . . .": H. Zotenberg, "Mémoire sur la chronique byzantine de Jean, évêque de Nikiou," *Journal asiatique* 7 (1879), 383, quoted in André Raymond, *Cairo*, trans. Willard Wood (Cambridge, Mass.: Harvard University Press, 2000), 10.

52 another monophysite history: It was written by Michael the Syrian, a twelfth-century monophysite.

52 "The God of vengeance . . .": Quoted in Raymond, *Cairo*, 7.

52 "I will send to Madina a camel train so long . . .": Quoted in Raymond, *Cairo*, 16.

53 the oldest continuously inhabited city on earth: Aleppo, its eternal rival, also makes this claim.

53 Mentioned by name by none other than God himself: Saul, soon to be Paul, stayed in a house there just after being blinded on the road to Damascus. Ananias, the man destined to restore his sight, is given divine directions to the house: "The Lord told him: 'Go to the house of Judas on Straight Street and ask for a man from Tarsus named Saul, for he is praying.'" See Acts 9:11, *The Holy Bible: New International Version* (London: Hodder and Stoughton, 1979), 1115. Older versions of this passage have God saying, "Arise, and go into the street which is called Straight."

54 Qasyun Hill: This is the anglicized version of Jabal Qasiyun. Other authors call it Mount Qassiun. The verdant hinterland of Damascus, fed by seven streams, is known as the Ghuta.

54 Caliph Uthman authorized raids into the Cyrenaica, today's Libya: This act represented a clear break from those of his predecessors, one of whom declared north Africa west of Egypt as "the country that leads men astray." See Charles-André Julien, *Histoire de l'Afrique du Nord, Des origines à 1830* (Paris: Payot, 1994), 344.

56 Yamina: Julien, *Histoire de l'Afrique du Nord*, discounts this story as legendary (345) but cites E. F. Gautier's claim that it underscores the revulsion felt by the Greek aristocracy for these marauding nomads. The invaders, led by Ibn Sa'd, were encouraged to return to Egypt thanks to an enormous bribe raised by the Byzantines of northern Tunisia.

56 "If a ship lies still . . .": Cited in Ernle Bradford, *Mediterranean: Portrait of a Sea* (New York: Harcourt Brace Jovanovich, 1971), 309. Lewis, in *Arabs in History*, writes: "The Arab

historians tell us that the first Caliphs were unwilling to authorize expeditions across the sea, and Umar is quoted as forbidding his generals to advance to any place 'which I cannot reach on my camel' " (126).

57 the magnetic compass: Bradford, *Mediterranean*, 316–18.

57 By 649 Muawiya . . . had weighed anchor: Francesco Gabrieli, *Muhammad and the Conquests of Islam*, trans. Virginia Luling and Rosamund Linell (New York: McGraw-Hill, 1968), 176. The sea battle of Phoenix is known in Arab historiography as Dint as-Sawari.

57 Nine hundred pack-camels: Ostrogorsky, *Byzantine State*, 104.

57 switching clothes: The anecdote is related by Theophanus in *Chronographia*, quoted in George Ostrogorsky, *History of the Byzantine State*, trans. Joan Hussey (Oxford: Blackwell, 1968), 104.

58 he was the second or third convert to Islam: L. Veccia Vaglieri, "Ali b. Abi Talib," *Encylopedia of Islam* (Leiden: Brill, 1960), 1:381–86. Veccia Vaglieri states that Ali would have to have been ten or eleven years of age at the time of his conversion to rival Abu Bekr in seniority.

59 Following months of negotiation: If not years. The tenor, length, and location of the negotiations are among the most controversial elements of subsequent Islamic historiography. See Hugh Kennedy, *The Prophet and the Age of the Caliphates: The Islamic Near East from the Sixth to the Eleventh Centuries* (London: Longman, 1986), 78–79.

59 The son of Abu Sufyan and Hind became the caliph: Muawiya may have styled himself caliph, but later Arab historians, in an attempt to discredit the Umayyads, refer to his descendants as kings, reserving the title of caliph for the Abbasids and their successors.

60 though one historian playfully suggests: Norwich, *Byzantium*, 99–100: "On 15 September 668, while he was lathering himself in his bath, one of his Greek attendants, in a fit of uncontrollable nostalgia, felled him with the soap-dish." Warren Treadgold, *A History of the Byzantine State and Society* (Stanford, Calif.: Stanford University Press, 1997), states that Constans demanded an "extraordinary amount of revenue and obedience from the Sicilians"; hence their wish to see him out of the way (322).

60 the exact nature of its constituent ingredients will never be known: As might be expected, Greek fire has excited the imagination of many historical sleuths. See in particular C. Zenghelis, "Le feu grégeois et les armes à feu des Byzantins," *Byzantion* 7 (1932).

60 one recent historian of the Byzantines sees Gibbon, then raises him one: Norwich, *Byzantium*, 100.

61 "The last of the Merovingians . . .": Henri Focillon, *L'An Mil* (Paris: Denoël, 1984), 7.

61 52,000 Christian soldiers: Walter E. Kaegi, *Byzantium and the Early Islamic conquests* (Cambridge: Cambridge University Press, 1995), 125. Fredegarius wrote: "But during the very night the army of Heraclius was smitten by the sword of the Lord: 52,000 of his men died where they slept." Kaegi notes that "the sword of the Lord" might be a reference to Khalid ibn al Walid's sobriquet.

62 *rois fainéants*, or do-nothing monarchs: The term came into usage in the nineteenth century. The story goes that their laziness was such that they couldn't be bothered to get around on horseback; instead they sat in a cart pulled by four oxen. Hence Focillon's remark cited above.

62 a nursery rhyme that has him putting his breeches on backward: The song, which has many verses depicting the ineptitude of the king, apparently dates from the French Revolution

and was obviously composed to make the monarchy look ridiculous: "Le bon roi Dagobert / A mis sa culotte à l'envers; / Le grand saint Eloi/Lui dit: Ô mon roi! / Votre Majesté/Est mal culottée. / C'est vrai, lui dit le roi, / Je vais la remettre à l'endroit." (Good King Dagobert / Put his breeches on backward / The great St. Eloi/Said to him: "O my King! / Your Majesty / Is badly breeched." / "Tis true," the king replied, / "I'll put them right way round.")

62 many of the Franks' Germanic cousins clung to their traditional beliefs: This was true throughout Christendom, even in Rome. Peter Brown writes: "In the city with the longest Christian tradition in the Latin west, collective memory still looked past the great basilica-shrine of Saint Peter to the world of Romulus and Remus. . . . On reaching the top of the flight of steps that led up to the courtyard of St. Peter's, many Catholic Christians would still turn their backs to the saint's basilica, to bow, with a reverential gesture, to the rising sun." *Rise of Western Christendom*, 95.

62 Karl Martiaux: This was his name at baptism. Thus the idea that he was given the sobriquet of Martel after the battle of Poitiers—an etymology repeated since the Middle Ages—is misleading. See Lucien-Jean Bord's *Les Mérovingiens: Les rois inconnus* (Vouillé: Editions de Chiré, 1981), 217.

62 unholy man of war: Bord, in *Les Mérovingiens*, gives a laundry list of Martel's depredations (237).

63 al-maghrib: Also al-Maghreb. See Hussain Monès, "La conquête de l'Afrique du Nord et la résistance berbère," *L'Histoire générale de l'Afrique* (Paris: UNESCO, 1990), maintains that it means "west of the land of Islam" (3:251). For Baltasar Porcel in his lyrical *Méditerranée: Tumultes de la Houle*, trans. Nelly Lhermillier (Paris: Actes Sud, 1998), the term is an abbreviation of Jazirat al-Maghrib, "the island where the sun sets." Most reference books refer to it merely as meaning "the west," as in sunset.

63 The forces of his son: Muawiya's son, and Huseyn's enemy, was Caliph Yazid.

63 built on Jewish holy ground by Christian artisans for the glory of Islam: No other rock on earth has as great a bibliography. I recommend a superb and erudite historical fiction: Kanan Makiya, *The Rock: A Tale of Seventh-Century Jerusalem* (New York: Pantheon, 2001).

64 according to quasi-legendary accounts: The famous ride is not disputed. Just how far Ukba went, however, is. V. Christides, "Ukba b. Nafi," *Encyclopedia of Islam* (Leiden: Brill, 2000), 10:789–90.

64 "My God I call you to witness . . .": Gabrieli, *Conquests of Islam*, 182.

64 one historian dryly notes: Julien, *Histoire de l'Afrique du Nord*, 350.

64 Abd al-Rahman Ibn Khaldun: The historian lived 1332–1406. His monumental work on the Berbers is Ibn Khaldun, *Histoire des Berbères et des dynasties musulmanes de l'Afrique septentrionale*, trans. Baron de Slane, 4 vols. (Paris: P. Geuthner, 1925–26).

64 the most remarkable personage of the century leading to Poitiers: Monès, "La conquête de l'Afrique du Nord": "Mi-reine, mi-sorcière, le teint sombre, la chevelure abondante, des yeux immenses, qui, d'après les auteurs anciens, viraient au rouge tandis que ses cheveux se dressaient sur sa tête lorqu'elle était en colère ou poussée par ses démons, c'était un vrai personnage de légende" (265). (Half-queen, half-witch, with a dark complexion and flowing hair, as well as huge eyes, which, according to ancient authors, turned red as her hair stood on end whenever she was angered or possessed by her demons, she was a true character of legend.)

66 rotten egg: The baroque tale is told in many Arab chronicles, but it has left some historians entirely skeptical and others slightly ambivalent. The "Julian-is-fiction" argument is given in Roger Collins, *The Arab Conquest of Spain: 710–797* (Oxford: Blackwell, 1989), 35–36; the call for cautious acceptance of at least some of the story is found in Joseph F. O'Callaghan, *A History of Medieval Spain* (Ithaca, N.Y.: Cornell University Press, 1973), 52.

66 two French historians: Jean-Henri Roy and Jean Devoisse, *La bataille de Poitiers, octobre 733* (Paris: Gallimard, 1966). I have relied extensively on this exhaustive and painstaking work to reconstruct the events of the battle.

69 he disappears from history at this point: Bernard F. Reilly, *The Medieval Spains* (Cambridge: Cambridge University Press, 1993), 52. Rodrigo's wife, however, does not disappear. She weds the son of Musa ibn Nusayr, who became the emir of al-Andalus.

70 eighteen hundred vessels (and 120,000 besiegers): Treadgold, *Byzantine State*, 304. The staggering numbers are generally accepted by most historians.

70 "Here you are, o sons of Ishmael . . .": Quoted by Evariste Lévi-Provençal in *La Péninsule ibérique au Moyen Age d'après le Kitab ar-rawd al-Mi'tar al-Aktar, d'Ibn Abd al-Mun'im al-Himyari* (Leiden: Brill, 1938), 34. The chronicler al-Himyari also claimed that Musa Ibn Nusayr planned on heading back to Damascus by land, fighting his way all around the north shore of the Mediterranean.

70 a cool-headed young commander named Abd al-Rahman al-Ghafiqi: This information appears in the Arab chronicles covering the period as well as the all-important Mozarab *Chronicle of 754*. See Philippe Sénac's *Les Carolingiens et al-Andalus: VIIIe–IXe siècles* (Paris: Maisonneuve et Larose, 2002), 17.

70 one papal source: The figure appears in the *Liber Pontificalis* of Pope Gregory II. The pope is said to have sent three holy sponges to Duke Eudo prior to the battle, thereby making him one of the first papally sanctioned warriors for Christ and Christendom.

70 lightning strikes up the Rhône Valley: And beyond. The Burgundian city of Autun was sacked in 725, marking the northernmost point of advance in this century of conquest.

71 Othello meets Desdemona: Another story of love across the lines of religion has yet another Munuza falling in love with the daughter of Pelayo, the victor at the battle of Covadonga, which prevented the Muslims from overrunning Asturias. (Covadonga, in nationalist histories, is taken to be the first battle of the reconquista, the Christian reconquest of Iberia.) In the story, Pelayo's daughter, not enamored of this Munuza, poisons herself to escape his attentions.

71 for to his north his troubles were multiple, and they all stemmed from one root: Charles Martel: On Martel and Eudo, see Paul Fouracre, *The Age of Charles Martel* (Harlow: Pearson, 2000), 81–89.

71 Martel's greatest apologist: The chronicle of Fredegarius was continued at the behest of Martel's half-brother, Count Childebrand. Thus whoever wrote the continuation had a very good reason to make the actions of the Franks look good.

72 their allies hunted down Munuza and killed him: Or they forced him to commit suicide. Hugh Kennedy, *Muslim Spain and Portugal: A Political History of al Andalus* (London: Longman, 1996), 24. In the *Chronicle of 754* Munuza throws himself from a cliff to escape capture. See Kenneth Baxter-Wolf, ed. and trans., *Conquerors and Chroniclers of Early Medieval Spain* (Liverpool: Liverpool University Press, 1990), 143.

72 Lampégie . . . was packed off to the women's quarters on Straight Street: She subsequently married the son of Caliph Hisham. See Syed Imaduddin, *A Political History of Muslim Spain* (Karachi: Najmah, 1984), 41.

72 the caliph raised Abd al-Rahman: Caliph Hisham, one of the last of the Umayyads of Syria (724–43).

73 in 732 or, according to some, 733: There has been considerable debate about the precise date. The two candidates are October 25, 732, and October 17, 733. The *Chronicle of 754* mentions that it took place on a Saturday in October. Most of the Frankish annals concerning the period give 732 as the date. But eleventh-century Arab chronicles—the battle is late in appearing in Arab histories—vary on which year after the hijra the battle took place. All concede that it was in the first days of the month of the Ramadan. Proponents of 733 also state that Abd al-Rahman called for the gathering in Pamplona for 732 and thus would probably have set out the following year. As no argument seems definitive, I have kept the "traditional" date of 732—that is, the one given in the annals composed in the years immediately after the battle.

73 Little else is known with certainty: My reconstruction of the battle relies principally on Roy and Devoisse, *La bataille de Poitiers*, 212–235, and on the *Chronicle of 754*, in Baxter-Wolf, *Conquerors and Chroniclers*, 144–45.

74 Mozarab: The term is derived from the Arabic *musta'rib*, which means "Arabized."

CHAPTER 3: CÓRDOBA

78 *Convivencia*: The term is mostly used for descriptions of medieval Spanish polities ruled by Christians but showing tolerance for Muslim subjects and neighboring Muslim emirates. I think it is a particularly evocative term, so I have used it throughout this book to describe any place where Muslim, Christian, and Jew got along, regardless of who was in power. The term came into general usage through the work of historian Américo Castro in the 1940s, who boldly maintained in his classic *España en su historia* that Spanish history was the story of intermingling rather than an endless crusade in the search for Christian unity.

78 its Carolingian stirring under Martel's grandson Charlemagne all too brief: Charlemagne's achievement was irreparably truncated in 843 at the Treaty of Verdun, when a three-way division of his kingdom was decided, thereby guaranteeing more than a millennium of intra-European warfare.

79 by the Irish or whomever: See Thomas Cahill, *How the Irish Saved Civilization* (New York: Anchor, 1996).

79 "In the name of the most merciful God . . .": Cited in Ernle Bradford's *Mediterranean: Portrait of a Sea* (New York: Harcourt Brace Jovanovich, 1971), 328. The caliph's displeasure was incurred when Nicephorus decided to stop paying tribute money to the Muslims in exchange for peace in Anatolia. This Nicephorus (reigned 802–11) is thought to have been of Ghassanid Arab descent—the same people who fought and lost alongside the Byzantines at Yarmuk.

80 not one left the table alive: The well-known tale is told best in Adolf Friedrich von Schack's *Poesia y arte de los Arabes en España y Sicilia* (Madrid: Hiperion, 1988).

80 the black flag of revolt: The instigator of the revolt was one Abu Muslim, an Iranian. He rallied many shia to his standard, promising them a restoration of the legitimate line of descent from the Prophet. Both he and they were betrayed by the Abbasids, who, after an initial flirtation with shia messianism, kept to their sunni ways. Bernard Lewis, magisterial as usual, sums up the displacement of the Umayyads by the Abbasids in his *The Arabs in History* (Oxford: Oxford University Press, 1993): "It came about not as the result of a palace conspiracy or *coup d'état*, but by the action of an extensive and successful revolutionary propaganda and organization, representing and expressing the dissatisfactions of important elements of the populations with the previous regime, and built up over a long period of time. Like most revolutionary movements it was a coalition of different interests, held together by a common desire to overthrow the existing order, but doomed to break up into conflicting groups once victory was obtained. One of the first tasks of the victorious Abbasids was to crush the disappointed extremist wing of the movement which had brought them to power. Abu Muslim, the chief architect of the revolution, and several of his companions were executed and an *émeute* by their followers suppressed" (84).

81 an enormous classical corpus of Greek and Roman thought: It is thought that Nestorian Christians, persecuted by their former Byzantine masters, were instrumental in translating these works into Arabic and Persian. See Richard E. Rubenstein, *Aristotle's Children: How Christians, Muslims, and Jews Rediscovered Ancient Wisdom and Illuminated the Middle Ages* (New York: Harcourt, 2003), 77. Of the contribution of the Nestorians, Rubenstein writes: "The result was a transfer of culture similar, in some respects, to that caused by alternating waves of refugees from Nazi- and Communist-dominated lands in the twentieth century."

81 "We should not be ashamed to acknowledge truth . . .": Ya'qub ibn Ishaq al-Kindi's profession of intellectual faith is cited in Albert Hourani's invaluable *A History of the Arab Peoples* (New York: Warner Books, 1991), 76.

81 Baghdad's many contributions to mathematics: *Algorithm* comes from a contraction of the name of al-Khwarizmi, one of the most capable of all mathematicians. He lived in Baghdad from about 780 to 850 and was a scholar at the House of Wisdom there. He dedicated his famous treatise on algebra *Hisab al-jabr w'al-muqabala* to Caliph al-Mamun, under whose patronage he worked. Our word *algebra* comes from the word *al-jabr* in the title (which means "completion"). This operation, together with the other main operation *al-muqabala*, meaning "balancing," and also mentioned in the title, were the main procedures in solving linear and quadratic equations.

81 siren song of reason: Hourani, *Arab Peoples*, briefly discusses Abu Bakr al-Razi, another ninth-century Baghdadi thinker, whose respect for reason led him to the audacious conclusion that "human reason alone could give certain knowledge, the path of philosophy was open to all uses, the claims of revelation were false and religions were dangerous" (78).

81 Abul Abbas: Charlemagne was apparently grief-stricken when the elephant died in July 810. See Franco Cardini's *Europe and Islam*, trans. Caroline Beamish (Oxford: Blackwell, 1999), 14–15.

82 Abd al-Rahman ibn Muawiya al-Dakhil: Given the name of the Arab protagonist at Poitiers, yet another Abd al-Rahman in our narrative might seem providentially confusing. It is, in fact, a fairly common name meaning "servant" or "slave" (*abd*) of the Merciful One (*al-Rahman*). Khalid ibn al-Walid's son, who was Muawiya's standard-bearer at the battle at Siffin, was named Abd al-Rahman. So too, more recently, was the "blind sheikh" behind the first plot to blow up the World Trade Center in New York City.

82 his brother turned back in midstream: This sad story is told with great brio by Antonio Muñoz Molina in *Córdoba de los Omeyas* (Barcelona: Planeta, 2003), 63–64. Almost all our information on the life of Abd al-Rahman I comes from *Akhbar Madjmua*, an anonymous tenth-century compilation of traditions. For a brief historiographical discussion on its reliability as a source, see Pierre Guichard's *Al-Andalus 711–1492* (Paris: Hachette, 2000), 46–47.

82 distaff kinsmen in Morocco: His mother's tribe were called the Nafza, who lived near Ceuta—which had already served as a jumping-off point for the conquest of Iberia. It carried no stigma to be the son of a concubine or captive, as long as one's father was of the ruling Arab tribe. In fact, the concubine was immediately "promoted" to full-fledged status within the clan once she had produced a son and therefore an heir.

82 crucified between a pig and a dog: The poor fellow was Abd al-Malik ibn Qatan. See Guichard, *Al-Andalus*, 41. Apparently this method of execution was not an isolated incident of malevolent genius. According to Richard Fletcher's *Moorish Spain* (Berkeley: University of California Press, 1993), a rebel allied with Ibn Hafsun met the same grotesque fate at the hands of the Cordobans in 888 (48).

82 the troubled shores of al-Andalus: Tradition holds that the momentous disembarkation occurred on the beach at Almuñécar.

83 Zaragoza took care of the Franks: The story of Zaragoza (or Saragossa) is slightly more baroque. In fact, the Zaragozans first solicited Charlemagne as *an ally* against Abd al-Rahman. It was only when the Christian king arrived in Iberia that they had a sudden change of heart. Charlemagne was forced to lay siege to the city, which he quickly raised when he learned of a revolt against him in Saxony. He decided, fatefully, to return home via Ronces-valles.

83 set off with the severed heads salted away in his baggage: Evariste Lévi-Provençal, *Histoire de l'Espagne musulmane: La conquête et l'Emirat hispano-umaiyade 710–912* (Paris: Mason-neuve, 1950), 1:110–11. Although subsequent scholarship has questioned some of Lévi-Provençal's findings, this monumental work is fundamental to our knowledge of al-Andalus. It was, to twentieth-century understanding of Muslim Spain, what the work of Reinhart Dozy (*Histoire des Musulmans d'Espagne, jusqu'à la conquête de l'Andalousie par les Almoravides*) was to the nineteenth century. For Dozy, Abd al-Rahman I was "un despote perfide, cruel, vindicatif et impitoyable." Whatever the truth, Dozy gets expertly skewered by Edward Said in *Orientalism* (New York: Vintage, 1979), 151.

83 a majority of the populace of al-Andalus until about 950: Richard Fletcher, in *Moorish Spain* (36–37), summarizes the argument laid out by Richard W. Bulliet's *Conversion to Islam in the Medieval Period* (Cambridge, Mass.: Harvard University Press, 1979). Pierre Guichard (*Al-Andalus*) disagrees with these conclusions and estimates that Muslims were in the majority by the mid–ninth century.

83n his head, as delivered to Salome: In the Syrian rivalry for the location of the head (there are other candidates elsewhere), Damascus comes out the better, for the Umayyad Mosque has an impressive shrine in its interior. Aleppo, however, also lays claim to the head of Zachariah, John the Baptist's father. He has his own prominent shrine within the walls of that city's Great Mosque, which is sometimes called Jami Zachariyé (the Mosque of Zachariah).

84 the monastic vineyards in the suburbs became destinations of choice: There was even a

wine market in Secunda, the mawali (or as Andalusi usage has it, *muwallad*) suburb of Córdoba that was razed after its revolt in 818.

84 Sefarad, hence the term *sephardic*: The word originally comes from the Bible. Obadiah 20 reads: "This company of Israelite exiles who are in Canaan will possess the land as far as Zarephath; the exiles from Jerusalem who are in Sepharad will possess the towns of the Negev." See *Holy Bible, New International Version* (London: Hoddard and Stoughton, 1973). *Sepharad* was eventually taken to mean "Spain."

84 Shmuel HaNagid: Although it is outside the subject matter of this book, mention should be made of a superb new translation of this man's work, which opens a window onto Andalusi life of the time. See *Selected Poems of Shmuel HaNagid*, trans. Peter Cole (Princeton, N.J.: Princeton University Press, 1996).

85 a garden of earthly regrets: Abd al-Rahman's nostalgia for the country of his youth is expatiated upon with great sympathy in the chapter entitled "The Mosque and the Palm Tree" in María Rosa Menocal's scholarly love letter to al-Andalus, *The Ornament of the World* (Boston: Little, Brown, 2002).

85 "In the midst of Rusafa a palm . . ." *Selected Poems of Shmuel HaNagid*, trans. Peter Cole (Princeton, N.J.: Princeton University Press, 1996), xxvi.

85 some of the crops the Arab immigrants brought to Spain: For a brief discussion of the cornucopia of al-Andalus, see Syed Imamuddin, *Muslim Spain: 714–1492 A.D.: A Sociological Study* (Leiden: Brill, 1981), 84–94. See also Fletcher, *Moorish Spain*, 62–64.

85 One wonders what the Visigoths ate: This, of course, is unfair. The great Isidore of Seville, polymath and primate of Visigothic Spain in the early seventh century, supplied the answer in the prologue to his *History of the Goths, Vandals, and Suevi* (624 C.E.), wherein he sang the praises of Iberia: "Of all lands from the west to the Indies, you, Spain, O sacred and always fortunate mother of princes and peoples, are the most beautiful. . . . Indulgent nature has deservedly enriched you with an abundance of everything fruitful. You are rich with olives, overflowing with grapes, fertile with harvests. You are dressed in corn, shaded with olive trees, covered with the vine. Your fields are full of flowers, your mountains full of trees, your shores full of fish. You are located in the most favourable region in the world; neither are you parched by the summer heat of the sun, nor do you languish under icy cold, but girded by a temperate band of sky, you are nourished by fertile west winds. You bring forth the fruits of the fields, the wealth of the mines, and beautiful and useful plants and animals. Nor are you to be held inferior in rivers, which the brilliant fame of your fair flocks ennobles." Translated by Kenneth B. Wolf, in Olivia Remie Constable, ed., *Medieval Iberia* (Philadelphia: University of Pennsylvania Press, 1997), 3.

85 A tenth-century Iraqi visitor . . . gives an assessment of Andalusi prosperity: Ibn Hawkal, an itinerant merchant who traveled the length and breadth of the Mediterranean. We shall meet him again in Palermo. The passage from his work is quoted in Richard Fletcher, *The Quest for El Cid* (Oxford: Oxford University Press, 1989), 18.

86 Another traveler in al-Andalus: The poet al-Shaqundi. Although he is a much later source (thirteenth century), his marveling at al-Andalus is nonetheless useful in understanding the sophistication of the place. Al-Shaqundi is credited with saying that the destruction of the caliphate and the creation of the taifa states was "the breaking of the necklace and the scattering of the pearls."

86 the cultural commissar of the city: Fletcher, in *Moorish Spain*, calls Ziryab an "Andalusi Beau Brummel." I have relied on Muñoz Molina's colorful evocation, *Córdoba de los Omeyas*, chap. 5.

87 the game of chess: The jury is—and probably always will be—out over whether it was Ziryab who brought chess to Europe. It is plausible but not proven. A Dutch grandmaster has written an interesting essay on his inconclusive search to find out the truth: Ree Hans, "Ziryab the Musician," in *The Human Comedy of Chess: A Grandmaster's Chronicles* (Russell Enterprise, English Algebraic Notation, 1999).

88 Nicholas worked with a committee of local notables: Thomas Glick, *Islamic and Christian Spain in the Early Middle Ages* (Princeton, N.J.: Princeton University Press, 1979), 256.

88 Andalusi Arabic poets were ringing changes on the classical form: Salma Jayyusi, "Andalusi Poetry: The Golden Period," in Jayyusi, ed., *The Legacy of Muslim Spain* (Leiden: Brill, 1994), 1:326–27, 359.

88 "the last flowering . . .": Albert Hourani, *A History of the Arab Peoples* (New York: Warner Books, 1991), 194.

88 "For the first time since the age of the Scripture . . .": Peter Cole, *The Dream of the Poem: Hebrew Poetry from Muslim and Christian Spain, 950–1492* (Princeton, N.J.: Princeton University Press, forthcoming).

89 literary cottage industry still thriving: Anyone wishing to enter this lush jungle of polemic would be well advised to start at either www.answering-islam.org.co.uk or www.answering-christianity.com.

89 Abd al-Rahman III is said to have dyed his hair dark: Marilyn Higbee Walker, "Abd al-Rahman, Caliph of Cordoba," in E. Michael Gehl, ed., *Medieval Iberia: An Encyclopedia* (London: Routledge, 2003), 6.

89 "My fellow Christians love to read the poems and romances of the Arabs . . .": Quoted in Fred James Hill and Nicholas Awde, *A History of the Islamic World* (New York: Hippocrene, 2003), 74.

90 "What madness drove you to commit yourself to this fatal ruin . . .": Paul Alvarus, *Life of Eulogius* (859 C.E.), in C. M. Sage, *Paul Albar of Córdoba: Studies on His Life and Writings* (Washington: Catholic University of America Press, 1943); reproduced in "Eulogius and the Martyrs of Córdoba," in Constable, *Medieval Iberia*, 54.

91 The story goes that their leader, on disembarking, gave his men twelve full days: John Julius Norwich, *Byzantium: The Apogee* (New York: Penguin, 1993), 37. Norwich states forthrightly: "According to a venerable tradition—supported by both Byzantine and Arabic sources—their leader Abu Hafs gave them twelve days to plunder the island, after which they were to return to the harbour; on doing so, they found to their horror that he had ordered the destruction of all their ships."

92 fearing punishment for having had his dastardly way with a nun: The fellow in question was Euphemius of Sicily; his paramour, Homoniza. Norwich, *Apogee*, has Euphemius eloping with her (38). Euphemius' great schemes came to naught; he was slain by the Byzantines at Enna in 828. As for the conquest of Sicily, the Muslims had effective control of the island after the fall of Syracuse, even if minor strongholds held out here and there. Lovely Taormina fell only in 901.

92 Mazara del Vallo: Near the southwestern extremity of the island, Mazaro today very much retains its Ifriqiyan flavor, being the home of a large Tunisian immigrant population that works on the fishing fleet based in the port. Their neighborhood is called the Casbah. As for the town's name, *Vallo* is a corruption of the Arabic *wali* (province), of which Mazaro was the capital.

92 To retail all the raids conducted: This statement should be qualified. Georges Jehel, in *L'Italie et le Maghreb au Moyen Age* (Paris: Presses Universitaires de France, 2001) manages to avoid numbness altogether (13–36). I have relied on his account and chronology to reconstruct these eventful years.

92 the scene of endemic feuding among local Lombard lords: Southern Italy was a mess at this time. The Carolingian Franks, allies of the papacy, had pushed the Lombards down into the Mezzogiorno. Since there was no overarching, recognized authority governing the petty dukedoms that sprang up, a permanent free-for-all took place. Much of the action was centered on Naples, Salerno, and the duchy of Benevento. Matters became further confused when the Byzantines arrived to reestablish their claim to the area.

93 The next pope, Leo IV, closed the barn door behind them by building a string of fortifications: The area enclosed is still called the Leonine City. And the pope had something of the lion in him: in 849, three years after the raid, he personally led a fleet of Christian vessels and inflicted a stinging defeat on the Muslims off Ostia. He would be the last competent pope for more than a century. See Paul Hetherington, *Medieval Rome: A Portrait of the City and Its Life* (New York: St. Martin's, 1994), 13.

93 every woman and child of Genoa was ensnared in an Andalusi slaving dragnet: The historiographical controversies surrounding this episode—it is mentioned in several Arab chronicles—are discussed in Jehel, *L'Italie et le Maghreb*, 30 (and notes).

93 prominent churchman Mayeul, head of the vigorous Burgundian monastic movement: Interestingly enough, more than a century later Pope Urban II prayed at the tomb of Mayeul in Souvigny before going on to Clermont to give his famous speech that would launch the era of the crusades. Did he swear to avenge Mayeul in his prayers? Piers Paul Read, *The Templars* (New York: St. Martin's, 1999), 68.

94 La Garde–Freinet was, literally, a thorn in the side of Mediterranean Christendom: Emmanuel Dufourcq's *La vie quotidienne dans l'Europe médiévale sous domination arabe* (Paris: Hachette, 1978), 26–27. Dufourcq relies on the chronicle of Liutprand of Cremona (page 7 of the 1839 edition of *Monumenta Historica Germanica*). The area remains a thorn in the side of conservative Christendom: it overlooks the hedonist goings-on in the Bay of St. Tropez.

94 The German monk-ambassadors were placed under house arrest for three full years: It was the invaluable Hasday ibn Shaprut who managed to spare their lives until the letters could be rewritten.

94 Madinat az-Zahra: Popular wisdom holds that the city-palace (it housed twelve thousand) was named after the caliph's beloved wife, Zahara. It has many transliterations, the one used by the modern Spanish government being Medina Azahara.

95 the ruling families of north Africa: The Aghlabids.

95 founded in 973 . . . by the Fatimid caliph: Caliph al-Mu'izz.

95 twelve thousand loaves of bread: Every historian of the Umayyads seems to love this

statistic, though only Richard Fletcher quips, "Perhaps the loaves were extremely small." See *Moorish Spain*, 66. Otherwise his evocation of the Madinat is admirable.

96 it was discovered in a library of Fez, Morocco, in 1938: The discovery was made by the great historian Evariste Lévi-Provençal. See Muñoz Molina, *Córdoba de los Omeyas*, 211.

96 Medinaceli's Roman arch of triumph: Admirers of the arch can take some solace that its silhouette is familiar even to the most oblivious modern, as it is used as a logo throughout Spain on road signs indicating monuments from antiquity.

97 City of Salim: Salim ibn Warghamal al-Masmudi was a Berber leader during the eighth-century Muslim conquest of Iberia.

98 Algeciras: From al-Jazeera al-Khadra, "the Green Island."

98 the unfortunate poet: Al-Ramadi. See Muñoz Molina, *Córdoba de los Omeyas*, 230–31.

99 Almanzor undertook, at one count, fifty-two campaigns: The figure is Ibn Khaldun's and is widely accepted.

101 "Gone was her radiant beauty . . .": Ibn Hazm, *The Ring of the Dove* (eleventh century), trans. A. J. Arberry (London: Luzac and Co., 1953); reproduced in "On Forgetting a Beloved" in Constable, ed., *Medieval Iberia*, 79.

CHAPTER 4: MANZIKERT 1071

102 what would you do if our positions were reversed: In Edward Gibbon's words: "'And what,' continued the sultan, 'would have been your own behaviour had fortune smiled on your arms?' The reply of the Greek betrays a sentiment which prudence, and even gratitude, should have taught him to suppress. 'Had I vanquished,' he fiercely said, 'I would have inflicted on thy body many a stripe.'" See *The Decline and Fall of the Roman Empire* (New York: Random House, 2003), 3: 404–05. The historical sources, though their wordings are different, essentially concur about this exchange. For the Greek side, the invaluable contemporary account is that of Michael Attaliates, whose *Histories* detail the travails of Byzantium from 1039 to 1074. He was a friend of Romanus and accompanied him on the Manzikert campaign. The memoir of a grandson and namesake of Romanus' principal general, Nicephorus Bryennius, is the other principal source for this encounter. While Bryennius (the grandson), in his own *Histories*, may have been repeating old family rationalizations for the defeat, his is nonetheless an important account. Interestingly, his wife was the consummate memoirist, Anna Comnena. The twelfth-century Armenian Matthew of Edessa (*Chronicles*) borrows heavily from these two Greeks, although he is, given his nationality, less than charitable to the Byzantine aristocrats who had impoverished his country in the eleventh century. A contemporary, John Scylitzes (*Breviarum Historicum*), is similarly indebted to Attaliates and Bryennius. All can be found in the *Corpus Scriptorum Historiae Byzantinae* (Bonn, 1829–97), with various English or French translations signaled in the bibilographical notices of Alfred Friendly's *The Dreadful Day: The Battle of Manzikert, 1071* (London: Hutchinson, 1981). As for the Muslim sources—less reliable since they were composed several centuries after the event—they are best studied and compared by the grand old man of early Turkey studies, Claude Cahen. His findings for Manzikert were summarized in "La Campagne de Manzikert d'après les sources musulmanes," which appeared in *Byzantion* 9

(Brussels, 1934), 628–642, but they can be read, along with a collection of Cahen's groundbreaking work on the region, in the one-volume *Turcobyzantina et Oriens Christianus* (London: Variorum, 1974). The best discussion I have seen on the reliability of the various sources occurs in the work of Speros Vryonis, Jr. The title of the volume in which Vryonis discusses Manzikert should tell the reader where to go to find related material on the battle's aftermath: *The Decline of Medieval Hellenism in Asia Minor and the Process of Islamization from the Eleventh through the Fifteenth Century* (Berkeley: University of California Press, 1971). I have relied on Vryonis and Cahen for background and, like Norwich in his study of Byzantium, on Friendly for a reconstruction of the battle.

104 *an exquisite medieval monastery:* The church in question is the Holy Cross, which dates from about 921. Constructed during the halcyon years of Armenian independence under King Gagik, it is adorned with bas-relief sculptures of biblical scenes that have few peers anywhere in the world. The church's tawny red stone, set off against the blue of Lake Van and the snow-capped mountains, make this an Armenian monument of the highest order. Perhaps in recognition of its beauty, the subsequent peoples who inhabited the area did not deface it. For the sadder fate of other Armenian churches, consult William Dalrymple's extraordinary *From the Holy Mountain: A Journey in the Shadow of Byzantium* (London: Flamingo, 1998).

104 *rode only geldings and mares into battle:* Erik Hildinger, *Warriors of the Steppe: A Military History of Central Asia, 500 B.C. to 1700 A.D.* (Cambridge, Mass.: Da Capo Press, 1997), 18. The other details of nomad life in this chapter derive from Hildinger and from Archibald R. Lewis, *Nomads and Crusaders: A.D. 1000–1368* (Bloomington: Indiana University Press, 1988).

106 *"white mantle of churches":* Radulf Glaber, *Histories*, II: 1,4. The famous passage goes: "One could have said that the very world . . . was stripping off its old raiment and reclothing itself everywhere with a white robe of churches. At that time [ca. 1000] almost all churches in the episcopal sees, those of the monasteries dedicated to all kinds of saints, and even the little village chapels, were rebuilt by the faithful to make them more beautiful." Quoted and discussed in Georges Duby, *L'An Mil* (Paris: Gallimard, 1980), p. 248.

106 *led by a warrior named Seljuk: Saljuq* is a frequently seen variant.

107 *Buyids . . . from near the southern shores of the Caspian Sea:* Also spelled *Buwayids*. The dynasty was founded by three brothers, Ali, Hasan, and Ahmad, from Daylam, to the southwest of the Caspian. The Buyid ascendancy coincided with that of the Fatimids of Egypt. The tenth century may be seen as the zenith of shia power, before the removal of the Buyids by the Seljuks (1056) and the Fatimids by the Ayyubids under Saladin (1171). Sicily and the Maghrib thew off the shia version of the faith in the middle of the eleventh century.

108 *"King of the East and West":* Friendly, *Dreadful Day*, 54.

108 *"holder of power":* There are many English renderings of the word *sultan*, but I have gone with that given by the authoritative Albert Hourani's *A History of the Arab Peoples* (New York: Warner Books, 1991), 83.

109 *blinding fourteen thousand vanquished enemies:* Or so goes the story of the battle of Clidion, in the valley of the Struma. Basil is said to have left one in every hundred men with one eye so that he could guide his fellows home. On seeing his great army so savagely mutilated, the Bulgarian tsar, Samuel, is supposed to have died of a heart attack. Of course, this story has had its debunkers. The most recent is Paul Stephenson, in *The Legend of Basil the Bulgar-Slayer* (Cambridge: Cambridge University Press, 2003), who argues convincingly that Basil's reputation as a

ferocious victor was cooked up by Greek nationalists in the nineteenth century, when the competition over who would get which slice of the Balkans was at its greatest. Still, most Byzantinists still stand by the story, as it is recounted in several historical sources.

110 At midcentury the basileus disbanded the thematic army of Armenia: That amounted to about fifty thousand men, or about one-fifth of the entire Byzantine army. Although all the Byzantinists consulted have much to say on this era of mismanagement, I have found particularly useful Warren Treadgold's *A History of the Byzantine State and Society* (Stanford, Calif.: Stanford University Press, 1997), 583–612.

110 the author of *Chronographia*: The highly entertaining and opinionated memoir of Michael Psellus is available to the general reader in the Penguin Classic edition entitled *Fourteen Byzantine Rulers*, trans. E.R.A. Sewter (London: Penguin, 1966).

110 The reign of Constantine X Ducas made that of his predecessor look like a heyday of good governance: There was a brief attempt at reform between these two reigns under the stewardship of Isaac I Comnenus, but he died prematurely (shortly after being forced to abdicate). His family would later save the empire from itself following the disorders attendant upon Manzikert. The great basileus Alexius I Comnenus (1081–1118) was his nephew.

111 "History provides few such vivid examples . . .": Friendly, *Dreadful Day*, 97.

111 "pestiferous pimp": Cited in John Julius Norwich's *Byzantium: The Apogee* (New York: Penguin, 1993), 320. Norwich, a first-rate storyteller, gives an unusually impassioned account of the Great Schism (315–22), in which he lays the blame squarely on the Latins.

112 "the harmony and grace of the Greek language . . .": The writer was Michael Choniates, the metropolitan of Athens, quoted in Paul Johnson's *A History of Christianity* (London: Pelican, 1980), 184.

113 the Hautevilles: They were from the village of Hauteville, near Coutances. Their early careers fall outside the scope of the present work, which is unfortunate, given all of their colorful adventures. For an excellent recent scholarly treatment, consult G. A. Loud's *The Age of Robert Guiscard* (Harlow: Pearson, 2000).

113 one of the greatest arrivistes of the Middle Ages: Norwich, *Apogee*, calls Guiscard "the most dazzling military adventurer between Julius Caesar and Napoleon" (307).

113 "of obscure origin, with an overbearing character and a villainous mind": Anna Comnena *The Alexiad of Anna Comnena*, trans. E.R.A. Sewter (London: Penguin, 1969), 54.

115 her uncle had been the patriarch: That was Michael Cerularius, a choleric intriguer of the first order and perhaps the most powerful of all patriarchs of Constantinople. He was partly responsible for the rise of the able Isaac Comnenus, only to be disappointed when he found he could not control the new basileus. Cerularius was eventuallly banished to an island in the Aegean, where he died, in 1058, in misery.

116 "streams of tears fell from her eyes.": Both passages are from Attaliates, quoted in Friendly, *Dreadful Day*, 152.

116 Psellus, in his memoir, fairly spits out his contempt for the new man on the throne: See Psellus, *Fourteen Byzantine Rulers*, 352. Never a shrinking violent, Psellus continues about Romanus: "He agreed that in all matters connected with literature he was my inferior (I am referring here to the sciences), but where military strategy was concerned it was his ambition to surpass me. The knowledge that I was thoroughly conversant with the science of military

tactics . . . moved him not only to admiration, but to envy. So far as he could, he argued against me, and tried to outdo me in these debates."

118 "make a stranger of himself . . .": cited in Friendly, *Dreadful Day*, 168. Psellus and Scylitzes echo these charges.

119 No consensus of opinion, or definitive answer: Of all the discussions of this mystifying episode, the one found in Friendly, *Dreadful Day*, is, to my mind, the clearest and most accessible (175–77).

119 that day in August 1071: There is, as usual, some dispute over the exact date. It is known that the battle took place on a Friday in August 1071. European historians have tended toward the nineteenth; Turkish, toward the twenty-sixth. Friendly, in *Dreadful Day*, discusses the discrepancy at length (178) and comes down on the side of the Turks. A significant passage from Attaliates states that a night just previous to the battle was moonless. If he did not mean overcast, then the twenty-sixth is the logical date, given the date of the new moon that month.

120 the indigenous inhabitants of Anatolia would, over centuries, change identities: Vryonis, *Decline of Medieval Hellenism*, shows that this was a gradual and incremental process.

120 Romanus summoned Nicephorus Bryennius and instructed him to take a small force out to investigate: For my reconstruction of the battle itself, I have relied principally on Attaliates, Bryennius, and Scylitzes, via Friendly, Norwich, and Vryonis.

121 composite bows: As opposed to bows made of single piece of wood. The nomad variety, composed of a central stave of wood laminated with sinew on the back and cattle horn on its interior, could withstand greater amounts of tension and compression. It was, in short, a better weapon. For a discussion of its merits, see Hildinger, *Warriors of the Steppe*, 21–23.

122 "Either I shall be victorious and fulfill my goal": Quoted in Mehmet Alta Koymen, "The Importance of the Malazgirt Victory with Special Reference to Iran and Turkey," *Journal of the Regional Cultural Institute* [Ankara] 5, no. 1 (1972), 9, and used as an epigraph by Friendly, *Dreadful Day*, 163. On the switch of Alp Arslan from sultan fighting a defensive war to jihadist prosecuting an offensive one, Vryonis remarks that the Battle of Manzikert was a turning point in Muslim historiography. As many of these subsequent histories were composed when crusaders were camped out in Syria and Palestine, such a switch is understandable. See Speros Vryonis, Jr., "A Personal History of the History of the Battle of Manzikert," *Byzantine Asia Minor (Sixth/Twelfth Centuries)* (Athens, 1998), 226–44.

123 the shape of the crescent that they would soon bequeath to Islamic iconography: It is generally accepted that the Turks gave Islam the crescent, and perhaps the crescent and the star. There are, of course, dissenters arguing that it was the symbol of a pre-Islamic moon cult in Arabia, holding it to be a celestial conjunction viewed by the Prophet shortly before his first revelation, and advancing any of a number of esoteric theories. What is certain is that Turkic tribes used it in the very early medieval period and that the Ottomans made it the symbol both of their empire and of Islam. The croissant, the crescent-shaped pastry that originated in central Europe, is said to date from about the time the Ottomans were repulsed at the gates of Vienna. This too may be apocryphal.

123 a feat of over-the-shoulder bowmanship: The old Romans knew this as "the Parthian shot," after their dextrous bowmen enemies in the east. Some claim that this is the origin of the phrase "parting shot," but I find that a bit of a stretch.

124 "It was like an earthquake": Attaliates, quoted in Norwich, *Apogee*, 352–53.

128 heterogeneous crowds of thirteenth-century Konya: On Rumi's death in 1273, his son wrote of the mourning in Konya: "The people of the city, young and old / Were all lamenting, crying, sighing loud, / The villagers as well as Turks and Greeks, / They tore their shirts from grief for the great man. / 'He was our Jesus!'—thus the Christians spoke. / 'He was our Moses!' said the Jews of him." Quoted in Annemarie Schimmel, *Rumi's World* (Boston: Shambhala, 2001), 31.

128 he could see only the light of his Lord Saviour: This supremely distasteful story is related in George Ostrogorsky, *History of the Byzantine State*, trans. Joan Hussey (Oxford: Blackwell, 1969), 345.

CHAPTER 5: PALERMO AND TOLEDO

131 George Maniakes: George Ostrogorsky, *History of the Byzantine State*, trans. Joan Hussey (Oxford: Blackwell, 1968), 293–94.

131 the great general fell victim to a whispering campaign: Maniakes, enraged at being relieved of command, raised an army and marched on Constantinople. He died en route in Bulgaria, felled by a lucky archer.

131 the tenth-century Iraqi traveler Ibn Hawkal: He seemed to have liked Palermo less than he did al-Andalus. In his description of Palermo he laments not seeing anyone of any distinction, claims that the religious houses on the city's outskirts are just havens for layabouts, and complains that the Palermitans are too fond of raw onions. For the relevant passages of Ibn Hawkal, I consulted a portion of Michèle Amari's 1845 translation, reproduced as "Métropole de l'islam mediterranéen," in Henri Bresc and Geneviève Bresc-Bautier, eds., *Palerme 1070–1492, Mosaïque de peuples, nation rebelle: La naissance violente de l'identité sicilienne* (Paris: Autrement, 1993), 49–51.

131 cotton, hemp, papyrus, sugarcane, oranges, lemons: Aziz Ahmad *La Sicile islamique*, trans. Yves Thoraval (Paris: Publisud, 1975), 44.

132 The scars of the modern era: The scars, and the reasons for them, are artfully described in Peter Robb, *Midnight in Sicily* (Boston: Faber and Faber, 1998).

132 only now being restored to stem the tide of *fatiscente*: The historic center was repeatedly bombed by the Allies in 1943, destroying or damaging many old buildings. The go-go years of irresponsible development, much of it sponsored by Mafia interests, lasted until the late 1980s. In 1997 a master plan for the City of Palermo was adopted. Its aim is to curb the construction of tower blocks and breezeways and to pour money into restoring the extensive old quarters of the city. See Adriana Chirco, *Palermo*, trans. Maria Letizia Pellerito, ed. David Russell (Palermo: Dario Flaccovio, 1998). I found it to be by far the best of the concise guides to the architectural heritage of the city.

133 a summer pavilion of Norman kings: It was commissioned by Roger's son, William I, but was finished only in the reign of William II, probably in 1167. The term *azzizatu* in the Sicilian dialect means "well-dressed."

134 "In the park there is also a great palace . . .": Benjamin of Tudela, *The Itinerary of Benjamin*

of Tudela, trans. M.N. Adler and A. Asher (New York: Joseph Simon, 1983), 137–38. It is thought that Benjamin visited Palermo in about the year 1170.

134 at the village of Balhara: Gianni Pirrone, "Eau et jardins, l'invention du paradis," trans. Henri Bresc and Evelyne Hubert, in Bresc and Bresc-Bautier, *Palerme 1070–1492*, 60.

134 scores of biblical and devotional scenes: There are also contemporaneous scenes, including the portrait of the building's benefactor, King William II, who reigned from 1166 to 1189. One of the more interesting features of these scenes is a portrait of Thomas Becket, the archbishop of Canterbury murdered on the orders of King Henry II of England in 1170. Since the church was under construction at the time, this mosaic must be one of the very first representations of Becket, who became one of the most popular saints of the Middle Ages. In a further twist, King William's queen was Joanna (or Joan) Plantagenet, schooled in Poitiers by her mother, Eleanor of Aquitaine, and sent out to be married at age seven to Sicily, escorted by her big brother Richard Lionheart. Her father was Henry II, the monarch who had had Becket killed. The pride of place given Becket at Monreale might have been a gesture of atonement on the part of Joanna. The relations are discussed, entertainingly, in Mary Taylor Simeti's *Travels with a Medieval Queen* (London: Phoenix, 2002), 67–70, and in John Julius Norwich's *The Kingdom in the Sun* (New York: Harper and Row, 1970), 320. On her husband's death in 1189, the still-young Joanna was taken under the wing of the crusading Richard Lionheart, who proposed that she marry the brother of Saladin. This wild idea came to nothing, and Joanna ended up wedding Raymond VI of Toulouse, the count who would be set upon for his pro-Cathar leanings in the Albigensian Crusade. Their son, Raymond VII, put up the last great resistance to the swallowing-up of Languedoc by the kings of France.

135 Some claim that the liturgy in many Norman Sicilian churches: Henri Bresc bases this claim about Arabic liturgies on the account of a fourteenth-century German wayfarer, Ludolph de Sudheim. See Henri Bresc, "Une culture solide, un Etat faible," in Bresc and Bresc-Bautier, *Palerme 1070–1492*, 34.

135 "dressed in robes of gold-embroidered silk . . .": Ibn Jubayr, *The Travels of Ibn Jubayr: A Mediaeval Spanish Muslim visits Makkah, Madinah, Egypt, Cities of the Middle East and Sicily*, trans. Roland Broadhurst (New Delhi: Goodword, 2003), 350. After admiring the Christian women, he adds guiltily, "We invoke God's protection for this description which enters the gates of absurdity and leads to the vanities of indulgence, and seek protection also from the bewitchment that leads to dotage." A page later he asks God for something somewhat different, in describing a town near Trapani: "Near to it [a fortress] on the mountain the Rum have a large town, the women of which are said to be the fairest of all the island. God grant that they be made captives of the Muslims."

135 by backing a rival contender to the throne of St. Peter: Anacletus II (1130–38). Although this "anti-pope" had more support than the man who gained official sanction (Innocent II), he ran up against the formidable opposition of Bernard of Clairvaux and the Germanic emperor. The deal with Roger, no friend of the Germans, was simple: Anacletus would make him a king, and Roger would recognize him as pope. Anacletus fades from history eventually, but Roger's claim to kingship would eventually be recognized, politics obliging, by the legitimate succession of popes. See J.N.D. Kelly, *The Oxford History of Popes* (Oxford: Oxford University Press, 1986), 169–70.

135 "King Roger, powerful through the grace of Allah": *al-malik Rujar al mu'tazz b-llah*.

Quoted in Houben, *Roger II*, 121. He writes of this particular coinage: "On the reverse there was a cross with the Greek legend, 'Jesus Christ conquers' (IC XC NI KA). This new form of [coin] was a compromise between the title of a Muslim sovereign and a Christian motto."

135 George of Antioch: A shadowy but very powerful figure in Roger's realm. Prior to being hired by the Normans, he had commanded the forces of the Zirid dynasty based in Mahdia, Tunisia. His career may be taken as a sign of the competitive market for learned and able officials among Christian and Muslim states. It is unclear to which faith he subscribed at the beginning of his life.

135 *amir al-umara*: Ahmad, *La Sicile islamique*, 69.

137 "king of Sicily, of the duchy of Apulia and of the principality of Capua": Hubert Houben, *Roger II of Sicily: A Ruler between East and West*, trans. Graham A. Loud and Diane Milburn (Cambridge: Cambridge University Press, 1992), 67.

137 distinctly unorthodox Islamic figurative scenes: Norwich, *Kingdom in the Sun*, calls the ceiling stalactites "the most unexpected covering to any Christian church on earth." His entertaining passage on the scenes depicted is worth quoting at length: "By the middle of the twelfth century certain schools of Arabic art had been jockeyed—principally by the Persians, who had never shared their scruples—out of their old abhorrence of the human form, and the tolerant atmosphere of Palermo led them to experiment still further. The details of the paintings are difficult to make out from floor level, but a pair of pocket binoculars will reveal, amid a welter of animal and vegetable ornamentation and Kufic inscriptions in praise of the King, countless delightful little scenes of oriental life and mythology. Some people are riding camels, others killing lions, yet others enjoying picnics with their harems; everywhere, it seems, there is a great deal of eating and drinking going on. Dragons and monsters abound; one man—Sinbad perhaps?—is being carried off on the back of a huge four-legged bird straight out of Hieronymus Bosch" (76).

137 Sainte Chapelle: This thirteenth-century sanctuary—thus a century younger than the Palatine Chapel—was commissioned by King Louis IX (St. Louis) of France. By an odd coincidence, pieces of Louis are enshrined in an altar in Monreale—he died on crusade in Tunisia in 1270 and his remains were taken to Sicily.

137 "This was made in the royal factory for the good fortune . . .": The translation is by Jeremy Johns, quoted in Houben's *Roger II*, 125. As given in this source, the translation puts in square brackets all the possessive pronouns; I have taken the liberty of eliminating the brackets for the sake of readability. The cloak or *mantellum* may be viewed at the treasury of the Hofburg in Vienna.

137 (many of which were handled by Arab civil servants): The Norman Sicilian exchequer was known as the *diwan*, an Arabic term that gave Italian *aduana* and French *douane*. For a scholarly overview of its functioning, see Donald Matthew, *The Norman Kingdom of Sicily* (Cambridge: Cambridge University Press, 1992), 219–28.

138 "His knowledge of mathematics and applied science was boundless": Al-Idrisi, from the preface to the *Book of Roger*, quoted in Houben, *Roger II*, 104.

139 Salerno translators: The most famous of them was Constantine the African. An eleventh-century Arab Christian born in Carthage, he eventually became a monk at Montecassino and produced a prolific amount of work culled from Arabic medical libraries.

139 Although his origins are disputed: Houben, *Roger II*, states that al-Idrisi was a descendant of the last Hammadid prince of Málaga but then allows in a note that some scholars believe he

was a native Sicilian from Mazara or perhaps a Moroccan (102–03). Whatever his provenance, it is his destination—Palermo—that is important.

139 *The delight of he who looks to travel throughout the world*: There are many, many different renderings of the original Arabic title *Nuzhat al-Mushtaq fi Ikhtiraq al-Afaq*, which range from *The Delight of Him Who Desires to Journey through the Climates* to *The Avocation of a Man Desirous of a Full Knowledge of the Different Countries of the World*. Jon Fasman's novel, *The Geographer's Library* (New York: Penguin, 2005), has great fun with al-Idrisi's work.

139 he appears to have truly loved his wife: See Houben, *Roger II*, 65–66. Roger remarried fifteen years after the death of Elvira, having satisfied himself only with mistresses before then. Elvira died in February 1135.

140 not much is known for certain about Roger's beloved queen: Norwich, *Kingdom in the Sun*, quotes the chronicler Alexander of Telese as having said that she was renowned for her piety and generosity to the poor (36). This, as Norwich comments, is just a customary tribute and says absolutely nothing about her.

140 Alfonso inspecting the city's fortifications for weaknesses: Historian Lévi-Provençal called Alfonso's confinement a "prison doré" (a golden prison). A legend holds that Alfonso may have abused the hospitality of his host to examine the city's defenses and find out how he might one day capture it. Julián Montemayor, "Alphonse VI et Bernard d'Agen ou la consécration frustrée," in Louis Cardaillac, ed., *Tolède: XIIe–XIIIe: Musulmans, chrétiens et juifs: Le savoir et la tolérance* (Paris: Autrement, 1991), 69.

140 the greatest agronomes of the age: Ibn Bassal and Ibn Wafid. See Richard Fletcher, *Moorish Spain* (Berkeley: University of California, 1993), 89.

141 humiliated on returning from Toledo by a vassal of the murdered Sancho: See Richard Fletcher, *The Quest for El Cid* (Oxford: Oxford University Press, 1989). Our best recent source for the life of El Cid, the author comes squarely down on the side of this story being an invention of later myth-makers (118–19).

141 The Cid, like Robert Guiscard, was an opportunist: David Wasserstein, *The Rise and Fall of the Party-Kings: Politics and Society in Islamic Spain, 1002–1086* (Princeton, N.J.: Princeton University Press, 1985): "[The Cid] acted less as a Christian attempting to wear down the Muslims than as a warrior exploiting all the methods of winning success current in his times" (262).

143 "How many rivals did I kill . . .": Quoted in Fletcher, *El Cid*, 35.

143 a protection racket: The characterization is not mine. See "Protection Rackets and Crusaders, c. 1000–1212" in Angus McKay, *Spain in the Middle Ages: From Frontier to Empire, 1000–1500* (New York: St. Martin's Press, 1977), chap. 1.

143 the endowment of monasteries as far afield as Cluny: Wasserstein, *Party-Kings*, notes that Alfonso gave Cluny an amazing 240 ounces of gold per annum (272).

144 Alfonso permitted the mosque to be transformed into a cathedral: The changeover was done while he was away from the city. Annoyed, he accepted the fait accompli. See McKay, *Spain in the Middle Ages*, 21.

145 the Muslim king of Granada: Abu Muhammad Abd Allah al-Ghassal.

145 "sent a great tremor through all al-Andalus": Quoted in Wasserstein, *Party-Kings*, 279.

145 these desert fanatics: H. T. Norris and P. Chalmeta, in "Al-Murabitun," *Encyclopedia of Islam* (Leiden: Brill, 1993), 7:583–91, quote an assessment of the Almoravids by the great English

historian Stanley Lane-Poole (*The Moors in Spain* [London, 1887]): "The reign of the Puritans had come, and without a Milton to soften its austerity" (181).

146 "I would rather be a camel-driver in Morocco . . .": Quoted in Fletcher, *Moorish Spain*, 111.

147 Out of their union was born Elvira of Castile: Although all historians agree that Alfonso VI was her father, some are less sure who her mother was. Houben, *Roger II*, states explicitly that it was Zaida (35). Another recent biographer, Pierre Aubé, in *Roger II de Sicile: Un Normand en Méditerranée* (Paris: Payot et Rivages, 2001), gives only her paternity (112). Some maintain, based on the chronicles from Alfonso's reign, that Zaida and Alfonso fell in love. See Bernhard Whishaw and Ellen M. Whishaw, *Arabic Spain: Sidelights on Her History and Art* (London: John Murray, 1912), 256.

148 Aristotle mattered most: See Richard E. Rubenstein, *Aristotle's Children: How Christians, Muslims, and Jews Rediscovered Ancient Wisdom and Illuminated the Middle Ages* (New York: Harcourt, 2003), 78–84.

149 Gerard of Cremona: A recent work on the translators of Toledo, particularly useful for its biographical sketches of more than a dozen of them, is Clara Foz, *Le Traducteur, L'Eglise et le Roi* (Ottawa: Université d'Ottawa, 1998). Foz maintains that there were two main periods: the twelfth-century sponsored by the Church, and the thirteenth, by King Alfonso X the Wise. Also useful: Danielle Jacquart, "L'école des traducteurs," in Cardillac, *Tolède*, 177–91.

151 later chroniclers set down its gist: Only one, Fulcher of Chartres, actually heard the speech.

152 "The defenders fled along the walls . . .": The anonymous chronicle of the First Crusade known as *Gesta Francorum* (Deeds of the Franks) is quoted in August C. Krey, *The First Crusade: The Accounts of Eye-Witnesses and Participants* (Gloucester, Mass.: Peter Smith, 1958), 256.

152 "After a very great and cruel slaughter of Saracens . . .": Albert of Aachen, *Historia Hierosolymitana*, quoted in Thomas Asbridge, *The First Crusade: A New History* (Oxford, Oxford University Press, 2004), 317. As its subtitle indicates, this work incorporates much of the recent scholarship about this crusade. It is now believed, for example, that not all of the population of Jerusalem met their deaths on that horrible day, as was previously thought.

152 thousands who had been butchered were carted outside the fortifications: Asbridge, *First Crusade*, 320.

154 massacring Jews they encountered en route: According to Asbridge, the notion that the perpetrators were uncontrolled peasant mobs, as historians have long insisted, is no longer sustainable. Several noblemen led these pogroms, most notably Emicho, count of Leiningen, and Count Hartmann of Dillingen. But why this violence? Asbridge, *First Crusade*, again: "Characterising Muslims, the expedition's projected enemies, as a sub-human species, the pope harnessed society's inclination to define itself in contrast to an alien 'other.' But tapping into this innate well-pool of discrimination and prejudice was akin to opening Pandora's Box. A potentially uncontrollable torrent of racial and religious intolerance was unleashed" (85). Further, Urban and the popular preachers framed the whole enterprise as a war to punish Islam for imagined crimes against Christendom. This warping of the reality—avenging slights where none existed—was easily transferred onto the "crimes" supposedly committed by Judaism toward Christianity, such as deicide. In 1096, then, the malevolent genie got out of the bottle.

154 exalted peasants and monks: To be fair, although the great mass of the People's Crusade was not unlike a mob, there were knights and foot soldiers among them, led by one Walter Sansavoir. Still, in comparison to the second wave of crusaders, they were little more than a rabble. They caused chaos as they marched through Hungary and the Balkans since, in their disorganization, the only way to provision themselves was by looting.

154 the toughened knights from northern France: The concept of knighthood at this time was rudimentary. The ethic of chivalry and the elaborate knightly ceremonial arose much later. "Warrior who could afford armor, horse, and grooms" might be a more accurate way of describing these "knights." Still, the leaders of this crusade were indisputably grandees: Raymond of Saint-Gilles, count of Toulouse; Duke Godfrey of Bouillon, Baldwin of Boulogne (Godfrey's brother), Bohemond of Taranto, Tancred of Hauteville (Bohemond's nephew), Robert of Normandy, Robert of Flanders, Stephen of Blois.

154 he had barely managed to turn back Robert Guiscard: Comnenus, it will be remembered, had to fight Robert Guiscard in the Balkans in the early 1080s. When Guiscard was called back to Italy to quell revolts, it was Bohemond of Taranto and Sichelgaita who prosecuted the war against the Byzantines. Now this same Bohemond was in Constantinople, pledging his allegiance to the basileus.

155 Baldwin of Boulogne: He seems to have been a nasty piece of work, joining the crusade at the very last minute, then striking off on his own the moment he saw a chance at carving out a kingdom for himself. He took no part in the siege of Antioch or the campaign into Palestine, which after all was the whole point of the exercise. He later became king of Jerusalem, the same king who shabbily discarded Roger II's mother, Adelaide.

155 the principals stripped to the waist in a public embrace: Steven Runciman, *A History of the Crusades*, vol. 1, *The First Crusade and the Foundation of the Kingdom of Jerusualem* (Cambridge: Cambridge University Press, 1957), 205.

155 the lance that had pierced the side of Jesus' body: The so-called Holy Lance was discovered in a church of Antioch. Asbridge, *First Crusade*, is commendably clear on the taking of Antioch (153–240).

156 the Frankish count of Edessa allied with the emir of Mosul: See Amin Maalouf, *The Crusades Through Arab Eyes*, trans. Jon Rothschild (London: Al Saqi, 1984), 72. Maalouf nicely underlines the strangeness of these alliances, which were formed only a decade or so after the atrocities of the First Crusade.

157 according to both Christian and Muslim chroniclers: The event is well documented. See Asbridge, *First Crusade*: "Some, desperate to find money wherever they could, 'ripped up the bodies of the [Muslim] dead, because they used to find coins hidden in their entrails.' Others took more savage steps: 'Here our men suffered from excessive hunger. I shudder to say that many of our men, terribly tormented by the madness of starvation, cut pieces of flesh from the buttocks of Saracens lying there dead. These pieces they cooked and ate, savagely devouring the flesh while it was insufficiently roasted.' Another account that is perhaps more disturbing asserted that, 'food shortage became so acute that the Christians ate with gusto many rotten Saracen bodies which they had pitched into the swamps three weeks before. This spectacle disgusted as many crusaders as it did strangers'" (274).

CHAPTER 6: HATTIN 1187

158 a behemoth rising 360 meters: The Hospitalers took over Marqab (also Margat) in 1186, one year prior to Hattin. See Hugh Kennedy, *Crusader Castles* (Cambridge: Cambridge University Press, 1994), 163. Tim Mackintosh-Smith, in his witty and acerbic *Travels with a Tangerine: A Journey in the Footnotes of Ibn Battutah* (London: Picador, 2001), says about Marqab: "The Hospitallers' basalt command-centre seems unreasonably massive and fascistical . . . a piece of sheer skinhead effrontery" (179).

160 a large statue of the late Syrian president Hafez al-Assad . . . the second homes of the rich and well connected: The area around Latakia and Tartus is the power base of the Assad family, the majority of its inhabitants being Alawis, a split-off movement of shia Islam to which the Assads and many of their Baathist colleagues belong. The beliefs of the Alawis are little understood; their knowledge transmitted through the generations by a select elite known as the "Babs," or Doors.

160 whence, it was once thought, the name *hashishi*, or Assassin: The epithet "hash-eater" or "hash-smoker" is now thought to be a sunni insult about the Nizaris, whom they thought to be slightly insane or touched in the head. Perhaps an equivalent would be calling someone a "stoner" or a "space cadet." Bernard Lewis, in *The Assassins: A Radical Sect in Islam* (New York: Basic Books, 1968), traces the outlines of the myth, then debunks the fond stories of hash parties in the Jebel Ansariye (11–12).

161 Count Raymond of Tripoli met a similar fate at the hands of the Assassins: The Count Raymond in question was the father of Count Raymond III of Tripoli who played a large role in the events at Hattin.

162 "To shed the blood of a heretic . . .": A Persian text that appeared in a scholarly paper published by the University of Tabriz, quoted in Lewis, *Assassins*, 48.

162 The Assassins possessed a dozen or so castles there: The descendants of the Assassins, the Ismailis under the Aga Khan, are now restoring some of these magnificent castles. They may be viewed online at the website of the Aga Khan Trust for Culture: www.akdn.org/agency/aktc_hcsp.html.

164 a natural lozenge-shaped hill that stretches fifty-five meters into the air: Ross Burns, *Monuments of Syria: An Historical Guide* (London: I.B. Tauris, 1992), 32.

164 "In less than an hour": Ibn al-Qalanisi, from his appendix to *The History of Damascus* (sometimes called *The Damascus Chronicle of the Crusades*), the most valuable Arabic source for the first half of the twelfth century. See Francesco Gabrieli, *Arab Historians of the Crusades*, trans. E.J. Costello (Berkeley: University of California Press, 1984), 39.

165 When he sobered up three weeks later: The tale is well known, but in my reading only Amin Maalouf, in his invaluable *Crusades Through Arab Eyes*, hazards a guess at the duration of the hangover (95).

165 a valley known as the Homs Gap: To westerners, of course. It is also called Buqeia.

165 Husn al-Akrad, Fortress of the Kurds: Warwick Bell, *Syria: A Historical and Architectural Guide* (Essex: Scorpion, 1994), 93. Bell quotes T. E. Lawrence on the Krak: "perhaps the best preserved and most wholly admirable castle in the world." In the surrounding valleys there is still a large Christian population.

168 nine thousand lordships and manors in the west: Terence Wise, *The Knights of Christ* (Oxford: Osprey, 1984), 6.

168 that could be redeemed, for a fee, in Outremer: The same system held true for travel within Europe.

169 he could not resist cuckold stories: Who can? Here is one of Usamah's best: "One day [a] Frank [of Nablus] went home and found a man with his wife in the same bed. He asked him, 'What could have made thee enter into my wife's room?' The man replied, 'I was tired, so I went into rest.' 'But how,' asked he, 'didst thou get into my bed?' The other replied, 'I found a bed that was spread, so I slept in it.' But said he, 'My wife was sleeping together with thee!' The other replied, 'Well, the bed is hers. How could I therefore have prevented her from using her own bed?' 'By the truth of my religion,' said the husband, 'if thou shouldst do it again, thou and I would have a quarrel.' Such was for the Frank the entire expression of his disapproval and the limit of his jealousy." Usamah ibn Munqidh, *An Arab-Syrian Gentleman and Warrior in the Period of the Crusades: Memoirs of Usamah ibn-Munqidh*, trans. Philip K. Hitti (1929; New York: Columbia University Press, 2000), 165.

169 *poulains* ("children" or "kids"): The modern French word means "colts" or "foals," which would make the heroes of the First Crusade stallions. For a discussion of the term, see M. R. Morgan, *The Chronicle of Ernoul and the Continuations of William of Tyre* (Oxford: Oxford University Press, 1973), 194–95.

169 Everyone who is a fresh emigrant from the Frankish lands: Ibn Munqidh, *An Arab-Syrian Gentleman*, 163–64.

170 eight upper-case Crusades: They are, with the major incidents: First (1095–99), in which crusaders capture Jerusalem; Second (1146–48), in which crusaders fail before Damascus; Third (1187–93), in which Richard Lionheart fails to recapture Jerusalem, and Frederick Barbarossa drowns en route to the Levant; Fourth (1202–04), in which crusaders sack Constantinople; Fifth (1217–21), in which crusaders are defeated before Damietta, Egypt; Sixth (1223–29), in which a temporary cession of Jerusalem to Frederick II is negotiated; Seventh (1245–50), in which Louis IX is defeated at Mansurah, Egypt, taken captive, then ransomed; and Eighth (1263–70), in which Edward of England negotiates a truce for the Latins of Outremer, and Louis IX dies off Tunis.

171 "This dreadful new military order": Quoted in Desmond Seward, *The Monks of War: The Military Religious Orders* (London: Penguin, 1995), 36.

171 a brother would read aloud from the Books of Joshua: Seward, *Monks of War*, 38–40.

171 "It is useless indeed for us to attack exterior enemies . . .": Quoted in Piers Paul Read, *The Templars* (New York: St. Martin's Press, 1999), 105.

172 The Quran has thirty-five verses: Jean Flori, *Guerre sainte, jihad, croisade: Violence et religion dans le christianisme et l'islam* (Paris: Seuil, 2002), 72. Flori counts only those with the root *jhd*. His discussion of the origins and elaboration of the doctrine of jihad is throughgoing and dispassionate (71–113). In my reading I have been more than once surprised by the willingness on the part of otherwise scrupulous western historians to settle for profoundly partisan generalizations about jihad. For the context of jihad in eleventh-century Outremer, I have relied on Carole Hillenbrand, *The Crusades: Islamic Perspectives* (New York: Routledge, 1999), 89–170; Robert Irwin, "Islam and the Crusades; 1096–1699," in Jonathan Riley-Smith, ed., *The Oxford Illustrated History of the Crusades* (Oxford: Oxford University Press, 1995), 223–33.

173 a short-lived shia dynasty of Aleppo: The Hamdanids, whose most famous ruler was Sayf al-Dawla (ruled 944–67).

173 *mujahadeen* or *ghaʐi*: The former is a volunteer for jihad—it has been transliterated in any number of ways and, recently, has been used to refer to almost any armed Muslim with a cause to defend. For our purposes, it means a volunteer for an officially sanctioned jihad. A ghazi is a "raider," generally understood as one at the borders of the dar al-Islam who launches religious sorties into the lands of the infidel. The Byzantine border warriors on the other side, often with a similar religious gloss, were known as *akritai*. Ghazi often grouped themselves in a *ribat*, the type of monastic fortress outpost from which the Almoravids drew their name. It is not too much of a stretch to consider the Krak des Chevaliers as the Christian equivalent of a ribat.

173 two revivalists—one each from Damascus and Aleppo: The Damascene qadi was Abu Saad al-Harawi, who arrived in Baghdad in August 1099, just weeks after the crusader sack of Jerusalem. His mission is nicely dramatized in the prologue to Maalouf's *Crusade Through Arab Eyes*. Al-Harawi became a prominent sunni qadi in Iraq and was thus a target of the Assasssins. They got to him in 1124 in Hamadan, in what is now Iran. (Hamadan is also the burial place of Avicenna.) The Aleppan Abdu Fadl Ibn al-Khashab caused a pro-jihad riot in Baghdad in 1111. On the death of Ridwan, the leader of Aleppo, in 1113, al-Khashab purged the city of his Assassin allies, killing more than two hundred of them, thereby earning the undying enmity of the survivors. Al-Khashab was also instrumental in bringing in the Turcoman il-Ghazi to rule the city and was present, exhorting the troops to jihad, at the Field of Blood. He was finally murdered by the Assassins in 1123.

174 at the town of Tikrit on the Tigris: Tikrit is latterly famous as the hometown of Saddam Hussein, who fully exploited his coincidental link with Saladin for propaganda purposes.

174 "The villages and towns are deserted . . .": From "Letter 257" of St. Bernard in *Patrologie Latine*, t. 182, col. 447, cited by Andre Vauchez, "Saint Bernard, un prédicateur irrésistible," in Robert Delort, ed., *Les croisades* (Paris: Seuil, 1988), 46–47.

175 Dorylaeum: Thought to be present-day Eskisehir, Turkey, in what was the province of Phrygia. The site of Second Crusade's devastating defeat was, ironically, the same battlefield on which the First Crusaders had routed the Rum Seljuks. Mention of the battle of Dorylaeum usually refers to the earlier encounter.

175 Humiliated, Louis dragged Eleanor away from Antioch: The messy episode is gleefully summed up in Read, *Templars*, 122–23.

177 the Geniza archive: A cache of some 250,000 documents kept at the Ben Ezra synagogue in Cairo. As it was forbidden to destroy any manuscript that contained the name of God, or even Hebrew letters, leather-bound documents had been chucked into a storage space for centuries. Forgotten, then discovered in 1864 by Jacob Saphir, an intrepid Lithuanian Talmudist, the whole lot was eventually sold off in bits and pieces by the impecunious Jews of Cairo, until in 1913 not one document was left in the city. Much of the great cache was corraled by Cambridge University. For an entertaining evocation of this scholarly gold rush, see Max Rodenbeck, *Cairo: The City Victorious* (New York: Vintage, 2000), 72–74.

177 "they were led past colonnades": Steven Runciman, *A History of the Crusades*, vol. 2, *The Kingdom of Jerusalem and the Frankish East, 1100–1187* (Cambridge: Cambridge University Press, 1952), 373. In one sentence Runciman admirably sums up a long passage in the chronicle of William, archbishop of Tyre, one of our main primary sources for this period. The original

may be found in William of Tyre, *A History of Deeds Done Beyond the Sea*, trans. Emily Atwater Babcock (New York: Columbia University Press, 1943), 2:319–21. The monumental Runciman remains our main secondary source for the crusades.

180 This atrocity got Cairo off the fence: Runciman holds that the deed was primarily done by a group of newcomers to the Levant from Nevers, France, whose count had died and were therefore uncontrollable. Whatever the case, a small westerner flotilla arrived shortly thereafter at the Coptic delta town of Tanis and performed the same merciless slaughter of every inhabitant. Runciman, *History of the Crusades*, 2:381.

180 in a conflagration, according to the chroniclers, that lasted two months: An admirable summation of this event occurs in André Raymond, Cairo, trans. Willard Wood (Cambridge, mass.: Harvard University Press, 2000): "The Frankish troops arrived before Cairo on 13 November. According to Arab historical tradition, Shawar [the vizier], unable to defend the unwalled city of Fustat, ordered its population to be evacuated. The residents responded with alacrity, having heard the terrible fate of the people of Bilbays. Then Shawar ordered Fustat to be torched so that it could not serve as a base of operations for the Franks in their attack on Qahira [Cairo]. . . . Arab historians . . . have given detailed and highly colored accounts of this patriotic incident, which has overtones of Rostopchin's order to burn Moscow at Napoleon's approach in 1812. Shawar is said to have had 20,000 jars of naphtha and 10,000 torches set in Fustat. The conflagration lasted for fifty-four days, and looters ran riot. From that time on, writes Marqizi, Fustat became the ruin known today as the *kiman* [little mounds]" (75).

180 Raymond's skull, set in a silver case: Runciman, *History of the Crusades*, 2:326. Based on the William of Tyre, *History of Deeds*, 2:199. William says that Raymond's right arm had also been cut off and sent to the caliph of Baghdad. After he saw this grisly duo of head and arm, "it was then sent to all the other Turkish satraps throughout the Orient."

181 his demise from dysentery: P. H. Newby, *Saladin in His Times* (London: Phoenix, 1983), 65.

182 a younger brother from a small fief in the Loire Valley: Reynaud (anglicized as Reginald in some studies) was a younger son of Geoffrey, count of Gien-sur-Loire, and took his name from Châtillon-sur-Loire. See Read, *Templars*, 142. The sleepy Sologne village of Gien-sur-Loire would be the scene of campaigning by Joan of Arc in 1429.

182 "a woman so eminent, so distinguished and powerful": William of Tyre, *History of Deeds*, 2:224.

183 Reynaud rounded up all the Orthodox priests of Cyprus: Maalouf, *Crusades Through Arab Eyes*, 157.

184 "The Christians impose a tax on the Muslims . . .": Abu l-Husayn Muhammad ibn Ahmad ibn Jubayr, *The Travels of Ibn Jubayr: A Mediaeval Spanish Muslim visits Makkah, Madinah, Egypt, Cities of the Middle East and Sicily*, trans. Roland Broadhurst (1952; New Delhi: Goodword, 2003), 301.

184 They were subsequently beheaded: Ibn Jubayr was in Alexandria when some of the imprisoned raiders were brought into town. He appears to have questioned them himself, before their execution. He states that one of their aims was to steal the body of Muhammad from its grave. If this is true, Reynaud was truly a sociopath. Ibn Jubayr, *Travels of Ibn Jubayr*, 51–53.

185 "the people . . . gave way to iniquity and debauchery": Kemal al-Din, quoted in Lewis, *Assassins*, 111.

186 "He [the messenger] said . . .": Lewis, *Assassins*, 116–17.

186 On the death of Nur al-Din's son, al Salih: In 1181. Al-Salih was only eighteen on his death. The pro-Zengid chronicler Ibn al-Athir (1160–1233), in *Sum of World History*, claims that he refused, as a good Muslim, a medicinal glass of wine and as a result expired. Maalouf, *Crusades Through Arab Eyes*, 183–84.

186 Toward the end of 1186 an enormous caravan: A rousing and imaginative reconstruction of this raid can be found in James Reston, Jr., *Warriors of God: Richard the Lionheart and Saladin in the Third Crusade* (New York: Doubleday, 2001), 23–25. Reston maintains, against the current historical consensus, that Saladin's sister was among the captives. The chronicle *Estoire d'Eracles*, a continuation of William of Tyre, is the source of this tale of Saladin's sister, but Runciman, *History of the Crusades*, debunks it (2:450, 454).

187 Sea of Galilee: This body of water is also known as Lake Tiberias and Lake Kinneret, the latter from the Hebrew word for "harp," which some see as the shape of the lake.

187 Cana: This could read, "What is believed by many biblical scholars to be the location of Cana." As with most biblical sites, generations of academics and archaeologists have squabbled over what happened where. It is now called Kafr Cana.

188 Sibylla's mother: Agnes of Courtenay, a daughter of the count of Edessa (Joscelin II), who lost that city to Zengi. Agnes married four times, once to King Amalric of Jerusalem, by whom she had Sibylla and Baldwin IV (the leper king).

188 the widowed heiress of Botrun: Botrun was a wealthy port south of Tripoli. The payment was ten thousand besants of gold, paid after her husband ungallantly put her on a scale. Runciman, *History of the Crusades*, punctiliously estimates that Lucia's "weight would have been about 10 stone" or 140 pounds (2:406n).

189 "This crown compensates for the Botrun marriage": *Estoire d'Eracles*, cited in Régine Pernoud, ed., *The Crusades*, trans. Enid McLeod (New York: G.P. Putnam's Sons, 1962), 154.

189 By midday of May 1: A certain Ernoul, squire to a great poulain lord, Balian of Ibelin, may have been an eyewitness to the events. His chronicle—published as *Chronique d'Ernoul et de Bernard le Trésorier* (ed. Mas Latrie, Paris, 1871)—provides, along with the continuator of William of Tyre through the *Estoire d'Eracles*, much of the information on the politics of the kingdom of Jerusalem and the course of events during that fateful summer.

190 "You love your blond head . . . !": *Estoire d'Eracles*, quoted in Runciman, *History of the Crusades*, 2:453.

191 Zippori: Ehud Netzer and Zeev Weiss, *Zippori* (Jerusalem: Israel Exploration Society, 1994).

192 Raymond argued that, if anything, the siege was a ploy: The fateful parley is recounted in many sources, Arab and Frank, with remarkably little difference in its details.

192 "It is not for you to ask me . . .": *Estoire d'Eracles*, quoted in Pernoud, *Crusades*, 164.

192 Balian of Ibelin: Moviegoers will recognize the name as that of the protagonist in Ridley Scott's *Kingdom of Heaven* (2005). The great battle whose aftermath is seen in the film— thousands of bodies, vultures wheeling—is Hattin. Although the script takes immense liberties with who did what and where, Balian did indeed lead the defense of Jerusalem and negotiate a humane surrender to Saladin. His presence in Jerusalem is an interesting story: after Hattin Saladin gave him safe passage there to retrieve his wife and children, but on his arrival the populace implored him to stay and organize the defense. He asked Saladin to be released from his promise

to depart along with his kin. Saladin not only granted this breaking of a vow but arranged for Balian's family to be taken to safety before the siege began.

193 The order was given to bypass Tauran: Geoffrey Regan, *Saladin and the Fall of Jerusalem* (North Ryde, Australia: Croom Helm, 1987), 121.

194 "Ah! Lord God, the battle is over! . . .": Ralph of Coggeshall, *Libellus de Expugnatione Terrae Sanctae per Saladinum*. Ralph, although not considered an eyewitness, is thought to have been an Englishman who participated in the defense of Jerusalem and thus would have heard the stories from the survivors of Hattin. Quoted in James A. Brundage, *The Crusades: A Documentary Survey* (Milwaukee, Wisc.: Marquette University Press, 1962), 157.

194 Kibbutz Lavi: My stay there, and the conversation with Mr. Aldubi, took place in June 2003.

197 Saladin's men ostentatiously poured streams of water: Ralph of Coggeshall, quoted in Brundage, *Crusades*, 157.

197 goatskins filled with water: Jean Richard, *The Crusades, c. 1071–1291*, trans. Jean Burrell (Cambridge: Cambridge University Press, 1999), 205.

197 they ran headlong from the columns: *Estoire d'Eracles* also speaks of five knights conspicuously defecting from the Christian side and telling Saladin of the disarray in the crusader army. See Pernoud, *Crusades*, 166.

197 "We are not coming down . . .": Ralph of Coggeshall, quoted in Brundage, *Crusades*, 157.

199 the disciplined formations of Taliq al-Din parted: Ibn al-Athir, quoted in Gabrieli, *Arab Historians*, 122.

199 "The Frankish king had retreated to the hill . . .": Saladin's son, al-Afad, gave this account to Ibn al-Athir, who was not present at the battle. Still, the chronicler is thought to be the most level-headed of the Arab sources. See Gabrieli, *Arab Historians*, 122–23.

200 "A king does not kill a king": The chronicler Beha ed-Din, quoted in Runciman, *History of the Crusades*, 2:460.

200 in killings often gruesomely botched by the amateur swordsmen: The chronicler Imad ed-Din, an eyewitness and faithful servant of Saladin, quoted in Newby, *Saladin*, 118.

201 Irony would be served: The Christian monument at Hattin gives the relevant passage from the New Testament: "And he goeth up into a mountain and calleth unto him whom he would and they came unto him." Imad ed-Din's description of the place gives a contrast: "The dead were scattered over the mountain and valleys, lying immobile on their sides. Hittin [Hattin] shrugged off their carcasses, and the perfume of victory was thick with the stench of them. I passed by them and saw the limbs of the fallen cast naked in the field of battle, scattered in pieces over the site of the encounter, lacerated and disjointed, with heads cracked open, throats split, spines broken, necks shattered, feet in pieces, noses mutilated, extremities torn off, members dismembered, parts shredded, eyes gouged out, stomachs disembowelled, hair coloured with blood, the praccordium slashed, fingers sliced off, the thorax shattered, the ribs broken, the joints disjointed, bones broken, tunics torn off, faces lifeless, wounds gaping, skin flayed, fragments chopped off, hair lopped, backs skinless, bodies dismembered, teeth knocked out, blood spilt, life's last breath exhaled, necks lolling, joints slackened, pupils liquefied, heads hanging, livers crusted, ribs staved in, heads shattered, breasts flayed, spirits flown, their very ghosts crushed, like stones among stones, a lesson to the wise." Gabrieli, *Arab Historians*, 135.

201 the sultan insisted that the bargain be kept: Runciman, *History of the Crusades*, 2:466.

204 he was long remembered more in the west than he was in Islamic countries: Hillenbrand, *Crusades*, 589–616.

CHAPTER 7: LAS NAVAS DE TOLOSA 1212

207 "to free most of the soil of Spain from its alien invaders": Paul Fregosi, *Jihad in the West: Muslim Conquests from the Seventh to the Twenty-first Centuries* (New York: Prometheus, 1998), 195.

208 a French adventurer given Alfonso's daughter in marriage: Henry of Burgundy (1066–1112) married Teresa of León, Alfonso VI's illegitimate daughter, and became count of Coimbra. Their son, Alfonso Henriques, had himself crowned the first king of Portugal in 1139 and is styled, in Portuguese, Afonso I.

209 Of the twenty-nine battles he won against them: Derek Lomax, *The Reconquest of Spain* (New York: Longman, 1978), 82.

209 ten thousand Christians of Granada . . . the grandfather of Averroes: Lomax, *Reconquest*, 85.

209 the sophisticated cities of al-Andalus were a mouthwatering prize: Bernard F. Reilly, in *The Medieval Spains* (Cambridge: Cambridge University Press, 1993), points out that Alfonso the Battler's conquest of the taifa state resulted in the kingdom of Aragon doubling in size and increasing in population from 125,000 to 500,000 (110). Similar gains could be made by capturing other Muslim cities. There obviously was more to the reconquista than just piety.

209 quite possibly impotent Alfonso the Battler: Reilly, *Medieval Spains*, 109.

209 *Rubet ensis sanguine Arabum:* Desmond Seward, *The Monks of War: The Military Religious Orders* (London: Penguin, 1995), 152.

209 In endowering Zaida with this necklace of fortresses: Reilly, *Medieval Spains*, 72.

210 the heresy of ascribing anthropomorphic attributes: Roger Le Tourneau, *The Almohad Movement in North Africa in the Twelfth and Thirteenth Centuries* (Princeton, N.J.: Princeton University Press, 1969), 46.

210 *mahdi*: In sunni Islam, the mahdi is an important figure but not a messiah. For the shia, the mahdi is a far more eschatological personage, announcing the end of time. We have seen in Chapter 6 that the shia Nizari Ismailis of Alamut (and Syria) believed that the laws of Islam were irrevocably abrogated when their leader proclaimed himself a mahdi. The elevation of Ibn Tumart, the sunni Almohad, would have been a heady boost to morale but would not have occasioned wild excesses.

212 "not only the universal church but the whole world to govern": Cited in J.N.D. Kelly, "Innocent III," in *The Oxford Dictionary of Popes* (Oxford: Oxford University Press, 1986), 186.

213 Enrico Dandolo: It will be remembered from the Introduction that Dandolo's body was eventually interred in the wall of a gallery in the Hagia Sophia under an inscription marked "Henricus Dandolo." When the Greeks regained control of the city in 1261, his remains were unceremoniously chucked out into the street.

213 When the Latins burst through the gates on April 12, 1204, mayhem ensued: A superb new account of this incredible episode of Christian history, which this present work can only evoke in passing, can be found in Jonathan Phillips, *The Fourth Crusade and the Sack of Constantinople* (New York: Viking, 2004). Finding an arresting metaphor to describe the moment the walls were

breached, Phillips writes, "The crusaders spread into the city like a deadly virus running through the veins of a weak old man: they shut down movement and then they ended life" (259).

214 A partial inventory: Phillips, *Fourth Crusade*, 262–63.

215 "foxes in the vineyard of the Lord": A fairly common image for heresy in the Middle Ages, it derives from a passage in the Song of Songs (2:15). Benedict XVI, elected pope in 2005, used a variant in his inaugural address when he spoke of toiling "in the vineyards of the Lord."

215 Innocent finally had the pretext to goad the northern nobility: It is often stated, erroneously, that the pope first came up with the idea of an attack on Languedoc after the assassination of his legate, that the crime in some way forced his hand. Innocent had, in fact, been lobbying for an assault for several years prior to the murder. See Stephen O'Shea, *The Perfect Heresy: The Revolutionary Life and Death of the Medieval Cathars* (London: Profile; New York: Walker; Vancouver: Douglas & McIntyre, 2000), 57.

215n From taking the Latin word used by the chroniclers, *puer*, to mean, literally, "boy": The distinguished French historians Philippe Ariès and Georges Duby pointed out the faulty translation. This and other information about the crusade comes from Peter Raedts, "La Croisade des enfants a-t-elle eu lieu?" in Robert Delort, ed., *Les croisades* (Paris: Seuil, 1988), 55–71.

217 Madrid, Ávila, Segovia, Medina del Campo, Cuenca, Huete, Uclés, Valladolid, and Soria: María Dolores Rosado Llamas and Manuel Gabriel López Payer, *La Batalla de las Navas de Tolosa: Historia y mito* (Jaén: Caja Rural Jaén, 2001), 112. Also mentioned are a dozen lesser municipalities. *La Batalla* is the most comprehensive study of the campaign and its legacy published to date, and I have relied on its meticulous analysis of the different, sometimes contradictory historical sources and on its reconstruction of the battle. The events on which there is a historical consensus are not signaled in these notes.

217 "Kill them all, God will know his own": This utterance, generally thought to be apocryphal, was supposedly uttered at the siege of Béziers in 1209. For a discussion of scholars backing away from the idea that the phrase was simply invented by a later chronicler, see O'Shea, *Perfect Heresy*, 269n.

217 a thirty-year-old whose red beard and penetrating blue eyes: The chronicler Abd al-Walid al-Marrakushi states of the caliph, "He had a clear complexion, a red beard, dark blue eyes, plump cheeks, average height; he often kept his eyes downcast and was very silent, most due to the faulty articulation [stuttering] from which he suffered; he was inscrutable, but at the same time mild, courageous, reluctant to shed blood, and not really disposed to undertake anything unless he had carefully studied it; he was charged with avarice." Quoted in Le Tourneau, *Almohad Movement*, 80. Reinhart Dozy, a pioneer of the study of Islamic Spain, translated some of the relevant Almohad chronicles in the late nineteenth century. Al-Marrakushi's chronicle is thought to be useful in that he was a native of Marrakesh and a contemporary of the events he describes. Perhaps most important, he is thought to have composed his work in Baghdad, far from the long arm of Almohad reprisal. The idea that the caliph inherited his looks not from Berber genes but from his mother's is widespread.

217 The Muslims may have numbered as many as thirty thousand: Estimates range up to 600,000. It is known that both sides had large armies, but the 100,000-plus figures usually given do not bear up under scrutiny. Rosado Llamas and López Payer, *La Batalla de las Navas de Tolosa*, 109–11.

221 The governor, according to a chronicler: The fourteenth-century Arab chronicler Ibn Abi Zar. His work is translated into Spanish by Ambrosio Huici Miranda, whose *Las grandes batallas de la Reconquista* (1956) and *Historia politica del Emperio Almohade* (1957) laid the groundwork for later scholarship.

222 Two Arab chroniclers: Ibn Abi Zar (see preceding note) and Ibn Abd Allah al-Himyari, another fourteenth-century chronicler. Spanish translation by Pilar Maestro González; French, by Evariste Lévi-Provençal.

223 Alfonso . . . advocated heading back up north to confront his treacherous neighbor: The source for this dramatic change of heart was Alfonso's daughter, Blanca, who wrote a detailed letter about the campaign to the countess of Champagne. Given the unflattering light it sheds on her father, the anecdote is generally considered trustworthy. Quoted in Rosado Llamas and López Payer, *La Batalla de las Navas de Tolosa*, 126–27.

223 "A thousand men . . . could hold it against all the men there are under heaven": Quoted in Rosado Llamas and López Payer, *La Batalla de las Navas de Tolosa*, 132; my translation.

224 later identified by legend as St. Isidoro: Later secular lore has him called Martín Halaja.

225 "the son of a coward": This story is told in *Crónica latina de los reyes de Castilla* and *Crónica de Veinte Reyes*. Both date from the thirteenth century. The former has been translated into French by G. Cirot as *Chronique latine des rois de Castille*, published as an offprint of *Bulletin Hispanique* no. 41.

226 "Archbishop, let us die here, you and I": Quoted in Rosado Llamas and López Payer, *La Batalla de las Navas de Tolosa*, 146.

226 A cross appeared in the sky: Perhaps the strangest miracle concerns what happened after the battle: the archbishop of Toledo maintained that the thousands of Muslim dead did not bleed or rot, thus sparing the Christian victors from pestilence.

226 One source speaks of the Andalusis on the wings of the formation running away: This appears in Arnold Amaury's letter to the Cistercians. Given his interest in exaggerating the prowess of the Christian army, this detail might be trustworthy, as it suggests demoralization as the victor rather than any feat of arms.

226 Others say that the soldiery's discontent: See Rosado Llamas and López Payer, *La Batalla de las Navas de Tolosa*, 157–61.

227 "Therefore ask Valencia what is the state of Murcia": Abu al-Baqa al-Rundi, "Lament for the Fall of Seville," in Olivia Remie Constable, ed., *Medieval Iberia: Readings from Christian, Muslim, and Jewish Sources* (Philadelphia: University of Pennsylvania Press, 1997), 221.

230 The Spaniards, alive to their history: This is my opinion. In my travels in the Mediterranean basin in the past twenty-five years, I have yet to visit any country except Spain where almost everyone—from waitress to tour guide through barkeep and bus driver—can hold forth at length about the past. The people of its cities celebrate Moors and Christians festivals with undiminished enthusiasm. In scholarly circles the discussion of Spain's singular history has been lively as well. From the 1940s on historians Américo Castro and Claudio Sánchez-Albornoz battled through their books about the meaning of Spain: the former argued that the mixing of creeds and peoples was the hallmark of the peninsula's past; the latter, that the Christian mission of Spain, unbroken from the time of the Visigoths, was paramount in a centuries-long quest for unity. It is an interesting debate, at the center of contemporary concerns about celebrating either

diversity or homogeneity. In the Spanish context, the Christian myths surrounding El Cid and Pelayo of Asturias have been sustained to the present day. See J. N. Hillgarth, "Spanish Historiography and Iberian Reality," *History and Theory* 24 (1985), 23–43, reproduced in Hillgarth, *Spain and the Mediterranean in the Later Middle Ages* (Aldershot: Ashgate, 2003). This witty and informative essay also speaks of the traditional self-image of Spaniards: "In 1629 there appeared a *Libro de las cinco excelencias del español*. These five 'excellencies' were passionate zeal for religion, military glory, purity of lineage, the monarchy, and extreme generosity. From the point of view of most non-Spaniards and even of some contemporaries inside Spain these virtues appear as fanaticism, one-sided pride, lust for dominion, rodomontade, and vulgar ostentation" (24).

230 the provincial government of Jaén announced: "El museo de la Batalla de Las Navas de Tolosa abrirá sus puertas en 2006," *El País*, July 9, 2004.

CHAPTER 8: THE SEA OF FAITH

231 "furious with indignation and wrath": Quoted in Geoffrey Regan, *Lionhearts: Richard I, Saladin, and the Third Crusade* (New York: Walker, 1998), 190.

232 "Then in the haughty presence of the Sultan . . .": *Dante Alighieri's Divine Comedy: Paradise*, trans. Mark Musa (Bloomington: Indiana University Press, 2004), 5:108–09 (Canto XI, 100–05).

233 eleventh-century Syrian poet: Abu Ala'a al-Ma'arri (973–1057), a one-eyed poet, sometimes called the Heretic, came from the town of Ma'arat al-Nu'man, later the scene of cannibalism during the First Crusade.

233 "It is a sign of God's love for us . . .": Andrew Palmer, Sebastian Brock, and Robert Hoyland, eds. and trans., *The Seventh Century in the West-Syrian Chronicles* (Liverpool: Liverpool University Press, 1993), xxi, quoted in John V. Tolan, *Saracens: Islam in the Medieval European Imagination* (New York: Columbia University Press, 2002), 37.

233 Hulegu, influenced by two of his Nestorian Christian wives: Erik Hildinger, *Warriors of the Steppe: A Military History of Central Asia, 500 B.C. to 1700 A.D.* (Cambridge, Mass.: Da Capo Press, 1997), 148–49. Hulegu, a Buddhist, had had a Nestorian mother as well.

234 a historian of genius: Ibn Khaldun stands out as a giant among historians, from any period. An empiricist rather than a speculative philosopher, but nonetheless a devout Muslim, he possessed an intellectual rigor that led him to some conclusions that were far ahead of his time, prefiguring Marx and other materialists. For example: "The basic causes of historical evolution are in fact to be sought in the economic and social structure" or "The differences which are seen between generations in their behaviour are only the expression of the differences which separate them in their economic way of life." See M. Talbi, "Ibn Khaldun, Wal al-Din Abd al-Rahman B. Muhammad B. Muhammad B. Abi Bakr Muhammad B. Al-Hasan," in *Encylopedia of Islam* (Leiden: Brill, 1971), 3:825–31.

234 the virtues and vices of *asabiyya*: Francesco Gabrieli, "Asabiyya," in *Encyclopedia of Islam* (Leiden: Brill, 1960), 1:681.

234 undisputed in Muslim doctrine: A full exposition of Islamic attitudes toward Jesus can be found in Kenneth Cragg, *Jesus and the Muslim: An Exploration* (Oxford: Oneworld, 1999).

234 "O you People of the Book . . .": Quoted in Jerome Murphy-O'Connor, *The Holy Land* (Oxford: Oxford University Press, 1998), 86.

235 the head of Cluny: Peter the Venerable (1092–1156).

235 the lush forest of medieval Christian polemic: The scholarship on the subject is similarly lush. Of particular value for my summary of the slanders were Tolan's *Saracens*; Norman Daniel, *Islam and the West: The Making of an Image* (Oxford: Oneworld, 2000); and Philippe Sénac, *L'Occident médiéval face à l'Islam* (Paris: Flammarion, 2000).

236 the use of concealed magnets: This claim was made in *Chanson d'Antioche*, an epic of the First Crusade by an unknown author. Alexandre Eckhardt, "Le cercueil flottant de Mahomet," *Mélanges de philologie romaine et de littérature médiévales offerts à E. Hoepffner*, Publication de la Faculté des Lettres de l'Université de Strasbourg, fasc. 113 (1949), 77–88, quoted in Tolan, *Saracens*, 121.

236 deflower the Virgin Mary: The claim was made by Eulogius, the most famous of the martyrs of Córdoba. Quoted in Tolan, *Saracens*, 93.

236 A thirteenth-century chronicler of León: Lucas de Tuy, in his *Chronicon mundi*, quoted in Tolan, *Saracens*, 182.

237 five friars were executed in Marrakesh . . . "to long for death for Christ . . .": Tolan, *Sarcens*, 218, 220.

238 Frederick was a polyglot artist: Dante called him "the father of Italian poetry."

238 an adept at oriental panache: "He [Frederick] traveled with a harem guarded by eunuchs, and with a menagerie which included camels, lions, panthers, white bears, monkeys and other animals. He had an enormous elephant, a gift from the sultan of Egypt, which was guarded by Saracen attendants. His bodyguard was composed of Sicilian Moslems, and he was accompanied by Ethiopian trumpeters and Moorish dancers and jongleurs." Joseph E. Strayer and Dana C. Munro, *The Middle Ages* (New York: Appleton-Century-Crofts, 1959), 334.

238 saw in him the Antichrist: Bernard McGinn, *Anti-Christ: Two Thousand Years of the Human Fascination with Evil* (New York: HarperCollins, 1994), 152–57. Frederick's reputation as the Beast was particularly strong among the followers of Joachim of Fiore, a thirteenth-century sect particularly popular among the more extreme elements of the Franciscans.

239 excommunicated for delaying his expedition to Outremer: He was supposed to have joined the Fifth Crusade of 1519 but delayed his departure for ten years to settle dynastic matters. Pope Gregory IX, a kinsman of Innocent III who freely treated Frederick as the Antichrist in his pronouncements, excommunicated him out of exasperation.

241 such borrowings from the Arab funduq: David Abulafia, "The Role of Trade in Muslim-Christian Contact During the Middle Ages," in Françoise Micheau, ed., *Les relations des pays d'Islam avec le monde latin: Du milieu du Xe siècle au milieu du XIIIe siècle* (Paris: Jacques Marseille, 2000), 304. Also useful in summarizing research on Christian-Muslim trade in the Mediterranean was the almost identically named: Georges Jehel and Philippe Racinet, *Les relations des pays d'Islam avec le monde latin: Du Xe siècle au milieu du XIIIe siècle* (Paris: Edition du Temps, 2000).

242 "Ah! What a great good fortune . . .": Ramon Llull, *Libre del gentil et los tres savis* (Book of the Gentile and the Three Wise Men), prologue, in A. Bonner, trans. and ed., *Doctor Illuminatus: A Ramon Llull Reader* (Princeton, N.J.: Princeton University Press, 1993), 90, quoted in Tolan, *Saracens*, 264.

243 On March 2, 1354, an earthquake flattened the fortress town: John Julius Norwich, *Byzantium: The Decline and Fall* (New York: Alfred A. Knopf, 1996), 320.

243 "a prodigy of decay": Jason Goodwin, *Lords of the Horizon: A History of the Ottoman Empire* (New York: Henry Holt, 1999), xiv.

245 a "Byzantine commonwealth" of religious and cultural expression: Dimitri Obolensky, *The Byzantine Commonwealth: Eastern Europe 500–1453* (New York: Praeger, 1971), chaps. 7–11.

245 deeply smitten: Norwich, *Decline and Fall*, prefers "besottedly in love" (302).

246 we can be certain only that the principal leader of the Serbian armies: For a thorough examination of all the sources, see Thomas A. Emmert, *Serbian Golgotha: Kosovo, 1389* (New York: Columbia University Press, 1990), a superbly researched monograph that separates what can be known from that which seems simply invented.

246 whom some historians unkindly believe to be a total fabrication: On this nettlesome matter, see Noel Malcolm, *Kosovo: A Short History* (New York: New York University Press, 1998), 68–74. After a lengthy examination of the matter, he is led to conclude, almost comically: "Without further evidence, the precise truth may never be known. But in the present state of knowledge, it is reasonable to think that Murat was in fact killed by someone, quite possibly a Hungarian, whose name either was, or sounded like, or was later adapted into, or meant the same as, Milos Kobilic" (74).

247 Kosovo's Shakespearean cocktail: André Gerolymatos, *The Balkan Wars: Conquest, Revolution, and Retribution from the Ottoman Era to the Twentieth Century and Beyond* (New York: Basic Books, 2002), chap. 1, for the interplay of the Kosovo myth and the events leading to the First World War.

247 the easing of the common man's feudal burden: Goodwin, *Lords of the Horizon*, 20. Goodwin has a nice passage: "Dusan of Serbia had let his lords exact two days' labour a week from their peasants. Under the Ottomans . . . peasants were only expected to work three days a year for the local spahi; beyond that small impost, and the tithe they paid as Christians amounting to ten per cent of their income, they were undisturbed in either their religion or their cultivation. . . . Peasants came back, if they had ever really left, to discover that all the weight of Balkan feudalism—the requisitions, corvées, serfdom, droit de seigneur—the whole bitter panoply of warriors in their castles and helpless villagers clustered at their foot, had been swept away. Turkish overlordship came even to the Orthodox as a kind of liberation."

248 the cause of boundless heartbreak: Philip Mansel, in his *Constantinople: City of the World's Desire, 1453–1924* (London: Penguin, 1997), quotes a Balkan lament (17):

> Be damned, O Emperor, be thrice damned
> For the evil you have done and the evil you do.
> You catch and shackle the old and the archpriests
> In order to take the children as Janissaries.
> Their parents weep and their sisters and brothers too
> And I cry until it pains me;
> As long as I live I shall cry,
> For last year it was my son and this year my brother.

249 "How Happy Is He . . .": The translation, and an explanation of this Kemalist republican motto, is found in Hugh Pope, *Sons of the Conquerors: The Rise of the Turkic World* (New York: Overlook Duckworth, 2005), 90.

250 the Genoese trading city of Galata: Also called Pera, from the Greek for "beyond."

250 an immense host of warriors from Wallachia, France, Germany, Poland, Italy, Spain, and England: See John Freely, *Istanbul: The Imperial City* (London: Penguin, 1998), 167.

250 exceeded all of their predecessors in the pursuit of atrocity: Regarding Timur's ferocity, there are, as in every subject of history, revisionists, notably Jean-Paul Roux, *Tamerlan* (Paris: Fayard, 1994).

251 Ibn Khaldun came away impressed with Timur's thoughtfulness: M. Talbi, "Ibn Khaldun, Wal al-Din Abd al-Rahman B. Muhammad B. Muhammad B. Abi Bakr Muhammad B. Al-Hasan," in *Encylopedia of Islam* (Leiden: Brill, 1971), 3:825–31.

252 which later legend made into a cage: Steven Runciman, *The Fall of Constantinople 1453* (Cambridge: Cambridge University Press, 1965), 42. According to that legend, Beyazit killed himself by smashing his head against the golden bars of the cage. It is uncertain how he died, but suicide is a good hypothesis.

252 Olivera, was relieved of her clothes: Repeated in most standard histories of this time, this story of poor Olivera (also called Despina) seems less incredible, given Timur's proclivities, than the fate of her husband.

252 decided to turn around and march across the world to conquer China: Timur never made it. He died en route, aged seventy-two.

CHAPTER 9: CONSTANTINOPLE 1453 AND KOSTANTINIYYE

253 The Ottomans ineffectually besieged Constantinople in 1422: The eighteen-year-old Murad, just having ascended the throne, cut his warrior teeth on this unsuccesssful siege. It lasted from June 10 to September 6.

254 after prudently having his infant stepbrother drowned in his bath: This was done, according to the Greek chronicler Michael Ducas, on Mehmet's order while he was comforting the child's mother on the grief she felt at the death of the sultan. Franz Babinger, whose monumental work of 1953, *Mehmed the Conqueror and His Time*, trans. Ralph Mannheim (Princeton, N.J.: Princeton University Press, 1978), forms the basis of much of our knowledge of Mehmet, states that Mehmet's action inaugurated the Ottoman custom of having one's male siblings strangled upon acceding to the throne (65–66). Later historians differ on Mehmet's responsibility in starting the custom, citing such examples as Beyazit at Kosovo. Whatever the origin, the custom thrived in a gruesome fashion—at some successions of the sixteenth and seventeenth centuries, scores of siblings and half-siblings were killed. A silken cord was used to strangle them so as not to shed royal blood.

254 Mehmet, conversant in Turkish, Greek, Hebrew, Arabic, Persian, and Latin: Steven Runciman, *The Fall of Constantinople 1453* (Cambridge: Cambridge University Press, 1965), 56. Other sources claim he spoke only three or four languages.

255 biographies of Alexander the Great: Mehmet's tastes went beyond the great Macedonian,

according to a western contemporary, Zorzi Dolfin, who wrote, "Daily he has Roman and other historical works read to him by a companion named Ciriaco of Ancona and another Italian. He has them read Laertius, Herodotus, Livy, Quintus Curtius, the chronicles of the popes, the emperors, the kings of France, and the Lombards." Quoted in Babinger, *Mehmed the Conqueror*, 112.

255 this fleshy-lipped, starry-eyed scion: Giovanni Maria Angiolello was a Venetian taken captive while still a youth during the Turkish conquest of Euboea (Negropont), the long island off the eastern coast of Greece. He became a page at the court of Mehmet and was later freed. In his *Historia Turchesa*, published in 1480 and avidly read throughout Europe, he gave the following description of the sultan in middle age: "of medium height, fat and fleshy; he had a wide forehead, large eyes with thick lashes, an aquiline nose, a small mouth with a round copious red-tinged beard, a short thick neck, a sallow complection, rather high shoulders and a loud voice." Quoted in Babinger, *Mehmed the Conqueror*, 424. Runciman, collating several contemporaneous descriptions of the man, writes that Mehmet was "of middle height but strongly built. His face was dominated by a pair of piercing eyes, under arched eyebrows, and a thin aquiline nose that curved over a mouth with full lips. In later life his features reminded men of a parrot about to eat ripe cherries." See *Fall of Constantinople*, 58.

258 one went as far afield as Paris and London: Manuel II Palaeologus, in 1400–01. He was the father of Constantine XI, the last basileus of the Byzantine Empire.

258 Peloponnesian province, Morea: The Latins had established an ephemeral province there following the carve-up of the Byzantine Empire after the sack of Constantinople in the Fourth Crusade. The Byzantines, in the mid–thirteenth century, recovered it, and what was known as a despotate came to be centered in Mystras, near Sparta. (Mystras, incidentally, is still a beautiful hillside covered with ruined Byzantine chapels.) The despots of Morea were usually of the ruling family of Constantinople and had almost complete autonomy from the capital. Another Greek holdout against the Ottoman advance was Trebizond, on the Black Sea coast of Anatolia, which had its own basileus.

259 Rome had lost much of its influence: The preceding century and a half had diminished papal power considerably. For seventy years in the fourteenth century the papacy had resided in Avignon, each successive pope a Frenchman in the orbit, if not the puppet, of the French Crown. Then from 1378 to 1415 a period of confusion ensued as European monarchies backed different contenders for the throne of St. Peter. Poland, Hungary, Germany, England, most of Italy, and the Scandinavian countries plumped for the Roman candidate. France, Scotland, Spain, southern Italy, and France sided with the cleric chosen in Avignon. The period is known as the Great Schism, not to be confused with the similarly named break between Latin and Orthodox churches that occurred in 1054. Mercifully, the politics of the latter Great Schism lie outside the scope of this work; its harm to papal influence, however, is germane to the events of 1453, as the papacy could no longer rally Christendom to a martial cause.

259 successive conclaves that ringingly announced the rift to be at an end: The most important of these was the Council of Florence in 1439.

259 "Better a sultan's turban than a cardinal's hat": The attribution to Notaras may be unjust, since he fought bravely during the siege. And if he did say such a thing, he was disastrously wrong, at least with regard to his personal destiny. Mehmet, however eager to repopulate

Kostantiniyye with Greeks, wasted no time in eliminating the civilian leadership of the defunct empire, Notaras included. One story of the days immediately after the conquest adds a personal, unsavory note to the bloody business of exterminating an elite: the sultan, on seeing Notaras' young son, immediately wanted the boy for his harem; on being rebuffed, the entire family was executed. Whatever the truth, it is known that a daughter, Anna Notaras, escaped the outrages immediately following the fall of Constantinople and lived out her life as a respectable noble-woman in Venice. Also, she is the heroine of Finnish novelist Mika Waltari's *The Dark Angel* (1952), a tolerably good tale of love between Latin and Greek set during the final days of Constantinople.

259 he was a Constantine, born of a Helena, as had been the first emperor of Constantinople: Constantine the Great's mother was St. Helen, credited with unearthing the True Cross—as well as many other relics—on a trip to Palestine in the fourth century. Constantine XI's mother was Helena Dragases, the daughter of a Serbian prince.

261 Under the guidance of a Bulgarian renegade: Baltaoglu Suleyman Bey. Not much is known of his early life, and he may have been a renegade under compulsion—that is, brought to Constantinople as a prisoner of war. He distinguished himself in an attack on the Genoese-controlled island of Lesbos. He was the Ottoman Empire's first admiral. David Nicolle, *Constantinople 1453: The End of Byzantium* (Oxford: Osprey, 2000), 21.

261 the headland of Constantinople: Now called Seraglio Point.

261 In the first week of April the Ottoman armies and their allies appeared: The events of the siege are well known, thanks to a wealth of primary sources. Foremost on the Christian side are the eyewitness chronicle of a Greek courtier, George Phrantzes; a Venetian surgeon, Nicolo Barbaro; and a Lesbosian archbishop, Leonard of Chios. There are other eyewitness accounts, as well as reconstructions done in the decades after the siege, most notably by Michael Ducas and Laonicus Chalcocondylas. On the Turkish side, the account of Tursun Bey, an eyewitness in the besieging army, was the most germane for our purposes, especially with regard to the Rumeli Hisari. Anthologies of primary sources consulted include J. R. Melville Jones, ed., *The Siege of Constantinople: Seven Contemporary Accounts* (Amsterdam: Hakkert, 1973), and Alain Servanite, ed., *Le Voyage à Istanbul: Byzance, Constantinople, Istanbul du Moyen Age au XX* *siècle* (Paris: Complexe, 2003). For the reconstruction of the siege, there is no shortage of excellent specialized histories. I have relied principally but not exclusively on Runciman, *Fall of Constantinople*; Nicolle, *Constantinople 1453*; the indispensable Babinger, *Mehmed the Conqueror*; Roger Crowley, *1453: The Holy War for Constantinople and the Clash of Islam and the West* (New York: Hyperion, 2005); and Nanami Shiono, *The Fall of Constantinople* (New York: Vertical, 2005). In addition to these works, every historian of the Byzantines and the Ottomans has had a crack at describing that momentous spring—their contributions are given where appropriate in these notes. I should add that, as always, the events on which a consensus exists are not flagged; those that are specific to one author, or that have been the cause of disagreement among scholars, are.

261 George Phrantzes: (1401–77), also Sphrantzes. His chronicle covers the years 1413–77. At the time of the siege he was grand logothete (chancellor) and personal secretary to the basileus.

262 two small Byzantine forts outside the walls: Studios, on the Marmara, and Therapia, on the Bosporus.

262 as every visitor past and present has realized: Du Loir, an aide-de-camp of a seventeenth-century French embassy to Kostantiniyye, wrote of the Golden Horn: "one would think it a waterway fashioned more by Art than by Nature." Quoted in Robert Mantran, *Istanbul au siècle de Soliman le Magnifique* (Paris: Hachetté, 1965), 52.

262 line of fortifications that ran from the Marmara to the Horn: Especially useful for this overview was Stephen Turnbull, *The Walls of Constantinople, AD 324–1453* (Oxford: Osprey, 2004).

263 a huge mausoleum for a modern-day Turkish prime minister: Adnan Menderes, who was the first prime minister (1950–60) not to be of the People's Republican Party that Ataturk had founded. He was overthrown by a military coup in 1960, tried for betraying the constitution, and hanged in 1961. The mausoleum was erected in 1990.

264 a basileus of the crusading era: The great Alexius I Comnenus, whose life works were recorded by his daughter Anna in the *Alexiad*.

264 a large stone plaque was affixed in 1953: Orhan Pamuk, in his memoir *Istanbul: Memories and the City*, trans. Maureen Freely (New York: Alfred A. Knopf, 2005), says the quincentenary was celebrated with a certain ambivalence: "Even in my own time, Turks committed to the idea of a westernized republic were wary of making too much of the conquest. Neither President Celal Bayar nor Prime Minister Adnan Menderes attended the 500th anniversary ceremony in 1953; although it had been many years in the planning, it was decided at the last moment that to do so might offend the Greeks and Turkey's western allies. The Cold War had just begun, and Turkey, a member of NATO, did not wish to remind the world about the conquest. It was, however, three years later that the Turkish state deliberately provoked what you might call 'conquest fever' by allowing mobs to rampage through the city, plundering the property of Greeks and other minorities. A number of churches were destroyed during the riots and a number of priests were murdered, so there are many echoes of the cruelties western historians describe in accounts of the 'fall' of Constantinople. In fact, both the Turkish and Greek states have been guilty of treating their respective minorities as hostages to geopolitics, and that is why more Greeks have left Istanbul over the past fifty years than in the fifty years following 1453" (172–73).

265 Porphyrogenitus: "Born into the Purple," that is, born of a reigning basileus and empress. This name was given to several grandees of Byzantium, the most famous being Constantine VII Porphyrogenitus, the tenth-century scholar-basileus whom we have encountered sending a botanical treatise to the Umayyad court in Córdoba.

266 a shrine was known to be there in Byzantine times: John Freely, *Istanbul* (London: A&C Black, 2000), 274. Freely, in this excellent Blue Guide, states that the shrine is the third holiest in all of Islam, after Mecca and Jersualem. The old Companion has given his name, Eyup, to the neighborhood at the head of the Golden Horn.

266 trundling barrels filled with stones: Within the first week the outer walls of the Lycus were destroyed. In addition to barrels, the defenders would have erected makeshift stockades, piled up sandbags, and thrown any sort of obstacle to blunt the attack.

267 a huge grain ship dispatched by the pope: Nicholas V, the "first of the Renaissance popes." See J.N.D. Kelly, *The Oxford Dictionary of Popes* (Oxford: Oxford University Press, 1986), 245. He was unable to rally Christendom to crusade both before and after the siege of Constantinople.

His main contribution was to welcome the scholarly Greek diaspora and found the Vatican Library.

268 he simply condemned the Bulgarian to a bastinado: A Turkish chronicle has him spared this punishment and leading the attack on the Blachernae in the final assault.

268 thereby inaugurating the era of the mortar: Nicolle, *Constantinople 1453*, 57.

268 bickering between the Genoese and the Venetians: The arguing over who should lead and contribute to the attack wasted precious days. It was only on April 28, a full six days after the Turks had arrived in the Golden Horn, that the attack was made. It was led by Giacomo Coco— he and many others died in the attempt, for which the Turks had had ample time to prepare.

269 Venice was proceeding cautiously: Venice, ever mindful of its own interests, had designs on Morea and wished to extract concessions from the extenuated Byzantines. The commander of the relief fleet left Venice only on May 7, and his force was to rendezvous with more ships from Crete off Euboea. By the time they had cleared all the logistical and diplomatic hurdles placed in their way by the Venetian Senate, it was too late.

269 a Latin volunteer named Johannes Grant: He was an engineer who had arrived with Giustiniani and was under the command of Lucas Notaras. See Runciman, *Fall of Constantinople*, 84, 118, 120.

269 they returned to the city they now knew to be doomed: A vote was taken by the crew members, while they were still in the safety of the Aegean, over whether to return. Only one sailor voted against the idea. Jason Goodwin, *Lords of the Horizon: A History of the Ottoman Empire* (New York: Henry Holt, 1999), 38.

270 Halil Pasha argued for lifting the siege: Runciman, as usual, delivers a stirring account: "The Vizier, Halil Pasha, relying on his record of long and distinguished public service, rose to his feet and demanded that the siege be abandoned. He had never approved of the campaign, and events had shown him to be right. The Turks had made no headway; instead, they had suffered some humiliating setbacks. At any time the princes of the West would come to the city's rescue. Venice had already dispatched a great fleet. Genoa, however unwillingly, would be forced to do likewise. Let the Sultan offer terms that would be acceptable to the Emperor and retire before worse disasters occurred. The venerable Vizier commanded respect. Many of his hearers, remembering how ineffectual the Turkish warships had shown themselves in battles against the Christians, must have shuddered at the thought of great Italian navies bearing down on them. The Sultan, after all, was only a boy of twenty-one. Was he imperilling his great heritage with the impetuous recklessness of youth?" *Fall of Constantinople*, 124–25. Halil was executed shortly after the siege.

270 the elements combined to give it an eerie send-off: In 1993 Kevin Pang, a scientist at NASA's Jet Propulsion Laboratory, hypothesized that an enormous volcanic eruption in early 1453 at Kuwae in the Pacific Ocean—an explosion the equivalent of two million Hiroshimas that lifted forty cubic kilometers of debris into the atmosphere—significantly altered the earth's climate that year and was, in all probability, the cause of the strange natural phenomena observed at Constantinople. For a summary of his claims, go to http://www.jpl.nasa.gov/releases/93/release_1993_1543.html. More conventional studies of portents include Louis Massignon, "Textes prémonitioires et commentaires mystiques rélatifs à la prise de Constantinople par les Turcs en 1953," *Oriens* 6 (1953), 10–17; and B. Lellouch and S. Yerasimos, *Les traditions apocalyptiques au*

tournant de la chute de Constantinople (Paris: Harmattan, 1999). A particularly spooky evocation is the chapter entitled "Omens and Portents" in Crowley, *1453*, 173–86.

270 the city's holiest icon: On a recent visit to the Greek Orthodox Patriarchate in Istanbul, an Arab-Christian guide from Antakya (Antioch) insisted that a magnificent eleventh-century icon in the otherwise modest church—Panagia Pammakristos (All-Blessed Mother of God)—was the icon carried in this unfortunate procession.

272 "Go on my falcons . . .": Crowley, *1453*, 212.

272 an Anatolian colossus named Hasan: Crowley, *1453*, 212.

273 a missile pierced the armor of Giustiniani Longo: It is unclear whether it was a bullet, and whether it shattered his breastplate or entered through the armhole. In any event, it was fatal. Runciman's wry comment on the sources: "Phrantzes says that he was wounded in the foot and Chalcocondylas in the hand, but Leonard by an arrow in the armpit and Critobulus by a ball that pierced his breastplate. It was probably a serious wound somewhere in his body. Barbaro, in his dislike of all Genoese, never mentions the wound at all, merely saying that he deserted his post. Otherwise, there is remarkable agreement between all sources." *Fall of Constantinople*, 224n.

273 The basileus pleaded with him to remain at his post: "My brother, fight bravely. Do not forsake us in our distress. The salvation of the City depends on you. Return to your post. Where are you going?" Nicolle, *Constantinople 1453*, 77.

274 At the vulnerable right angle of fortifications, a postern gate had apparently been left open: The Kerkoporta Postern, now a gap between the Theodosian and Blachernae walls adorned by a tree and facing an extramural soccer pitch.

274 In all likelihood, he and his faithful courtiers rushed to the breach of the Lycus, and died there: It is uncertain what exactly happened to Constantine. Later legend has him shouting out that he is the basileus, inviting death. Other stories have his body being recognized and his head cut off and presented to Mehmet, who dispatched it to other Islamic capitals. There are stories of his head being buried in the Ayasofya; and there was once a tomb in Istanbul that used to be shown off as his. Most likely, he was thrown into a mass grave. He was fifty-four.

274 The sultan sharply ordered one man to desist from prying a marble slab from the floor: Crowley, *1453*, 233. Fatih is thought to have struck the man with his sword.

275 "The spider served as the gatekeeper . . .": Tursun Bey, an eyewitness, cited in Servanite, *Le Voyage à Istanbul*, 135. Chosroes is the Greek version of Khusrau, a traditional regal name in Persia (Mehmet is not referring to the Chosroes who fought Heraclius), as is Afrasiyab. In Firdausi's *Shahnameh* (The Epic of Kings), a tenth-century monument of Persian literature (six thousand lines) recounting legendary events from a distant past, both kings—they were father and son—are among the protagonists. Hence Mehmet is referring to the great Firdausi and his Persian lore. In some accounts, such as Runciman's and Norwich's, Khusrau is translated as "Caesar," which, however beguiling, does not make much poetic sense, as it would entail mixing two entirely different traditions.

276 the eponymous Byzas: The story of the founding goes as follows: Byzas, a hero of the Attic city of Megara, travels to Delphi, where the oracle tells him that he must establish a colony "opposite the Land of the Blind." He travels to the Bosporus, realizes Chalcedon (founded 678 B.C.E.) must be that unfortunate land, and in 658 B.C.E. builds on the opposite shore the city named after him.

277 under the Ottomans most land belonged to the sultan: In contrast to western feudalism, most landholding was not hereditary. Lifelong leases were granted by the sultan.

277 Gennadios: Also Gennadius. As well as playing a pivotal role in establishing an Orthodox Church under the Islamic dispensation, he was a formidable scholar, most notably in bringing Aristotelian thought (and consequently that of Thomas Aquinas) to bear on Orthodox doctrine. Paradoxically, although derisively known as "the Latinist" by rival churchmen, he had been instrumental prior to the siege in resisting the proposed union of Greek and Latin churches.

277 another great church: The Church of the Holy Apostles. Second only to the Hagia Sophia in size, the church was the burial ground of Byzantine emperors. By 1453, however, it was largely a ruin, and its neighborhood became distinctly Turkish and Muslim. After only a year or so Gennadios moved the patriarchate to St. Mary Pammakaristos (the All-Blessed), where it remained for 138 years. The Church of the Holy Apostles was demolished to build the Fatih Mosque, the conqueror's religious complex and the first great Ottoman mosque of the city. Pammakaristos was taken from the Christians in 1586 by Sultan Murad III and became the Fethiye Camii (Mosque of Victory), so named for the conquest of Georgia by the Ottomans. Suleyman Kirimtayif, *Converted Byzantine Churches in Istanbul: Their Transformation into Mosques and Masjids* (Istanbul: Ege Yayinlari, 2001), 63–64.

277 out of bounds to imams in search of ready-made mosques: In time, however, Fatih's philohellene tendencies would disappear among his descendants and churches would be converted to mosques. Successive sultans appropriated Christian churches for their own purposes, and the ravages of time did the rest. St. Mary of the Mongols is the only preconquest church still in use as a Christian sanctuary. Further, as the first generations of genuine convivencia were forgotten, showy Christian buildings in the city became inadvisable. Discreet new churches were built in Christian areas, and the old Byzantine structures were left to the Ottoman rulers. That being said, by the nineteenth century the westerners resident in the city had few constraints in erecting elaborate churches in Galata. Runciman, in *Fall of Constaninople*, has a short, interesting appendix on the matter, "The Churches of Constantinople After the Conquest," 199–204.

278 a Greek sycophant of talent: Michael Kritovoulos, whose work nonetheless is a valuable source for our knowledge of Mehmet.

278 "from all parts of Asia and Europe . . .": Kritovoulos, quoted in Philip Mansel, *Constantinople: City of the World's Desire, 1453–1924* (London: Penguin, 1997), 8.

279 (The Venetians attempted to bribe Fatih's Jewish physician into poisoning him in 1471): Babinger, *Mehmed the Conqueror*, 291–92.

279 "If you wish to stand in high honor on the Sultan's threshold . . .": Quoted in Mansel, *Constantinople*, 24.

280 "You may well weep like a woman . . .": In Stanley Lane-Poole's *The Moors in Spain* (1887), the famous and probably apocryphal incident gets the full treatment: " 'Allahu akbar!' he said, 'God is most great,' as he burst into tears. His mother Ayesha stood beside him: 'You may well weep like a woman,' she said, 'for what you could not defend like a man.' The spot whence Boabdil took his sad farewell look at his city from which he was banished for ever, bears to this day the name of *el ultimo sospiro del Moro*, 'the last sigh of the Moor.' "

280 Arap Camii: It was built by the Dominicans in the early fourteenth century and is clearly recognizable as a Latin church.

281 For the rulers of Spain, the past had become an embarrassment: The past of convivencia, that is. The idea of a mystical continuity from the Visigoths to the fifteenth-century Spanish monarchs became an accepted narrative at the court. "The epic past was self-consciously reestablished," writes one historian, "accompanied by the wild enthusiasm of the reunited nation. Perhaps that was the only time in world history that an idealized past was programmatically restored and not just dreamed of." Stephen Gilman, "The Problem of the Spanish Renaissance," *Folio* 10 (1977), 49, quoted in J. N. Hillgarth, "Spanish Historiography and Iberian Reality," *History and Theory* 24 (1985), reproduced in Hillgarth, *Spain and the Mediterranean in the Later Middle Ages* (Aldershot: Ashgate, 2003), 29.

281 "They say Ferdinand is a wise monarch . . .": Quoted in Jason Goodwin, *Lords of the Horizon: A History of the Ottoman Empire* (New York: Henry Holt, 1998), 99.

281 menagerie of nationalities: Mansel, in *Constantinople*, 7, states that the capital contained seventy-two and a half nationalities ("Gypsies were considered half a nationality").

282 Joseph Nasi: Mansel, *Constantinople*, 124–26. Among his myriad business activities, Nasi supplied the wine to Sultan Selim the Sot.

282 believed to be of Anatolian Christian stock: Some say European stock. As far as I can determine, no one knows for certain.

284 a legacy of overwrought European travel writing: Western prurience toward Ottoman harems and sexual mores forms one of the strongest critiques of Orientalism as an artistic—and popular—movement. One of the greatest erotic best-sellers of nineteenth-century Britain was, for example, *The Lustful Turk*. This ground, already well trodden by modern scholarship, is lightly and entertainingly covered in Fatema Mernissi's refreshing *Scheherazade Goes West* (New York: Washington Square, 2001), a memoir of a feminist Moroccan intellectual on a book tour in the west. Mernissi, who was born in a harem, writes: "We can break the West into two camps as far as smiles are concerned: the Americans and the Europeans. The American men, upon hearing the word 'harem,' smiled with unadulterated and straightforward embarrassment. Whatever the word means for Americans hinges on something linked to shame. The Europeans, in contrast, responded with smiles that varied from polite reserve in the North to merry exuberance in the South, with subtleties fluctuating according to the distance of the journalists' origin from the Mediterranean. French, Spanish, and Italian men had a flirtatious, amused light in their eyes. Scandinavians and Germans, with the exception of the Danes, had astonishment in theirs— astonishment tinged with shock. 'Were you really born in a harem?' they would ask, looking intently at me with a mixture of apprehension and puzzlement" (11–12).

284 Fener district: also Phanar. It became a Greek city within a city in Kostantiniyye. Phanariot merchants grew very wealthy and at one time controlled Moldavia and Wallachia. It is here where the ghosts of the city's vanished Greek community are the most palpable, even if most of its members had deserted the quarter for Galata and airier neighborhoods along the Bosporus by the end of the nineteenth century.

284 St. Mary of the Mongols, so named for a Byzantine princess: Princess Maria Palaeologina, illegitimate daugher of Basileus Michael VIII. She had originally been packed off to Persia to marry Hulegu, the destroyer of Baghdad (1258), but he died before she arrived and she was wed to his son. She is supposed to have converted many Mongols of his court to Christianity. Upon her husband's assassination in 1281, she returned to Constantinople and refused to be sent off

again to marry another Mongol khan. She became a nun and underwrote the construction of the church. Fatih's firman, still on display, guaranteed the integrity of the sanctuary.

CHAPTER 10: MALTA 1565

287 the youthful Sultan, moved to magnanimity by the suicidal bravery of the knights: The siege of Rhodes, in 1522, was an epic six-month affair that pitted ninety thousand Ottoman troops against eight thousand defenders. As at Malta, the knights' resistance in the face of such great odds earned the admiration of Christian and Muslim alike. Charles V remarked that "nothing in the world was so well lost as Rhodes." The youthful Suleyman, on seeing Grand Master Philippe Villiers de l'Isle Adam, a seventy-year-old, board his ship for exile, is supposed to have said to his advisers, "It is not without some pain that I oblige this Christian at his age to leave his home."

287 the Spanish king (who was also the Holy Roman Emperor): Charles V, the same monarch who criticized the construction of the cathedral in Córdoba's Mezquita.

288 They would certainly have known the fate of John the Baptist: It will be recalled that mosques in Aleppo and Damascus have shrines to John and his father.

288 the admiral of the Turkish fleet: In his childhood Admiral Piali was found abandoned—on a plowshare, it was said—outside of Belgrade during Suleyman's successful siege of the city, which was then a Hungarian possession. Raised in the Topkapi, he became a trusted adviser of the sovereign, a friend of his son (who on Suleyman's death became Sultan Selim the Grim), and the husband of Selim's daughter. Aged thirty-five at the time of the siege, he shared command of the operation in its early stages with Mustapha Pasha and is generally thought to have insisted, disastrously, that the Turks take Fort St. Elmo before turning their attention to Birgu and Senglea.

289 give pause even to the most ardent admirers of the knights: Ernle Bradford, in his *The Great Siege: Malta 1565* (Penguin, London, 1964), cites the assessment of a nineteenth-century historian of the Order, Whitworth Porter, who, in *The History of the Knights of Malta* (London, 1883), wrote of the atrocity: "It would have been well for the reputation of La Valette, had he restrained the feelings of indignation which this disgraceful event (the decapitation of the Knights) had most naturally evoked within reasonable bonds; but unfortunately the chronicler is compelled to record that his retaliation was as savage, and as unworthy a Christian soldier, as was the original deed; nay, more so, for Mustapha had contented himself with mangling the insensible corpses of his foe, whilst La Valette, in the angry excitement of the moment, caused all his Turkish prisoners to be decapitated, and their heads to be fired from the guns of St. Angelo into the Ottoman camp. Brutal as was this act, and repulsive as it seems to the notions of the modern warrior, it was, alas! too much in accordance with the practice of the age to have been regarded with feelings of disapprobation, or even wonderment, by the chroniclers of those times. Still, the event casts a shadow over the fair fame of otherwise so illustrious a hero, which history regrets to record" (140).

289 "all the world might come here to sharpen its knives": Letter of May 24, 1920. Harry T. Moore, ed., *The Collected Letters of D.H. Lawrence* (London: Heinemann, 1962), 631.

290 the depredations of the Second World War: In 1942 Malta endured 157 days of continuous bombing by the Luftwaffe. Some thirty thousand buildings were destroyed. Simon Gaul, *Malta, Gozo and Comino* (London: Cadogan, 1993), 82.

291 Turkish fleets dropped anchor in Toulon: The Franco-Ottoman treaty was signed in 1536. As for the enmity between the Valois and the Habsburgs, France was at war with Charles V or his successor in 1515–29, 1536–37, 1542–44, 1552, and 1559. Michel Péronnet, *Le XVIᵉ siècle 1492–1620: Des grandes découvertes à la contre-Réformes* (Paris: Hachette, 2005), 182–83. The new seascape is spelled out in Maxime Rodinson, *Europe and the Mystique of Islam*, trans. Roger Veinus (Seattle: University of Washington Press, 1991): "In the fifteenth and sixteenth centuries European rulers did not consider Christian expansionism worth the sacrifice of their own political (and eventually national) interests; nor did the general public see this as justification for a call to arms throughout Europe, as earlier had been the case with the Crusaders. Henry VIII made all this quite clear to the Venetian ambassador in 1516. From then on, to the realists, the Ottoman Empire became a power like any other and even a European power . . . [a]nd therefore political relations with the Ottomans became essential. Whether it was to be alliance, neutrality, or outright war would depend on political factors quite separate from religion" (33).

291 "It is the great battle of the Cross and the Koran . . .": Quoted in Bradford, *Great Siege*, 54.

292 a scion of the great—and greatly conflicted—families of Toulouse: His adoring biographer and contemporary, the abbé de Brantôme, lists several consuls of the Valette family in the eleventh- and twelfth-century governance of that city.

292 "I do not come to Malta for wealth or honour . . .": Quoted in Bradford, *Great Siege*, 66.

292 the knights were organized into *langues*: They were Auvergne, Provence, France, Aragon, Castile, Germany, Italy, and England. The last-mentioned was a shadow of its former self, ever since Henry VIII had outlawed the Catholic knights. Still, Oliver Starkey, an English knight, played a prominent role in the siege as Valette's secretary and right-hand man.

292 "the most striking interior I have ever seen": Quoted in Gaul, *Malta, Gozo and Comino*, 114.

293 an audiovisual labyrinth: The advertising brochures for the show, called "The Great Siege of Malta and The Knights of St. John," are entertainingly tacky. One tag line reads: "Put yourself in mortal danger and enjoy every minute of it." Although the walk-through experience does not live up to that billing, it is amusing, even if its consistent demonization of the Muslim armies and leaders becomes tiresome. In fact, even the most recent histories of the siege (our chapter draws primarily from these western accounts) fall into the trap of "cheering" for the defenders and taking cheap shots at what is viewed as the fanaticism of Islam. That the knights, especially at St. Elmo, fought with a religious fanaticism equaling if not surpassing that of the Janissaries is passed over in silence. The usual device of denigration—on view in polemics published in present-day newspapers—is to use the word *Allah* instead of *God* when ascribing irrational and inhuman motives to adherents of Islam.

295 Ibrahim Pasha, the canny Greek who was Suleyman's grand vizier: In the early years of his career as grand vizier, Ibrahim was almost a cosultan with Suleyman, so great was his power and influence. Eventually the beautiful and immensely persuasive Ukrainian Roxelana (known to the Turks as Haseki Hurrem) intrigued against her rival for the sultan's admiration. He was so besotted of her that he abandoned all his other wives, and she convinced him that Ibrahim was

threat. On March 15, 1536, Suleyman and his vizier dined alone, after which the sultan had his deaf-mute retainers strangle the man and throw his body out of the Topkapi. Mansel, *Constantinople*, 88.

295 the noblewoman Julia Gonzaga: The lady's fame was in some part due to the admiration she inspired in Renaissance poets. Ludovico Ariosto, in *Orlando Furioso*, wrote: "Julia Gonzaga, she that wheresoe'er / She moves, where'er she turns her lucid eyes, / Not only is in charms without a peer, / But seems a goddess lighted from the skies" (canto 46:8). She later attained a measure of influence as the mistress of a Medici cardinal.

296 the defeat of Mark Antony and Cleopatra in 31 B.C.E.: The battle of Actium. The victor was Octavian, who would go on to be Augustus Caesar and usher in the Roman Empire. Actium is a cape that closes off the Ambracian Gulf; on the opposite shore is Preveza. The area is on the western coast of Greece, about ninety kilometers south of the Albanian border.

296 "Dragut is a lion . . .": Quoted in Jean Merrien, *Histoire des Corsaires* (St. Malo: L'Ancre de la Marine, 2000), 62.

296 severely punished by the Inquisition if captured: An altogether fascinating examination of some sixteen hundred renegades of the sixteenth and seventeenth centuries was recently published in France: Bartolomé Bennassar and Lucile Bennassar, *Les Chrétiens d'Allah: L'histoire extraordinaire des renégats, XVIᵉ-XVIIᵉ siècles* (Paris: Perrin, 2001). As yet untranslated into English, the book draws on Inquisition interrogations and trials throughout the Mediterranean world to reconstruct the reasoning behind some of the defections to Islam and, especially, to retrace some remarkable personal itineraries of these obscure historical figures.

296 The Habsburg monarch: Charles V.

297 "caravans": The odd name for a season-long campaign of seaborne piracy came from the order's earlier days, when knights accompanied caravans of pilgrims to Palestine. Participation in several caravans was necessary for promotion within the highly stratified order.

297 an even more powerful Ottoman princess: Mihrimah, the daughter of Roxelana and the wife of Grand Vizier Rustem Pasha. She was Suleyman's favorite daughter and used her influence in having her stepbrothers killed. Her mosque complex, a luminous masterpiece of Sinan's with an astounding 161 windows piercing the dome, lies just inside the Edirnekapi, or the Adrianople Gate, through which her great-great-grandfather, Fatih, made his first triumphal entrance into the city.

298 Birgu and Senglea: To reconstruct the very well-chronicled events of the siege, I have relied on the indispensable *Great Siege* by Ernle Bradford, as well as Tim Pickles, *Malta 1565: Last Battle of the Crusades* (Oxford: Osprey, 1998), and Catherine Desportes, *Le Siège de Malte: La grande défaite de Soliman le Magnifique 1565* (Paris: Perrin, 1999). The best contemporaneous source is Francesco Balbi di Correggio, *La Verdadera relaçion de todo lo que el año de MDXLV ha sucedido en la Isla de Malta* (Barcelona, 1568), which was published recently as *The Siege of Malta 1565*, trans. Ernle Bradford (London: Penguin, 1963).

301 "Even the rank and file wore scarlet robes": Balbi di Correggio, *Siege*, Balbi was a Spanish poet and arquebusier who fought on Senglea. His memoir was avidly read throughout Europe and remains an invaluable source for the events of 1565.

302 the attackers had suffered three thousand dead, the defenders, 250: Pickles, *Malta 1565*, 55.

303 the powerful Habsburg viceroy there had repeatedly promised: Don García de Toledo is

the whipping boy of historians favorable to the Order of St. John. He was in constant contact with La Valette throughout the siege, thanks to the ability of the local Maltese to slip past the Turkish lines and launch small boats from coves known only to them. García's correspondence is a litany of broken promises, though he did manage to send a small relief force at the end of June. Any credit the viceroy might gain in posterity's eyes for this gesture is diminished by the fact that the reinforcements got through to the knights only by disobeying his orders. García had explicitly told them to return to Sicily if, by the time they arrived, Fort St. Elmo had fallen (which it had). They ignored the order and shored up defenses, and morale, on Birgu and Senglea.

305 the modest city of Mdina: Mdina was the capital of Malta at the time and the home to its nobility. The Maltese leadership had been cool to the knights ever since their arrival, uninvited, twenty-five years earlier and remained above the fray during the siege. Their city, however, was garrisoned by the knights and was saved in late August from Turkish attack through the ruse of placing every man, woman, and child on the ramparts, dressed up as soldiers, to give the impression that the city was overflowing with warriors. The Turkish, disheartened by the end of the summer and thoroughly deceived, abandoned their plan of attack.

305 It tottered, then fell over into the ditch: This was not the end of the siege tower tactic. Another was built a week later, but it was commandeered by the defenders and used against the Turkish attackers.

307 Birgu is now known, quite reasonably in view of 1565, as Vittoriosa: "For its contribution to the final victory, Grand Master La Vallette renamed it Civitas Victoriosa which name in the Italian form, it still bears. The motto assigned on this great occasion was *Victricem palmam fero* (I bear the palms of Victory), while on the Main Gate leading to the city, a Latin quotation from the Bible was inscribed: *Obumbrasti Super caput meum in die belli*—Psalm 139 (Thou hast overshadowed my head in time of war)." Lorenzo Zahra, *Vittoriosa: A Brief Historical Guide to the City of Birgu* (Birgu: Birgu Local Council, 1999).

308 once again near the Ionian locale of Mark Antony and Cleopatra: Lepanto, now Navpaktos, is on the Gulf of Patras, opposite Patras. For a stirring account of the battle in the context of Muslim-Christian relations, see the first chapter of Andrew Wheatcroft's *Infidels: The Conflict between Christendom and Islam 638–2002* (London: Viking Penguin, 2003), and the seventh chapter of Victor Davis Hanson, *Carnage and Culture: Landmark Battles in the Rise of Western Power* (New York: Doubleday, 2001). Hanson hews to the view, in keeping with his thesis of western superiority, that Lepanto was a watershed, proving the virtues of capitalism. For the medieval millennium of this present work, which concerns itself with the confessional geography of the Mediterranean, the great battle came as a postscript, for the Ottoman Empire was a multinational state par excellence.

308 Cervantes, who almost met his death there: Miguel de Cervantes Saavedra was badly wounded in the left hand during the combat, which earned him the nickname *el manco de Lepanto* (the one-handed man of Lepanto). The injury to his left hand was, Cervantes said, "to the greater glory of his right."

BIBLIOGRAPHY

Editions cited are those consulted. Many works have earlier publication dates.

Ahmad, Aziz. *La Sicile islamique*. Translated by Yves Thoraval. Paris: Publisud, 1975.

Akkari, Hatem, ed. *La Méditerranée médiévale*. Tunis: Alif-Les Editions de la Méditerranée, 2002.

Alighieri, Dante. *Dante Alighieri's Divine Comedy*. Translated by Mark Musa. Bloomington: Indiana University Press, 2004.

Arberry, A. J. *The Koran Interpreted*. London: Allen and Unwin, 1955.

Armstrong, Karen. *Islam: A Short History*. New York: Modern Library, 2000.

―――. *Holy War: The Crusades and Their Impact on Today's World*. New York: Anchor, 2001.

Asbridge, Thomas. *The First Crusade: A New History*. Oxford: Oxford University Press, 2004.

Ash, John. *A Byzantine Journey*. New York: Random House, 1995.

Aubé, Pierre. *Roger II de Sicile: Un Normand en Méditerranée*. Paris: Payot et Rivages, 2001.

Babinger, Franz. *Mehmed the Conqueror and His Time*. Translated by Ralph Mannheim. 1953; Princeton, N.J.: Princeton University Press, 1978.

Balard, Michel, et al. *Islam et monde latin (Milieu Xᵉ–Milieu XIIIᵉ): Espaces et enjeux*. Paris: Association pour le développement de l'histoire économique, 2001.

Balbi di Correggio, Francisco. *The Siege of Malta 1565*. Translated by Ernle Bradford. London: Penguin, 1963.

Baxter-Wolf, Kenneth, ed. and trans. *Conquerors and Chroniclers of Early Medieval Spain*. Liverpool: Liverpool University Press, 1990.

Bell, Warwick. *Syria: A Historical and Architectural Guide*. Essex: Scorpion, 1994.

Benjamin of Tudela. *The Itinerary of Benjamin of Tudela: Travels in the Middle Ages*. Translated by M. N. Adler and A. Asher. Malibu: Joseph Simon, 1983.

Bennassar, Bartolomé, and Lucile Bennassar. *Les Chrétiens d'Allah: L'histoire extraordinaire des renégats, XVIᵉ-XVIIᵉ siècles*. Paris: Perrin, 2001.

Bianquis, Thierry. "L'Egypte depuis la conquête arabe jusqu'à la fin de l'Empire fatimide (1171)." *L'Histoire générale de l'Afrique*, vol. 3. Paris: UNESCO, 1990.

Bible, The Holy: New International Version. London: Hodder and Stoughton, 1979.

Bloeme, Jacques. *L'Europe avant l'An Mil*, vol. 2. Paris: L'Harmattan, 2001.

Bonnassie, Pierre. "Le Temps de Wisigoths." In *Histoire des Espagnols*. Edited by Bartolomé Bennassar. Paris: Robert Laffont, 1992.

Bord, Lucien-Jean. *Les Mérovingiens: Les Rois Inconnus.* Vouillé: Editions de Chiré, 1981.

Bowersock, G. W. "Seeing the Voice of the Lord." *New York Times Book Review.* April 6, 2003.

Bradford, Ernle. *The Great Siege: Malta 1565.* Penguin: London, 1964.

————. *Mediterranean: Portrait of a Sea.* New York: Harcourt Brace Jovanovich, 1971.

————. *The Shield and the Sword: The Knights of St. John.* London: Penguin, 2002.

Braudel, Fernand. *Memory and the Mediterranean.* Translated by Siân Reynolds. New York: Vintage, 2001.

Bresc, Henri, and Geneviève Bresc-Bautier, eds. *Palerme 1070–1492, Mosaïque de peuples, nation rebelle: La naissance violente de l'identité sicilienne.* Paris: Autrement, 1993.

Brown, Peter. *The Rise of Western Christendom.* Oxford: Blackwell, 1996.

Brundage, James A. *The Crusades: A Documentary Survey.* Milwaukee, Wisc.: Marquette University Press, 1962.

Buhl, F. "Hind Bit Utba." *Encyclopedia of Islam*, vol. 3. Leiden: Brill, 1973.

————. "Muhammad." *Encyclopedia of Islam*, vol. 7. Leiden: Brill, 1993.

Bulliet, Richard W. *Conversion to Islam in the Medieval Period.* Cambridge, Mass.: Harvard University Press, 1979.

————. *The Case for Islamo-Christian Civilization.* New York: Columbia University Press, 2004.

Burns, Ross. *Monuments of Syria: An Historical Guide.* London: I.B. Tauris, 1992.

Butor, Michel. *The Spirit of Mediterranean Places.* Translated by Lydia Davis. Evanston, Ill.: Marlboro/Northwestern, 1997.

Cahen, Claude. *Turcobyzantina et Oriens Christianus.* London: Variorum, 1974.

Cahill, Thomas. *How the Irish Saved Civilization.* New York: Anchor, 1996.

Camps, Gabriel. "Les Berbères." *Encylopédie de la Mediterranée.* Tunis: Alif-Les Editions de la Mediterranée, 1996.

Cardaillac, Louis, ed. *Tolède: XIIᵉ–XIIIᵉ: Musulmans, chrétiens et juifs: Le savoir et la tolérance.* Paris: Autrement, 1991.

Cardini, Franco. *Europe and Islam.* Translated by Caroline Beamish. Oxford: Blackwell, 2001.

Carpentier, Elisabeth. *Les Batailles de Poitiers: Charles Martel et les Arabes.* La Crèche: Geste, 2000.

Chalmeta, P. "Al-Mansur bi'illah." *Encyclopedia of Islam*, vol. 6. Leiden: Brill, 1986.

Chambers, James. *The Devil's Horsemen: The Mongol Invasion of Europe.* London: Phoenix, 1979.

Chejne, Anwar G. *Muslim Spain: Its History and Culture.* Minneapolis: University of Minnesota Press, 1974.

Chirco, Adriana. *Palermo.* Translated by Maria Letizia Pellerito, edited by David Russell. Palermo: Dario Flaccovio, 1998.

Christides, V. "Misr." *Encyclopedia of Islam*, vol. 7. Leiden: Brill, 1993.

————. "Ukba b. Nafi." *Encyclopedia of Islam*, vol. 10. Leiden: Brill, 2000.

Cole, Peter. *The Dream of the Poem: Hebrew Poetry from Muslim and Christian Spain, 950–1492.* Princeton, N.J.: Princeton University Press, forthcoming.

Collins, Roger. *Early Medieval Spain.* New York: St. Martin's Press, 1983.

————. *The Arab Conquest of Spain: 710–797*. Oxford: Blackwell, 1989.

Comnena, Anna. *The Alexiad of Anna Comnena*. Translated by E.R.A. Sewter. London: Penguin, 1969.

Constable, Olivia Remie, ed. *Medieval Iberia*. Philadelphia: University of Pennsylvania Press, 1997.

Cook, Michael. *Muhammad*. Oxford: Oxford University Press, 1983.

Cragg, Kenneth, trans. and ed. *Readings in the Qur'an*. Brighton: Sussex Academic, 1999.

————. *Jesus and the Muslim: An Exploration*. Oxford: Oneworld, 1999.

Crone, P. "Khalid b. Al-Walid." *Encyclopedia of Islam*, vol. 4. Leiden: Brill, 1978.

Crowley, Roger. *1453: The Holy War for Constantinople and the Clash of Islam and the West*. New York: Hyperion, 2005.

Dalrymple, William. *From the Holy Mountain: A Journey in the Shadow of Byzantium*. London: Flamingo, 1998.

Daniel, Norman. *Islam and the West: The Making of an Image*. Oxford: Oneworld, 2000.

Delort, Robert, ed. *Les croisades*. Paris: Seuil, 1988.

Desportes, Catherine. *Le Siège de Malte: La grande défaite de Soliman le Magnifique 1565*. Paris: Perrin, 1999.

Dodds, Jerrilynn D., ed. *Al-Andalus: The Art of Islamic Spain*. New York: Metropolitan Museum of Art, 1992.

Donner, Fred McGraw. *The Early Islamic Conquests*. Princeton, N.J.: Princeton University Press, 1981.

Dozy, Reinhart. *Histoire des Musulmans d'Espagne, jusqu'à la conquête de l'Andalousie par les Almoravides*. Leiden: Brill, 1932.

Duby, Georges. *L'An Mil*. Paris: Gallimard, 1980.

Dufourcq, Charles-Emmanuel. *La vie quotidienne dans l'Europe médiévale sous la domination arabe*. Paris: Hachette, 1978.

Durand, Robert. *Musulmans et Chrétiens en Méditerranée occidentale: X^e–XIIIe siècles. Contacts et échanges*. Rennes: Presses Universitaires de Rennes, 2000.

El Sheikh, Nadia Maria. *Byzantium Viewed by the Arabs*. Cambridge, Mass.: Harvard University Press, 2004.

Elisséef, Nikita. *L'Orient musulman au Moyen Age*. Paris: Armand Colin, 1977.

Emmert, Thomas A. *Serbian Golgotha: Kosovo, 1389*. New York: Columbia University Press, 1990.

Fasman, Jon. *The Geographer's Library*. New York: Penguin, 2005.

Fletcher, Richard. *The Quest for El Cid*. Oxford: Oxford University Press, 1989.

————. *Moorish Spain*. Berkeley: University of California Press, 1993.

————. *The Cross and the Crescent: Christianity and Islam from Muhammad to the Reformation*. London: Penguin, 2003.

Flori, Jean. *Guerre sainte, jihad, croisade: Violence et religion dans le christianisme et l'islam*. Paris: Seuil, 2002.

Focillon, Henri. *L'An Mil*. Paris: Denoël, 1984.

Fouracre, Paul. *The Age of Charles Martel*. Harlow: Pearson, 2000.

Foz, Clara. *Le Traducteur, L'Eglise et le Roi*. Ottawa: Université d'Ottawa, 1998.

Freely, John. *Istanbul: The Imperial City*. London: Penguin, 1998.

————. *Istanbul*. London: A&C Black, 2000.

Fregosi, Paul. *Jihad in the West: Muslim Conquests from the Seventh to the Twenty-first Centuries*. New York: Prometheus, 1998.

Friendly, Alfred. *The Dreadful Day: The Battle of Manzikert, 1071*. London: Hutchinson, 1981.

Gabrieli, Francesco. "Asabiyya." *Encyclopedia of Islam*, vol. 1. Leiden: Brill, 1960.

————. *Muhammad and the Conquests of Islam*. Translated by Virginia Luling and Rosamund Linell. New York: McGraw-Hill, 1968.

————. *Arab Historians of the Crusades*. Translated by E. J. Costello. Berkeley: University of California Press, 1984.

Gaul, Simon. *Malta, Gozo and Comino*. London: Cadogan, 1993.

George, Leonard. *The Encylopedia of Heresies and Heretics*. London: Robson, 1995.

Gerolymatos, André. *The Balkan Wars: Conquest, Revolution, and Retribution from the Ottoman Era to the Twentieth Century and Beyond*. New York: Basic Books, 2002.

Gibbon, Edward. *The Decline and Fall of the Roman Empire*. New York: Random House, 2003.

Glick, Thomas. *Islamic and Christian Spain in the Early Middle Ages*. Princeton, N.J.: Princeton University Press, 1979.

Goodwin, Jason. *Lords of the Horizon: A History of the Ottoman Empire*. New York: Henry Holt, 1999.

Gourdin, P., et al. *Pays d'Islam et monde latin*. Neuilly: Atlande, 2001.

Guerdan, René. *Byzantium: Its Triumphs and Tragedy*. Translated by D.L.B. Hartley. New York: G.P. Putnam's Sons, 1957.

Guichard, Pierre. *Al-Andalus*. Paris: Hachette, 2000.

HaNagid, Shmuel. *Selected Poems of Shmuel HaNagid*. Translated and edited by Peter Cole. Princeton, N.J.: Princeton University Press, 1996.

Hanson, Victor Davis. *Carnage and Culture: Landmark Battles in the Rise of Western Power*. New York: Doubleday, 2001.

Heer, Friedrich. *The Medieval World, 1100–1350*. Translated by Janet Sondheimer. New York: New American Library, 1961.

Hetherington, Paul. *Medieval Rome: A Portrait of the City and Its Life*. New York: St. Martin's Press, 1994.

Hildinger, Erik. *Warriors of the Steppe: A Military History of Central Asia, 500 B.C. to 1700 A.D.* Cambridge, Mass.: Da Capo Press, 1997.

Hill, Fred James, and Nicholas Awde. *A History of the Islamic World*. New York: Hippocrene, 2003.

Hillenbrand, Carole. *The Crusades: Islamic Perspectives*. New York: Routledge, 1999.

Hillgarth, J.N. *Spain and the Mediterranean in the Later Middle Ages*. Aldershot: Ashgate, 2003.

Hitti, Philip K. *History of the Arabs*. New York: St. Martin's Press, 1970.

Houben, Hubert. *Roger II of Sicily: A Ruler between East and West*. Translated by G. A. Loud and Diane Milburn. Cambridge: Cambridge University Press, 1992.

Hourani, Albert. *A History of the Arab Peoples*. New York: Warner Books, 1991.

Huntington, Samuel P. *The Clash of Civilizations and the Remaking of World Order*. New York: Touchstone, 1996.

Ibn Ishaq, Muhammad. *The Life of Muhammad*. Translated by A. Guillaume. Oxford: Oxford University Press, 1955.

Ibn Jubayr, Ahmad. *The Travels of Ibn Jubayr: A Mediaeval Spanish Muslim visits Makkah, Madinah, Egypt, Cities of the Middle East and Sicily*. Translated by Roland Broadhurst. New Delhi: Goodword, 2003.

Ibn Khaldun. *Histoire des Berbères et des dynasties musulmanes de l'Afrique septentrionale*. 4 vols. Translated by Baron de Slane. Paris: P. Geuthner, 1925–26.

Ibn Munqidh, Usamah. *An Arab-Syrian Gentleman & Warrior in the Period of the Crusades: Memoirs of Usamah ibn-Munqidh*. Translated by Philip K. Hitti. New York: Columbia University Press, 2000.

Imamuddin, Syed. *Muslim Spain: 714–1492 A.D.: A Sociological Study*. Leiden: Brill, 1981.

———. *A Political History of Muslim Spain*. Karachi: Najmah, 1984.

Jansen, Philippe, Annliese Nef, and Christophe Picard. *La Mediterranée entre pays d'Islam et monde latin*. Paris: Sedes, 2000.

Jayyusi, Salma. "Andalusi Poetry: The Golden Period." In *The Legacy of Muslim Spain*, vol. 1. Edited by Salma Jayyusi. Leiden: Brill, 1994.

Jehel, Georges. *La Méditerranée médiévale de 350 à 1450*. Paris: Armand Colin, 1992.

———. *L'Italie et le Maghreb au Moyen Age*. Paris: Presses Universitaires de France, 2001.

Jehel, Georges, and Philippe Racinet. *Les relations des pays d'Islam avec le monde latin: Du Xe siècle au milieu du XIIIe siècle*. Paris: Edition du Temps, 2000.

Johnson, Paul. *A History of Christianity*. London: Pelican, 1980.

Julien, Charles-André. *Histoire de l'Afrique du Nord, Des origines à 1830*. Paris: Payot, 1994.

Juynboll, G.H.A. *Muslim Tradition: Studies in Chronology, Provenance, and Authorship of Early Hadith*. Cambridge: Cambridge University Press, 1983.

Kaegi, Walter E. *Byzantium and the Early Islamic Conquests*. Cambridge: Cambridge University Press, 1995.

———. *Heraclius: Emperor of Byzantium*. Cambridge: Cambridge University Press, 2003.

Kelly, J.N.D. *The Oxford History of Popes*. Oxford: Oxford University Press, 1986.

Kennedy, Hugh. *The Prophet and the Age of the Caliphates: The Islamic Near East from the Sixth to the Eleventh Centuries*. London: Longman, 1986.

———. *Crusader Castles*. Cambridge: Cambridge University Press, 1994.

———. *Muslim Spain and Portugal: A Political History of al Andalus*. London: Longman, 1996.

———. *The Armies of the Caliphs: Military and Society in the Early Islamic State*. London: Routledge, 2001.

Kinkade, Richard P. "Rodrigo, Legend of the Last Visigothic King." In *Medieval Iberia: An Encyclopedia*. Edited by E. Michael Gehl. London: Routledge, 2003.

Kirimtayif, Suleyman. *Converted Byzantine Churches in Istanbul: Their Transformation into Mosques and Masjids*. Istanbul: Ege Yayinlari, 2001.

Krey, August C. *The First Crusade: The Accounts of Eye-Witnesses and Participants*. Gloucester, Mass.: Peter Smith, 1958.

Krone, P. "Khalid b. Al-Walid." *Encyclopedia of Islam*, vol. 4. Leiden: Brill, 1978.

Lane-Poole, Stanley. *The Story of the Moors in Spain*. New York: G.P. Putnam's, 1887.

Le Tourneau, Roger. *The Almohad Movement in North Africa in the Twelfth and Thirteenth Centuries*. Princeton, N.J.: Princeton University Press, 1969.

Lellouch, B., and S. Yerasimos. *Les traditions apocalyptiques au tournant de la chute de Constantinople*. Paris: Harmattan, 1999.

Lévi-Provençal, Evariste. *La Péninsule ibérique au Moyen Age d'après le Kitab ar-rawd al-Mi'tar al-Aktar, d'Ibn Abd al-Mun'im al-Himyari*. Leiden: Brill, 1938.

————. *Histoire de l'Espagne musulmane: La conquête et l'Emirat hispano-umaiyade 710–912*, vol. 1. Paris: Masonneuve, 1950.

Lewis, Archibald R. *Nomads and Crusaders: A.D. 1000–1368*. Bloomington: Indiana University Press, 1988.

Lewis, Bernard. *Islam and the West*. Oxford: Oxford University Press, 1993.

————. *The Arabs in History*. Oxford: Oxford University Press, 1993.

————. *The Muslim Discovery of Europe*. New York: Norton, 2001.

————. *The Assassins: A Radical Sect in Islam*. New York: Basic Books, 2003.

Lewis, Bernard, ed. *A Middle East Mosaic: Fragments of Life, Letters and History*. New York: Modern Library, 2001.

Llull, Ramon. *Doctor Illuminatus: A Ramon Llull Reader*. Translated and edited by A. Bonner. Princeton, N.J.: Princeton University Press, 1993.

Lomax, Derek. *The Reconquest of Spain*. New York: Longman, 1978.

Loud, G.A. *The Age of Robert Guiscard*. Harlow: Pearson, 2000.

Maalouf, Amin. *The Crusades Through Arab Eyes*. Translated by Jon Rothschild. London: Al Saqi, 1984.

Mackintosh-Smith, Tim. *Travels with a Tangerine: A Journey in the Footnotes of Ibn Battutah*. London: Picador, 2001.

Madden, Thomas F., ed. *The Crusades: The Essential Reading*. Oxford: Blackwell, 2002.

Makiya, Kanan. *The Rock: A Tale of Seventh-Century Jerusalem*. New York: Pantheon, 2001.

Malcolm, Noel. *Kosovo: A Short History*. New York: New York University Press, 1998.

Mansel, Philip Mansel. *Constantinople: City of the World's Desire, 1453–1924*. London: Penguin, 1997.

Mantran, Robert. *Istanbul au siècle de Soliman le Magnifique*. Paris: Hachette, 1965.

Martin-Chauffier, Gilles. *Le Roman de Constantinople*. Paris: Rocher, 2005.

Matthew, Donald. *The Norman Kingdom of Sicily*. Cambridge: Cambridge University Press, 1992.

Matvejevitch, Predrag. *Bréviaire méditerranéen*. Translated by Evaine Le Calvé-Ivicevic. Paris: Fayard, 1992.

McGinn, Bernard. *Anti-Christ: Two Thousand Years of the Human Fascination with Evil*. New York: HarperCollins, 1994.

McKay, Angus. *Spain in the Middle Ages: From Frontier to Empire, 1000–1500*. New York: St. Martin's Press, 1977.

Melville Jones, J.R., ed. *The Siege of Constantinople: Seven Contemporary Accounts*. Amsterdam: Hakkert, 1973.

Menocal, María Rosa. *The Ornament of the World*. Boston: Little, Brown, 2002.

Mernissi, Fatema. *Scheherazade Goes West*. New York: Washington Square Press, 2001.

Merrien, Jean. *Histoire des Corsaires*. St. Malo: L'Ancre de la Marine, 2000.

Micheau, Françoise, ed. *Les relations des pays d'Islam avec le monde latin: Du milieu du Xe siècle au milieu du XIIIe siècle*. Paris: Jacques Marseille, 2000.

Monès, Hussain. "Al-Ikab." *Encyclopedia of Islam*, vol. 3. Leiden: Brill, 1971.

———. "La conquête de l'Afrique du Nord et la résistance berbère." *L'Histoire générale de l'Afrique*, vol. 3. Paris: UNESCO, 1990.

Morgan, M. R. *The Chronicle of Ernoul and the Continuations of William of Tyre*. Oxford: Oxford University Press, 1973.

Muñoz Molina, Antonio. *Córdoba de los Omeyas*. Barcelona: Planeta, 2003.

Murphy-O'Connor, Jerome. *The Holy Land*. Oxford: Oxford University Press, 1998.

Muscat, Joseph. *The Carrack of the Order*. Malta: Pubblikazzjonijiet Indipendenza, 2000.

Netzer, Ehud, and Zeev Weiss. *Zippori*. Jerusalem: Israel Exploration Society, 1994.

Newby, P. H. *Saladin in His Times*. London: Phoenix, 1983.

Nicephorus. *Short History*. Translated and edited by C. Mango. Washington: Dumbarton Oaks, 1990.

Nicolle, David. *Yarmuk 636 A.D.: The Muslim Conquest of Syria*. Oxford: Osprey, 1994.

———. *Medieval Warfare Source Book: Christian Europe and Its Neighbours*. London: Brockhampton, 1998.

———. *Constantinople 1453: The End of Byzantium*. Oxford: Osprey, 2000.

———. *Saladin and the Saracens*. Oxford: Osprey, 2001.

———. *Hattin 1187: Saladin's Greatest Victory*. Oxford: Osprey, 2002.

Norris, H.T., and P. Chalmeta. "Al-Murabitun." *Encyclopedia of Islam*, vol. 7. Leiden: Brill, 1993.

Norwich, John Julius. *The Kingdom in the Sun*. New York: Harper and Row, 1970.

———. *Byzantium: The Early Centuries*. New York: Alfred A. Knopf, 1989.

———. *Byzantium: The Apogee*. New York: Penguin, 1993.

———. *Byzantium: The Decline and Fall*. New York: Alfred A. Knopf, 1996.

———. *A Short History of Byzantium*. New York: Vintage, 1997.

Obolensky, Dimitri. *The Byzantine Commonwealth: Eastern Europe 500–1453*. New York: Praeger, 1971.

O'Callaghan, Joseph. *A History of Medieval Spain*. Ithaca: Cornell University Press, 1973.

O'Shea, Stephen. *The Perfect Heresy: The Revolutionary Life and Death of the Medieval Cathars*. London: Profile; New York: Walker; Vancouver: Douglas & McIntyre, 2000.

Ostrogorsky, George. *History of the Byzantine State*. Translated by Joan Hussey. Oxford: Blackwell, 1968.

Pamuk, Orhan. "The White Sea Is Azure." *Istanbul, Many Worlds, Mediterraneans* 10 (Winter 1997–98).

———. *Istanbul: Memories and the City*. Translated by Maureen Freely. New York: Alfred A. Knopf, 2005.

Partner, Peter. *God of Battles: Holy Wars of Christianity and Islam*. Princeton, N.J.: Princeton University Press, 1997.

Pernoud, Régine, ed. *The Crusades*. Translated by Enid McLeod. New York: G.P. Putnam's Sons, 1962.

Péronnet, Michel. *Le XVI° siècle 1492–1620: Des grandes découvertes à la contre-Réformes*. Paris: Hachette, 2005.

Perry, Mary Elizabeth. *The Handless Maiden: Moriscos and the Politics of Religion in Early Modern Spain*. Princeton, N.J.: Princeton University Press, 2005.

Peters, F. E. *A Reader on Classical Islam*. Princeton, N.J.: Princeton University Press, 1994.

Phillips, Jonathan. *The Crusades: 1095–1197*. Harlow: Pearson, 2002.

———. *The Fourth Crusade and the Sack of Constantinople*. New York: Viking, 2004.

Pickles, Tim. *Malta 1565: Last Battle of the Crusades*. Oxford: Osprey, 1998.

Pope, Hugh. *Sons of the Conquerors: The Rise of the Turkic World*. New York: Overlook Duckworth, 2005.

Porcel, Baltasar. *Méditerranée: Tumultes de la Houle*. Translated by Nelly Lhermillier. Paris: Actes Sud, 1998.

Psellus, Michael. *Fourteen Byzantine Rulers*. Translated by E.R.A. Sewter. London: Penguin, 1966.

Raymond, André. *Cairo*. Translated by Willard Wood. Cambridge, Mass.: Harvard University Press, 2000.

Read, Piers Paul. *The Templars*. New York: St. Martin's Press, 1999.

Regan, Geoffrey. *Saladin and the Fall of Jerusalem*. North Ryde, Australia: Croom Helm, 1987.

———. *Lionhearts: Richard I, Saladin, and the Third Crusade*. New York: Walker, 1998.

Reilly, Bernard F. *The Contest of Christian and Muslim Spain, 1031–1157*. Oxford: Blackwell, 1992.

———. *The Medieval Spains*. Cambridge: Cambridge University Press, 1993.

Reston, Jr., James. *Warriors of God: Richard the Lionheart and Saladin in the Third Crusade*. New York: Doubleday, 2001.

Richard, Jean. *The Crusades, c. 1071–1291*. Translated by Jean Burrell. Cambridge: Cambridge University Press, 1999.

Riley-Smith, Jonathan, ed. *The Oxford Illustrated History of the Crusades*. Oxford: Oxford University Press, 1995.

Riley-Smith, Jonathan. *The Knights of St. John in Jerusalem and Cyprus, c. 1050–1310*. New York: St. Martin's Press, 1967.

Robb, Peter. *Midnight in Sicily*. Boston: Faber and Faber, 1998.

Robinson, Neal. *Islam: A Concise Introduction*. Richmond, Surrey: Curzon, 1999.

Rodenbeck, Max. *Cairo: The City Victorious*. New York: Vintage, 2000.

Rodinson, Maxime. *Europe and the Mystique of Islam*. Translated by Roger Veinus. Seattle: University of Washington Press, 1991.

———. *Muhammad*. Translated by Anne Carter. New York: New Press, 2002.

Rosado Llamas, María Dolores, and Manuel Gabriel López Payer. *La Batalla de las Navas de Tolosa: Historia y mito*. Jaén: Caja Rural de Jaén, 2001.

Roux, Jean-Paul. *Tamerlan*. Paris: Fayard, 1994.

Roy, Jean-Henri, and Jean Devoisse. *La bataille de Poitiers, octobre 733*. Paris: Gallimard, 1966.

Rubenstein, Richard E. *Aristotle's Children: How Christians, Muslims, and Jews Rediscovered Ancient Wisdom and Illuminated the Middle Ages*. New York: Harcourt, 2003.

Runciman, Steven. *A History of the Crusades*. Vol. 1, *The First Crusade and the Foundation of the Kingdom of Jerusalem*. Cambridge: Cambridge University Press, 1957.

————. *A History of the Crusades.* Vol. 2, *The Kingdom of Jerusalem and the Frankish East, 1100–1187.* Cambridge: Cambridge University Press, 1952.

————. *The Fall of Constantinople 1453.* Cambridge: Cambridge University Press, 1965.

Sachar, Howard M. *Farewell España: The World of the Sephardim Remembered.* New York: Vintage, 1995.

Sage, C. M. *Paul Albar of Córdoba: Studies on His Life and Writings.* Washington, D.C.: Catholic University of America, 1943.

Said, Edward. *Orientalism.* New York: Vintage, 1979.

Santosousso, Antonio. *Barbarians, Marauders, and Infidels: The Ways of Medieval Warfare.* Boulder, Colo.: Westview Press, 2004.

Schimmel, Annemarie. *Rumi's World.* Boston: Shambhala, 2001.

Sénac, Philippe. *L'Occident médiéval face à l'Islam.* Paris: Flammarion, 2000.

————. *Les Carolingiens et al-Andalus: VIIIe–IXe siècles.* Paris: Maisonneuve et Larose, 2002.

Servanite, Alain, ed. *Le Voyage à Istanbul: Byzance, Constantinople, Istanbul du Moyen Age au XXe siècle.* Paris: Complexe, 2003.

Seward, Desmond. *The Monks of War: The Military Religious Orders.* London: Penguin, 1995.

Shatzmiller, M. "Al-Muwahhidun." *Encylopedia of Islam,* vol. 7. Leiden: Brill, 1993.

Shiono, Nanami. *The Fall of Constantinople.* New York: Vertical, 2005.

Simeti, Mary Taylor. *Travels with a Medieval Queen.* London: Phoenix, 2002.

Sire, H.J.A. *The Knights of Malta.* New Haven, Conn.: Yale University Press, 1994.

Stephenson, Paul. *The Legend of Basil the Bulgar-Slayer.* Cambridge: Cambridge University Press, 2003.

Storey, R.L. *Chronology of the Medieval World, 800–1491.* New York: Simon and Schuster, 1994.

Strayer, Joseph E., and Dana C. Munro. *The Middle Ages.* New York: Appleton-Century-Crofts, 1959.

Sutton, Kenneth M., and Marshall W. Baldwin, eds. *A History of the Crusades: The First Hundred Years,* vol. 1. Madison: University of Wisconsin, 1969.

Talbi, M. "Ibn Khaldun, Wal al-Din Abd al-Rahman B. Muhammad B. Muhammad B. Abi Bakr Muhammad B. Al-Hasan." *Encylopedia of Islam,* vol. 3. Leiden: Brill, 1971.

————. "Al-Kahina." *Encyclopedia of Islam,* vol. 4. Leiden: Brill, 1978.

Theophanes. *The Chronicle of Theophanes: An English Translation of Anni Mundi 6095–6305 (A.D. 602–813).* Translated by Harry Turtledove. Philadelphia: University of Pennsylvania Press, 1982.

Theroux, Paul. *The Pillars of Hercules: A Grand Tour of the Mediterranean.* London: Penguin, 1995.

Tolan, John V. *Saracens: Islam in the Medieval European Imagination.* New York: Columbia University, 2002.

Treadgold, Warren. *A History of the Byzantine State and Society.* Stanford, Calif.: Stanford University Press, 1997.

Turnbull, Stephen. *The Walls of Constantinople, AD 324–1453.* Oxford: Osprey, 2004.

Van den Graven, Robert. *Byzantine Istanbul.* Istanbul: Citlembik, 2001.

Veccia Vaglieri, L. "Ali b. Abi Talib." *Encyclopedia of Islam,* vol. 1. Leiden: Brill, 1960.

Von Schack, Adolf Friedrich. *Poesia y arte de los Arabes en España y Sicilia*. Madrid: Hiperion, 1988.

Vryonis, Jr., Speros. *The Decline of Medieval Hellenism in Asia Minor and the Process of Islamization from the Eleventh through the Fifteenth Century*. Berkeley: University of California Press, 1971.

———. "A Personal History of the History of the Battle of Manzikert." *Byzantine Asia Minor (Sixth/Twelfth Centuries)*. Athens, 1998.

Walker, Marilyn Higbee. "Abd al-Rahman, Caliph of Cordoba." In *Medieval Iberia: An Encyclopedia*. Edited by E. Michael Gehl. London: Routledge, 2003.

Wasserstein, David. *The Rise and Fall of the Party-Kings: Politics and Society in Islamic Spain, 1002–1086*. Princeton, N.J.: Princeton University Press, 1985.

Wheatcroft, Andrew. *Infidels: The Conflict between Christendom and Islam 638–2002*. London: Viking Penguin, 2003.

Whishaw, Bernhard, and Ellen M. Whishaw. *Arabic Spain: Sidelights on Her History and Art*. London: John Murray, 1912.

William of Tyre. *A History of Deeds Done Beyond the Sea*. Translated by Emily Atwater Babcock. New York: Columbia University Press, 1943.

Wise, Terence. *The Knights of Christ*. Oxford: Osprey, 1984.

———. *Armies of the Crusades*. Oxford: Osprey, 2004.

Zahra, Lorenzo. *Vittoriosa: A Brief Historical Guide to the City of Birgu*. Birgu: Birgu Local Council, 1999.

Zenghelis, C. "Le feu grégeois et les armes à feu des Byzantins." *Byzantion* 7 (1932).

ACKNOWLEDGMENTS

Before all else, I thank my family for their support and patience in the years this book was in preparation. Jill Pearlman—partner, spouse, fellow traveler, and writer—has endured yet another of my spells of monomania with grace, good humor, and gentle resignation. I cannot ever thank her enough. And my boisterous young daughters, Rachel and Eve, helped remind me that there is more to life than scimitars and catapults. As always, my two brothers and my father have been encouraging, if bemused. My mother, whose final illness came in 2004, might have, I hope, enjoyed this book. Then again, her kindness and love were such that she would never have told me if she hadn't. I will always be grateful to my parents, Anne Conlon and Daniel O'Shea, for crossing their own sea of faith from Ireland to Canada in 1949.

This book was written in Providence, Rhode Island, and in a farmhouse near Perpignan, France. Research required some eccentric travel around the Mediterranean; thus I have had help in many places and from many people.

For his searingly effective editorial advice, I thank novelist Eli Gottlieb, an old friend from our New York days together and ever the deft prose surgeon. In matters writerly, Allen Kurzweil has also been a great help. Allen is one of several Providence area denizens past and present who have aided me in ways large and small. Among them: Ernesto Aparicio, Denis Baldwin-Beneich, Popanha Brandes, Anna Cousins, Jill Donnelly, Claude Goldstein, Vladimir Golstein, Paule Khoury, Barbara Ann Markel, Brendan McCaughey, Todd Mennillo, Elli Mylonas, Bruno Schneider, William Viall, and the staff at the Rockefeller Library at Brown University and at the Providence Athenaeum. In the Rousillon region of southern France, we were once again surrounded by warm Catalans, whose greeting of *Ça va, le bouquin?* (Done with the book yet?) became a not-so-private joke. My thanks to neighbor Henri Fabresse for pulling us out of ditches and plowing the land for a vegetable garden, to Francis and Martine Péron for their unflagging interest, to Peter Turkie for the loan of exactly the right book, and to Suzanne Lowry for her enthusiastic support. But most of all, my gratitude goes to the Djurovic family of Thuir: Vladimir, Yovanka, and the late Roselyne, whose untimely disappearance still shocks. We miss Roselyne, our friend and *complice*, terribly.

For my foray to Poitiers, I thank my hosts Graziella Ibañez and Matthew von Piepenburg. In Spain, Bautista Martínez Ceprian helped enormously in the research, even when that meant pulling me over the brambles of Las Navas de Tolosa. For the Córdoba chapter, the advice of Peter Cole, poet and translator, was acutely useful. For Malta, I thank David Brussat for his informed heads-up and, in Valletta, Alberto Nocera, for sharing his encyclopedic knowledge of the island over a few drinks at the bar. For Palermo, the advice of Eduardo Fichera on his native city proved invaluable.

Istanbul became the center of my travels around the eastern Med, and here my cup runneth over. Ayda Manukyan, a musical Armenian who knows every nook and cranny of her hometown, squired me around Istanbul with expert ease. Scholar Feridun Özgümüs showed me the city's land walls, columnist Figen Batur its Bosporus night. Archaeologist Gül Pulhan led me to where I wanted to go in both eastern Anatolian and southern Syria, her unflappable irony in the face of my tenderfoot Orientalism a source of much laughter. She has been a great help and a good friend. Thanks also to Melek Taylan, Aydin Ugur, John Freely, John Ash, Niels Stoltenborg—and to Fatih, the little boy who knew where the mosque of Rumi was.

In eastern Anatolia, thanks are due to my driver, Abidin, and to Ali Ihsan, a representative of the Ministry of Culture in Malazgirt. In Aleppo, the staff at the Baron Hotel, where every guest seems, disconcertingly, to be a writer, was unfailingly kind. The affable Walid Malah drove me to Assassin hideouts of the Jebel Ansariye in Aziza, his lovingly maintained 1955 Studebaker Commander; driver Adnan Kadour used ingenuity in getting around checkpoints in navigating the Syrian approaches to the Golan. In Israel, Davide Silvera proved to be an exceptional dragoman, totally unfazed at the prospect of a client solely interested in twelfth-century Galilee.

Thanks too to my publishers and editors—Peter Carson, Andrew Franklin, George Gibson, Scott McIntyre—for their encouragement and patience. I'm also indebted to agents Chuck Verrill and Liz Darhansoff. And a very big debt of gratitude to Profile's Kate Griffin, who with her family has done the improbable—made London feel like home to me. In Paris, Sandy and Elisabeth Whitelaw, along with Valérie Chassigneux, Cathy Nolan, Heidi Ellison, Scott Blair, Randy Koral, Ruth Marshall, Mitchell Feinberg, and Valli and Pierre Budestchu, have always been warm and welcoming to their prodigal friend. The staff at the Bibliothèque Nationale and the library of the Institut du Monde Arabe in Paris were unfailingly helpful as well. My thanks, too, to Mourad Wahba. And in New York, George Lange gave cheerfully of his talents to make me look quasi-presentable in a photograph.

All of these people, helpful in so many ways, are of course in no way responsible for the inaccuracies and infelicities that this book undoubtedly contains. They, alas, are my fault alone. Vertot, an eighteenth-century French historian of the Ottoman siege of Rhodes, turned away documents that arrived too late on his desk with the famously insouciant rejection *Mon siège est fait* (My siege is finished). As my sea is now finished, I hope that readers will be indulgent if I missed the boat a couple of times.

INDEX

Note: Page numbers in *italic* indicate illustrations.

A NOTE ON THE AUTHOR

A historian, journalist, and translator, Stephen O'Shea is the author of *Back to the Front: An Accidental Historian Walks the Trenches of World War I* and *The Perfect Heresy: The Revolutionary Life and Death of the Medieval Cathars*. He lives in Providence, Rhode Island.